CONTEMPORARY
AMERICAN POETRY

THIRD EDITION

Edited by A. Poulin, Jr.

State University College at Brockport
State University of New York

HOUGHTON MIFFLIN COMPANY   BOSTON
Dallas   Geneva, Illinois   Hopewell, New Jersey
Palo Alto   London

Cover Calligraphy by Jean Evans

Acknowledgments begin on page 601.

Printed in the U.S.A.

Library of Congress Catalog Card Number: 79–91632

ISBN: 0–395–28635–2

PS
613
.P68
1980

AMERICAN POETRY

Whatever it is, it must have
A stomach that can digest
Rubber, coal, uranium, moons, poems.

Like the shark, it contains a shoe.
It must swim for miles through the desert
Uttering cries that are almost human.

—Louis Simpson

for Basilike and Daphne

Contents

CONTENTS

CONTENTS

CONTENTS

CONTENTS

CONTENTS

CONTENTS

CONTENTS

CONTENTS

Preface

The forty poets represented in this anthology are among those who have shaped the contours and the direction of poetry in this country from about World War II to the present. While achieving an individual and collective distinction all their own, they have contributed to and expanded American poetic traditions.

Some critics may still be honing or inventing sharper tools with which to evaluate American poetry published since 1945; they already weigh our poets for greatness—grading them like eggs. Eventually literary history may arrive at its own harsher retrospective conclusions. However, today, for us, these poets are clearly—in John Berryman's words—among "the high ones" of poetry in this country; and one hopes this book reflects the quality of our communal experiences for some four decades as much as it testifies to the vitality of our own imagination and of our poetry.

My primary concern while preparing this book has been to offer an anthology that is both discriminatingly representative and generously selective—admittedly, a most delicate balance. Thus I've selected poets whose work is representative of the full vitality and rich diversity of contemporary American poetry. And I've attempted to represent each poet as fully and as equitably as possible, selecting works that reflect the poet's characteristic subjects, themes, and styles. In time, I hope this anthology will be even more comprehensive—in order that it may include the work of poets whose absence is presently most noticeable.

Various poets in this book share a number of characteristics, and they might have been grouped accordingly. However, I have chosen to arrange them in a simple alphabetical order. No contemporary poet belongs to one "school" exclusively; some belong to no school at all. And attempts to categorize poets in such a fashion often simply convince the discriminating reader that so-and-so isn't just a confessional, Beat, New York, or Projectivist poet. Besides, such an approach also may predispose the reader to a given set of anticipations, thereby violating the integrity of the individual poem, the uniqueness of the individual poet, and the spontaneity of the reader's own response.

For much the same reasons, I've placed all critical apparatus at the back of the book, where a handful of readers may turn should they feel uncontrollably compelled to do so. For each poet, I've supplied a selected bibliography of primary and secondary works and a brief biographical and critical note sketching some of the prominent features of each writer's work. In these notes, I've taken schools into account now and then, but primarily I've let the poet's work—and not any set of critical assumptions—serve as my point of departure.

In my essay on "The Radical Tradition," I've attempted to delineate the major characteristics of contemporary poetry and to view it in a critical and historical perspective—in the hope of providing readers with a sense of how and why today's poetry is both new and a continuation of various American literary traditions. Lastly I've supplied a selected bibliography of the more substantial works of criticism devoted to American poetry since 1945.

Serious readers of poetry know full well that, regardless of how representative and generous it is meant to be, any anthology is necessarily no more than an *introduction*. The only way any reader can appreciate the true richness of today's poetry is by eventually setting this anthology aside and turning to the individual poet's own books. Indeed, the genuine measure of this anthology's effectiveness and "success" will be the extent to which it encourages readers to buy and read and respond to the books published by the poets represented. Thus I offer this anthology only as a gathering, an introduction, a door . . .

Readers should know that, in selecting poets and poems for this anthology, I am not insensitive to the measure of responsibility that such activity places on me; I hope that I have lived up to that responsibility. Readers should also know that this anthology quite literally would have been impossible without the generous cooperation of many of the poets, their agents, and their publishers, especially in the intricate negotiations for permissions to reprint poems. To those poets and their representatives I'm profoundly grateful.

I trust readers will agree with my belief that the full-page photographs of the poets add a human dimension to this book that isn't found very often in anthologies. I want to thank the photographers for supplying me with so many stunning photographs.

Obviously I'm indebted to a long list of other individuals who ought to be mentioned by name—poets, friends, colleagues, assistants, strangers. To name one would necessitate naming them all; trying to name all necessarily would result in overlooking too many. However, they should know that the absence of their names in this preface does not reflect an absence from my thoughts . . .

. . . and Basilike and Daphne, spouse, daughter, friends, to whom this book continues to be dedicated, to whom I continue to owe all.

A. Poulin, Jr.
Brockport, New York

CONTEMPORARY
AMERICAN POETRY

A. R. Ammons

APOLOGIA PRO VITA SUA

I started picking up the stones
throwing them into one place
and by sunrise I was going far away
for the large ones
always turning to see never lost
the cairn's height
lengthening my radial reach:

the sun watched with deep concentration
and the heap through the hours grew
and became by nightfall
distinguishable from all the miles around
of slate and sand:

during the night the wind falling
turned earthward its lofty freedom and speed
and the sharp blistering sound muffled
toward dawn and the blanket was
drawn up over a breathless face:

even so you can see in full dawn
the ground there lifts
a foreign thing desertless in origin.

CORSONS INLET

I went for a walk over the dunes again this morning
to the sea,
then turned right along
    the surf
                rounded a naked headland
                and returned

along the inlet shore:

it was muggy sunny, the wind from the sea steady and high,
crisp in the running sand,
      some breakthroughs of sun
    but after a bit

continuous overcast:

the walk liberating, I was released from forms,
from the perpendiculars,
      straight lines, blocks, boxes, binds
of thought
into the hues, shadings, rises, flowing bends and blends
        of sight:

              I allow myself eddies of meaning:
yield to a direction of significance
running
like a stream through the geography of my work:
  you can find
in my sayings
           swerves of action
           like the inlet's cutting edge:
      there are dunes of motion,
organizations of grass, white sandy paths of remembrance
in the overall wandering of mirroring mind:

but Overall is beyond me: is the sum of these events
I cannot draw, the ledger I cannot keep, the accounting
beyond the account:

in nature there are few sharp lines: there are areas of
primrose
    more or less dispersed;
disorderly orders of bayberry; between the rows

of dunes,
irregular swamps of reeds,
though not reeds alone, but grass, bayberry, yarrow, all . . .
predominantly reeds:

A. R. AMMONS

I have reached no conclusions, have erected no boundaries,
shutting out and shutting in, separating inside
    from outside: I have
    drawn no lines:
    as

manifold events of sand
change the dune's shape that will not be the same shape
tomorrow,

so I am willing to go along, to accept
the becoming
thought, to stake off no beginnings or ends, establish
    no walls:

by transitions the land falls from grassy dunes to creek
to undercreek: but there are no lines, though
    change in that transition is clear
    as any sharpness: but "sharpness" spread out,
allowed to occur over a wider range
than mental lines can keep:

the moon was full last night: today, low tide was low:
black shoals of mussels exposed to the risk
of air
and, earlier, of sun,
waved in and out with the waterline, waterline inexact,
caught always in the event of change:
    a young mottled gull stood free on the shoals
    and ate
to vomiting: another gull, squawking possession, cracked a crab,
picked out the entrails, swallowed the soft-shelled legs, a ruddy
turnstone running in to snatch leftover bits:

risk is full: every living thing in
siege: the demand is life, to keep life: the small
white blacklegged egret, how beautiful, quietly stalks and spears
    the shallows, darts to shore
        to stab—what? I couldn't
    see against the black mudflats—a frightened
    fiddler crab?

A. R. AMMONS

the news to my left over the dunes and
reeds and bayberry clumps was
        fall: thousands of tree swallows
        gathering for flight:
        an order held
        in constant change: a congregation
rich with entropy: nevertheless, separable, noticeable
        as one event,
                not chaos: preparations for
flight from winter,
cheet, cheet, cheet, cheet, wings rifling the green clumps,
beaks
at the bayberries
    a perception full of wind, flight, curve,
    sound:
    the possibility of rule as the sum of rulelessness:
the "field" of action
with moving, incalculable center:

in the smaller view, order tight with shape:
blue tiny flowers on a leafless weed: carapace of crab:
snail shell:
        pulsations of order
        in the bellies of minnows: orders swallowed,
broken down, transferred through membranes
to strengthen larger orders: but in the large view, no
lines or changeless shapes: the working in and out, together
        and against, of millions of events: this,
                so that I make
                no form
                formlessness:

orders as summaries, as outcomes of actions override
or in some way result, not predictably (seeing me gain
the top of a dune,

the swallows
could take flight—some other fields of bayberry
        could enter fall
        berryless) and there is serenity:

no arranged terror: no forcing of image, plan,
or thought:
no propaganda, no humbling of reality to precept:

terror pervades but is not arranged, all possibilities
of escape open: no route shut, except in
   the sudden loss of all routes:

     I see narrow orders, limited tightness, but will
not run to that easy victory:
     still around the looser, wider forces work:
     I will try
  to fasten into order enlarging grasps of disorder, widening
scope, but enjoying the freedom that
Scope eludes my grasp, that there is no finality of vision,
that I have perceived nothing completely,
     that tomorrow a new walk is a new walk.

LASER

    An image comes
    and the mind's light, confused
    as that on surf
    or ocean shelves,
    gathers up,
    parallelizes, focuses
    and in a rigid beam illuminates the image:

    the head seeks in itself
    fragments of left-over light
    to cast a new
    direction,
    any direction,
    to strike and fix
    a random, contradicting image:

but any found image falls
back to darkness or
the lesser beams splinter and
go out:
the mind tries to
dream of diversity, of mountain
rapids shattered with sound and light,

of wind fracturing brush or
bursting out of order against a mountain
range: but the focused beam
folds all energy in:
the image glares filling all space:
the head falls and
hangs and cannot wake itself.

HE HELD RADICAL LIGHT

He held radical light
as music in his skull: music
turned, as
over ridges immanences of evening light
rise, turned
back over the furrows of his brain
into the dark, shuddered,
shot out again
in long swaying swirls of sound:

reality had little weight in his transcendence
so he
had trouble keeping
his feet on the ground, was
terrified by that
and liked himself, and others, mostly
under roofs:
nevertheless, when the
light churned and changed

A. R. AMMONS

his head to music, nothing could keep him
off the mountains, his
head back, mouth working,
wrestling to say, to cut loose
from the high, unimaginable hook:
released, hidden from stars, he ate,
burped, said he was like any one
of us: demanded he
was like any one of us.

WORKING WITH TOOLS

I make a simple assertion
like a nice piece of stone
and you
alert to presence and entrance
man your pick and hammer

and by chip and deflection
distract simplicity
and cut my assertion
back to mangles, little heaps:

well, baby, that's the way
you get along: it's all right,
I understand such
ways of being afraid:
sometimes you want my come-on

hard, something to
take in and be around:
sometimes you want
a vaguer touch: I understand
and won't give assertion up.

THE UNIFYING PRINCIPLE

Ramshackles, archipelagoes, loose constellations
are less fierce, subsidiary centers, with the
attenuations of interstices, roughing the salience,

jarring the outbreak of too insistent commonalty:
a board, for example, not surrendering the rectitude
of its corners, the island of the oaks an

admonishment to pines, underfigurings (as of the Bear)
that take identity on: this motion is against
the grinding oneness of seas, hallows distinction

into the specific: but less lovely, too, for how
is the mass to be amassed, by what sanction
neighbor touch neighbor, island bear resemblance,

how are distinction's hard lines to be dissolved
(and preserved): what may all the people turn to,
the old letters, the shaped, characteristic peak

generations of minds have deflected and kept:
a particular tread that sometimes unweaves, taking
more shape on, into dance: much must be

tolerated as out of timbre, out of step, as being not
in its time or mood (the hiatus of the unconcerned)
and much room provided for the wretched to find caves

to ponder way off in: what then can lift the people
and only when they choose to rise or what can make
them want to rise, though business prevents: the

unifying principle will be a
phrase shared, an old cedar long known, general
wind-shapes in a usual sand: those objects single,

single enough to be uninterfering, multiple by
the piling on of shared sight, touch, saying:
when it's found the people live the small wraths of ease.

A. R. AMMONS

CUT THE GRASS

The wonderful workings of the world: wonderful,
wonderful: I'm surprised half the time:
ground up fine, I puff if a pebble stirs:

I'm nervous: my morality's intricate: if
a squash blossom dies, I feel withered as a stained
zucchini and blame my nature: and

when grassblades flop to the little red-ant
queens burring around trying to get aloft, I blame
my not keeping the grass short, stubble

firm: well, I learn a lot of useless stuff, meant
to be ignored: like when the sun sinking in the
west glares a plane invisible, I think how much

revelation concealment necessitates: and then I
think of the ocean, multiple to a blinding
oneness and realize that only total expression

expresses hiding: I'll have to say everything
to take on the roundness and withdrawal of the deep dark:
less than total is a bucketful of radiant toys.

THE CITY LIMITS

When you consider the radiance, that it does not withhold
itself but pours its abundance without selection into every
nook and cranny not overhung or hidden; when you consider

that birds' bones make no awful noise against the light but
lie low in the light as in a high testimony; when you consider
the radiance, that it will look into the guiltiest

swervings of the weaving heart and bear itself upon them,
not flinching into disguise or darkening; when you consider
the abundance of such resource as illuminates the glow-blue

bodies and gold-skeined wings of flies swarming the dumped
guts of a natural slaughter or the coil of shit and in no
way winces from its storms of generosity; when you consider

that air or vacuum, snow or shale, squid or wolf, rose or lichen,
each is accepted into as much light as it will take, then
the heart moves roomier, the man stands and looks about, the

leaf does not increase itself above the grass, and the dark
work of the deepest cells is of a tune with May bushes
and fear lit by the breadth of such calmly turns to praise.

THE ETERNAL CITY

After the explosion or cataclysm, that big
display that does its work but then fails
out with destructions, one is left with the

pieces: at first, they don't look very valuable,
but nothing sizable remnant around for
gathering the senses on, one begins to take

an interest, to sort out, to consider closely
what will do and won't, matters having become
not only small but critical: bulbs may have been

uprooted: they should be eaten, if edible, or
got back in the ground: what used to be garages,
even the splinters, should be collected for

fires: some unusually deep holes or cleared
woods may be turned to water supplies or
sudden fields: ruinage is hardly ever a

pretty sight but it must when splendor goes
accept into itself piece by piece all the old
perfect human visions, all the old perfect loves.

© Gerard Malanga

John Ashbery

THE PICTURE OF LITTLE J. A. IN A PROSPECT OF FLOWERS

He was spoilt from childhood by the future, which he mastered rather early and apparently without great difficulty.

Boris Pasternak

I

Darkness falls like a wet sponge
And Dick gives Genevieve a swift punch
In the pajamas. "Aroint thee, witch."
Her tongue from previous ecstasy
Releases thoughts like little hats.

"He clap'd me first during the eclipse.
Afterwards I noted his manner
Much altered. But he sending
At that time certain handsome jewels
I durst not seem to take offense."

In a far recess of summer
Monks are playing soccer.

II

So far is goodness a mere memory
Or naming of recent scenes of badness
That even these lives, children,
You may pass through to be blessed,
So fair does each invent his virtue.

And coming from a white world, music
Will sparkle at the lips of many who are
Beloved. Then these, as dirty handmaidens
To some transparent witch, will dream

13

Of a white hero's subtle wooing,
And time shall force a gift on each.

That beggar to whom you gave no cent
Striped the night with his strange descant.

III

Yet I cannot escape the picture
Of my small self in that bank of flowers:
My head among the blazing phlox
Seemed a pale and gigantic fungus.
I had a hard stare, accepting

Everything, taking nothing,
As though the rolled-up future might stink
As loud as stood the sick moment
The shutter clicked. Though I was wrong,
Still, as the loveliest feelings

Must soon find words, and these, yes,
Displace them, so I am not wrong
In calling this comic version of myself
The true one. For as change is horror,
Virtue is really stubbornness

And only in the light of lost words
Can we imagine our rewards.

"THEY DREAM ONLY OF AMERICA"

They dream only of America
To be lost among the thirteen million pillars of grass:
"This honey is delicious
Though it burns the throat."

And hiding from darkness in barns
They can be grownups now
And the murderer's ash tray is more easily—
The lake a lilac cube.

JOHN ASHBERY

He holds a key in his right hand.
"Please," he asked willingly.
He is thirty years old.
That was before

We could drive hundreds of miles
At night through dandelions.
When his headache grew worse we
Stopped at a wire filling station.

Now he cared only about signs.
Was the cigar a sign?
And what about the key?
He went slowly into the bedroom.

"I would not have broken my leg if I had not fallen
Against the living room table. What is it to be back
Beside the bed? There is nothing to do
For our liberation, except wait in the horror of it.

And I am lost without you."

LEAVING THE ATOCHA STATION

The arctic honey blabbed over the report causing darkness
And pulling us out of there experiencing it
he meanwhile . . . And the fried bats they sell there
dropping from sticks, so that the menace of your prayer folds . . .
Other people . . .   flash
the garden are you boning
and defunct covering . . . Blind dog expressed royalties . . .
comfort of your perfect tar grams nuclear world bank tulip
Favorable to   near the night pin
loading formaldehyde.   the table torn from you
Suddenly   and we are close
Mouthing the root   when you think
generator   homes enjoy leered

The worn stool blazing   pigeons from the roof
                driving tractor to squash
Leaving the Atocha Station   steel

infected bumps the screws
    everywhere   wells
abolished top ill-lit
scarecrow falls   Time, progress and good sense
strike of shopkeepers dark blood
no forest you can name drunk scrolls
the completely new Italian hair . . .
Baby . . .   ice falling off the port
The centennial   Before we can

                 old   eat
members with their chins
          so high up   rats
    relaxing the cruel discussion
  suds   the painted corners
white   most aerial
      garment crow
              and when the region took us back
the person left us like birds
  it was fuzz on the passing light
over disgusted heads, far into amnesiac
permanent house depot   amounts he can
      decrepit mayor . . .   exalting flea
for that we turn around
experiencing it is not to go into
the epileptic prank forcing bar
to borrow out onto tide-exposed fells
over her morsel, she chasing you
and the revenge he'd get
establishing the vultural over
rural area cough protection
murdering quintet. Air pollution terminal
the clean fart genital enthusiastic toe prick album serious evening flames
the lake over your hold   personality
      lightened . . .   roar
You are freed
      including barrels
head of the swan   forestry
the night and stars fork
That is, he said
    and rushing under the hoops of
equations probable
      absolute mush   the right

JOHN ASHBERY

    entity   chain store   sewer opened their books
           The flood dragged you
           I coughed to the window
last month: juice, earlier
like the slacks   to be declining
    the peaches   more
  fist
sprung expecting the cattle
false loam   imports
          next time around

THESE LACUSTRINE CITIES

These lacustrine cities grew out of loathing
Into something forgetful, although angry with history.
They are the product of an idea: that man is horrible, for instance,
Though this is only one example.

They emerged until a tower
Controlled the sky, and with artifice dipped back
Into the past for swans and tapering branches,
Burning, until all that hate was transformed into useless love.

Then you are left with an idea of yourself
And the feeling of ascending emptiness of the afternoon
Which must be charged to the embarrassment of others
Who fly by you like beacons.

The night is a sentinel.
Much of your time has been occupied by creative games
Until now, but we have all-inclusive plans for you.
We had thought, for instance, of sending you to the middle of the desert,

To a violent sea, or of having the closeness of the others be air
To you, pressing you back into a startled dream
As sea-breezes greet a child's face.
But the past is already here, and you are nursing some private project.

The worst is not over, yet I know
You will be happy here. Because of the logic

Of your situation, which is something no climate can outsmart.
Tender and insouciant by turns, you see.

You have built a mountain of something,
Thoughtfully pouring all your energy into this single monument,
Whose wind is desire starching a petal,
Whose disappointment broke into a rainbow of tears.

EVENING IN THE COUNTRY

I am still completely happy.
My resolve to win further I have
Thrown out, and am charged by the thrill
Of the sun coming up. Birds and trees, houses,
These are but the stations for the new sign of being
In me that is to close late, long
After the sun has set and darkness come
To the surrounding fields and hills.
But if breath could kill, then there would not be
Such an easy time of it, with men locked back there
In the smokestacks and corruption of the city.
Now as my questioning but admiring gaze expands
To magnificent outposts, I am not so much at home
With these memorabilia of vision as on a tour
Of my remotest properties, and the eidolon
Sinks into the effective "being" of each thing,
Stump or shrub, and they carry me inside
On motionless explorations of how dense a thing can be,
How light, and these are finished before they have begun
Leaving me refreshed and somehow younger.
Night has deployed rather awesome forces
Against this state of affairs: ten thousand helmeted footsoldiers,
A Spanish armada stretching to the horizon, all
Absolutely motionless until the hour to strike
But I think there is not too much to be said or be done
And that these things eventually take care of themselves
With rest and fresh air and the outdoors, and a good view of things.
So we might pass over this to the real
Subject of our concern, and that is
Have you begun to be in the context you feel
Now that the danger has been removed?

JOHN ASHBERY

Light falls on your shoulders, as is its way,
And the process of purification continues happily,
Unimpeded, but has the motion started
That is to quiver your head, send anxious beams
Into the dusty corners of the rooms
Eventually shoot out over the landscape
In stars and bursts? For other than this we know nothing
And space is a coffin, and the sky will put out the light.
I see you eager in your wishing it the way
We may join it, if it passes close enough:
This sets the seal of distinction on the success or failure of your attempt.
There is growing in that knowledge
We may perhaps remain here, cautious yet free
On the edge, as it rolls its unblinking chariot
Into the vast open, the incredible violence and yielding
Turmoil that is to be our route.

DEFINITION OF BLUE

The rise of capitalism parallels the advance of romanticism
And the individual is dominant until the close of the nineteenth century.
In our own time, mass practices have sought to submerge the personality
By ignoring it, which has caused it instead to branch out in all directions
Far from the permanent tug that used to be its notion of "home."
These different impetuses are received from everywhere
And are as instantly snapped back, hitting through the cold atmosphere
In one steady, intense line.

There is no remedy for this "packaging" which has supplanted the old
    sensations.
Formerly there would have been architectural screens at the point where
    the action became most difficult
As a path trails off into shrubbery—confusing, forgotten, yet continuing
    to exist.
But today there is no point in looking to imaginative new methods
Since all of them are in constant use. The most that can be said for them
    further
Is that erosion produces a kind of dust or exaggerated pumice
Which fills space and transforms it, becoming a medium
In which it is possible to recognize oneself.

Each new diversion adds its accurate touch to the ensemble, and so
A portrait, smooth as glass, is built up out of multiple corrections
And it has no relation to the space or time in which it was lived.
Only its existence is a part of all being, and is therefore, I suppose, to be
    prized
Beyond chasms of night that fight us
By being hidden and present.

And yet it results in a downward motion, or rather a floating one
In which the blue surroundings drift slowly up and past you
To realize themselves some day, while, you, in this nether world that could
    not be better
Waken each morning to the exact value of what you did and said, which
    remains.

AS YOU CAME FROM THE HOLY LAND

of western New York state
were the graves all right in their bushings
was there a note of panic in the late August air
because the old man had peed in his pants again
was there turning away from the late afternoon glare
as though it too could be wished away
was any of this present
and how could this be
the magic solution to what you are in now
whatever has held you motionless
like this so long through the dark season
until now the women come out in navy blue
and the worms come out of the compost to die
it is the end of any season

you reading there so accurately
sitting not wanting to be disturbed
as you came from that holy land
what other signs of earth's dependency were upon you
what fixed sign at the crossroads
what lethargy in the avenues
where all is said in a whisper
what tone of voice among the hedges
what tone under the apple trees

JOHN ASHBERY

the numbered land stretches away
and your house is built in tomorrow
but surely not before the examination
of what is right and will befall
not before the census
and the writing down of names

remember you are free to wander away
as from other times other scenes that were taking place
the history of someone who came too late
the time is ripe now and the adage
is hatching as the seasons change and tremble
it is finally as though that thing of monstrous interest
were happening in the sky
but the sun is setting and prevents you from seeing it

out of night the token emerges
its leaves like birds alighting all at once under a tree
taken up and shaken again
put down in weak rage
knowing as the brain does it can never come about
not here not yesterday in the past
only in the gap of today filling itself
as emptiness is distributed
in the idea of what time it is
when that time is already past

FOREBODING

A breeze off the lake—petal-shaped
Luna-park effects avoid the teasing outline
Of where we would be if we were here.
Bombed out of our minds, I think
The way here is too close, too packed
With surges of feeling. It can't be.
The wipeout occurs first at the center,
Now around the edges. A big ugly one
With braces kicking the shit out of a smaller one
Who reaches for a platinum axe stamped excalibur:
Just jungles really. The daytime bars are
Packed but night has more meaning

JOHN ASHBERY

In the pockets and side vents. I feel as though
Somebody had just brought me an equation.
I say, "I can't answer this—I know
That it's true, please believe me,
I can see the proof, lofty, invisible
In the sky far above the striped awnings. I just see
That I want it to go on, without
Anybody's getting hurt, and for the shuffling
To resume between me and my side of night."

THE ICE-CREAM WARS

Although I mean it, and project the meaning
As hard as I can into its brushed-metal surface,
It cannot, in this deteriorating climate, pick up
Where I leave off. It sees the Japanese text
(About two men making love on a foam-rubber bed)
As among the most massive secretions of the human spirit.
Its part is in the shade, beyond the iron spikes of the fence,
Mixing red with blue. As the day wears on
Those who come to seem reasonable are shouted down
(*Why you old goat!* Look who's talkin'. Let's see you
Climb off that tower—the waterworks architecture, both stupid and
Grandly humorous at the same time, is a kind of mask for him,
Like a seal's face. Time and the weather
Don't always go hand in hand, as here: sometimes
One is slanted sideways, disappears for awhile.
Then later it's forget-me-not time, and rapturous
Clouds appear above the lawn, and the rose tells
The old old story, the pearl of the orient, occluded
And still apt to rise at times.)
                              A few black smudges
On the outer boulevards, like squashed midges
And the truth becomes a hole, something one has always known,
A heaviness in the trees, and no one can say
Where it comes from, or how long it will stay—

A randomness, a darkness of one's own.

JOHN ASHBERY

STREET MUSICIANS

One died, and the soul was wrenched out
Of the other in life, who, walking the streets
Wrapped in an identity like a coat, sees on and on
The same corners, volumetrics, shadows
Under trees. Farther than anyone was ever
Called, through increasingly suburban airs
And ways, with autumn falling over everything:
The plush leaves the chattels in barrels
Of an obscure family being evicted
Into the way it was, and is. The other beached
Glimpses of what the other was up to:
Revelations at last. So they grew to hate and forget each other.

So I cradle this average violin that knows
Only forgotten showtunes, but argues
The possibility of free declamation anchored
To a dull refrain, the year turning over on itself
In November, with the spaces among the days
More literal, the meat more visible on the bone.
Our question of a place of origin hangs
Like smoke: how we picnicked in pine forests,
In coves with the water always seeping up, and left
Our trash, sperm and excrement everywhere, smeared
On the landscape, to make of us what we could.

© Thomas Victor

Imamu Amiri Baraka (LeRoi Jones)

DUNCAN SPOKE OF A PROCESS

And what I have learned
of it, to repeat, repeated
as a day will repeat
its color, the tired sounds
run off its bones. In me, a balance.

Before that, what came easiest. From
wide poles, across the greenest earth,
eyes locked on, where they could live, and
whatever came from there, where the hand
could be offered, like Gideon's young troops
on their knees at the water.

                   I test myself,
with memory. A live bloody skeleton. Hung as softly
as summer. Sways like words' melody, as ugly as any
lips, or fingers stroking lakes, or flesh like a
white frightened scream.

What comes, closest, is
closest. Moving, there
is a wreck of spirit,
               a heap of broken feeling. What

was only love
or in those cold rooms,
opinion. Still, it made
color. And filled me
as no one will. As, even
I cannot fill
myself.

        I see what I love most and will not
leave what futile lies
I have. I am where there
is nothing, save myself. And go out to
what is most beautiful. What some noncombatant Greek

or soft Italian prince
would sing, "Noble Friends."
                                Noble Selves. And which one
is truly
to rule here? And
what country is this?

THE DEAD LADY CANONIZED

                        (A thread
of meaning. Meaning light. The quick
response. To breath, or the virgins
sick odor against the night.

                        (A trail
of objects. Dead nouns, rotted faces
propose the night's image. Erect
for that lady, a grave of her own.

                        (The stem
of the morning, sets itself, on
each window (of thought, where it
goes. The lady is dead, may the Gods,

                        (those others
beg our forgiveness. And Damballah, kind father,
sew up
her bleeding hole.

A GUERILLA HANDBOOK

In the palm
the seed
is burned up
in the wind.
                In their rightness
the tree trunks are socialists
leaves murder the silence and are brown
and old when they blow to the sea.
                            Convinced
of the lyric. Convinced

of the man's image (since
he will not look at substance
other than his ego. Flowers, grapes
the shadows of weeds, as the weather
is colder, and women walk
with their heads down.
                    Silent political rain
against the speech
of friends. (We love them
trapped in life, knowing no way out
except description. Or black soil
floating in the arm.
                    We must convince the living
                    that the dead
                    cannot sing.

DEATH IS NOT AS NATURAL
AS YOU FAGS SEEM TO THINK

I hunt
the black puritan.
                  (Half-screamer

in dull tones
of another forest.

Respecter of power. That it transform, and enlarge
Hierarchy crawls over earth (change exalting space
Dried mud to mountain, cape and whip, swirled
Walkers, and riders and flyers.
Language spread into darkness. Be Vowel
                        and value

                Consonant
                    and direction.

Rather the lust of the thing
than across to droop at its energies. In melted snows
the leather cracks, and pure men claw at their bodies.
Women laugh delicately, delicately rubbing their thighs.

And the dead king laughs, looking out the hole
in his tomb. Seeing the poor
singing his evil songs.

IMAMU AMIRI BARAKA (LEROI JONES)

LEGACY

(For Blues People)

In the south, sleeping against
the drugstore, growling under
the trucks and stoves, stumbling
through and over the cluttered eyes
of early mysterious night. Frowning
drunk waving moving a hand or lash.
Dancing kneeling reaching out, letting
a hand rest in shadows. Squatting
to drink or pee. Stretching to climb
pulling themselves onto horses near
where there was sea (the old songs
lead you to believe). Riding out
from this town, to another, where
it is also black. Down a road
where people are asleep. Towards
the moon or the shadows of houses.
Towards the songs' pretended sea.

CONFIRMATION

The blood in me, assumes a beautiful shape, it assumes
that I can write, and that I am the great mind of my own
soul, in a fit of fall flashing bells, the great booms
and machines that make the world worth exploding and re-
building, for whatever we agree on is most honorable.

There is no struggle to speak if you want to.
There is no slowness or stupidity we must bear.
There is perfection! There is grace! There are
all those things they talked about . . . but different!
Jesus Christ, how different! How much bullshit did they
put into our way, how much ugliness we canonized, dazed
and dazzing in
The Music is so strong,
it smashes through the boards. It questions
the beat of my mind, where the soul beats against the iron badges

IMAMU AMIRI BARAKA (LEROI JONES)

of a cage. How hateful can be anything. How it can turn you, resur-
rect your errors as if the mind laughed at what it hated to use, and
used the fingers of your consciousness to dazzle yourself with madness.

We can be used by everything. We are not in danger of being wrong.
Only stupid, in the quiet despotic night. Oh, how the freaks of this
adventure sadden, the old ladies walking by scared and scaring, not
even caring that the world is falling apart, and even the intellectuals
will be killed. Oh, Christ you don't understand. I don't understand
what the problem has to do with this woman's lips, or that woman's
understanding of why is the world is finally so ugly, even though
you're right. The world is the most perfect thing in the soul. The world
is a soul, and we are souls if we remember the murmurs of the spirit.

POEM FOR HALFWHITE COLLEGE STUDENTS

Who are you, listening to me, who are you
listening to yourself? Are you white or
black, or does that have anything to do
with it? Can you pop your fingers to no
music, except those wild monkies go on
in your head, can you jerk, to no melody,
except finger poppers get it together
when you turn from starchecking to checking
yourself. How do you sound, your words, are they
yours? The ghost you see in the mirror, is it really
you, can you swear you are not an imitation greyboy,
can you look right next to you in that chair, and swear,
that the sister you have your hand on is not really
so full of Elizabeth Taylor, Richard Burton is
coming out of her ears. You may even have to be Richard
with a white shirt and face, and four million negroes
think you cute, you may have to be Elizabeth Taylor, old lady,
if you want to sit up in your crazy spot dreaming about dresses,
and the sway of certain porters' hips. Check yourself, learn who it is
speaking, when you make some ultrasophisticated point, check yourself,
when you find yourself gesturing like Steve McQueen, check it out, ask
in your black heart who it is you are, and is that image black or white,

you might be surprised right out the window, whistling dixie on the way in.

IMAMU AMIRI BARAKA (LEROI JONES)

BLACK PEOPLE: THIS IS OUR DESTINY

The road runs straight with no turning, the circle
runs complete as it is in the storm of peace, the all
embraced embracing in the circle complete turning road
straight like a burning straight with the circle complete
as in a peaceful storm, the elements, the niggers' voices
harmonized with creation on a peak in the holy black man's
eyes that we rise, whose race is only direction up, where
we go to meet the realization of makers knowing who we are
and the war in our hearts but the purity of the holy world
that we long for, knowing how to live, and what life is, and
who God is, and the many revolutions we must spin through in our
seven adventures in the endlessness of all existing feeling, all
existing forms of life, the gases, the plants, the ghost minerals
the spirits the souls the light in the stillness where the storm
the glow the nothing in God is complete except there is nothing
to be incomplete the pulse and change of rhythm, blown flight
to be anything at all . . . vibration holy nuance beating against
itself, a rhythm a playing re-understood now by one of the 1st race
the primitives the first men who evolve again to civilize the
world

KA 'BA

A closed window looks down
on a dirty courtyard, and black people
call across or scream across or walk across
defying physics in the stream of their will

Our world is full of sound
Our world is more lovely than anyone's
tho we suffer, and kill each other
and sometimes fail to walk the air

We are beautiful people
with african imaginations
full of masks and dances and swelling chants
with african eyes, and noses, and arms,
though we sprawl in grey chains in a place
full of winters, when what we want is sun.

IMAMU AMIRI BARAKA (LEROI JONES)

We have been captured,
brothers. And we labor
to make our getaway, into
the ancient image, into a new

correspondence with ourselves
and our black family. We need magic
now we need the spells, to raise up
return, destroy, and create. What will be

the sacred words?

REVOLUTIONARY LOVE

Black Revolutionary Woman
In love w/ Revolution
Your man better be a revolution
for you to love him
Black Revolutionary woman
the care of the world
is yours, in your hands is
entrusted all the new beauty
created here on earth
Black revolutionary woman
were you my companion I'd
call you Amina, Afrikan faith
and inspiration, were
you my comrade in struggle, I'd still
call you lady, great lady
Bibi, Black Revolutionary Woman
were you my woman, and even in the pit
of raging struggle, we need what we love,
we need what we desire to create, were you
my woman, I'd call you companion, comrade,
sister, black lady, Afrikan faith, I'd call you
house, Black Revolutionary woman
I'd call you wife.

© Rollie McKenna

John Berryman

from **THE DREAM SONGS**

1

Huffy Henry hid   the day,
unappeasable Henry sulked.
I see his point,—a trying to put things over.
It was the thought that they thought
they could *do* it made Henry wicked & away.
But he should have come out and talked.

All the world like a woolen lover
once did seem on Henry's side.
Then came a departure.
Thereafter nothing fell out as it might or ought.
I don't see how Henry, pried
open for all the world to see, survived.

What he has now to say is a long
wonder the world can bear & be.
Once in a sycamore I was glad
all at the top, and I sang.
Hard on the land wears the strong sea
and empty grows every bed.

4

Filling her compact & delicious body
with chicken páprika, she glanced at me
twice.
Fainting with interest, I hungered back
and only the fact of her husband & four other people
kept me from springing on her

or falling at her little feet and crying
'You are the hottest one for years of night
Henry's dazed eyes
have enjoyed, Brilliance.' I advanced upon

33

(despairing) my spumoni. —Sir Bones: is stuffed,
de world, wif feeding girls.

—Black hair, complexion Latin, jewelled eyes
downcast . . . The slob beside her   feasts . . . What wonders is
she sitting on, over there?
The restaurant buzzes. She might as well be on Mars.
Where did it all go wrong? There ought to be a law against Henry.
—Mr Bones: there is.

8

      The weather was fine. They took away his teeth,
      white & helpful; bothered his backhand;
      halved his green hair.
      They blew out his loves, his interests. 'Underneath,'
      (they called in iron voices) 'understand,
      is nothing. So there.'

      The weather was very fine. They lifted off
      his covers till he showed, and cringed & pled
      to see himself less.
      They installed mirrors till he flowed. 'Enough'
      (murmured they) 'if you will watch Us instead,
      yet you may saved be. Yes.'

      The weather fleured. They weakened all his eyes,
      and burning thumbs into his ears, and shook
      his hand like a notch.
      They flung long silent speeches. (Off the hook!)
      They sandpapered his plumpest hope. (So capsize.)
      They took away his crotch.

9

      Deprived of his enemy, shrugged to a standstill
      horrible Henry, foaming. Fan their way
      toward him who will
      in the high wood: the officers, their rest,
      with p. a. echoing: his girl comes, say,
      conned in to test

      if he's still human, see: she love him, see,
      therefore she get on the Sheriff's mike & howl

JOHN BERRYMAN

'Come down, come down'.
Therefore he un-budge, furious. He'd flee
but only Heaven hangs over him foul.
At the crossways, downtown,

he dreams the folks are buying parsnips & suds
and paying rent to foes. He slipt & fell.
It's golden here in the snow.
A mild crack: a far rifle. Bogart's duds
truck back to Wardrobe. Fancy the brain from hell
held out so long. Let go.

13

God bless Henry. He lived like a rat,
with a thatch of hair on his head
in the beginning.
Henry was not a coward. Much.
He never deserted anything; instead
he stuck, when things like pity were thinning.

So may be Henry was a human being.
Let's investigate that.
. . . We did; okay.
He is a human American man.
That's true. My lass is braking.
My brass is aching. Come & diminish me, & map my way.

God's Henry's enemy. We're in business . . . Why,
what business must be clear.
A cornering.
I couldn't feel more like it. —Mr Bones,
as I look on the saffron sky,
you strikes me as ornery.

14

Life, friends, is boring. We must not say so.
After all, the sky flashes, the great sea yearns,
we ourselves flash and yearn,
and moreover my mother told me as a boy
(repeatedly) 'Ever to confess you're bored
means you have no

Inner Resources.' I conclude now I have no
inner resources, because I am heavy bored.
Peoples bore me,
literature bores me, especially great literature,
Henry bores me, with his plights & gripes
as bad as achilles,

who loves people and valiant art, which bores me.
And the tranquil hills, & gin, look like a drag
and somehow a dog
has taken itself & its tail considerably away
into mountains or sea or sky, leaving
behind: me, wag.

29

There sat down, once, a thing on Henry's heart
só heavy, if he had a hundred years
& more, & weeping, sleepless, in all them time
Henry could not make good.
Starts again always in Henry's ears
the little cough somewhere, an odour, a chime.

And there is another thing he has in mind
like a grave Sienese face a thousand years
would fail to blur the still profiled reproach of. Ghastly,
with open eyes, he attends, blind.
All the bells say: too late. This is not for tears;
thinking.

But never did Henry, as he thought he did,
end anyone and hacks her body up
and hide the pieces, where they may be found.
He knows: he went over everyone, & nobody's missing.
Often he reckons, in the dawn, them up.
Nobody is ever missing.

45

He stared at ruin. Ruin stared straight back.
He thought they was old friends. He felt on the stair
where her papa found them bare
they became familiar. When the papers were lost

rich with pals' secrets, he thought he had the knack
of ruin. Their paths crossed

and once they crossed in jail; they crossed in bed;
and over an unsigned letter their eyes met,
and in an Asian city
directionless & lurchy at two & three,
or trembling to a telephone's fresh threat,
and when some wired his head

to reach a wrong opinion, 'Epileptic'.
But he noted now that: they were not old friends.
He did not know this one.
This one was a stranger, come to make amends
for all the imposters, and to make it stick.
Henry nodded, un-.

46

I am, outside. Incredible panic rules.
People are blowing and beating each other without mercy.
Drinks are boiling. Iced
drinks are boiling. The worse anyone feels, the worse
treated he is. Fools elect fools.
A harmless man at an intersection said, under his breath: "Christ!"

That word, so spoken, affected the vision
of, when they trod to work next day, shopkeepers
who went & were fitted for glasses.
Enjoyed they then an appearance of love & law.
Millenia whift & waft—one, one—er, er . . .
Their glasses were taken from them, & they saw.

Man has undertaken the top job of all,
son fin. Good luck.
I myself walked at the funeral of tenderness.
Followed other deaths. Among the last,
like the memory of a lovely fuck,
was: *Do, ut des.*

55

Peter's not friendly. He gives me sideways looks.
The architecture is far from reassuring.
I feel uneasy.
A pity,—the interview began so well:
I mentioned fiendish things, he waved them away
and sloshed out a martini

strangely needed. We spoke of indifferent matters—
God's health, the vague hell of the Congo,
John's energy,
anti-matter matter. I felt fine.
Then a change came backward. A chill fell.
Talk slackened,

died, and he began to give me sideways looks.
'Christ,' I thought 'what now?' and would have askt for another
but didn't dare.
I feel my application   failing. It's growing dark,
some other sound is overcoming. His last words are:
'We betrayed me.'

230

There are voices, voices. Light's dying. Birds have quit.
He lied about me, months ago. His friendly wit
now slid to apology.
I am sorry that senior genius remembered it.
I am nothing, to occupy his thought
one moment. We

went at his bidding to his cabin, three,
in two bodies; and he spoke like Jove.
I sat there full of love,
salt with attention, while his jokes like nods
pierced for us our most strange history. He
seemed to be in charge of the odds:

hurrah. Three. Three. I must remember that.
I love great men I love. Nobody's great.
I must remember that.
We all fight. Having fought better than the rest,
he sings, & mutters & prophesies in the West
and is our flunked test.

I always come in prostrate; Yeats & Frost.

266

Dinch me, dark God, having smoked me out.
Let Henry's ails fail, pennies on his eyes
never to open more,
the shires are voting him out of time & place,
they'll drop his bundle, drunkard & Boy Scout,
where he was once before:

nowhere, nowhere. Was then the thing all planned?
I mention what I do not understand.
I mention for instance Love:
God loves his creatures when he treats them so?
Surely one grand *exception* here below
his presidency of

the widespread galaxies might once be made
for perishing Henry, whom let not then die.
He can advance no claim,
save that he studied thy Word & grew afraid,
work & fear be the basis for his terrible cry
not to forget his name.

382

At Henry's bier let some thing fall out well:
enter there none who somewhat has to sell,
the music ancient & gradual,
the voices solemn but the grief subdued,
no hairy jokes but everybody's mood
subdued, subdued,

until the Dancer comes, in a short short dress
hair black & long & loose, dark dark glasses,
uptilted face,
pallor & strangeness, the music changes
to 'Give!' & 'Ow!' and how! the music changes,
she kicks a backward limb

on tiptoe, pirouettes, & she is free
to the knocking music, sails, dips, & suddenly
returns to the terrible gay
occasion hopeless & mad, she weaves, it's hell,
she flings to her head a leg, bobs, all is well,
she dances Henry away.

384

The marker slants, flowerless, day's almost done,
I stand above my father's grave with rage,
often, often before
I've made this awful pilgrimage to one
who cannot visit me, who tore his page
out: I come back for more,

I spit upon this dreadful banker's grave
who shot his heart out in a Florida dawn
O ho alas alas
When will indifference come, I moan & rave
I'd like to scrabble till I got right down
away down under the grass

and ax the casket open ha to see
just how he's taking it, which he sought so hard
we'll tear apart
the mouldering grave clothes ha & then Henry
will heft the ax once more, his final card,
and fell it on the start.

JOHN BERRYMAN

from ELEVEN ADDRESSES TO THE LORD

1

Master of beauty, craftsman of the snowflake,
inimitable contriver,
endower of Earth so gorgeous & different from the boring Moon,
thank you for such as it is my gift.

I have made up a morning prayer to you
containing with precision everything that most matters.
'According to Thy will' the thing begins.
It took me off & on two days. It does not aim at eloquence.

You have come to my rescue again & again
in my impassable, sometimes despairing years.
You have allowed my brilliant friends to destroy themselves
and I am still here, severely damaged, but functioning.

Unknowable, as I am unknown to my guinea pigs:
how can I 'love' you?
I only as far as gratitude & awe
confidently & absolutely go.

I have no idea whether we live again.
It doesn't seem likely
from either the scientific or the philosophical point of view
but certainly all things are possible to you,

and I believe as fixedly in the Resurrection-appearances to Peter & to Paul
as I believe I sit in this blue chair.
Only that may have been a special case
to establish their initiatory faith.

Whatever your end may be, accept my amazement.
May I stand until death forever at attention
for any your least instruction or enlightenment.
I even feel sure you will assist me again, Master of insight & beauty.

6

Under new management, Your Majesty:
Thine. I have solo'd mine since childhood, since
my father's suicide when I was twelve
blew out my most bright candle faith, and look at me.

I served at Mass six dawns a week from five,
adoring Father Boniface & you,
memorizing the Latin he explained.
Mostly we worked alone. One or two women.

Then my poor father frantic. Confusions & afflictions
followed my days. Wives left me.
Bankrupt I closed my doors. You pierced the roof
twice & again. Finally you opened my eyes.

My double nature fused in that point of time
three weeks ago day before yesterday.
Now, brooding thro' a history of the early Church,
I identify with everybody, even the heresiarchs.

11

Germanicus leapt upon the wild lion in Smyrna,
wishing to pass quickly from a lawless life.
The crowd shook the stadium.
The proconsul marvelled.

'Eighty & six years have I been his servant,
and he has done me no harm.
How can I blaspheme my King who saved me?'
Polycarp, John's pupil, facing the fire.

Make too me acceptable at the end of time
in my degree, which then Thou wilt award.
Cancer, senility, mania,
I pray I may be ready with my witness.

JOHN BERRYMAN

HENRY'S UNDERSTANDING

He was reading late, at Richard's, down in Maine,
aged 32? Richard & Helen long in bed,
my good wife long in bed.
All I had to do was strip & get into my bed,
putting the marker in the book, & sleep,
& wake to a hot breakfast.

Off the coast was an island, P'tit Manaan,
the bluff from Richard's lawn was almost sheer.
A chill at four o'clock.
It only takes a few minutes to make a man.
A concentration upon now & here.
Suddenly, unlike Bach,

& horribly, unlike Bach, it occurred to me
that *one* night, instead of warm pajamas,
I'd take off all my clothes
& cross the damp cold lawn & down the bluff
into the terrible water & walk forever
under it out toward the island.

© *Thomas Victor*

Elizabeth Bishop

THE MAP

Land lies in water; it is shadowed green.
Shadows, or are they shallows, at its edges
showing the line of long sea-weeded ledges
where weeds hang to the simple blue from green.
Or does the land lean down to lift the sea from under,
drawing it unperturbed around itself?
Along the fine tan sandy shelf
is the land tugging at the sea from under?

The shadow of Newfoundland lies flat and still.
Labrador's yellow, where the moony Eskimo
has oiled it. We can stroke these lovely bays,
under a glass as if they were expected to blossom,
or as if to provide a clean cage for invisible fish.
The names of seashore towns run out to sea,
the names of cities cross the neighboring mountains
—the printer here experiencing the same excitement
as when emotion too far exceeds its cause.
These peninsulas take the water between thumb and finger
like women feeling for the smoothness of yard-goods.

Mapped waters are more quiet than the land is,
lending the land their waves' own conformation:
and Norway's hare runs south in agitation,
profiles investigate the sea, where land is.
Are they assigned, or can the countries pick their colors?
—What suits the character or the native waters best.
Topography displays no favorites; North's as near as West.
More delicate than the historians' are the map-makers' colors.

ELIZABETH BISHOP

THE MAN-MOTH*

      Here, above,
cracks in the buildings are filled with battered moonlight.
The whole shadow of Man is only as big as his hat.
It lies at his feet like a circle for a doll to stand on,
and he makes an inverted pin, the point magnetized to the moon.
He does not see the moon; he observes only her vast properties,
feeling the queer light on his hands, neither warm nor cold,
of a temperature impossible to record in thermometers.

      But when the Man-Moth
pays his rare, although occasional, visits to the surface,
the moon looks rather different to him. He emerges
from an opening under the edge of one of the sidewalks
and nervously begins to scale the faces of the buildings.
He thinks the moon is a small hole at the top of the sky,
proving the sky quite useless for protection.
He trembles, but must investigate as high as he can climb.

      Up the façades,
his shadow dragging like a photographer's cloth behind him,
he climbs fearfully, thinking that this time he will manage
to push his small head through that round clean opening
and be forced through, as from a tube, in black scrolls on the light.
(Man, standing below him, has no such illusions.)
But what the Man-Moth fears most he must do, although
he fails, of course, and falls back scared but quite unhurt.

      Then he returns
to the pale subways of cement he calls his home. He flits,
he flutters, and cannot get aboard the silent trains
fast enough to suit him. The doors close swiftly.
The Man-Moth always seats himself facing the wrong way
and the train starts at once at its full, terrible speed,
without a shift in gears or a gradation of any sort.
He cannot tell the rate at which he travels backwards.

* Newspaper misprint for "mammoth."

Each night he must
be carried through artificial tunnels and dream recurrent dreams.
Just as the ties recur beneath his train, these underlie
his rushing brain. He does not dare look out the window,
for the third rail, the unbroken draught of poison,
runs there beside him. He regards it as a disease
he has inherited the susceptibility to. He has to keep
his hands in his pockets, as others must wear mufflers.

If you catch him,
hold up a flashlight to his eye. It's all dark pupil,
an entire night itself, whose haired horizon tightens
as he stares back, and closes up the eye. Then from the lids
one tear, his only possession, like the bee's sting, slips.
Slyly he palms it, and if you're not paying attention
he'll swallow it. However, if you watch, he'll hand it over,
cool as from underground springs and pure enough to drink.

THE FISH

I caught a tremendous fish
and held him beside the boat
half out of water, with my hook
fast in a corner of his mouth.
He didn't fight.
He hadn't fought at all.
He hung a grunting weight,
battered and venerable
and homely. Here and there
his brown skin hung in strips
like ancient wallpaper,
and its pattern of darker brown
was like wallpaper:
shapes like full-blown roses
stained and lost through age.
He was speckled with barnacles,
fine rosettes of lime,

and infested
with tiny white sea-lice,
and underneath two or three
rags of green weed hung down.
While his gills were breathing in
the terrible oxygen
—the frightening gills,
fresh and crisp with blood,
that can cut so badly—
I thought of the coarse white flesh
packed in like feathers,
the big bones and the little bones,
the dramatic reds and blacks
of his shiny entrails,
and the pink swim-bladder
like a big peony.
I looked into his eyes
which were far larger than mine
but shallower, and yellowed,
the irises backed and packed
with tarnished tinfoil
seen through the lenses
of old scratched isinglass.
They shifted a little, but not
to return my stare.
—It was more like the tipping
of an object toward the light.
I admired his sullen face,
the mechanism of his jaw,
and then I saw
that from his lower lip
—if you could call it a lip—
grim, wet, and weaponlike,
hung five old pieces of fish-line,
or four and a wire leader
with the swivel still attached,
with all their five big hooks
grown firmly in his mouth.
A green line, frayed at the end
where he broke it, two heavier lines,
and a fine black thread
still crimped from the strain and snap
when it broke and he got away.

ELIZABETH BISHOP

Like medals with their ribbons
frayed and wavering,
a five-haired beard of wisdom
trailing from his aching jaw.
I stared and stared
and victory filled up
the little rented boat,
from the pool of bilge
where oil had spread a rainbow
around the rusted engine
to the bailer rusted orange,
the sun-cracked thwarts,
the oarlocks on their strings,
the gunnels—until everything
was rainbow, rainbow, rainbow!
And I let the fish go.

LETTER TO N. Y.

for Louise Crane

In your next letter I wish you'd say
where you are going and what you are doing;
how are the plays, and after the plays
what other pleasures you're pursuing:

taking cabs in the middle of the night,
driving as if to save your soul
where the road goes round and round the park
and the meter glares like a moral owl,

and the trees look so queer and green
standing alone in big black caves
and suddenly you're in a different place
where everything seems to happen in waves,

and most of the jokes you just can't catch,
like dirty words rubbed off a slate,
and the songs are loud but somehow dim
and it gets so terribly late,

and coming out of the brownstone house
to the gray sidewalk, the watered street,
one side of the buildings rises with the sun
like a glistening field of wheat.

—Wheat, not oats, dear. I'm afraid
if it's wheat it's none of your sowing,
nevertheless I'd like to know
what you are doing and where you are going.

QUESTIONS OF TRAVEL

There are too many waterfalls here; the crowded streams
hurry too rapidly down to the sea,
and the pressure of so many clouds on the mountaintops
makes them spill over the sides in soft slow-motion,
turning to waterfalls under our very eyes.
—For if those streaks, those mile-long, shiny, tearstains,
aren't waterfalls yet,
in a quick age or so, as ages go here,
they probably will be.
But if the streams and clouds keep travelling, travelling,
the mountains look like the hulls of capsized ships,
slime-hung and barnacled.

Think of the long trip home.
Should we have stayed at home and thought of here?
Where should we be today?
Is it right to be watching strangers in a play
in this strangest of theatres?
What childishness is it that while there's a breath of life
in our bodies, we are determined to rush
to see the sun the other way around?
The tiniest green hummingbird in the world?
To stare at some inexplicable old stonework,
inexplicable and impenetrable,
at any view,

instantly seen and always, always delightful?
Oh, must we dream our dreams
and have them, too?
And have we room
for one more folded sunset, still quite warm?

But surely it would have been a pity
not to have seen the trees along this road,
really exaggerated in their beauty,
not to have seen them gesturing
like noble pantomimists, robed in pink.
—Not to have had to stop for gas and heard
the sad, two-noted, wooden tune
of disparate wooden clogs
carelessly clacking over
a grease-stained filling-station floor.
(In another country the clogs would all be tested.
Each pair there would have identical pitch.)
—A pity not to have heard
the other, less primitive music of the fat brown bird
who sings above the broken gasoline pump
in a bamboo church of Jesuit baroque:
three towers, five silver crosses.
—Yes, a pity not to have pondered,
blurr'dly and inconclusively,
on what connection can exist for centuries
between the crudest wooden footwear
and, careful and finicky,
the whittled fantasies of wooden cages.
—Never to have studied history in
the weak calligraphy of songbirds' cages.
—And never to have had to listen to rain
so much like politicians' speeches:
two hours of unrelenting oratory
and then a sudden golden silence
in which the traveller takes a notebook, writes:

"Is it lack of imagination that makes us come
to imagined places, not just stay at home?
Or could Pascal have been not entirely right
about just sitting quietly in one's room?

Continent, city, country, society:
the choice is never wide and never free.
And here, or there . . . No. Should we have stayed at home,
wherever that may be?"

THE ARMADILLO

for Robert Lowell

This is the time of year
when almost every night
the frail, illegal fire balloons appear.
Climbing the mountain height,

rising toward a saint
still honored in these parts,
the paper chambers flush and fill with light
that comes and goes, like hearts.

Once up against the sky it's hard
to tell them from the stars—
planets, that is—the tinted ones:
Venus going down, or Mars,

or the pale green one. With a wind,
they flare and falter, wobble and toss;
but if it's still they steer between
the kite sticks of the Southern Cross,

receding, dwindling, solemnly
and steadily forsaking us,
or, in the downdraft from a peak,
suddenly turning dangerous.

Last night another big one fell.
It splattered like an egg of fire
against the cliff behind the house.
The flame ran down. We saw the pair

of owls who nest there flying up
and up, their whirling black-and-white
stained bright pink underneath, until
they shrieked up out of sight.

The ancient owl's nest must have burned.
Hastily, all alone,
a glistening armadillo left the scene,
rose-flecked, head down, tail down,

and then a baby rabbit jumped out,
short-eared, to our surprise.
So soft!—a handful of intangible ash
with fixed, ignited eyes.

Too pretty, dreamlike mimicry!
O falling fire and piercing cry
and panic, and a weak mailed fist
clenched ignorant against the sky!

NORTH HAVEN

(*In Memoriam: Robert Lowell*)

I can make out the rigging of a schooner
a mile off; I can count
the new cones on the spruce. It is so still
the pale bay wears a milky skin; the sky
no clouds except for one long, carded horse's tail.

The islands haven't shifted since last summer,
even if I like to pretend they have—
drifting, in a dreamy sort of way,
a little north, a little south, or sidewise—
and that they're free within the blue frontiers of bay.

This month our favorite one is full of flowers:
buttercups, red clover, purple vetch,
hawkweed still burning, daisies pied, eyebright,
the fragrant bedstraw's incandescent stars,
and more, returned, to paint the meadows with delight.

The goldfinches are back, or others like them,
and the white-throated sparrow's five-note song,
pleading and pleading, brings tears to the eyes.
Nature repeats herself, or almost does:
repeat, repeat, repeat; revise, revise, revise.

Years ago, you told me it was here
(in 1932?) you first "discovered *girls*"
and learned to sail, and learned to kiss.
You had "such fun," you said, that classic summer.
("Fun"—it always seemed to leave you at a loss . . .)

You left North Haven, anchored in its rock,
afloat in mystic blue . . . And now—you've left
for good. You can't derange, or rearrange,
your poems again. (But the sparrows can their song.)
The words won't change again. Sad friend, you cannot change.

ONE ART

The art of losing isn't hard to master;
so many things seem filled with the intent
to be lost that their loss is no disaster.

Lose something every day. Accept the fluster
of lost door keys, the hour badly spent.
The art of losing isn't hard to master.

Then practice losing farther, losing faster:
places, and names, and where it was you meant
to travel. None of these will bring disaster.

ELIZABETH BISHOP

I lost my mother's watch. And look! my last, or
next-to-last, of three loved houses went.
The art of losing isn't hard to master.

I lost two cities, lovely ones. And, vaster,
some realms I owned, two rivers, a continent.
I miss them, but it wasn't a disaster.

—Even losing you (the joking voice, a gesture
I love) I shan't have lied. It's evident
the art of losing's not too hard to master
though it may look like (*Write* it!) like disaster.

Robert Bly

SURPRISED BY EVENING

There is unknown dust that is near us,
Waves breaking on shores just over the hill,
Trees full of birds that we have never seen,
Nets drawn down with dark fish.

The evening arrives; we look up and it is there,
It has come through the nets of the stars,
Through the tissues of the grass,
Walking quietly over the asylums of the waters.

The day shall never end, we think:
We have hair that seems born for the daylight;
But, at last, the quiet waters of the night will rise,
And our skin shall see far off, as it does under water.

WAKING FROM SLEEP

Inside the veins there are navies setting forth,
Tiny explosions at the water lines,
And seagulls weaving in the wind of the salty blood.

It is the morning. The country has slept the whole winter.
Window seats were covered with fur skins, the yard was full
Of stiff dogs, and hands that clumsily held heavy books.

Now we wake, and rise from bed, and eat breakfast!—
Shouts rise from the harbor of the blood,
Mist, and masts rising, the knock of wooden tackle in the sunlight.

Now we sing, and do tiny dances on the kitchen floor.
Our whole body is like a harbor at dawn;
We know that our master has left us for the day.

ROBERT BLY

POEM IN THREE PARTS

I

Oh, on an early morning I think I shall live forever!
I am wrapped in my joyful flesh,
As the grass is wrapped in its clouds of green.

II

Rising from a bed, where I dreamt
Of long rides past castles and hot coals,
The sun lies happily on my knees;
I have suffered and survived the night
Bathed in dark water, like any blade of grass.

III

The strong leaves of the box-elder tree,
Plunging in the wind, call us to disappear
Into the wilds of the universe,
Where we shall sit at the foot of a plant,
And live forever, like the dust.

SNOWFALL IN THE AFTERNOON

I

The grass is half-covered with snow.
It was the sort of snowfall that starts in late afternoon,
And now the little houses of the grass are growing dark.

II

If I reached my hands down, near the earth,
I could take handfuls of darkness!
A darkness was always there, which we never noticed.

III

As the snow grows heavier, the cornstalks fade farther away,
And the barn moves nearer to the house.
The barn moves all alone in the growing storm.

IV

The barn is full of corn, and moving toward us now,
Like a hulk blown toward us in a storm at sea;
All the sailors on deck have been blind for many years.

IN A TRAIN

There has been a light snow.
Dark car tracks move in out of the darkness.
I stare at the train window marked with soft dust.
I have awakened at Missoula, Montana, utterly happy.

DRIVING TO TOWN LATE TO MAIL A LETTER

It is a cold and snowy night. The main street is deserted.
The only things moving are swirls of snow.
As I lift the mailbox door, I feel its cold iron.
There is a privacy I love in this snowy night.
Driving around, I will waste more time.

WATERING THE HORSE

How strange to think of giving up all ambition!
Suddenly I see with such clear eyes
The white flake of snow
That has just fallen in the horse's mane!

AFTER LONG BUSYNESS

I start out for a walk at last after weeks at the desk.
Moon gone, plowing underfoot, no stars; not a trace of light!
Suppose a horse were galloping toward me in this open field?
Every day I did not spend in solitude was wasted.

THE BUSY MAN SPEAKS

Not to the mother of solitude will I give myself
Away, not to the mother of love, nor to the mother of conversation,
Nor to the mother of art, nor the mother
Of tears, nor the mother of the ocean;
Not to the mother of sorrow, nor the mother
Of the downcast face, nor the mother of the suffering of death;
Not to the mother of the night full of crickets,
Nor the mother of the open fields, nor the mother of Christ.

But I will give myself to the father of righteousness, the father
Of cheerfulness, who is also the father of rocks,
Who is also the father of perfect gestures;
From the Chase National Bank
An arm of flame has come, and I am drawn
To the desert, to the parched places, to the landscape of zeros;
And I shall give myself away to the father of righteousness,
The stones of cheerfulness, the steel of money, the father of rocks.

ROBERT BLY

WAR AND SILENCE

The bombers spread out, temperature steady
A Negro's ear sleeping in an automobile tire
Pieces of timber float by saying nothing

*

Bishops rush about crying, There is no war,
And bombs fall,
Leaving a dust on the beech trees

*

One leg walks down the road and leaves
The other behind, the eyes part
And fly off in opposite directions

*

Filaments of death grow out.
The sheriff cuts off his black legs
And nails them to a tree

COUNTING SMALL-BONED BODIES

Let's count the bodies over again.

If we could only make the bodies smaller,
The size of skulls,
We could make a whole plain white with skulls in the moonlight!

If we could only make the bodies smaller,
Maybe we could get
A whole year's kill in front of us on a desk!

If we could only make the bodies smaller,
We could fit
A body into a finger-ring, for a keepsake forever.

ROBERT BLY

LOOKING INTO A FACE

Conversation brings us so close! Opening
The surfs of the body,
Bringing fish up near the sun,
And stiffening the backbones of the sea!

I have wandered in a face, for hours,
Passing through dark fires.
I have risen to a body
Not yet born,
Existing like a light around the body,
Through which the body moves like a sliding moon.

THE HERMIT

Darkness is falling through darkness,
Falling from ledge
To ledge.
There is a man whose body is perfectly whole.
He stands, the storm behind him,
And the grass blades are leaping in the wind.
Darkness is gathered in folds
About his feet.
He is no one. When we see
Him, we grow calm,
And sail on into the tunnels of joyful death.

COME WITH ME

Come with me into those things that have felt this despair for so long—
Those removed Chevrolet wheels that howl with a terrible loneliness,
Lying on their backs in the cindery dirt, like men drunk, and naked,

Staggering off down a hill at night to drown at last in the pond.
Those shredded inner tubes abandoned on the shoulders of thruways,
Black and collapsed bodies, that tried and burst,
And were left behind;
And the curly steel shavings, scattered about on garage benches,
Sometimes still warm, gritty when we hold them,
Who have given up, and blame everything on the government,
And those roads in South Dakota that feel around in the darkness . . .

SHACK POEM

1

I don't even know these roads I walk on,
I see the backs of white birds.
Whales rush by, their teeth ivory.

2

Far out at the edge of the heron's wing,
where the air is disturbed by the last feather,
there is the Kingdom. . . .

3

Hurrying to brush between the Two Fish,
the wild woman flies on . . .
blue glass stones a path on earth mark her going.

4

I sit down and fold my legs. . . .
The half dark in the room is delicious.
How marvelous to be a thought entirely surrounded by brains!

LOOKING INTO A TIDE POOL

It is a tide pool, shallow, water coming in, clear, tiny white shell-people on the bottom, asking nothing, not even directions! On the surface the noduled seaweed, lying like hands, slowly drawing back and returning, hands laid on fevered bodies, moving back and forth, as the healer sings wildly, shouting to Jesus and his dead mother.

WHEN THE WHEEL DOES NOT MOVE

There is a dense energy that pools in the abdomen and wants to move and does not! It lies there fierce and nomadic, blocking the road, preventing anyone else from going by.

When the sperm wants to move and does not, then it is as if the earth were not made for me at all, and I cannot walk with the cricket voyaging over his Gobi of wood chips; he is too free for me. I hear a howling in the air.

And what the soul offers, we never see clearly, though the spears fly through the air, crossing above our heads . . . and the naked old man walks by the ecstatically grieving sea, by the tumbling waters. . . . And how can the soul walk without its body? When its own seed stops the wheel, then the body lets nothing through its pores, it longs to groan and stretch out, to walk in procession shaking the sistrum, to disappear into the fog. . . .

And it is knotted. The sun hunches over and walks with its eyes on the ground, the moon hardens, it will not pass away, it refuses to become the sickle, but holds up its face at the window. . . . The water goes back disappointed to the root, the house of sticks falls, we stand alone on the plain. . . .

INSECT HEADS

These insects, golden
and Arabic, sailing in the husks of galleons,
their octagonal heads also
hold sand paintings of the next life.

ROBERT BLY

PASSING AN ORCHARD BY TRAIN

Grass high under apple trees.
The bark of the trees rough and sexual,
the grass growing heavy and uneven.

We cannot bear disaster, like
the rocks—
swaying nakedly
in open fields.

One slight bruise and we die!
I know no one on this train.
A man comes walking down the aisle.
I want to tell him
that I forgive him, that I want him
to forgive me.

© Thomas Victor

Gwendolyn Brooks

from **A STREET IN BRONZEVILLE**

to David and Keziah Brooks

kitchenette building

We are things of dry hours and the involuntary plan,
Grayed in, and gray. "Dream" makes a giddy sound, not strong
Like "rent," "feeding a wife," "satisfying a man."

But could a dream send up through onion fumes
Its white and violet, fight with fried potatoes
And yesterday's garbage ripening in the hall,
Flutter, or sing an aria down these rooms

Even if we were willing to let it in,
Had time to warm it, keep it very clean,
Anticipate a message, let it begin?

We wonder. But not well! not for a minute!
Since Number Five is out of the bathroom now,
We think of lukewarm water, hope to get in it.

the mother

Abortions will not let you forget.
You remember the children you got that you did not get,
The damp small pulps with a little or with no hair,
The singers and workers that never handled the air.
You will never neglect or beat
Them, or silence or buy with a sweet.
You will never wind up the sucking-thumb
Or scuttle off ghosts that come.
You will never leave them, controlling your luscious sigh,
Return for a snack of them, with gobbling mother-eye.

I have heard in the voices of the wind the voices of my dim killed
    children.
I have contracted. I have eased
My dim dears at the breasts they could never suck.
I have said, Sweets, if I sinned, if I seized
Your luck
And your lives from your unfinished reach,
If I stole your births and your names,
Your straight baby tears and your games,
Your stilted or lovely loves, your tumults, your marriages, aches, and your
    deaths,
If I poisoned the beginnings of your breaths,
Believe that even in my deliberateness I was not deliberate.
Though why should I whine,
Whine that the crime was other than mine?—
Since anyhow you are dead.
Or rather, or instead,
You were never made.
But that too, I am afraid,
Is faulty: oh, what shall I say, how is the truth to be said?
You were born, you had body, you died.
It is just that you never giggled or planned or cried.

Believe me, I loved you all.
Believe me, I knew you, though faintly, and I loved, I loved you
All.

a song in the front yard

I've stayed in the front yard all my life.
I want a peek at the back
Where it's rough and untended and hungry weed grows.
A girl gets sick of a rose.

I want to go in the back yard now
And maybe down the alley,
To where the charity children play.
I want a good time today.

They do some wonderful things.
They have some wonderful fun.
My mother sneers, but I say it's fine
How they don't have to go in at quarter to nine.
My mother, she tells me that Johnnie Mae

Will grow up to be a bad woman.
That George'll be taken to Jail soon or late
(On account of last winter he sold our back gate).

But I say it's fine. Honest, I do.
And I'd like to be a bad woman, too,
And wear the brave stockings of night-black lace
And strut down the streets with paint on my face.

the ballad of chocolate Mabbie

It was Mabbie without the grammar school gates.
And Mabbie was all of seven.
And Mabbie was cut from a chocolate bar.
And Mabbie thought life was heaven.

The grammar school gates were the pearly gates,
For Willie Boone went to school.
When she sat by him in history class
Was only her eyes were cool.

It was Mabbie without the grammar school gates
Waiting for Willie Boone.
Half hour after the closing bell!
He would surely be coming soon.

Oh, warm is the waiting for joys, my dears!
And it cannot be too long.
Oh, pity the little poor chocolate lips
That carry the bubble of song!

Out came the saucily bold Willie Boone.
It was woe for our Mabbie now.
He wore like a jewel a lemon-hued lynx
With sand-waves loving her brow.

It was Mabbie alone by the grammar school gates.
Yet chocolate companions had she:
Mabbie on Mabbie with hush in the heart.
Mabbie on Mabbie to be.

the independent man

Now who could take you off to tiny life
In one room or in two rooms or in three
And cork you smartly, like the flask of wine
You are? Not any woman. Not a wife.
You'd let her twirl you, give her a good glee
Showing your leaping ruby to a friend.
Though twirling would be meek. Since not a cork
Could you allow, for being made so free.

A woman would be wise to think it well
If once a week you only rang the bell.

of De Witt Williams on his way to Lincoln Cemetery

He was born in Alabama.
He was bred in Illinois.
He was nothing but a
Plain black boy.

Swing low swing low sweet sweet chariot.
Nothing but a plain black boy.

Drive him past the Pool Hall.
Drive him past the Show.
Blind within his casket,
But maybe he will know.

Down through Forty-seventh Street:
Underneath the L,
And Northwest Corner, Prairie,
That he loved so well.

Don't forget the Dance Halls—
Warwick and Savoy,
Where he picked his women, where
He drank his liquid joy.

Born in Alabama.
Bred in Illinois.
He was nothing but a
Plain black boy.

Swing low swing low sweet sweet chariot.
Nothing but a plain black boy.

NEGRO HERO

to suggest Dorie Miller

I had to kick their law into their teeth in order to save them.
However I have heard that sometimes you have to deal
Devilishly with drowning men in order to swim them to shore.
Or they will haul themselves and you to the trash and the fish beneath.
(When I think of this, I do not worry about a few
Chipped teeth.)

It is good I gave glory, it is good I put gold on their name.
Or there would have been spikes in the afterward hands.
But let us speak only of my success and the pictures in the Caucasian
   dailies
As well as the Negro weeklies. For I am a gem.
(They are not concerned that it was hardly The Enemy my fight was
   against
But them.)

It was a tall time. And of course my blood was
Boiling about in my head and straining and howling and singing me on.
Of course I was rolled on wheels of my boy itch to get at the gun.
Of course all the delicate rehearsal shots of my childhood massed in
   mirage before me.
Of course I was child
And my first swallow of the liquor of battle bleeding black air dying and
   demon noise
Made me wild.

It was kinder than that, though, and I showed like a banner my kindness.
I loved. And a man will guard when he loves.
Their white-gowned democracy was my fair lady.
With her knife lying cold, straight, in the softness of her sweet-flowing
   sleeve.
But for the sake of the dear smiling mouth and the stuttered promise I
   toyed with my life.
I threw back!—I would not remember
Entirely the knife.

Still—am I good enough to die for them, is my blood bright enough to
be spilled,
Was my constant back-question—are they clear
On this? Or do I intrude even now?
Am I clean enough to kill for them, do they wish me to kill
For them or is my place while death licks his lips and strides to them
In the galley still?

(In a southern city a white man said
Indeed, I'd rather be dead;
Indeed, I'd rather be shot in the head
Or ridden to waste on the back of a flood
Than saved by the drop of a black man's blood.)

Naturally, the important thing is, I helped to save them, them and a part
of their democracy.
Even if I had to kick their law into their teeth in order to do that for
them.
And I am feeling well and settled in myself because I believe it was a
good job,
Despite this possible horror: that they might prefer the
Preservation of their law in all its sick dignity and their knives
To the continuation of their creed
And their lives.

WE REAL COOL

The Pool Players.
Seven at the Golden Shovel.

We real cool. We
Left school. We

Lurk late. We
Strike straight. We

Sing sin. We
Thin gin. We

Jazz June. We
Die soon.

GWENDOLYN BROOKS

THE LOVERS OF THE POOR

arrive. The Ladies from the Ladies' Betterment
        League
Arrive in the afternoon, the late light slanting
In diluted gold bars across the boulevard brag
Of proud, seamed faces with mercy and murder hinting
Here, there, interrupting, all deep and debonair,
The pink paint on the innocence of fear;
Walk in a gingerly manner up the hall.
Cutting with knives served by their softest care,
Served by their love, so barbarously fair.
Whose mothers taught: You'd better not be cruel!
You had better not throw stones upon the wrens!
Herein they kiss and coddle and assault
Anew and dearly in the innocence
With which they baffle nature. Who are full,
Sleek, tender-clad, fit, fiftyish, a-glow, all
Sweetly abortive, hinting at fat fruit,
Judge it high time that fiftyish fingers felt
Beneath the lovelier planes of enterprise.
To resurrect. To moisten with milky chill.
To be a random hitching-post or plush.
To be, for wet eyes, random and handy hem.
        Their guild is giving money to the poor.
The worthy poor. The very very worthy
And beautiful poor. Perhaps just not too swarthy?
Perhaps just not too dirty nor too dim
Nor—passionate. In truth, what they could wish
Is—something less than derelict or dull.
Not staunch enough to stab, though, gaze for gaze!
God shield them sharply from the beggar-bold!
The noxious needy ones whose battle's bald
Nonetheless for being voiceless, hits one down.
        But it's all so bad! and entirely too much for
            them.
The stench; the urine, cabbage, and dead beans,
Dead porridges of assorted dusty grains,
The old smoke, *heavy* diapers, and, they're told,
Something called chitterlings. The darkness. Drawn
Darkness, or dirty light. The soil that stirs.
The soil that looks the soil of centuries.
And for that matter the *general* oldness. Old

Wood. Old marble. Old tile. Old old old.
Not homekind Oldness! Not Lake Forest, Glencoe.
Nothing is sturdy, nothing is majestic,
There is no quiet drama, no rubbed glaze, no
Unkillable infirmity of such
A tasteful turn as lately they have left,
Glencoe, Lake Forest, and to which their cars
Must presently restore them. When they're done
With dullards and distortions of this fistic
Patience of the poor and put-upon.
          They've never seen such a make-do-ness as
Newspaper rugs before! In this, this "flat,"
Their hostess is gathering up the oozed, the rich
Rugs of the morning (tattered! the bespattered. . . .)
Readies to spread clean rugs for afternoon.
Here is a scene for you. The Ladies look,
In horror, behind a substantial citizeness
Whose trains clank out across her swollen heart.
Who, arms akimbo, almost fills a door.
All tumbling children, quilts dragged to the floor
And tortured thereover, potato peelings, soft-
Eyed kitten, hunched-up, haggard, to-be-hurt.
          Their League is alloting largesse to the Lost.
But to put their clean, their pretty money, to put
Their money collected from delicate rose-fingers
Tipped with their hundred flawless rose-nails seems . . .
          They own Spode, Lowestoft, candelabra,
Mantels, and hostess gowns, and sunburst clocks,
Turtle soup, Chippendale, red satin "hangings,"
Aubussons and Hattie Carnegie. They Winter
In Palm Beach; cross the Water in June; attend,
When suitable, the nice Art Institute;
Buy the right books in the best bindings; saunter
On Michigan, Easter mornings, in sun or wind.
Oh Squalor! This sick four-story hulk, this fibre
With fissures everywhere! Why, what are bringings
Of loathe-love largesse? What shall peril hungers
So old old, what shall flatter the desolate?
Tin can, blocked fire escape and chitterling
And swaggering seeking youth and the puzzled wreckage
Of the middle-passage, and urine and stale shames
And, again, the porridges of the underslung
And children children children. Heavens! That
Was a rat, surely, off there, in the shadows? Long

And long-tailed? Gray? The Ladies from the Ladies'
Betterment League agree it will be better
To achieve the outer air that rights and steadies,
To hie to a house that does not holler, to ring
Bells elsetime, better presently to cater
To no more Possibilities, to get
Away. Perhaps the money can be posted.
Perhaps they two may choose another Slum!
Some serious sooty half-unhappy home!—
Where loathe-love likelier may be invested.
              Keeping their scented bodies in the center
Of the hall as they walk down the hysterical hall,
They allow their lovely skirts to graze no wall,
Are off at what they manage of a canter,
And, resuming all the clues of what they were,
Try to avoid inhaling the laden air.

RIOT

A riot is the language of the unheard.

              Martin Luther King

John Cabot, out of Wilma, once a Wycliffe,
all whitebluerose below his golden hair,
wrapped richly in right linen and right wool,
almost forgot his Jaguar and Lake Bluff;
almost forgot Grandtully (which is The
Best Thing That Ever Happened to Scotch); almost
forgot the sculpture at the Richard Gray
and Distelheim; the kidney pie at Maxim's,
the Grenadine de Boeuf at Maison Henri.

Because the Negroes were coming down the street.

Because the Poor were sweaty and unpretty
(not like Two Dainty Negroes in Winnetka)
and they were coming toward him in rough ranks.
In seas. In windsweep. They were black and loud.
And not detainable. And not discreet.

Gross. Gross. "*Que tu es grossier!*" John Cabot
itched instantly beneath the nourished white
that told his story of glory to the World.
"Don't let It touch me! the blackness! Lord!" he whispered
to any handy angel in the sky.

But, in a thrilling announcement, on It drove
and breathed on him: and touched him. In that breath
the fume of pig foot, chitterling and cheap chili,
malign, mocked John. And, in terrific touch, old
averted doubt jerked forward decently,
cried "Cabot! John! You are a desperate man,
and the desperate die expensively today."

John Cabot went down in the smoke and fire
and broken glass and blood, and he cried "Lord!
Forgive these nigguhs that know not what they do."

AN ASPECT OF LOVE,
ALIVE IN THE ICE AND FIRE

LaBohem Brown

It is the morning of our love.

In a package of minutes there is this We.
How beautiful.
Merry foreigners in our morning,
we laugh, we touch each other,
are responsible props and posts.

A physical light is in the room.

Because the world is at the window
we cannot wonder very long.

You rise. Although
genial, you are in yourself again.
I observe
your direct and respectable stride.
You are direct and self-accepting as a lion
in African velvet. You are level, lean,
remote.

There is a moment in Camaraderie
when interruption is not to be understood.
I cannot bear an interruption.
This is the shining joy;
the time of not-to-end.

On the street we smile.
We go
in different directions
down the imperturbable street.

TO DON AT SALAAM

I like to see you lean back in your chair
so far you have to fall but do not—
your arms back, your fine hands
in your print pockets.

Beautiful. Impudent.
Ready for life.
A tied storm.

I like to see you wearing your boy smile
whose tribute is for two of us or three.

Sometimes in life
things seem to be moving
and they are not
and they are not
there.
You are there.

Your voice is the listened-for music.
Your act is the consolidation.

I like to see you living in the world.

© Gerard Malanga

Robert Creeley

THE BUSINESS

To be in love is like going out-
side to see what kind of day

it is. Do not
mistake me. If you love

her how prove she
loves also, except that it

occurs, a remote chance on
which you stake

yourself? But barter for
the Indian was a means of sustenance.

There are records.

I KNOW A MAN

As I sd to my
friend, because I am
always talking,—John, I

sd, which was not his
name, the darkness sur-
rounds us, what

can we do against
it, or else, shall we &
why not, buy a goddamn big car,

ROBERT CREELEY

drive, he sd, for
christ's sake, look
out where yr going.

A FORM OF WOMEN

I have come far enough
from where I was not before
to have seen the things
looking in at me through the open door

and have walked tonight
by myself
to see the moonlight
and see it as trees

and shapes more fearful
because I feared
what I did not know
but have wanted to know.

My face is my own, I thought.
But you have seen it
turn into a thousand years.
I watched you cry.

I could not touch you.
I wanted very much to
touch you
but could not.

If it is dark
when this is given to you,
have care for its content
when the moon shines.

My face is my own.
My hands are my own.
My mouth is my own
but I am not.

Moon, moon,
when you leave me alone
all the darkness is
an utter blackness,

a pit of fear,
a stench,
hands unreasonable
never to touch.

But I love you.
Do you love me.
What to say
when you see me.

A WICKER BASKET

Comes the time when it's later
and onto your table the headwaiter
puts the bill, and very soon after
rings out the sound of lively laughter—

Picking up change, hands like a walrus,
and a face like a barndoor's,
and a head without any apparent size,
nothing but two eyes—

So that's you, man,
or me. I make it as I can,
I pick up, I go
faster than they know—

Out the door, the street like a night,
any night, and no one in sight,
but then, well, there she is,
old friend Liz—

And she opens the door of her cadillac,
I step in back,
and we're gone.
She turns me on—

ROBERT CREELEY

There are very huge stars, man, in the sky,
and from somewhere very far off someone hands me a slice of
                apple pie,
with a gob of white, white ice cream on top of it,
and I eat it—

Slowly. And while certainly
they are laughing at me, and all around me is racket
of these cats not making it, I make it

in my wicker basket.

THE FLOWER

I think I grow tensions
like flowers
in a wood where
nobody goes.

Each wound is perfect,
encloses itself in a tiny
imperceptible blossom,
making pain.

Pain is a flower like that one,
like this one,
like that one,
like this one.

THE RAIN

All night the sound had
come back again,
and again falls
this quiet, persistent rain.

ROBERT CREELEY

What am I to myself
that must be remembered,
insisted upon
so often? Is it

that never the ease,
even the hardness,
of rain failing
will have for me

something other than this,
something not so insistent—
am I to be locked in this
final uneasiness.

Love, if you love me,
lie next to me.
Be for me, like rain,
the getting out

of the tiredness, the fatuousness, the semi-
lust of intentional indifference.
Be wet
with a decent happiness.

THE MEMORY

Like a river she was,
huge roily mass of water
carrying tree trunks
and divers drunks.

Like a Priscilla, a feminine Benjamin,
a whore gone right over
the falls,
she was.

Did you know her.
Did you love her, brother.
Did wonder pour down
on the whole goddamn town.

ROBERT CREELEY

THE RESCUE

The man sits in a timelessness
with the horse under him in time
to a movement of legs and hooves
upon a timeless sand.

Distance comes in from the foreground
present in the picture as time
he reads outward from
and comes from that beginning.

A wind blows in
and out and all about the man
as the horse ran
and runs to come in time.

A house is burning in the sand.
A man and horse are burning.
The wind is burning.
They are running to arrive.

THE LANGUAGE

Locate *I*
love you some-
where in

teeth and
eyes, bite
it but

take care not
to hurt, you
want so

much so
little. Words
say everything,

ROBERT CREELEY

I
love you
again,

then what
is emptiness
for. To

fill, fill.
I heard words
and words full

of holes
aching. Speech
is a mouth.

THE WINDOW

Position is where you
put it, where it is,
did you, for example, that

large tank there, silvered,
with the white church along-
side, lift

all that, to what
purpose? How
heavy the slow

world is with
everything put
in place. Some

man walks by, a
car beside him on
the dropped

road, a leaf of
yellow color is
going to

ROBERT CREELEY

fall. It
all drops into
place. My

face is heavy
with the sight. I can
feel my eye breaking.

THE ACT OF LOVE

for Bobbie

Whatever constitutes
the act of love,
save physical

encounter, you are
dear to me,
not value as

with banks—
but a meaning self-
sufficient, dry

at times as sand,
or else the trees,
dripping with

rain. How shall
one, this so-
called person,

say it? He
loves, his mind
is occupied, his

hands move
writing words
which come

into his head.
Now here,
the day surrounds

ROBERT CREELEY

this man
and woman
sitting a small

distance apart.
Love will not
solve it—but

draws closer,
always, makes
the moisture of their

mouths and bodies
actively
engage. If I

wanted
a dirty picture,
would it always

be of a
woman straddled?
Yes

and no, these
are true opposites,
a you and me

of non-
sense,
for our love.

Now, one
says, the wind
lifts, the sky

is very blue, the
water just
beyond me makes

its lovely sounds.
How *dear*
you are

ROBERT CREELEY

to me, how love-
ly all your
body *is*, how

all these
senses do
commingle, so

that in your very
arms I still
can think of you.

ON VACATION

Things seem empty
on vacation if the labors
have not been physical,

if tedium was rather
a daily knot, a continuum,
if satisfaction was almost

placid. On Sundays the restlessness
grows, on weekends, on
months of vacation myself grows

vacuous. Taking walks, swimming,
drinking, I am always afraid
of having more. Hence a true

Puritan, I shall never rest from my labors
until all rest with me, until I am
driven by that density home.

ROBERT CREELEY

MOMENT

Whether to *use* time, or to *kill* time, either
still preys on my mind.

One's come now to the graveyard,
where the bones of the dead are.

All roads *have* come
here, truly common—

except the body is moved,
still, to some other use.

© Terry Parke

James Dickey

THE HEAVEN OF ANIMALS

Here they are. The soft eyes open.
If they have lived in a wood
It is a wood.
If they have lived on plains
It is grass rolling
Under their feet forever.

Having no souls, they have come,
Anyway, beyond their knowing.
Their instincts wholly bloom
And they rise.
The soft eyes open.

To match them, the landscape flowers,
Outdoing, desperately
Outdoing what is required:
The richest wood,
The deepest field.

For some of these,
It could not be the place
It is, without blood.
These hunt, as they have done,
But with claws and teeth grown perfect,

More deadly than they can believe.
They stalk more silently,
And crouch on the limbs of trees,
And their descent
Upon the bright backs of their prey

May take years
In a sovereign floating of joy.
And those that are hunted
Know this as their life,
Their reward: to walk

Under such trees in full knowledge
Of what is in glory above them,
And to feel no fear,
But acceptance, compliance.
Fulfilling themselves without pain

At the cycle's center,
They tremble, they walk
Under the tree,
They fall, they are torn,
They rise, they walk again.

IN THE LUPANAR AT POMPEII

There are tracks which belong to wheels
Long since turned to air and time.
Those are the powerful chariots
I follow down cobblestones,
Not being dragged, exactly,
But not of my own will, either,
Going past the flower sellers'
And the cindery produce market
And the rich man's home, and the house
Of the man who kept a dog
Set in mosaic.

As tourist, but mostly as lecher,
I seek out the dwelling of women
Who all expect me, still, because
They expect anybody who comes.
I am ready to pay, and I do,
And then go in among them
Where on the dark walls of their home
They hold their eternal postures,
Doing badly drawn, exacting,
Too-willing, wide-eyed things
With dry-eyed art.

I sit down in one of the rooms
Where it happened again and again.
I could be in prison, or dead,

JAMES DICKEY

Cast down for my sins in a cell
Still filled with a terrible motion
Like the heaving and sighing of earth
To be free of the heat it restrains.
I feel in my heart how the heart
Of the mountain broke, and the women
Fled onto the damp of the walls
And shaped their embraces

To include whoever would come here
After the stone-cutting chariots.
I think of the marvel of lust
Which can always, at any moment,
Become more than it believed,
And almost always is less:
I think of its possible passing
Beyond, into tender awareness,
Into helplessness, weeping, and death:
It must be like the first
Soft floating of ash,

When, in the world's frankest hands,
Someone lay with his body shaken
Free of the self: that amazement—
For we who must try to explain
Ourselves in the house of this flesh
Never can tell the quick heat
Of our own from another's breathing,
Nor yet from the floating of feathers
That form in our lungs when the mountain
Settles like odd, warm snow against
Our willing limbs.

We never can really tell
Whether nature condemns us or loves us
As we lie here dying of breath
And the painted, unchanging women,
Believing the desperate dead
Where they stripped to the skin of the soul
And whispered to us, as to
Their panting, observing selves:
"Passion. Before we die
Let us hope for no longer
But truly know it."

JAMES DICKEY

A SCREENED PORCH IN THE COUNTRY

All of them are sitting
Inside a lamp of coarse wire
And being in all directions
Shed upon darkness,
Their bodies softening to shadow, until
They come to rest out in the yard
In a kind of blurred golden country
In which they more deeply lie
Than if they were being created
Of Heavenly light.

Where they are floating beyond
Themselves, in peace,
Where they have laid down
Their souls and not known it,
The smallest creatures,
As every night they do,
Come to the edge of them
And sing, if they can,
Or, if they can't, simply shine
Their eyes back, sitting on haunches,

Pulsating and thinking of music.
Occasionally, something weightless
Touches the screen
With its body, dies,
Or is unmurmuringly hurt,
But mainly nothing happens
Except that a family continues
To be laid down
In the midst of its nightly creatures,
Not one of which openly comes

Into the golden shadow
Where the people are lying,
Emitted by their own house
So humanly that they become
More than human, and enter the place
Of small, blindly singing things,
Seeming to rejoice

JAMES DICKEY

Perpetually, without effort,
Without knowing why
Or how they do it.

THE HOSPITAL WINDOW

I have just come down from my father.
Higher and higher he lies
Above me in a blue light
Shed by a tinted window.
I drop through six white floors
And then step out onto pavement.

Still feeling my father ascend,
I start to cross the firm street,
My shoulder blades shining with all
The glass the huge building can raise.
Now I must turn round and face it,
And know his one pane from the others.

Each window possesses the sun
As though it burned there on a wick.
I wave, like a man catching fire.
All the deep-dyed windowpanes flash,
And, behind them, all the white rooms
They turn to the color of Heaven.

Ceremoniously, gravely, and weakly,
Dozens of pale hands are waving
Back, from inside their flames.
Yet one pure pane among these
Is the bright, erased blankness of nothing.
I know that my father is there,

In the shape of his death still living.
The traffic increases around me
Like a madness called down on my head.
The horns blast at me like shotguns,
And drivers lean out, driven crazy—
But now my propped-up father

Lifts his arm out of stillness at last.
The light from the window strikes me
And I turn as blue as a soul,
As the moment when I was born.
I am not afraid for my father—
Look! He is grinning; he is not

Afraid for my life, either,
As the wild engines stand at my knees
Shredding their gears and roaring,
And I hold each car in its place
For miles, inciting its horn
To blow down the walls of the world

That the dying may float without fear
In the bold blue gaze of my father.
Slowly I move to the sidewalk
With my pin-tingling hand half dead
At the end of my bloodless arm.
I carry it off in amazement,

High, still higher, still waving,
My recognized face fully mortal,
Yet not; not at all, in the pale,
Drained, otherworldly, stricken,
Created hue of stained glass.
I have just come down from my father.

IN THE MOUNTAIN TENT

I am hearing the shape of the rain
Take the shape of the tent and believe it,
Laying down all around where I lie
A profound, unspeakable law.
I obey, and am free-falling slowly

Through the thought-out leaves of the wood
Into the minds of animals.
I am there in the shining of water
Like dark, like light, out of Heaven.

I am there like the dead, or the beast
Itself, which thinks of a poem—
Green, plausible, living, and holy—
And cannot speak, but hears,
Called forth from the waiting of things,

A vast, proper, reinforced crying
With the sifted, harmonious pause,
The sustained intake of all breath
Before the first word of the Bible.

At midnight water dawns
Upon the held skulls of the foxes
And weasels and tousled hares
On the eastern side of the mountain.
Their light is the image I make

As I wait as if recently killed,
Receptive, fragile, half-smiling,
My brow watermarked with the mark
On the wing of a moth

And the tent taking shape on my body
Like ill-fitting, Heavenly clothes.
From holes in the ground comes my voice
In the God-silenced tongue of the beasts.
"I shall rise from the dead," I am saying.

THE FIREBOMBING

*Denke daran, dass nach den grossen Zerstörungen
Jedermann beweisen wird, dass er unshuldig war.*

—*Günter Eich*

Or hast thou an arm like God?

—*The Book of Job*

Homeowners unite.

All families lie together, though some are burned alive.
The others try to feel
For them. Some can, it is often said.

Starve and take off

Twenty years in the suburbs, and the palm trees willingly leap
Into the flashlights,
And there is beneath them also
A booted crackling of snailshells and coral sticks.
There are cowl flaps and the tilt cross of propellers,
The shovel-marked clouds' far sides against the moon,
The enemy filling up the hills
With ceremonial graves. At my somewhere among these,

Snap, a bulb is tricked on in the cockpit

And some technical-minded stranger with my hands
Is sitting in a glass treasure-hole of blue light,
Having potential fire under the undeodorized arms
Of his wings, on thin bomb-shackles,
The "tear-drop-shaped" 300-gallon drop-tanks
Filled with napalm and gasoline.

Thinking forward ten minutes
From that, there is also the burst straight out
Of the overcast into the moon; there is now
The moon-metal-shine of propellers, the quarter-
moonstone, aimed at the waves,
Stopped on the cumulus.

There is then this re-entry
Into cloud, for the engines to ponder their sound.
In white dark the aircraft shrinks; Japan

Dilates around it like a thought.
Coming out, the one who is here is over
Land, passing over the all-night grainfields,
In dark paint over
The woods with one silver side,
Rice-water calm at all levels
Of the terraced hill.
                              Enemy rivers and trees
Sliding off me like snakeskin,
Strips of vapor spooled from the wingtips
Going   invisible   passing   over   on
Over   bridges   roads for nightwalkers
Sunday night in the enemy's country   absolute

Calm   the moon's face   coming   slowly
About
            the inland sea
Slants   is woven with wire thread
Levels out   holds together like a quilt
Off the starboard wing   cloud flickers
At my glassed-off forehead   the moon's now and again
Uninterrupted face going forward
Over the waves in a glide-path
Lost into land.

Going: going with it

Combat booze by my side in a cratered canteen,
Bourbon frighteningly mixed
With GI pineapple juice,
Dogs trembling under me for hundreds of miles, on many
Islands, sleep-smelling that ungodly mixture
Of napalm and high-octane fuel,
Good bourbon and GI juice.

Rivers circling behind me around
Come to the fore, and bring
A town with everyone darkened.
Five thousand people are sleeping off
An all-day American drone.
Twenty years in the suburbs have not shown me
Which ones were hit and which not.

Haul on the wheel   racking slowly
The aircraft blackly around
In a dark dream   that   that is
That is like flying inside someone's head

Think of this   think of this

I did not think of my house
But think of my house now

Where the lawn mower rests on its laurels
Where the diet exists
For my own good   where I try to drop
Twenty years, eating figs in the pantry
Blinded by each and all

Of the eye-catching cans that gladly have caught my wife's eye
Until I cannot say
Where the screwdriver is   where the children
Get off the bus   where the new
Scoutmaster lives   where the fly
Hones his front legs   where the hammock folds
Its erotic daydreams   where the Sunday
School text for the day has been put   where the fire
Wood is   where the payments
For everything under the sun
Pile peacefully up,

But in this half-paid-for pantry
Among the red lids that screw off
With an easy half-twist to the left
And the long drawers crammed with dim spoons,
I still have charge—secret charge—
Of the fire developed to cling
To everything: to golf carts and fingernail
Scissors as yet unborn   tennis shoes
Grocery baskets   toy fire engines
New Buicks stalled by the half-moon
Shining at midnight on crossroads   green paint
Of jolly garden tools   red Christmas ribbons:

Not atoms, these, but glue inspired
By love of country to burn,
The apotheosis of gelatin.

Behind me having risen the Southern Cross
Set up by chaplains in the Ryukyus—
Orion, Scorpio, the immortal silver
Like the myths of king-
insects at swarming time—
One mosquito, dead drunk
On altitude, drones on, far under the engines,
And bites between
The oxygen mask and the eye.
The enemy-colored skin of families
Determines to hold its color
In sleep, as my hand turns whiter
Than ever, clutching the toggle—
The ship shakes   bucks
Fire hangs   not yet fire

In the air above Beppu
For I am fulfilling

An "anti-morale" raid upon it.
All leashes of dogs
Break under the first bomb, around those
In bed, or late in the public baths: around those
Who inch forward on their hands
Into medicinal waters.
Their heads come up with a roar
Of Chicago fire:
Come up with the carp pond showing
The bathhouse upside down,
Standing stiller to show it more
As I sail artistically over
The resort town followed by farms,
Singing and twisting
All the handles in heaven   kicking
The small cattle off their feet
In a red costly blast
Flinging jelly over the walls
As in a chemical war-
fare field demonstration.
With fire of mine like a cat

Holding onto another man's walls,
My hat should crawl on my head
In streetcars, thinking of it,
The fat on my body should pale.

Gun down
The engines, the eight blades sighing
For the moment when the roofs will connect
Their flames, and make a town burning with all
American fire.
                    Reflections of houses catch;
Fire shuttles from pond to pond
In every direction, till hundreds flash with one death.
With this in the dark of the mind,
Death will not be what it should;
Will not, even now, even when
My exhaled face in the mirror
Of bars, dilates in a cloud like Japan.
The death of children is ponds

Shutter-flashing; responding mirrors; it climbs
The terraces of hills
Smaller and smaller, a mote of red dust
At a hundred feet; at a hundred and one it goes out.
That is what should have got in
To my eye
And shown the insides of houses, the low tables
Catch fire from the floor mats,
Blaze up in gas around their heads
Like a dream of suddenly growing
Too intense for war. Ah, under one's dark arms
Something strange-scented falls—when those on earth
Die, there is not even sound;
One is cool and enthralled in the cockpit,
Turned blue by the power of beauty,
In a pale treasure-hole of soft light
Deep in aesthetic contemplation,
Seeing the ponds catch fire
And cast it through ring after ring
Of land: O death in the middle
Of acres of inch-deep water!   Useless

Firing   small arms
Speckles   from the river
Bank   one ninety-millimeter
Misses   far down   wrong petals   gone

It is this detachment,
The honored aesthetic evil,
The greatest sense of power in one's life,
That must be shed in bars, or by whatever
Means, by starvation
Visions in well-stocked pantries:
The moment when the moon sails in between
The tail-booms   the rudders nod   I swing
Over   directly over the heart
The *heart* of the fire. A mosquito burns out on my cheek
With the cold of my face   there are the eyes
In blue light   bar light
All masked but them   the moon
Crossing from left to right   in the streams below
Oriental fish form quickly
In the chemical shine,

In their eyes one tiny seed
Of deranged, Old Testament light.

Letting go   letting go
The plane rises gently   dark forms
Glide off me   long water   pales
In safe zones   a new cry enters
The voice box of chained family dogs

We buck   leap over something
Not there   settle back
Leave it   leave it clinging and crying
It consumes them in a hot
Body-flash, old age or menopause
Of children, clings and burns
                          eating through
And when a reed mat catches fire
From me, it explodes through field after field
Bearing its sleeper   another

Bomb finds a home
And clings to it like a child. And so

Goodbye to the grassy mountains
To cloud streaming from the night engines
Flags   pennons   curved silks
Of air   myself streaming also
My body covered
With flags, the air of flags
Between the engines.
Forever I do sleep in that position,
Forever in a turn
For home that breaks out streaming banners
From my wingtips,
Wholly in position to admire.

O then I knock it off
And turn for home over the black complex thread worked through
The silver night-sea,
Following the huge, moon-washed steppingstones
Of the Ryukyus south,
The nightgrass of mountains billowing softly

In my rising heat.
                    Turn and tread down
The yellow stones of the islands
To where Okinawa burns,
Pure gold, on the radar screen,
Beholding, beneath, the actual island form
In the vast water-silver poured just above solid ground,
An inch of water extending for thousands of miles
Above flat ploughland. Say "down," and it is done.

All this, and I am still hungry,
Still twenty years overweight, still unable
To get down there or see
What really happened.
                    But it may be that I could not,
If I tried, say to any
Who lived there, deep in my flames: say, in cold
Grinning sweat, as to another
As these homeowners who are always curving
Near me down the different-grassed street: say
As though to the neighbor
I borrowed the hedge-clippers from
On the darker-grassed side of the two,
Come in, my house is yours, come in
If you can, if you
Can pass this unfired door. It is that I can imagine
At the threshold nothing
With its ears crackling off
Like powdery leaves,
Nothing with children of ashes, nothing not
Amiable, gentle, well-meaning,
A little nervous for no
Reason   a little worried   a little too loud
Or too easygoing   nothing I haven't lived with
For twenty years, still nothing not as
American as I am, and proud of it.

Absolution? Sentence? No matter;
The thing itself is in that.

JAMES DICKEY

SLED BURIAL, DREAM CEREMONY

While the south rains, the north
Is snowing, and the dead southerner
Is taken there. He lies with the top of his casket
Open, his hair combed, the particles in the air
Changing to other things. The train stops

In a small furry village, and men in flap-eared caps
And others with women's scarves tied around their heads
And business hats over those, unload him,
And one of them reaches inside the coffin and places
The southerner's hand at the center

Of his dead breast. They load him onto a sled,
An old-fashioned sled with high-curled runners,
Drawn by horses with bells, and begin
To walk out of town, past dull red barns
Inching closer to the road as it snows

Harder, past an army of gunny-sacked bushes,
Past horses with flakes in the hollows of their sway-backs,
Past round faces drawn by children
On kitchen windows, all shedding basic-shaped tears.
The coffin top still is wide open;

His dead eyes stare through his lids,
Not fooled that the snow is cotton. The woods fall
Slowly off all of them, until they are walking
Between rigid little houses of ice-fishers
On a plain which is a great plain of water

Until the last rabbit track fails, and they are
At the center. They take axes, shovels, mattocks,
Dig the snow away, and saw the ice in the form
Of his coffin, lifting the slab like a door
Without hinges. The snow creaks under the sled

As they unload him like hay, holding his weight by ropes.
Sensing an unwanted freedom, a fish
Slides by, under the hole leading up through the snow
To nothing, and is gone. The coffin's shadow
Is white, and they stand there, gunny-sacked bushes,

JAMES DICKEY

Summoned from village sleep into someone else's dream
Of death, and let him down, still seeing the flakes in the air
At the place they are born of pure shadow
Like his dead eyelids, rocking for a moment like a boat
On utter foreignness, before he fills and sails down.

THE SHEEP CHILD

Farm boys wild to couple
With anything   with soft-wooded trees
With mounds of earth   mounds
Of pinestraw   will keep themselves off
Animals by legends of their own:
In the hay-tunnel dark
And dung of barns, they will
Say   I have heard tell

That in a museum in Atlanta
Way back in a corner somewhere
There's this thing that's only half
Sheep   like a woolly baby
Pickled in alcohol   because
Those things can't live   his eyes
Are open   but you can't stand to look
I heard from somebody who . . .

But this is now almost all
Gone. The boys have taken
Their own true wives in the city,
The sheep are safe in the west hill
Pasture   but we who were born there
Still are not sure. Are we,
Because we remember, remembered
In the terrible dust of museums?

Merely with his eyes, the sheep-child may

Be saying   saying

I am here, in my father's house.
I who am half of your world, came deeply

JAMES DICKEY

To my mother in the long grass
Of the west pasture, where she stood like moonlight
Listening for foxes. It was something like love
From another world that seized her
From behind, and she gave, not lifting her head
Out of dew, without ever looking, her best
Self to that great need. Turned loose, she dipped her face
Farther into the chill of the earth, and in a sound
Of sobbing   of something stumbling
Away, began, as she must do,
To carry me. I woke, dying,

In the summer sun of the hillside, with my eyes
Far more than human. I saw for a blazing moment
The great grassy world from both sides,
Man and beast in the round of their need,
And the hill wind stirred in my wool,
My hoof and my hand clasped each other,
I ate my one meal
Of milk, and died
Staring. From dark grass I came straight

To my father's house, whose dust
Whirls up in the halls for no reason
When no one comes   piling deep in a hellish mild corner,
And, through my immortal waters,
I meet the sun's grains eye
To eye, and they fail at my closet of glass.
Dead, I am most surely living
In the minds of farm boys: I am he who drives
Them like wolves from the hound bitch and calf
And from the chaste ewe in the wind.
They go into woods   into bean fields   they go
Deep into their known right hands. Dreaming of me,
They groan   they wait   they suffer
Themselves, they marry, they raise their kind.

ADULTERY

We have all been in rooms
We cannot die in, and they are odd places, and sad.
Often Indians are standing eagle-armed on hills

JAMES DICKEY

In the sunrise   open wide to the Great Spirit
Or gliding in canoes   or cattle are browsing on the walls
Far away   gazing down with the eyes of our children

Not far away   or there are men driving
The last railspike, which has turned
Gold in their hands. Gigantic forepleasure lives

Among such scenes, and we are alone with it
At last. There is always some weeping
Between us   and someone is always checking

A wrist watch by the bed to see how much
Longer we have left. Nothing can come
Of this   nothing can come

Of us: of me with my grim techniques
Or you who have sealed your womb
With a ring of convulsive rubber:

Although we come together,
Nothing will come of us. But we would not give
It up, for death is beaten

By praying Indians   by distant cows   historical
Hammers   by hazardous meetings that bridge
A continent. One could never die here

Never die   never die
While crying. My lover, my dear one
I will see you next week

When I'm in town. I will call you
If I can. Please get hold of   please don't
Oh God, Please don't any more I can't bear . . . Listen:

We have done it again   we are
Still living. Sit up and smile,
God bless you. Guilt is magical.

JAMES DICKEY

DEER AMONG CATTLE

Here and there in the searing beam
Of my hand going through the night meadow
They all are grazing

With pins of human light in their eyes.
A wild one also is eating
The human grass,

Slender, graceful, domesticated
By darkness, among the bred-
for-slaughter,

Having bounded their paralyzed fence
And inclined his branched forehead onto
Their green frosted table,

The only live thing in this flashlight
Who can leave whenever he wishes,
Turn grass into forest,

Foreclose inhuman brightness from his eyes
But stands here still, unperturbed,
In their wide-open country,

The sparks from my hand in his pupils
Unmatched anywhere among cattle,

Grazing with them the night of the hammer
As one of their own who shall rise.

© *Thomas Victor*

Alan Dugan

LOVE SONG: I AND THOU

Nothing is plumb, level, or square:
　　the studs are bowed, the joists
are shaky by nature, no piece fits
　　any other piece without a gap
or pinch, and bent nails
　　dance all over the surfacing
like maggots. By Christ
　　I am no carpenter. I built
the roof for myself, the walls
　　for myself, the floors
for myself, and got
　　hung up in it myself. I
danced with a purple thumb
　　at this house-warming, drunk
with my prime whiskey: rage.
　　Oh I spat rage's nails
into the frame-up of my work:
　　it held. It settled plumb,
level, solid, square and true
　　for that great moment. Then
it screamed and went on through,
　　skewing as wrong the other way.
God damned it. This is hell,
　　but I planned it, I sawed it,
I nailed it, and I
　　will live in it until it kills me.
I can nail my left palm
　　to the left-hand crosspiece but
I can't do everything myself.
　　I need a hand to nail the right,
a help, a love, a you, a wife.

ALAN DUGAN

TRIBUTE TO KAFKA FOR
SOMEONE TAKEN

The party is going strong.
The doorbell rings. It's
for someone named me.
I'm coming. I take
a last drink, a last
puff on a cigarette,
a last kiss at a girl,
and step into the hall,
                          bang,
shutting out the laughter. "Is
your name you?" "Yes."
"Well come along then."
"See here. See here. See here."

ELEGY

I know but will not tell
you, Aunt Irene, why there
are soapsuds in the whiskey:
Uncle Robert had to have
a drink while shaving. May
there be no bloodshed in your house
this morning of my father's death
and no unkept appearance
in the living, since he has
to wear the rouge and lipstick
of your ceremony, mother,
for the first and last time:
father, hello and goodbye.

TO A RED-HEADED DO-GOOD WAITRESS

Every morning I went to her charity and learned
to face the music of her white smile so well
that it infected my black teeth as I escaped,

ALAN DUGAN

and those who saw me smiled too and went in
the White Castle, where she is the inviolable lady.

There cripples must be bright, and starvers noble:
no tears, no stomach-cries, but pain made art
to move her powerful red pity toward philanthropy.
So I must wear my objectively stinking poverty
like a millionaire clown's rags and sing, "Oh I

got plenty o' nuttin'," as if I made
a hundred grand a year like Gershwin, while
I get a breakfast every day from her for two
weeks and nothing else but truth: she has
a policeman and a wrong sonnet in fifteen lines.

FOR MASTURBATION

I have allowed myself
this corner and am God.
Here in the must
beneath their stoop
I will do as I will,
either as act as act,
or dream for the sake of dreams,
and if they find me out
in rocket ships or jets
working to get away,

then let my left great-toe-
nail grow into the inside knob
of my right ankle bone and let
my fingernails make eight new moons
temporarily in the cold salt marches of my palms!
THIS IS THE WAY IT IS, and if
it is "a terrible disgrace"
it is as I must will,
because I am not them
though I am theirs to kill.

FABRICATION OF ANCESTORS

For old Billy Dugan, shot in the ass in the Civil War, my father said.

The old wound in my ass
has opened up again, but I
am past the prodigies
of youth's campaigns, and weep
where I used to laugh
in war's red humors, half
in love with silly-assed pains
and half not feeling them.
I have to sit up with
an indoor unsittable itch
before I go down late
and weeping to the storm-
cellar on a dirty night
and go to bed with the worms.
So pull the dirt up over me
and make a family joke
for Old Billy Blue Balls,
the oldest private in the world
with two ass-holes and no
place more to go to for a laugh
except the last one. Say:
The North won the Civil War
without much help from me
although I wear a proof
of the war's obscenity.

AMERICAN AGAINST SOLITUDE

Ah to be alone and uninhibited!
To make mistakes in private, then
to show a good thing! But that's
not possible: it's in the Close of life
that towering Virtù happens. Why
be absent from the wheeling world?
It is an education! Act by act,
Futures materialize! So, go deal,
old bones, enjoy it while you may!:

ALAN DUGAN

eat, drink, think, and love; oh even work!,
as if all horrors are mistakes,
and make the social product: new
invisible skies arriving! full
of life, death, insanity, and grace!

POEM

What's the balm
for a dying life,
dope, drink, or Christ,
is there one?

I puke and choke
with it and find
no peace of mind
in flesh, and no hope.

It flows away
in mucous juice.
Nothing I can do
can make it stay,

so I give out
and water the garden: it
is all shit
for the flowers anyhow.

ELEGY FOR A PURITAN CONSCIENCE

I closed my ears with stinging bugs
and sewed my eyelids shut
but heard a sucking at the dugs
and saw my parents rut.

I locked my jaw with rusty nails
and cured my tongue in lime
but ate and drank in garbage pails
and said these words of crime.

ALAN DUGAN

I crushed my scrotum with two stones
and drew my penis in
but felt your wound expect its own
and fell in love with sin.

PRAYER

God, I need a job because I need money.
Here the world is, enjoyable with whiskey,
women, ultimate weapons, and class!
But if I have no money, then my wife
gets mad at me, I can't drink well,
the armed oppress me, and no boss
pays me money. But when I work,
Oh I get paid!, the police are courteous,
and I can have a drink and breathe air.
I feel classy. I am where the arms are.
The wife is wife in deed. The world
is interesting!, except I have to be
indoors all day and take shit, and make
weapons to kill outsiders with. I miss
the air and smell that paid work stinks
when done for someone else's profit, so I quit,
enjoy a few flush days in air, drunk, then
I need a job again. I'm caught in a steel cycle.

ON LEAVING TOWN

This must be a bad dream. We will wake up
tomorrow naked in the prior garden, each
entwined in his particular love. We will
get up to natural water, fruits, and what?,
a gambol with the lions? Nonsense. This
is petrified obsession, perfect in tautology,
visible in the smoke, the layout of the streets,
and prison buildings. The city has put on
glass armor in rock war against its death,
which is internal. It rides out radiate

on country roads to ride down enemy foliage.
Why? There's nothing left in it to kill
except its people, and they look thoroughly every way—
left, right, front, back, up, down, and in—
before they cross another, or its streets. Such animals,
joyful of desolate beauties, they are so tough, the live ones,
that they stand around like Easter Island statues of survival won
by casual struggle, proud of their tension or their craft.
Oh I reject the dream but not the city. I
have loved its life and left it and I am
a better animal for having learned its ways;
but it is not enough to be a captive animal,
social in town. Escaped emotions: boredom and fear.

MORAL DREAM

A little girl in white, gold-haired,
came to my dream and brought a gift:
it was the doll of Christ. I was elect!
not by my virtù but by dreams equipped
to take the gift. Oh Gift-Taker, Sir
Equipment to the goddess Pedophilia,
she came to my bed in long gold hair,
and what I did with her I do not know
because I slept in sleep. When I awoke,
asleep, I found her head balled in the bone
crux of my elbow's calipers. She had
a dead man's face to measure: young
Hitler's, curdled in the flesh, with black
straight hair and two front teeth
knocked out: he was the dead doll of Christ.
I felt an instantaneous tree of ice
invade my nervous system and connect
dreams' dreams to an historical reality.
Thus, I expected subsequent atrocities
and woke for whiskey and an armed life.

© Gerard Malanga

Robert Duncan

OFTEN I AM PERMITTED TO RETURN
TO A MEADOW

as if it were a scene made-up by the mind,
that is not mine, but is a made place,

that is mine, it is so near to the heart,
an eternal pasture folded in all thought
so that there is a hall therein

that is a made place, created by light
wherefrom the shadows that are forms fall.

Wherefrom fall all architectures I am
I say are likenesses of the First Beloved
whose flowers are flames lit to the Lady.

She it is Queen Under The Hill
whose hosts are a disturbance of words within words
that is a field folded.

It is only a dream of the grass blowing
east against the source of the sun
in an hour before the sun's going down

whose secret we see in a children's game
of ring a round of roses told.

Often I am permitted to return to a meadow
as if it were a given property of the mind
that certain bounds hold against chaos,

that is a place of first permission,
everlasting omen of what is.

ROBERT DUNCAN

THE STRUCTURE OF RIME II

What of the Structure of Rime? I said.

The Messenger in guise of a Lion roard: *Why does man retract his song from the impoverished air? He brings his young to the opening of the field. Does he so fear beautiful compulsion?*

I in the guise of a Lion roard out great vowels and heard their amazing patterns.

A lion without disguise said: He that sang to charm the beasts was false of tongue. There is a melody within this surfeit of speech that is most man.
What of the Structure of Rime? I asked.

An absolute scale of resemblance and disresemblance establishes measures that are music in the actual world.

The Lion in the Zodiac replied:

The actual stars moving are music in the real world. This is the meaning of the music of the spheres.

POETRY, A NATURAL THING

Neither our vices nor our virtues
further the poem. "They came up
and died
just like they do every year
on the rocks."

The poem
feeds upon thought, feeling, impulse,
to breed   itself,
a spiritual urgency at the dark ladders leaping.

This beauty is an inner persistence
toward the source

striving against (within) down-rushet of the river,
    a call we heard and answer
in the lateness of the world
    primordial bellowings
from which the youngest world might spring,

salmon not in the well where the
    hazelnut falls
but at the falls battling, inarticulate,
    blindly making it.

This is one picture apt for the mind.

A second: a moose painted by Stubbs,
where last year's extravagant antlers
    lie on the ground.
The forlorn moosey-faced poem wears
    new antler-buds,
    the same,

"a little heavy, a little contrived",

his only beauty to be
    all moose.

INGMAR BERGMAN'S *SEVENTH SEAL*

This is the way it is. We see
three ages in one: the child Jesus
innocent of Jerusalem and Rome
—magically at home in joy—
that's the year from which
our inner persistence has its force.

The second, Bergman shows us,
carries forward image after image
of anguish, of the Christ crossd
and sends up from open sores of the plague
(shown as wounds upon His corpse)

from lacerations in the course of love
(the crown of whose kingdom tears the flesh)

. . . There is so much suffering!
What possibly protects us
from the emptiness, the forsaken cry,
the utter dependence, the vertigo?
Why do so many come to love's edge
only to be stranded there?

The second face of Christ, his
evil, his Other, emaciated, pain and sin.
Christ, what a contagion!
What a stink it spreads round

our age! It's our age!
and the rage of the storm is abroad.
The malignant stupidity of statesmen rules.
The old riders thru the forests race
        shouting: the wind! the wind!
Now the black horror cometh again.

And I'll throw myself down
as the clown does in Bergman's *Seventh Seal*
to cower as if asleep with his wife and child,
hid in the caravan under the storm.

Let the Angel of Wrath pass over.
Let the end come.
War, stupidity and fear are powerful.
We are only children. To bed! to bed!
        To play safe!

To throw ourselves down
helplessly, into happiness,
        into an age of our own, into
        our own days.
There where the Pestilence roars,
where the empty riders of the horror go.

ROBERT DUNCAN

SUCH IS THE SICKNESS OF MANY A GOOD THING

Was he then Adam of the Burning Way?
hid away in the heat like wrath
    conceald in Love's face,
or the seed, Eris in Eros,
    key and lock
of what I was?   I could not speak
    the releasing
word.   For into a dark
    matter he came
and askt me to say what
    I could not say.   "I . ."

All the flame in me stopt
    against my tongue.
My heart was a stone, a dumb
    unmanageable thing in me,
a darkness that stood athwart
    his need
for the enlightening, the
    "I love you" that has
only this one quick in time,
    this one start
when its moment is true.

Such is the sickness of many a good thing
that now into my life from long ago this
refusing to say I love you has bound
the weeping, the yielding, the
    yearning to be taken again,
into a knot, a waiting, a string

so taut it taunts the song,
it resists the touch. It grows dark
to draw down the lover's hand
from its lightness to what's
    underground.

ROBERT DUNCAN

BENDING THE BOW

We've our business to attend Day's duties,
bend back the bow in dreams as we may
til the end rimes in the taut string
with the sending. Reveries are rivers and flow
where the cold light gleams reflecting the window upon the
    surface of the table,
the presst-glass creamer, the pewter sugar bowl, the litter
    of coffee cups and saucers,
carnations painted growing upon whose surfaces. The whole
composition of surfaces leads into the other
               current disturbing
what I would take hold of. I'd been

in the course of a letter—I am still
in the course of a letter—to a friend,
who comes close in to my thought so that
the day is hers. My hand writing here
there shakes in the currents of . . . of air?
of an inner anticipation of . . . ?   reaching to touch
ghostly exhilarations in the thought of her.

       At the extremity of this
          design
"there is a connexion working in both directions, as in
          the bow and the lyre"—
only in that swift fulfillment of the wish
         that sleep
       can illustrate my hand
        sweeps the string.

You stand behind the where-I-am.
The deep tones and shadows I will call a woman.
The quick high notes . . . You are a girl there too,
   having something of sister and of wife,
         inconsolate,
and I would play Orpheus for you again,

       recall the arrow or song
       to the trembling daylight
       from which it sprang.

ROBERT DUNCAN

from the Emperor Julian, *Hymn to the Mother of the Gods:*

*And Attis encircles the heavens like a tiara, and thence
sets out as though to descend to earth.*

*For the even is bounded, but the uneven is without bounds
and there is no way through or out of it.*

TRIBAL MEMORIES   **PASSAGES 1**

And to Her-Without-Bounds, I send,
wherever She wanders,   by what
          campfire at evening,

among tribes setting each the City where
                    we Her people are
at the end of a day's reaches   here
          the Eternal
lamps lit, here   the wavering human
     sparks of heat and light
glimmer, go out, and reappear.

For this is the company of the living
and the poet's voice speaks from no
          crevice in the ground between
               mid-earth and underworld
breathing fumes of what is deadly to know,
               news larvae in tombs
          and twists of time do feed upon,

but from the hearth stone, the lamp light,
               the heart of the matter where the

                    house is held

yet here, the warning light at the edge of town!

The City will go out in time, will go out
          into time, hiding even its embers.
And we were scatterd thruout the countries and times of man

for we took alarm in ourselves,
                    rumors of the enemy
spread among the feathers of the wing that coverd us.

Mnemosyne, they named her, the
                    Mother with the whispering
        featherd wings.   Memory,
the great speckled bird who broods over the
                    nest of souls, and her egg,
        the dream in which all things are living,
I return to, leaving my self.

I am beside myself with this
        thought of the One in the World-Egg,
enclosed,   in a shell of murmurings,

                    rimed round,
                    sound-chamberd child.

It's that first!   The forth-going to be
                    bursts into green as the spring
        winds blow watery from the south
and the sun returns north.   He hides

        fire among words in his mouth

and comes racing out of the zone of dark and storm

                    towards us.

I sleep in the afternoon, retreating from work,
reading and dropping away from the reading,
as if I were only a seed of myself,
        unawakend,   unwilling
                    to sleep or wake.

STRUCTURE OF RIME XXIII

   Only passages of a poetry, no more. No matter how many times the
cards are handled and laid out to lay out their plan of the future—a
fortune—only passages of what is happening. Passages of moonlight upon
a floor.

Let me give you an illusion of grieving. In the room at the clean sweep of moonlight a young man stands looking down. An agony I have spoken of overtakes him, waves of loss and return.

But he would withdraw from the telling. We cannot tell whether rage (which rimes) or grief shakes him. Let me give you an illusion of not grieving.

MY MOTHER WOULD BE A FALCONRESS

My mother would be a falconress,
And I, her gay falcon treading her wrist,
would fly to bring back
from the blue of the sky to her, bleeding, a prize,
where I dream in my little hood with many bells
jangling when I'd turn my head.

My mother would be a falconress,
and she sends me as far as her will goes.
She lets me ride to the end of her curb
where I fall back in anguish.
I dread that she will cast me away,
for I fall, I mis-take, I fail in her mission.

She would bring down the little birds.
And I would bring down the little birds.
When will she let me bring down the little birds,
pierced from their flight with their necks broken,
their heads like flowers limp from the stem?

I tread my mother's wrist and would draw blood.
Behind the little hood my eyes are hooded.
I have gone back into my hooded silence,
talking to myself and dropping off to sleep.

For she has muffled my dreams in the hood she has made me,
sewn round with bells, jangling when I move.
She rides with her little falcon upon her wrist.
She uses a barb that brings me to cower.

ROBERT DUNCAN

She sends me abroad to try my wings
and I come back to her.   I would bring down
the little birds to her
I may not tear into, I must bring back perfectly.

I tear at her wrist with my beak to draw blood,
and her eye holds me, anguisht, terrifying.
She draws a limit to my flight.
Never beyond my sight, she says.

She trains me to fetch and to limit myself in fetching.
She rewards me with meat for my dinner.
But I must never eat what she sends me to bring her.

Yet it would have been beautiful, if she would have carried me,
always, in a little hood with the bells ringing,
at her wrist, and her riding
to the great falcon hunt, and me
flying up to the curb of my heart from her heart
to bring down the skylark from the blue to her feet,
straining, and then released for the flight.

My mother would be a falconress,
and I her gerfalcon, raised at her will,
from her wrist sent flying, as if I were her own
pride, as if her pride
knew no limits, as if her mind
sought in me flight beyond the horizon.

Ah, but high, high in the air I flew.
And far, far beyond the curb of her will,
were the blue hills where the falcons nest.
And then I saw west to the dying sun—
it seemd my human soul went down in flames.

I tore at her wrist, at the hold she had for me,
until the blood ran hot and I heard her cry out,
far, far beyond the curb of her will

to horizons of stars beyond the ringing hills of the world where
    the falcons nest
I saw, and I tore at her wrist with my savage beak.
I flew, as if sight flew from the anguish in her eye beyond her sight,
sent from my striking loose, from the cruel strike at her wrist,
striking out from the blood to be free of her.

ROBERT DUNCAN

My mother would be a falconress,
and even now, years after this,
when the wounds I left her had surely heald,
and the woman is dead,
her fierce eyes closed, and if her heart
were broken, it is stilld   ·

I would be a falcon and go free.
I tread her wrist and wear the hood,
talking to myself, and would draw blood.

THE TORSO   PASSAGES 18

Most beautiful!   the red-flowering eucalyptus,
            the madrone, the yew

Is he . . .

So thou wouldst smile, and take me in thine arms
The sight of London to my exiled eyes
Is as Elysium to a new-come soul

If he be Truth
I would dwell in the illusion of him

His hands unlocking from chambers of my male body

such an idea in man's image

rising tides that sweep me towards him

. . . *homosexual?*

and at the treasure of his mouth

pour forth my soul

his soul   commingling

ROBERT DUNCAN

I thought a Being more than vast, His body leading
    into Paradise,   his eyes
                quickening a fire in me,   a trembling

    hieroglyph: At the root of the neck

  the clavicle, for the neck is the stem of the great artery
        upward into his head that is beautiful

                At the rise of the pectoral muscles

  the nipples, for the breasts are like sleeping fountains
        of feeling in man, waiting above the beat of his heart,
        shielding the rise and fall of his breath, to be
        awakend

                At the axis of his mid hriff

  the navel, for in the pit of his stomach the chord from
        which first he was fed has its temple

                At the root of the groin

  the pubic hair, for the torso is the stem in which the man
        flowers forth and leads to the stamen of flesh in which
        his seed rises

a wave of need and desire over   taking me

                cried out my name

(This was long ago.   It was another life)

                and said,

    What do you want of me?

I do not know, I said.   I have fallen in love.   He
    has brought me into heights and depths my heart
            would fear   without him.   His look

    pierces my side   ·   fire eyes   ·

I have been waiting for you, he said:
            I know what you desire

        you do not yet know   but through me   ·

    And I am with you everywhere.   In your falling

I have fallen from a high place.   I have raised myself

            from darkness in your   rising

                    wherever you are

        my hand in your hand   seeking   the locks, the keys

I am there.   Gathering me, you gather

        your Self   ·

    For my Other is not a woman but a man

    the King upon whose bosom let me lie.

© Gerard Malanga

Lawrence Ferlinghetti

[CONSTANTLY RISKING ABSURDITY]

Constantly risking absurdity
                                and death
                whenever he performs
                                above the heads
                                                of his audience
        the poet like an acrobat
                                climbs on rime
                                        to a high wire of his own making
and balancing on eyebeams
                                above a sea of faces
                paces his way
                                to the other side of day
        performing entrechats
                                and sleight-of-foot tricks
and other high theatrics
                                and all without mistaking
                any thing
                                for what it may not be

        For he's the super realist
                                who must perforce perceive
                taut truth
                                before the taking of each stance or step
        in his supposed advance
                                toward that still higher perch
where Beauty stands and waits
                                with gravity
                                        to start her death-defying leap

        And he
                a little charleychaplin man
                                who may or may not catch
                her fair eternal form
                                spreadeagled in the empty air
                of existence

LAWRENCE FERLINGHETTI

[SOMETIME DURING ETERNITY]

Sometime during eternity
                            some guys show up
and one of them
                    who shows up real late
                                        is a kind of carpenter
            from some square-type place
                                like Galilee
        and he starts wailing
                            and claiming he is hep
            to who made heaven
                            and earth
                                        and that the cat
            who really laid it on us
                                is his Dad

And moreover
        he adds
                It's all writ down
                            on some scroll-type parchments
        which some henchmen
                            leave lying around the Dead Sea somewheres
                a long time ago
                            and which you won't even find
for a coupla thousand years or so
                            or at least for
    nineteen hundred and fortyseven
                                of them
                to be exact
                            and even then
        nobody really believes them
                            or me
                                for that matter

You're hot
            they tell him

And they cool him

They stretch him on the Tree to cool

LAWRENCE FERLINGHETTI

And everybody after that
                              is always making models
          of this Tree
                         with Him hung up
and always crooning His name
                              and calling Him to come down
          and sit in
                         on their combo
          as if he is the king cat
                              who's got to blow
or they can't quite make it

Only he don't come down
                              from His Tree

Him just hang there
                    on His Tree
                              looking real Petered out
                    and real cool
                              and also
          according to a roundup
                              of late world news
from the usual unreliable sources
                              real dead

[THE PENNYCANDYSTORE BEYOND THE EL]

The pennycandystore beyond the El
is where I first
               fell in love
                         with unreality
Jellybeans glowed in the semi-gloom
of that september afternoon
A cat upon the counter moved among
                              the licorice sticks
               and tootsie rolls
     and Oh Boy Gum

Outside the leaves were falling as they died

A wind had blown away the sun
A girl ran in
Her hair was rainy
Her breasts were breathless in the little room

Outside the leaves were falling
                    and they cried
                              Too soon! too soon!

I AM WAITING

I am waiting for my case to come up
and I am waiting
for a rebirth of wonder
and I am waiting for someone
to really discover America
and wail
and I am waiting
for the discovery
of a new symbolic western frontier
and I am waiting
for the American Eagle
to really spread its wings
and straighten up and fly right
and I am waiting
for the Age of Anxiety
to drop dead
and I am waiting
for the war to be fought
which will make the world safe
for anarchy
and I am waiting
for the final withering away
of all governments
and I am perpetually awaiting
a rebirth of wonder

I am waiting for the Second Coming
and I am waiting

LAWRENCE FERLINGHETTI

for a religious revival
to sweep thru the state of Arizona
and I am waiting
for the Grapes of Wrath to be stored
and I am waiting
for them to prove
that God is really American
and I am seriously waiting
for Billy Graham and Elvis Presley
to exchange roles seriously
and I am waiting
to see God on television
piped onto church altars
if only they can find
the right channel
to tune in on
and I am waiting
for the Last Supper to be served again
with a strange new appetizer
and I am perpetually awaiting
a rebirth of wonder

I am waiting for my number to be called
and I am waiting
for the living end
and I am waiting
for dad to come home
his pockets full
of irradiated silver dollars
and I am waiting
for the atomic tests to end
and I am waiting happily
for things to get much worse
before they improve
and I am waiting
for the Salvation Army to take over
and I am waiting
for the human crowd
to wander off a cliff somewhere
clutching its atomic umbrella
and I am waiting
for Ike to act
and I am waiting
for the meek to be blessed

and inherit the earth
without taxes
and I am waiting
for forests and animals
to reclaim the earth as theirs
and I am waiting
for a way to be devised
to destroy all nationalisms
without killing anybody
and I am waiting
for linnets and planets to fall like rain
and I am waiting for lovers and weepers
to lie down together again
in a new rebirth of wonder

I am waiting for the Great Divide to be crossed
and I am anxiously waiting
for the secret of eternal life to be discovered
by an obscure general practitioner
and save me forever from certain death
and I am waiting
for life to begin
and I am waiting
for the storms of life
to be over
and I am waiting
to set sail for happiness
and I am waiting
for a reconstructed Mayflower
to reach America
with its picture story and tv rights
sold in advance to the natives
and I am waiting
for the lost music to sound again
in the Lost Continent
in a new rebirth of wonder

I am waiting for the day
that maketh all things clear
and I am waiting
for Ole Man River
to just stop rolling along
past the country club
and I am waiting

LAWRENCE FERLINGHETTI

for the deepest South
to just stop Reconstructing itself
in its own image
and I am waiting
for a sweet desegregated chariot
to swing low
and carry me back to Ole Virginie
and I am waiting
for Ole Virginie to discover
just why Darkies are born
and I am waiting
for God to lookout
from Lookout Mountain
and see the Ode to the Confederate Dead
as a real farce
and I am awaiting retribution
for what America did
to Tom Sawyer
and I am perpetually awaiting
a rebirth of wonder

I am waiting for Tom Swift to grow up
and I am waiting
for the American Boy
to take off Beauty's clothes
and get on top of her
and I am waiting
for Alice in Wonderland
to retransmit to me
her total dream of innocence
and I am waiting
for Childe Roland to come
to the final darkest tower
and I am waiting
for Aphrodite
to grow live arms
at a final disarmament conference
in a new rebirth of wonder

I am waiting
to get some intimations
of immortality
by recollecting my early childhood
and I am waiting

LAWRENCE FERLINGHETTI

for the green mornings to come again
youth's dumb green fields come back again
and I am waiting
for some strains of unpremeditated art
to shake my typewriter
and I am waiting to write
the great indelible poem
and I am waiting
for the last long careless rapture
and I am perpetually waiting
for the fleeing lovers on the Grecian Urn
to catch each other up at last
and embrace
and I am awaiting
perpetually and forever
a renaissance of wonder

A PHOENIX AT FIFTY

At new age fifty
turn inward on old self
and rock on my back in a torn green hammock
deep in a ruined garden
where first the sweet birds sang
behind a white wood cottage
at Montecito Santa Barbara
sunk in sea-vine succulents
under huge old eucalyptrees
wind blows white sunlight thru
A mute ruined statue of a nymph dancing
turns in sun
as if to sing 'When day is done'
It is not
A helicopter flies
out of an angle of the sun
its windmill choppers waving
thru the waving treetops
thru which the hot wind blows & blows
pure desire made of light
I float on my back in the sea of it
and gaze straight up into eye-white sky

LAWRENCE FERLINGHETTI

as into eyes of one beloved whispering
                'Let
                        me
                              in'
Too bright
            too bright!
I close my eyes
lest sun thru such lenses
set me afire
but the blown light batters thru
lids and lashes
I burn and leave
no ashes

Yet will arise

POUND AT SPOLETO

I walked into a loge in the Teatro Melisso, the lovely Renaissance salle where the poetry readings and the chamber concerts were held every day of the Spoleto Festival, and suddenly saw Ezra Pound for the first time, still as a mandarin statue in a box in a balcony at the back of the theatre, one tier up from the stalls. It was a shock, seeing only a striking old man in a curious pose, thin and long haired, aquiline at 80, head tilted strangely to one side, lost in permanent abstraction.... After three younger poets on stage, he was scheduled to read from his box, and there he sat with an old friend (who held his papers) waiting. He regarded the knuckles of his hands, moving them a very little, expressionless. Only once, when everyone else in the full theatre applauded someone on stage, did he rouse himself to clap, without looking up, as if stimulated by sound in a void.... After almost an hour, his turn came. Or after a life.... Everyone in the hall rose, turned and looked back and up at Pound in his booth, applauding. The applause was prolonged and Pound tried to rise from his armchair. A microphone was partly in the way. He grasped the arms of the chair with his boney hands and tried to rise. He could not and he tried again and could not. His old friend did not try to help him. Finally she put a poem in his hand, and after at least a minute his voice came out. First the jaw moved and then the voice came out, inaudible. A young Italian pulled the mike up very close to his face and held it there and the voice came over, frail but stubborn, higher than I had expected, a thin, soft monotone. The hall had gone silent at a stroke. The voice knocked me down so soft, so thin, so frail, so stubborn still. I put my head on my arms on the velvet sill of the box. I was surprised to see a single tear drop on my knee. The thin, indomitable voice went on. I went blind from the box, through the back door of it, into the empty corridor of the theatre where they still sat turned to him, went down and out, into the sunlight, weeping. . . .

   Up above the town
             by the ancient aqueduct
   the chestnut trees
             were still in bloom
     Mute birds
        flew in the valley
             far below
    The sun shone
         on the chestnut trees
   and the leaves
        turned in the sun
     and turned and turned and turned
     And would continue turning
  His voice
     went on
       and on
          through the leaves. . . .

MONET'S LILIES SHUDDERING

  Monet never knew
     he was painting his 'Lilies' for
  a lady from the Chicago Art Institute
   who went to France and filmed
    today's lilies
     by the 'Bridge at Giverny'
       a leaf afloat among them
  the film of which now flickers
   at the entrance to his framed visions
    with a Debussy piano soundtrack
flooding with a new fluorescence (fleur-essence?)
  the rooms and rooms
     of waterlilies

LAWRENCE FERLINGHETTI

Monet caught a Cloud in a Pond
                              in 1903
          and got a first glimpse
                              of its lilies
     and for twenty years returned
          again and again to paint them
               which now gives us the impression
                    that he floated thru life on them
                                        and their reflections
          which he also didn't know
               we would have occasion
                         to reflect upon

Anymore than he could know
          that John Cage would be playing a
               'Cello with Melody-driven Electronics'
                    tonight at the University of Chicago
And making those Lilies shudder and shed
                                   black light

© *Thomas Victor*

Allen Ginsberg

HOWL

for Carl Solomon

I

I saw the best minds of my generation destroyed by madness, starving
   hysterical naked,
dragging themselves through the negro streets at dawn looking for an
   angry fix,
angelheaded hipsters burning for the ancient heavenly connection to the
   starry dynamo in the machinery of night,
who poverty and tatters and hollow-eyed and high sat up smoking in the
   supernatural darkness of cold-water flats floating across the tops of
   cities contemplating jazz,
who bared their brains to Heaven under the El and saw Mohammedan
   angels staggering on tenement roofs illuminated,
who passed through universities with radiant cool eyes hallucinating
   Arkansas and Blake-light tragedy among the scholars of war,
who were expelled from the academies for crazy & publishing obscene
   odes on the windows of the skull,
who cowered in unshaven rooms in underwear, burning their money in
   wastebaskets and listening to the Terror through the wall,
who got busted in their pubic beards returning through Laredo with a
   belt of marijuana for New York,
who ate fire in paint hotels or drank turpentine in Paradise Alley, death,
   or purgatoried their torsos night after night
with dreams, with drugs, with waking nightmares, alcohol and cock and
   endless balls,
incomparable blind streets of shuddering cloud and lightning in the mind
   leaping toward poles of Canada & Paterson, illuminating all the
   motionless world of Time between,
Peyote solidities of halls, backyard green tree cemetery dawns, wine drunk-
   enness over the rooftops, storefront boroughs of teahead joyride neon
   blinking traffic light, sun and moon and tree vibrations in the roaring
   winter dusks of Brooklyn, ashcan rantings and kind king light of mind,
who chained themselves to subways for the endless ride from Battery to
   holy Bronx on benzedrine until the noise of wheels and children

brought them down shuddering mouth-wracked and battered bleak of brain all drained of brilliance in the drear light of Zoo,

who sank all night in submarine light of Bickford's floated out and sat through the stale beer afternoon in desolate Fugazzi's, listening to the crack of doom on the hydrogen jukebox,

who talked continuously seventy hours from park to pad to bar to Bellevue to museum to the Brooklyn Bridge,

a lost battalion of platonic conversationalists jumping down the stoops off fire escapes off windowsills off Empire State out of the moon,

yacketayakking screaming vomiting whispering facts and memories and anecdotes and eyeball kicks and shocks of hospitals and jails and wars,

whole intellects disgorged in total recall for seven days and nights with brilliant eyes, meat for the Synagogue cast on the pavement,

who vanished into nowhere Zen New Jersey leaving a trail of ambiguous picture postcards of Atlantic City Hall,

suffering Eastern sweats and Tangerian bone-grindings and migraines of China under junk-withdrawal in Newark's bleak furnished room,

who wandered around and around at midnight in the railroad yard wondering where to go, and went, leaving no broken hearts,

who lit cigarettes in boxcars boxcars boxcars racketing through snow toward lonesome farms in grandfather night,

who studied Plotinus Poe St. John of the Cross telepathy and bop kaballa because the cosmos instinctively vibrated at their feet in Kansas,

who loned it through the streets of Idaho seeking visionary indian angels who were visionary indian angels,

who thought they were only mad when Baltimore gleamed in supernatural ecstasy,

who jumped in limousines with the Chinaman of Oklahoma on the impulse of winter midnight streetlight smalltown rain,

who lounged hungry and lonesome through Houston seeking jazz or sex or soup, and followed the brilliant Spaniard to converse about America and Eternity, a hopeless task, and so took ship to Africa,

who disappeared into the volcanoes of Mexico leaving behind nothing but the shadow of dungarees and the lava and ash of poetry scattered in fireplace Chicago,

who reappeared on the West Coast investigating the F.B.I. in beards and shorts with big pacifist eyes sexy in their dark skin passing out incomprehensible leaflets,

who burned cigarette holes in their arms protesting the narcotic tobacco haze of Capitalism,

who distributed Supercommunist pamphlets in Union Square weeping and undressing while the sirens of Los Alamos wailed them down, and wailed down Wall, and the Staten Island ferry also wailed,

who broke down crying in white gymnasiums naked and trembling before
the machinery of other skeletons,

who bit detectives in the neck and shrieked with delight in policecars for
committing no crime but their own wild cooking pederasty and
intoxication,

who howled on their knees in the subway and were dragged off the roof
waving genitals and manuscripts,

who let themselves be fucked in the ass by saintly motorcyclists, and
screamed with joy,

who blew and were blown by those human seraphim, the sailors, caresses
of Atlantic and Caribbean love,

who balled in the morning in the evenings in rosegardens and the grass
of public parks and cemeteries scattering their semen freely to whom-
ever come who may,

who hiccupped endlessly trying to giggle but wound up with a sob behind
a partition in a Turkish Bath when the blonde & naked angel came to
pierce them with a sword,

who lost their loveboys to the three old shrews of fate the one eyed shrew
of the heterosexual dollar the one eyed shrew that winks out of the
womb and the one eyed shrew that does nothing but sit on her ass
and snip the intellectual golden threads of the craftsman's loom,

who copulated ecstatic and insatiate with a bottle of beer a sweetheart a
package of cigarettes a candle and fell off the bed, and continued
along the floor and down the hall and ended fainting on the wall
with a vision of ultimate cunt and come eluding the last gyzym of
consciousness,

who sweetened the snatches of a million girls trembling in the sunset,
and were red eyed in the morning but prepared to sweeten the snatch
of the sunrise, flashing buttocks under barns and naked in the lake,

who went out whoring through Colorado in myriad stolen night-cars,
N.C., secret hero of these poems, cocksman and Adonis of Denver—
joy to the memory of his innumerable lays of girls in empty lots &
diner backyards, moviehouses' rickety rows, on mountaintops in caves
or with gaunt waitresses in familiar roadside lonely petticoat upliftings
& especially secret gas-station solipsisms of johns, & hometown alleys
too,

who faded out in vast sordid movies, were shifted in dreams, woke on a
sudden Manhattan, and picked themselves up out of basements
hungover with heartless Tokay and horrors of Third Avenue iron
dreams & stumbled to unemployment offices,

who walked all night with their shoes full of blood on the snowbank
docks waiting for a door in the East River to open to a room full of
steamheat and opium,

who created great suicidal dramas on the apartment cliff-banks of the Hudson under the wartime blue floodlight of the moon & their heads shall be crowned with laurel in oblivion,

who ate the lamb stew of the imagination or digested the crab at the muddy bottom of the rivers of Bowery,

who wept at the romance of the streets with their pushcarts full of onions and bad music,

who sat in boxes breathing in the darkness under the bridge, and rose up to build harpsichords in their lofts,

who coughed on the sixth floor of Harlem crowned with flame under the tubercular sky surrounded by orange crates of theology,

who scribbled all night rocking and rolling over lofty incantations which in the yellow morning were stanzas of gibberish,

who cooked rotten animals lung heart feet tail borsht & tortillas dreaming of the pure vegetable kingdom,

who plunged themselves under meat trucks looking for an egg,

who threw their watches off the roof to cast their ballot for Eternity outside of Time, & alarm clocks fell on their heads every day for the next decade,

who cut their wrists three times successively unsuccessfully, gave up and were forced to open antique stores where they thought they were growing old and cried,

who were burned alive in their innocent flannel suits on Madison Avenue amid blasts of leaden verse & the tanked-up clatter of the iron regiments of fashion & the nitroglycerine shrieks of the fairies of advertising & the mustard gas of sinister intelligent editors, or were run down by the drunken taxicabs of Absolute Reality,

who jumped off the Brooklyn Bridge this actually happened and walked away unknown and forgotten into the ghostly daze of Chinatown soup alleyways & firetrucks, not even one free beer,

who sang out of their windows in despair, fell out of the subway window, jumped in the filthy Passaic, leaped on negroes, cried all over the street, danced on broken wineglasses barefoot smashed phonograph records of nostalgic European 1930's German jazz finished the whiskey and threw up groaning into the bloody toilet, moans in their ears and the blast of colossal steamwhistles,

who barreled down the highways of the past journeying to each other's hotrod-Golgotha jail-solitude watch or Birmingham jazz incarnation,

who drove crosscountry seventytwo hours to find out if I had a vision or you had a vision or he had a vision to find out Eternity,

who journeyed to Denver, who died in Denver, who came back to Denver & waited in vain, who watched over Denver & brooded & loned in Denver and finally went away to find out the Time, & now Denver is lonesome for her heroes,

who fell on their knees in hopeless cathedrals praying for each other's
salvation and light and breasts, until the soul illuminated its hair for
a second,

who crashed through their minds in jail waiting for impossible criminals
with golden heads and the charm of reality in their hearts who sang
sweet blues to Alcatraz,

who retired to Mexico to cultivate a habit, or Rocky Mount to tender
Buddha or Tangiers to boys or Southern Pacific to the black loco-
motive or Harvard to Narcissus to Woodlawn to the daisychain or
grave,

who demanded sanity trials accusing the radio of hypnotism & were
left with their insanity & their hands & a hung jury,

who threw potato salad at CCNY lecturers on Dadaism and subsequently
presented themselves on the granite steps of the madhouse with
shaven heads and harlequin speech of suicide, demanding instanta-
neous lobotomy,

and who were given instead the concrete void of insulin metrasol elec-
tricity hydrotherapy psychotherapy occupational therapy pingpong &
amnesia,

who in humorless protest overturned only one symbolic pingpong table,
resting briefly in catatonia,

returning years later truly bald except for a wig of blood, and tears and
fingers, to the visible madman doom of the wards of the madtowns
of the East,

Pilgrim State's Rockland's and Greystone's foetid halls, bickering with
the echoes of the soul, rocking and rolling in the midnight solitude-
bench dolmen-realms of love, dream of life a nightmare, bodies turned
to stone as heavy as the moon,

with mother finally ******, and the last fantastic book flung out of the
tenement window, and the last door closed at 4 AM and the last
telephone slammed at the wall in reply and the last furnished room
emptied down to the last piece of mental furniture, a yellow paper
rose twisted on a wire hanger in the closet, and even that imaginary,
nothing but a hopeful little bit of hallucination—

ah, Carl, while you are not safe I am not safe, and now you're really in
the total animal soup of time—

and who therefore ran through the icy streets obsessed with a sudden
flash of the alchemy of the use of the ellipse the catalog the meter &
the vibrating plane,

who dreamt and made incarnate gaps in Time & Space through images
juxtaposed, and trapped the archangel of the soul between 2 visual
images and joined the elemental verbs and set the noun and dash of
consciousness together jumping with sensation of Pater Omnipotens
Aeterna Deus

to recreate the syntax and measure of poor human prose and stand before you speechless and intelligent and shaking with shame, rejected yet confessing out the soul to conform to the rhythm of thought in his naked and endless head,

the madman bum and angel beat in Time, unknown, yet putting down here what might be left to say in time come after death,

and rose reincarnate in the ghostly clothes of jazz in the goldhorn shadow of the band and blew the suffering of America's naked mind for love into an eli eli lamma lamma sabacthani saxophone cry that shivered the cities down to the last radio

with the absolute heart of the poem of life butchered out of their own bodies good to eat a thousand years.

II

What sphinx of cement and aluminum bashed open their skulls and ate up their brains and imagination?

Moloch! Solitude! Filth! Ugliness! Ashcans and unobtainable dollars! Children screaming under the stairways! Boys sobbing in armies! Old men weeping in the parks!

Moloch! Moloch! Nightmare of Moloch! Moloch the loveless! Mental Moloch! Moloch the heavy judger of men!

Moloch the incomprehensible prison! Moloch the crossbone soulless jailhouse and Congress of sorrows! Moloch whose buildings are judgement! Moloch the vast stone of war! Moloch the stunned governments!

Moloch whose mind is pure machinery! Moloch whose blood is running money! Moloch whose fingers are ten armies! Moloch whose breast is a cannibal dynamo! Moloch whose ear is a smoking tomb!

Moloch whose eyes are a thousand blind windows! Moloch whose skyscrapers stand in the long streets like endless Jehovahs! Moloch whose factories dream and croak in the fog! Moloch whose smokestacks and antennae crown the cities!

Moloch whose love is endless oil and stone! Moloch whose soul is electricity and banks! Moloch whose poverty is the specter of genius! Moloch whose fate is a cloud of sexless hydrogen! Moloch whose name is the Mind!

Moloch in whom I sit lonely! Moloch in whom I dream Angels! Crazy in Moloch! Cocksucker in Moloch! Lacklove and manless in Moloch!

Moloch who entered my soul early! Moloch in whom I am a consciousness without a body! Moloch who frightened me out of my natural ecstasy! Moloch whom I abandon! Wake up in Moloch! Light streaming out of the sky!

Moloch! Moloch! Robot apartments! invisible suburbs! skeleton treas-
    uries! blind capitals! demonic industries! spectral nations! invincible
    madhouses! granite cocks! monstrous bombs!
They broke their backs lifting Moloch to Heaven! Pavements, trees,
    radios, tons! lifting the city to Heaven which exists and is everywhere
    about us!
Visions! omens! hallucinations! miracles! ecstasies! gone down the Ameri-
    can river!
Dreams! adorations! illuminations! religions! the whole boatload of sensi-
    tive bullshit!
Breakthroughs! over the river! flips and crucifixions! gone down the flood!
    Highs! Epiphanies! Despairs! Ten years' animal screams and suicides!
    Minds! New loves! Mad generation! down on the rocks of Time!
Real holy laughter in the river! They saw it all! the wild eyes! the holy
    yells! They bade farewell! They jumped off the roof! to solitude!
    waving! carrying flowers! Down to the river! into the street!

III

Carl Solomon! I'm with you in Rockland
    where you're madder than I am
I'm with you in Rockland
    where you must feel very strange
I'm with you in Rockland
    where you imitate the shade of my mother
I'm with you in Rockland
    where you've murdered your twelve secretaries
I'm with you in Rockland
    where you laugh at this invisible humor
I'm with you in Rockland
    where we are great writers on the same dreadful typewriter
I'm with you in Rockland
    where your condition has become serious and is reported on the radio
I'm with you Rockland
    where the faculties of the skull no longer admit the worms of the senses
I'm with you in Rockland
    where you drink the tea of the breasts of the spinsters of Utica
I'm with you in Rockland
    where you pun on the bodies of your nurses the harpies of the Bronx
I'm with you in Rockland
    where you scream in a straightjacket that you're losing the game of
    the actual pingpong of the abyss
I'm with you in Rockland

where you bang on the catatonic piano the soul is innocent and
immortal it should never die ungodly in an armed madhouse
I'm with you in Rockland
where fifty more shocks will never return your soul to its body again
from its pilgrimage to a cross in the void
I'm with you in Rockland
where you accuse your doctors of insanity and plot the Hebrew
socialist revolution against the fascist national Golgotha
I'm with you in Rockland
where you will split the heavens of Long Island and resurrect your
living human Jesus from the superhuman tomb
I'm with you in Rockland
where there are twentyfive-thousand mad comrades all together singing
the final stanzas of the Internationale
I'm with you in Rockland
where we hug and kiss the United States under our bedsheets the
United States that coughs all night and won't let us sleep
I'm with you in Rockland
where we wake up electrified out of the coma by our own souls'
airplanes roaring over the roof they've come to drop angelic bombs
the hospital illuminates itself imaginary walls collapse   O skinny
legions run outside   O starry spangled shock of mercy the eternal war
is here   O victory forget your underwear we're free
I'm with you in Rockland
in my dreams you walk dripping from a sea-journey on the highway
across America in tears to the door of my cottage in the Western
night

San Francisco 1955–56

AMERICA

America I've given you all and now I'm nothing.
America two dollars and twentyseven cents January 17, 1956.
I can't stand my own mind.
America when will we end the human war?
Go fuck yourself with your atom bomb.
I don't feel good don't bother me.
I won't write my poem till I'm in my right mind.
America when will you be angelic?

When will you take off your clothes?
When will you look at yourself through the grave?
When will you be worthy of your million Trotskyites?
America why are your libraries full of tears?
America when will you send your eggs to India?
I'm sick of your insane demands.
When can I go into the supermarket and buy what I need with my
    good looks?
America after all it is you and I who are perfect not the next world.
Your machinery is too much for me.
You made me want to be a saint.
There must be some other way to settle this argument.
Burroughs is in Tangiers I don't think he'll come back it's sinister.
Are you being sinister or is this some form of practical joke?
I'm trying to come to the point.
I refuse to give up my obsession.
America stop pushing I know what I'm doing.
America the plum blossoms are falling.
I haven't read the newspapers for months, everyday somebody goes on
    trial for murder.
America I feel sentimental about the Wobblies.
America I used to be a communist when I was a kid I'm not sorry.
I smoke marijuana every chance I get.
I sit in my house for days on end and stare at the roses in the closet.
When I go to Chinatown I get drunk and never get laid.
My mind is made up there's going to be trouble.
You should have seen me reading Marx.
My psychoanalyst thinks I'm perfectly right.
I won't say the Lord's Prayer.
I have mystical visions and cosmic vibrations.
America I still haven't told you what you did to Uncle Max after he
    came over from Russia.

I'm addressing you.
Are you going to let your emotional life be run by Time Magazine?
I'm obsessed by Time Magazine.
I read it every week.
Its cover stares at me every time I slink past the corner candystore.
I read it in the basement of the Berkeley Public Library.
It's always telling me about responsibility. Businessmen are serious.
    Movie producers are serious. Everybody's serious but me.
It occurs to me that I am America.
I am talking to myself again.

Asia is rising against me.

I haven't got a chinaman's chance.

I'd better consider my national resources.

My national resources consist of two joints of marijuana millions of geni-
tals an unpublishable private literature that goes 1400 miles an hour
and twentyfive-thousand mental institutions.

I say nothing about my prisons nor the millions of underprivileged who
live in my flowerpots under the light of five hundred suns.

I have abolished the whorehouses of France, Tangiers is the next to go.

My ambition is to be President despite the fact that I'm a Catholic.

America how can I write a holy litany in your silly mood?

I will continue like Henry Ford my strophes are as individual as his auto-
mobiles more so they're all different sexes.

America I will sell you strophes $2500 apiece $500 down on your old
strophe

America free Tom Mooney

America save the Spanish Loyalists

America Sacco & Vanzetti must not die

America I am the Scottsboro boys.

America when I was seven momma took me to Communist Cell meetings
they sold us garbanzos a handful per ticket a ticket costs a nickel and
the speeches were free everybody was angelic and sentimental about
the workers it was all so sincere you have no idea what a good thing
the party was in 1835 Scott Nearing was a grand old man a real
mensch Mother Bloor made me cry I once saw Israel Amter plain.
Everybody must have been a spy.

America you don't really want to go to war.

America it's them bad Russians.

Them Russians them Russians and them Chinamen. And them Russians.

The Russia wants to eat us alive. The Russia's power mad. She wants to
take our cars from out our garages.

Her wants to grab Chicago. Her needs a Red Readers' Digest. Her wants
our auto plants in Siberia. Him big bureaucracy running our filling-
stations.

That no good. Ugh. Him make Indians learn read. Him need big black
niggers. Hah. Her make us all work sixteen hours a day. Help.

America this is quite serious.

America this is the impression I get from looking in the television set.

America is this correct?

I'd better get right down to the job.

It's true I don't want to join the Army or turn lathes in precision parts
factories, I'm nearsighted and psychopathic anyway.

America I'm putting my queer shoulder to the wheel.

ALLEN GINSBERG

LOVE POEM ON THEME BY WHITMAN

I'll go into the bedroom silently and lie down between the bridegroom
    and the bride,
those bodies fallen from heaven stretched out waiting naked and restless,
arms resting over their eyes in the darkness,
bury my face in their shoulders and breasts, breathing their skin,
and stroke and kiss neck and mouth and make back be open and known,
legs raised up crook'd to receive, cock in the darkness driven tormented
    and attacking
roused up from hole to itching head,
bodies locked shuddering naked, hot lips and buttocks screwed into each
    other
and eyes, eyes glinting and charming, widening into looks and abandon,
and moans of movement, voices, hands in air, hands between thighs,
hands in moisture on softened hips, throbbing contraction of bellies
till the white come flow in the swirling sheets,
and the bride cry for forgiveness, and the groom be covered with tears of
    passion and compassion,
and I rise up from the bed replenished with last intimate gestures and
    kisses of farewell—
all before the mind wakes, behind shades and closed doors in a darkened
    house
where the inhabitants roam unsatisfied in the night,
nude ghosts seeking each other out in the silence.

PSALM III

To God: to illuminate all men. Beginning with Skid Road.
Let Occidental and Washington be transformed into a
higher place, the plaza of eternity.
Illuminate the welders in shipyards with the brilliance of
their torches.
Let the crane operator lift up his arm for joy.
Let elevators creak and speak, ascending and descending in
awe.
Let the mercy of the flower's direction beckon in the eye.
Let the straight flower bespeak its purpose in straightness—
to seek the light.

Let the crooked flower bespeak its purpose in crookedness—
to seek the light.
Let the crookedness and straightness bespeak the light.
Let Puget Sound be a blast of light.
I feed on your Name like a cockroach on a crumb—this
cockroach is holy.

Seattle 1956

WALES VISITATION

White fog lifting & falling on mountain-brow
  Trees moving in rivers of wind
      The clouds arise
 as on a wave, gigantic eddy lifting mist
  above teeming ferns exquisitely swayed
       along a green crag
  glimpsed thru mullioned glass in valley raine—

Bardic, O Self, Visitacione, tell naught
 but what seen by one man in a vale in Albion,
  of the folk, whose physical sciences end in Ecology,
   the wisdom of earthly relations,
  of mouths & eyes interknit ten centuries visible
   orchards of mind language manifest human,
 of the satanic thistle that raises its horned symmetry
  flowering above sister grass-daisies' pink tiny
    bloomlets angelic as lightbulbs—

Remember 160 miles from London's symmetrical thorned tower
  & network of TV pictures flashing bearded your Self
 the lambs on the tree-nooked hillside this day bleating
 heard in Blake's old ear, & the silent thought of Wordsworth in
     eld Stillness
 clouds passing through skeleton arches of Tintern Abbey—
   Bard Nameless as the Vast, babble to Vastness!
All the Valley quivered, one extended motion, wind
   undulating on mossy hills
 a giant wash that sank white fog delicately down red runnels
    on the mountainside
 whose leaf-branch tendrils moved asway
    in granitic undertow down—

ALLEN GINSBERG

and lifted the floating Nebulous upward, and lifted the arms of the
trees
and lifted the grasses an instant in balance
and lifted the lambs to hold still
and lifted the green of the hill, in one solemn wave

A solid mass of Heaven, mist-infused, ebbs thru the vale,
a wavelet of Immensity, lapping gigantic through Llanthony
Valley,
the length of all England, valley upon valley under Heaven's ocean
tonned with cloud-hang,
Heaven balanced on a grassblade—
Roar of the mountain wind slow, sigh of the body,
One Being on the mountainside stirring gently
Exquisite scales trembling everywhere in balance,
one motion thru the cloudy sky-floor shifting on the million
feet of daisies,
one Majesty the motion that stirred wet grass quivering
to the farthest tendril of white fog poured down
through shivering flowers on the mountain's
head—
No imperfection in the budded mountain,
Valleys breathe, heaven and earth move together,
daisies push inches of yellow air, vegetables tremble
green atoms shimmer in grassy mandalas,
sheep speckle the mountainside, revolving their jaws with empty
eyes,

horses dance in the warm rain,
tree-lined canals network through live farmland,
blueberries fringe stone walls
on hill breasts nippled with hawthorn,
pheasants croak up meadow-bellies haired with fern—
Out, out on the hillside, into the ocean sound, into delicate
gusts of wet air,
Fall on the ground, O great Wetness, O Mother, No harm on
thy body!
Stare close, no imperfection in the grass,
each flower Buddha-eye, repeating the story,
the myriad-formed soul
Kneel before the foxglove raising green buds, mauve bells drooped
doubled down the stem trembling antennae,
& look in the eyes of the branded lambs that stare
breathing stockstill under dripping hawthorn—

I lay down mixing my beard with the wet hair of the mountainside,
    smelling the brown vagina-moist ground, harmless,
        tasting the violet thistle-hair, sweetness—
One being so balanced, so vast, that its softest breath
      moves every floweret in the stillness on the valley floor,
    trembles lamb-hair hung gossamer rain-beaded in the grass,
lifts trees on their roots, birds in the great draught
      hiding their strength in the rain, bearing same weight,

Groan thru breast and neck, a great Oh! to earth heart
        Calling our Presence together
    The great secret is no secret
      Senses fit the winds,
        Visible is visible,
    rain-mist curtains wave through the bearded vale,
      grey atoms wet the wind's Kaballah
Crosslegged on a rock in dusk rain,
    rubber booted in soft grass, mind moveless,
  breath trembles in white daisies by the roadside,
      Heaven breath and my own symmetric
    Airs wavering thru antlered green fern
drawn in my navel, same breath as breathes thru Capel-Y-Ffn,
      Sounds of Aleph and Aum
        through forests of gristle,
    my skull and Lord Hereford's Knob equal,
        All Albion one.
What did I notice? Particulars! The
    vision of the great One is myriad—
  smoke curls upward from ash tray,
    house fire burned low,
The night, still wet & moody black heaven
      starless
  upward in motion with wet wind.

July 29, 1967 (LSD)—August 3, 1967 (London)

ON NEAL'S ASHES

    Delicate eyes that blinked blue Rockies all ash
    nipples, Ribs I touched w/ my thumb are ash
    mouth my tongue touched once or twice all ash
    bony cheeks soft on my belly are cinder, ash

earlobes & eyelids, youthful cock tip, curly pubis
breast warmth, man palm,.high school thigh,
baseball bicept arm, asshole anneal'd to silken skin
     all ashes, all ashes again.

August 1968

FLASH BACK

In a car Grey smoke over Elmira
The vast boy reformatory brick factory
Valed below misty hills 25 years ago
I sat with Joe Army visiting and murmured green Grass.
Jack's just not *here* anymore, Neal's ashes
Loneliness makes old men moan, God's solitude,
O women shut up, yelling for baby meat more.

November 10, 1969

EGO CONFESSION

I want to be known as the most brilliant man in America
Introduced to Gyalwa Karmapa heir of the Whispered Transmission
 Crazy Wisdom Practice Lineage
as the secret young wise man who visited him and winked anonymously
 decade ago in Gangtok
Prepared the way for Dharma in America without mentioning Dharma—
 scribbled laughter
Who saw Blake and abandoned God
To whom the Messianic Fink sent messages darkest hour sleeping on steel
 sheets "somewhere in the Federal Prison system" Weathermen got no
 Moscow Gold
who went backstage to Cecil Taylor serious chat chord structure & Time
 in nightclub
who fucked a rose-lipped rock star in a tiny bedroom slum watched by a
 statue of Vajrasattva—
and overthrew the CIA with a silent thought—
Old Bohemians many years hence in Viennese beergardens'll recall

his many young lovers with astonishing faces and iron breasts
gnostic apparatus and magical observation of rainbow-lit spiderwebs
extraordinary cooking, lung stew & Spaghetti a la Vongole and recipe for
    salad dressing 3 parts oil one part vinegar much garlic and honey a
    spoonful
his extraordinary ego, at service of Dharma and completely empty
unafraid of its own self's spectre
parroting gossip of gurus and geniuses famous for their reticence—
Who sang a blues made rock stars weep and moved an old black guitarist
    to laughter in Memphis—
I want to be the spectacle of Poesy triumphant over trickery of the world
Omniscient breathing its own breath thru War tear gas spy hallucination
whose common sense astonished gaga Gurus and rich Artistes—
who called the Justice department & threaten'd to Blow the Whistle
Stopt Wars, turned back petrochemical Industries' Captains to grieve &
    groan in bed
Chopped wood, built forest houses & established farms
distributed monies to poor poets & nourished imaginative genius of the
    land
Sat silent in jazz roar writing poetry with an ink pen—
wasn't afraid of God or Death after his 48th year—
let his brains turn to water under Laughing Gas his gold molar pulled by
    futuristic dentists
Seaman knew ocean's surface a year
carpenter late learned bevel and mattock
son, conversed with elder Pound & treated his father gently
—All empty all for show, all for the sake of Poesy
to set surpassing example of sanity as measure for late generations
Exemplify Muse Power to the young avert future suicide
accepting his own lie & the gaps between lies with equal good humor
Solitary in worlds full of insects & singing birds all solitary
—who had no subject but himself in many disguises
some outside his own body including empty air-filled space forests &
    cities—
Even climbed mountains to create his mountain, with ice ax & crampons
    & ropes, over Glaciers—

October 1974

ALLEN GINSBERG

from CONTEST OF THE BARDS

The Rune

Where the years have gone,   where the clouds have flown
                    Where the rainbow shone
We vanish,   and we make no moan

Where the sun will blind   the delighting mind
                    in a diamond wind
We appear,   our beauty refined.

Icy intellect,   fir'y Beauty wreck
                    but Love's castled speck
of Moonbeam,   nor is Truth correct.

Wise bodies leave here   with the mind's false cheer,
                    Eternity near
as Beauty,   where we disappear.

When sufferings come,   when all tongues lie dumb
                    when Bliss is all numb
with knowledge,   a bony white sum,

We die neither blest   nor with curse confessed
                    wanting Earth's worst Best:
But return,   where all Beauties rest.

Jan. 17–22, 1977

© Thomas Victor

Donald Hall

MY SON, MY EXECUTIONER

My son, my executioner,
    I take you in my arms,
Quiet and small and just astir,
    And whom my body warms.

Sweet death, small son, our instrument
    Of immortality,
Your cries and hungers document
    Our bodily decay.

We twenty-five and twenty-two,
    Who seemed to live forever,
Observe enduring life in you
    And start to die together.

DIGGING

One midnight, after a day when lilies
lift themselves out of the ground while you watch them,
and you come into the house at dark
your fingers grubby with digging, your eyes
vague with the pleasure of digging,

let a wind raised from the South
climb through your bedroom window, lift you in its arms
—you have become as small as a seed—
and carry you out of the house, over the black garden,
spinning and fluttering,

and drop you in cracked ground.
The dirt will be cool, rough to your clasped skin
like a man you have never known.

You will die into the ground
in a dead sleep, surrendered to water.

You will wake suffering
a widening pain in your side, a breach
gapped in your right ribs
where a green shoot struggles to lift itself upwards
through the tomb of your dead flesh

to the sun, to the air of your garden
where you will blossom
in the shape of your own self, thoughtless
with flowers, speaking
to bees, in the language of green and yellow, white and red.

THE MAN IN THE DEAD MACHINE

High on a slope in New Guinea
the Grumman Hellcat
lodges among bright vines
as thick as arms. In 1942,
the clenched hand of a pilot
glided it here
where no one has ever been.

In the cockpit the helmeted
skeleton sits
upright, held
by dry sinews at neck
and shoulder, and webbing
that straps the pelvic cross
to the cracked
leather of the seat, and the breastbone
to the canvas cover
of the parachute.

Or say that the shrapnel
missed him, he flew
back to the carrier, and every
morning takes his chair, his pale

DONALD HALL

hands on the black arms, and sits
upright, held
by the firm webbing.

GOLD

Pale gold of the walls, gold
of the centers of daisies, yellow roses
pressing from a clear bowl. All day
we lay on the bed, my hand
stroking the deep
gold of your thighs and your back.
We slept and woke
entering the golden room together,
lay down in it breathing
quickly, then
slowly again,
caressing and dozing, your hand sleepily
touching my hair now.

We made in those days
tiny identical rooms inside our bodies
which the men who uncover our graves
will find in a thousand years,
shining and whole.

STORIES

I look at the rock and the house;
I look at the boat on the river;
I sit on the colored stone
and listen to stories:

the mountain shudders
at the breath of a lizard
and the stream disappears
in a tunnel of jewels;

the walk of a woman
into darkness stops
when a snake hisses
with the voice of a cavern;

when the rock turns to air
the sun touches
her body, and diamonds
and the talking lake:

cool air at noon,
light on deep water,
fire at night
in the squares of the winter.

THE TOWN OF HILL

Back of the dam, under
a flat pad

of water, church
bells ring

in the ears of lilies,
a child's swing

curls in the current
of a yard, horned

pout sleep
in a green

mailbox, and
a boy walks

from a screened
porch beneath

the man-shaped
leaves of an oak

down the street looking
at the town

of Hill that water
covered forty

years ago,
and the screen

door shuts
under dream water.

MAPLE SYRUP

August, goldenrod blowing. We walk
into the graveyard, to find
my grandfather's grave. Ten years ago
I came here last, bringing
marigolds from the round garden
outside the kitchen.
I didn't know you then.
            We walk
among carved names that go with photographs
on top of the piano at the farm:
Keneston, Wells, Fowler, Batchelder, Buck.
We pause at the new grave
of Grace Fenton, my grandfather's
sister. Last summer
we called on her at the nursing home,
eighty-seven, and nodding
in a blue housedress. We cannot find
my grandfather's grave.
            Back at the house
where no one lives, we potter
and explore the back chamber
where everything comes to rest: spinning wheels,
pretty boxes, quilts,
bottles, books, albums of postcards.
Then with a flashlight we descend
firm steps to the root cellar—black,
cobwebby, huge,

with dirt floors and fieldstone walls,
and above the walls, holding the hewn
sills of the house, enormous
granite foundation stones.
Past the empty bins
for squash, apples, carrots, and potatoes,
we discover the shelves for canning, a few
pale pints
of tomato left, and—what
is this?—syrup, maple syrup
in a quart jar, syrup
my grandfather made twenty-five
years ago
for the last time.
                    I remember
coming to the farm in March
in sugaring time, as a small boy.
He carried the pails of sap, sixteen-quart
buckets, dangling from each end
of a wooden yoke
that lay across his shoulders, and emptied them
into a vat in the saphouse
where fire burned day and night
for a week.
                    Now the saphouse
tilts, nearly to the ground,
like someone exhausted
to the point of death, and next winter
when snow piles three feet thick
on the roofs of the cold farm,
the saphouse will shudder and slide
with the snow to the ground.
                    Today
we take my grandfather's last
quart of syrup
upstairs, holding it gingerly,
and we wash off twenty-five years
of dirt, and we pull
and pry the lid up, cutting the stiff,
dried rubber gasket, and dip our fingers
in, you and I both, and taste
the sweetness, you for the first time,
the sweetness preserved, of a dead man
in the kitchen he left

DONALD HALL

when his body slid
like anyone's into the ground.

KICKING THE LEAVES

1

Kicking the leaves, October, as we walk home together
from the game, in Ann Arbor,
on a day the color of soot, rain in the air;
I kick at the leaves of maples,
reds of seventy different shades, yellow
like old paper; and poplar leaves, fragile and pale;
and elm leaves, flags of a doomed race.
I kick at the leaves, making a sound I remember
as the leaves swirl upward from my boot,
and flutter; and I remember
Octobers walking to school in Connecticut,
wearing corduroy knickers that swished
with a sound like leaves; and a Sunday buying
a cup of cider at a roadside stand
on a dirt road in New Hampshire; and kicking the leaves,
autumn 1955 in Massachusetts, knowing
my father would die when the leaves were gone.

2

Each fall in New Hampshire, on the farm
where my mother grew up, a girl in the country,
my grandfather and grandmother
finished the autumn work, taking the last vegetables in
from the cold fields, canning, storing roots and apples
in the cellar under the kitchen. Then my grandfather
raked leaves against the house
as the final chore of autumn.
One November I drove up from college to see them.
We pulled big rakes, as we did when we hayed in summer,
pulling the leaves against the granite foundations
around the house, on every side of the house,
and then, to keep them in place, we cut spruce boughs

and laid them across the leaves,
green on red, until the house
was tucked up, ready for snow
that would freeze the leaves in tight, like a stiff skirt.
Then we puffed through the shed door,
taking off boots and overcoats, slapping our hands,
and sat in the kitchen, rocking, and drank
black coffee my grandmother made,
three of us sitting together, silent, in gray November.

3

One Saturday when I was little, before the war,
my father came home at noon from his half day at the office
and wore his Bates sweater, black on red,
with the crossed hockey sticks on it, and raked beside me
in the back yard, and tumbled in the leaves with me,
laughing, and carried me, laughing, my hair full of leaves,
to the kitchen window
where my mother could see us, and smile, and motion
to set me down, afraid I would fall and be hurt.

4

Kicking the leaves today, as we walk home together
from the game, among crowds of people
with their bright pennants, as many and bright as leaves,
my daughter's hair is the red-yellow color
of birch leaves, and she is tall like a birch,
growing up, fifteen, growing older; and my son
flamboyant as maple, twenty,
visits from college, and walks ahead of us, his step
springing, impatient to travel
the woods of the earth. Now I watch them
from a pile of leaves beside this clapboard house
in Ann Arbor, across from the school
where they learned to read,
as their shapes grow small with distance, waving,
and I know that I
diminish, not them, as I go first
into the leaves, taking
the step they will follow, Octobers and years from now.

5

This year the poems came back, when the leaves fell.
Kicking the leaves, I heard the leaves tell stories,
remembering, and therefore looking ahead, and building
the house of dying. I looked up into the maples
and found them, the vowels of bright desire.
I thought they had gone forever
while the bird sang *I love you, I love you*
and shook its black head
from side to side, and its red eye with no lid,
through years of winter, cold
as the taste of chicken wire, the music of cinder block.

6

Kicking the leaves, I uncover the lids of graves.
My grandfather died at seventy-seven, in March
when the sap was running; and I remember my father
twenty years ago,
coughing himself to death at fifty-two in the house
in the suburbs. Oh, how we flung
leaves in the air! How they tumbled and fluttered around us,
like slowly cascading water, when we walked together
in Hamden, before the war, when Johnson's Pond
had not surrendered to houses, the two of us
hand in hand, and in the wet air the smell of leaves
burning;
and in six years I will be fifty-two.

7

Now I fall, now I leap and fall
to feel the leaves crush under my body, to feel my body
buoyant in the ocean of leaves, the night of them,
night heaving with death and leaves, rocking like the ocean.
Oh, this delicious falling into the arms of leaves,
into the soft laps of leaves!
Face down, I swim into the leaves, feathery,
breathing the acrid odor of maple, swooping
in long glides to the bottom of October—
where the farm lies curled against winter, and soup steams

its breath of onion and carrot
onto damp curtains and windows; and past the windows
I see the tall bare maple trunks and branches, the oak
with its few brown weathery remnant leaves,
and the spruce trees, holding their green.
Now I leap and fall, exultant, recovering
from death, on account of death, in accord with the dead,
the smell and taste of leaves again,
and the pleasure, the only long pleasure, of taking a place
in the story of leaves.

THE TOY BONE

Looking through boxes
in the attic at my mother's house in Hamden,
I find a model airplane, snapshots
of a dog wearing baby clothes,
a catcher's mitt—the oiled
pocket eaten
by mice—and I discover
the toy bone, the familiar smell of it.
*
I sat alone each day
after school, in the living room
of my parents' house in Hamden, ten
years old, eating
slices of plain white bread.
I listened to the record, Connie
Boswell singing
again and again, her voice
turning like a heel, "The Kerry Dancers",
and I knew she was crippled, and sang
from a wheelchair. I played
with Tommy, my red-and-white
Shetland collie, throwing
his toy bone
into the air and catching it, or letting it fall,
while he watched me
with intent, curious eyes.

DONALD HALL

I was happy
in the room dark with shades drawn.

OX CART MAN

In October of the year,
he counts potatoes dug from the brown field,
counting the seed, counting
the cellar's portion out,
and bags the rest on the cart's floor.

He packs wool sheared in April, honey
in combs, linen, leather
tanned from deerhide,
and vinegar in a barrel
hooped by hand at the forge's fire.

He walks by ox's head, ten days
to Porstmouth Market, and sells potatoes,
and the bag that carried potatoes,
flaxseed, birch brooms, maple sugar, goose
feathers, yarn.

When the cart is empty he sells the cart.
When the cart is sold he sells the ox,
harness and yoke, and walks
home, his pockets heavy
with the year's coin for salt and taxes,

and at home by fire's light in November cold
stitches new harness
for next year's ox in the barn,
and carves the yoke, and saws planks
building the cart again.

"Ox Cart Man" from *Kicking the Leaves* (Harper & Row). Reprinted by permission; © 1977 The New Yorker Magazine, Inc.

Robert Hayden

FREDERICK DOUGLASS

When it is finally ours, this freedom, this liberty, this beautiful
and terrible thing, needful to man as air,
usable as earth; when it belongs at last to all,
when it is truly instinct, brain matter, diastole, systole,
reflex action; when it is finally won; when it is more
than the gaudy mumbo jumbo of politicians:
this man, this Douglass, this former slave, this Negro
beaten to his knees, exiled, visioning a world
where none is lonely, none hunted, alien,
this man, superb in love and logic, this man
shall be remembered. Oh, not with statues' rhetoric,
not with legends and poems and wreaths of bronze alone,
but with the lives grown out of his life, the lives
fleshing his dream of the beautiful, needful thing.

"FROM THE CORPSE WOODPILES, FROM THE ASHES"

From the corpse woodpiles, from the ashes
and staring pits of Dachau,
Buchenwald they come—

O David, Hirschel, Eva,
cops and robbers with me once,
their faces are like yours—

From Johannesburg, from Seoul.
Their struggles are all horizons.
Their deaths encircle me.

Through target streets I run,
in light part nightmare
and part vision fleeing

What I cannot flee, and reach
that cold cloacal cell
where He, who is man beatified

And Godly mystery,
lies chained, His pain
our anguish and our anodyne.

THOSE WINTER SUNDAYS

Sundays too my father got up early
and put his clothes on in the blueblack cold,
then with cracked hands that ached
from labor in the weekday weather made
banked fires blaze. No one ever thanked him.

I'd wake and hear the cold splintering, breaking.
When the rooms were warm, he'd call,
and slowly I would rise and dress,
fearing the chronic angers of that house,

Speaking indifferently to him,
who had driven out the cold
and polished my good shoes as well.
What did I know, what did I know
of love's austere and lonely offices?

NIGHT, DEATH, MISSISSIPPI

I

A quavering cry. Screech-owl?
Or one of them?
The old man in his reek
and gauntness laughs—

ROBERT HAYDEN

One of them, I bet—
and turns out the kitchen lamp,
limping to the porch to listen
in the windowless night.

Be there with Boy and the rest
if I was well again.
Time was. Time was.
White robes like moonlight

In the sweetgum dark.
Unbucked that one then
and him squealing bloody Jesus
as we cut it off.

Time was. A cry?
A cry all right.
He hawks and spits,
fevered as by groinfire.

Have us a bottle,
Boy and me—
he's earned him a bottle—
when he gets home.

II

Then we beat them, he said,
beat them till our arms was tired
and the big old chains
messy and red.

O Jesus burning on the lily cross

Christ, it was better
than hunting bear
which don't know why
you want him dead.

O night, rawhead and bloodybones night

ROBERT HAYDEN

You kids fetch Paw
some water now so's he
can wash that blood
off him, she said.

O night betrayed by darkness not its own

MONET'S "WATERLILIES"

(for Bill and Sonja)

Today as the news from Selma and Saigon
poisons the air like fallout,
        I come again to see
the serene great picture that I love.

Here space and time exist in light
the eye like the eye of faith believes.
        The seen, the known
dissolve in iridescence, become
illusive flesh of light
        that was not, was, forever is.

O light beheld as through refracting tears.
Here is the aura of that world
        each of us has lost.
Here is the shadow of its joy.

SOLEDAD

(And I, I am no longer of that world)

Naked, he lies in the blinded room
chainsmoking, cradled by drugs, by jazz
as never by any lover's cradling flesh.

Miles Davis coolly blows for him:
O *pena negra,* sensual Flamenco blues;
the red clay foxfire voice of Lady Day

(lady of the pure black magnolias)
sobsings her sorrow and loss and fare you well,
dryweeps the pain his treacherous jailers

have released him from for awhile.
His fears and his unfinished self
await him down in the anywhere streets.

He hides on the dark side of the moon,
takes refuge in a stained-glass cell,
flies to a clockless country of crystal.

Only the ghost of Lady Day knows where
he is. Only the music. And he swings
oh swings: beyond complete immortal now.

THE NIGHT-BLOOMING CEREUS

And so for nights
we waited, hoping to see
the heavy bud
break into flower.

On its neck-like tube
hooking down from the edge
of the leaf-branch
nearly to the floor,

the bud packed
tight with its miracle swayed
stiffly on breaths
of air, moved

as though impelled
by stirrings within itself.
It repelled as much
as it fascinated me

ROBERT HAYDEN

sometimes—snake,
eyeless bird head,
beak that would gape
    with grotesque life-squawk.

But you, my dear,
conceded less to the bizarre
than to the imminence
    of bloom. Yet we agreed

we ought
to celebrate the blossom,
paint ourselves, dance
    in honor of

archaic mysteries
when it appeared. Meanwhile
we waited, aware
    of rigorous design.

Backster's
polygraph, I thought,
would have shown
    (as clearly as it had

a philodendron's
fear) tribal sentience
in the cactus, focused
    energy of will.

That belling of
tropic perfume—that
signalling
    not meant for us;

the darkness
cloyed with summoning
fragrance. We dropped
    trivial tasks

and marvelling
beheld at last the achieved
flower. Its moonlight
 petals were

 still unfold-
ing, the spike fringe of the outer
perianth recessing
 as we watched.

 Lunar presence,
foredoomed, already dying,
it charged the room
 with plangency

 older than human
cries, ancient as prayers
invoking Osiris, Krishna,
 Tezcátlipóca.

 We spoke
in whispers when
we spoke
 at all . . .

FOR A YOUNG ARTIST

Sprawled in the pigsty,
 snouts nudging snuffling him—
a naked old man
 with bloodstained wings.

 Fallen from the August sky?
Dead? Alive?
 But he twists away

from the cattle-prod, wings
        jerking, lifts his grizzled head,
regarding all
        with searching eyes.

Neither smiles nor threats,
dumbshow nor lingua franca
were of any use to those
trying for clues to him.

They could not make him hide
his nakedness
in their faded hand-me-downs.

Humane, if hostile and afraid,
they spread him a pallet
in the chicken-house.
The rooster pecked his wings.

Leftovers were set out for him;
he ate sunflowers
instead and the lice crawling his feathers.

Carloads of the curious paid
his clever hosts to see the
actual angel? carny freak?
in the barbedwire pen.

They crossed themselves and prayed
his blessing;
catcalled and chunked at him.

        In the dark his heavy wings
open and shut, stiffly spread
        like a wooden butterfly's.

        He leaps, board wings clum-
sily flapping, big sex
        flopping, falls.

        The hawk-haunted fowl
flutter and squawk;
        panic squeals in the sty.

He strains, an awk-
ward patsy, sweating strains
leaping falling. Then—

silken rustling in the air,
the angle of ascent
achieved.

(After the story, "A Very Old Man with Enormous Wings," by Gabriel García Márques)

© Thomas Victor

Richard Hugo

DEATH OF THE KAPOWSIN TAVERN

I can't ridge it back again from char.
Not one board left. Only ash a cat explores
and shattered glass smoked black and strung
about from the explosion I believe
in the reports. The white school up for sale
for years, most homes abandoned to the rocks
of passing boys—the fire, helped by wind
that blew the neon out six years before,
simply ended lots of ending.

A damn shame. Now, when the night chill
of the lake gets in a troller's bones
where can the troller go for bad wine
washed down frantically with beer?
And when wise men are in style again
will one recount the two-mile glide of cranes
from dead pines or the nameless yellow
flowers thriving in the useless logs,
or dots of light all night about the far end
of the lake, the dawn arrival of the idiot
with catfish—most of all, above the lake
the temple and our sanctuary there?

Nothing dies as slowly as a scene.
The dusty jukebox cracking through
the cackle of a beered-up crone—
wagered wine—sudden need to dance—
these remain in the black debris.
Although I know in time the lake will send
wind black enough to blow it all away.

G.I. GRAVES IN TUSCANY

They still seem G.I., the uniform lines
of white crosses, the gleam that rolls
white drums over the lawn. Machines

185

that cut the grass left their maneuvers plain.
Our flag doesn't seem silly though plainly
it flies only because there is wind.

Let them go by. I don't want to turn in.
After ten minutes I'd be sick of their names
or the names of their towns. Then
some guide would offer a tour
for two thousand lire, smiling the places
of battle, feigning hate for the Krauts.
I guess visitors come. A cross here and there
is rooted in flowers. Maybe in Scranton
a woman is saving. Maybe in books
what happened and why is worked out.

The loss is so damn gross. I remember
a washtub of salad in basic, blacktop acres
of men waiting to march, passing three hours
of bombers, en route to Vienna, and bombing
and passing two hours of planes, coming back.
Numbers are vulgar. If I stayed
I'd count the men in years of probable loss.

I'm a liar. I'm frightened to stop.
Afraid of a speech I might make,
corny over some stone with a name
that indicates Slavic descent—you there,
you must be first generation,
I'm third. The farm, I'm told, was hard
but it all means something. Think
of Jefferson, of the Constitution,
not of these children
beside me, bumming a smoke and laughing.

DEGREES OF GRAY IN PHILIPSBURG

You might come here Sunday on a whim.
Say your life broke down. The last good kiss
you had was years ago. You walk these streets

laid out by the insane, past hotels
that didn't last, bars that did, the tortured try
of local drivers to accelerate their lives.
Only churches are kept up. The jail
turned 70 this year. The only prisoner
is always in, not knowing what he's done.

The principal supporting business now
is rage. Hatred of the various grays
the mountain sends, hatred of the mill,
The Silver Bill repeal, the best liked girls
who leave each year for Butte. One good
restaurant and bars can't wipe the boredom out.
The 1907 boom, eight going silver mines,
a dance floor built on springs—
all memory resolves itself in gaze,
in panoramic green you know the cattle eat
or two stacks high above the town,
two dead kilns, the huge mill in collapse
for fifty years that won't fall finally down.

Isn't this your life? That ancient kiss
still burning out your eyes? Isn't this defeat
so accurate, the church bell simply seems
a pure announcement: ring and no one comes?
Don't empty houses ring? Are magnesium
and scorn sufficient to support a town,
not just Philipsburg, but towns
of towering blondes, good jazz and booze
the world will never let you have
until the town you came from dies inside?

Say no to yourself. The old man, twenty
when the jail was built, still laughs
although his lips collapse. Someday soon,
he says, I'll go to sleep and not wake up.
You tell him no. You're talking to yourself.
The car that brought you here still runs.
The money you buy lunch with,
no matter where it's mined, is silver
and the girl who serves you food
is slender and her red hair lights the wall.

RICHARD HUGO

MONTGOMERY HOLLOW

Birds here should have names so hard to say
you name them over. They finally found
the farmer hanging near the stream.
Only insect hum today and the purple odor
of thyme. You'd bet your throat against
the way a mind goes bad. You conquer loss
by going to the place it happened
and replaying it, saying the name
of the face in the open casket right.

People die in cities. Unless it's war
you never see the bodies. They die in print,
over phones in paramouric flats.
Here, you find them staring down the sun,
flies crawling them like bacon. Wives
scream two days running and the pain is gone.
Here, you find them living.

To know a road you own it, every bend
and pebble and the weeds along it,
dust that itches when the August hayrake
rambles home. You own the home.
You own the death of every bird you name.
To live good, keep your life and the scene.
Cow, brook, hay: these are names of coins.

for Stanley Kauffmann

MONTANA RANCH ABANDONED

Cracks in eight log buildings, counting sheds
and outhouse, widen and a ghost peeks out.
Nothing, tree or mountain, weakens wind
coming for the throat. Even wind must work
when land gets old. The rotting wagon tongue
makes fun of girls who begged to go to town.
Broken brakerods dangle in the dirt.

RICHARD HUGO

Alternatives were madness or a calloused moon.
Wood they carved the plowblade from
turned stone as nameless gray. Indifferent flies
left dung intact. One boy had to leave
when horses pounded night, and miles away
a neighbor's daughter puked. Mother's cry
to dinner changed to caw in later years.

Maybe raiding bears or eelworms made them quit,
or daddy died, or when they planted wheat
dead Flatheads killed the plant. That stove
without a grate can't warm the ghost.
Tools would still be good if cleaned, but mortar
flakes and log walls sag. Even if you shored,
cars would still boom by beyond the fence, no glance
from drivers as you till the lunar dust.

THE HOUSE ON 15TH S.W.

Cruelty and rain could be expected.
Any season. The talk was often German
and we cried at the death of strangers.
Potatoes mattered and neighbors who came
to marvel at our garden. I never helped
with the planting. I hid in woods these houses
built on either side replaced. Ponds
duplicated sky. I watched my face
play out dreams of going north with clouds.

North surely was soft. North was death
and women and the women soft. The tongue
there was American and kind. Acres of women
would applaud me as I danced, and acres
of graves would dance when sun announced
another cloud was dead. No grating scream
to meals or gratuitous beatings,
no crying, raging fists against closed doors,
twisted years I knew were coming at me,
hours alone in bars with honest mirrors,
being fun with strangers, being liked
so much the chance of jail was weak

from laughter, and my certainty of failure
mined by a tyrant for its pale perverted ore.

My pride in a few poems, my shame
of a wasted life, no wife, no children,
cancel out. I'm left neutral as this house,
not caring to go in. Light would be soft
and full, not harsh and dim remembered.
The children, if there are children inside,
would be normal, clean, not at all
the soiled freaks I had counted on.

FARMER, DYING

Seven thousand acres of grass have faded yellow
from his cough. These limp days, his anger,
legend forty years from moon to Stevensville,
lives on, just barely, in a Great Falls whore.
Cruel times, he cries, cruel winds. His geese roam
unattended in the meadow. The gold last leaves
of cottonwoods ride Burnt Fork creek away.
His geese grow fat without him. Same old insult.
Same indifferent rise of mountains south,
hunters drunk around the fire ten feet from his fence.

What's killing us is something autumn. Call it
war or fever. You know it when you see it: flare.
Vine and fire and the morning deer come half
a century to sip his spring, there, at the far end
of his land, wrapped in cellophane by light.
What lives is what he left in air, definite,
unseen, hanging where he stood the day he roared.
A bear prowls closer to his barn each day.
Farmers come to watch him die. They bring crude offerings
of wine. Burnt Fork creek is caroling. He dies white
in final anger. The bear taps on his pane.

And we die silent, our last day loaded with the scream
of Burnt Fork creek, the last cry of that raging farmer.
We have aged ourselves to stone trying to summon
mercy for ungrateful daughters. Let's live him

RICHARD HUGO

in ourselves, stand deranged on the meadow rim
and curse the Baltic back, moon, bear and blast.
And let him shout from his grave for us.

for Hank and Nancy

THE HILLTOP

I like bars close to home and home run down,
a signal to the world, I'm weak. I like a bar
to be a home. Take this one. Same men every night.
Same jokes. Traffic going by
fifteen feet away and punchboards never paying off.
Churn of memory and ulcer. Most of all
the stale anticipation of the girl
sure to walk in someday fresh from '39,
not one day older, holding out her arms.

Soon, I say to no one late each night,
I'll be all right. I put five dollars
in the jukebox and never hear a tune.
I take pride drinking alone and being kind.
When I walk in, people say my name.
By ten, the loveliest girl in Vegas
swims about the room, curving in and counter
to the flow of smoke. Her evil sister
swings her legs and giggles in my drink.

When I'm at home, the kitchen light stays on.
Help me, friend. By dawn, a hundred dogs
are gnawing at my throat. My gnarled phlegm
chokes up yellow. My empty room
revolves tornado and my relatives
are still unnamed. A dozen practiced gestures
get me through the day. By five, I'm crawling
up the hill, certain I'll live, my Hilltop smile
perfected and my coin naïve.

for Susan Zwinger

RICHARD HUGO

LETTER TO LOGAN FROM MILLTOWN

Dear John: This is a Dear John letter from booze.
With you, liver. With me, bleeding ulcer. The results
are the horrific same: as drunks we're done. Christ,
John, what a loss to those underground political
movements that count, the Degradationists,
the Dipsomaniacists, and that force gaining momentum
all over the world, the Deteriorationists. I hope
you know how sad this is. Once I quit drinking it was clear
to others, including our chairman (who incidentally
also had to quit drinking), that less 40 pounds
I look resolute and strong and on the surface appear
efficient. Try this for obscene development: they made me
director of creative writing. Better I'd gone on bleeding
getting whiter and whiter and finally blending
into the snow to be found next spring, a tragedy
that surely would increase my poetic reputation.
POET FOUND IN THAW   SNOWS CLAIM MISSOULA BARD
I'm in Milltown. You remember that bar, that beautiful bar
run by Harold Herndon where I pissed five years away
but pleasantly. And now I can't go in for fear
I'll fall sobbing to the floor. God, the ghosts in there.
The poems. Those honest people from the woods and mill.
What a relief that was from school, from that smelly
student-teacher crap and those dreary committees
where people actually say "considering the lateness
of the hour." Bad times too. That depressing summer
of '66 and that woman going—I've talked too often
about that. Now no bourbon to dissolve the tension,
to find self-love in blurred fantasies, to find the charm
to ask a woman home. What happens to us, John?
We are older than our scars. We have outlasted and survived
our wars and it turns out we're not as bad as we thought.
And that's really sad. But as a funny painter said
at a bash in Portland, and I thought of you then,
give Mother Cabrini another Martini. But not ever again
you and me. Piss on sobriety, and take care. Dick.

RICHARD HUGO

IN YOUR GOOD DREAM

From this hill they are clear, the people
in pairs emerging from churches, arm
in soft arm. And limb on green limb
the shade oaks lining the streets form
rainproof arches. All day festive tunes
explain your problems are over. You picnic
alone on clean lawn with your legend.
Girls won't make fun of you here.

Storms are spotted far off enough
to plan going home and home has fire.

It's been here forever. Two leisurely grocers
who never compete. At least ten elms
between houses and rapid grass refilling
the wild field for horses. The same mayor
year after year—no one votes anymore—
stocks bass in the ponds and monster trout
in the brook. Anger is outlawed.
The unpleasant get out. Two old policemen
stop children picking too many flowers
in May and give strangers directions.

You know they are happy. Best to stay
on the hill, drowsy witness, hearing
the music, seeing their faces beam
and knowing they marry forever, die late
and are honored in death. A local process,
no patent applied for, cuts name, born date
and died too deep in the headstone to blur.

© Gerard Malanga

David Ignatow

COMMUNION

Let us be friends, said Walt,
and buildings sprang up
quick as corn and people
were born into them, stock
brokers, admen, lawyers and doctors
and they contended
      among themselves
that they might know
      each other.

Let us be friends, said Walt.
We are one and occasionally two
of which the one is made
and cemeteries were laid out
miles in all directions
to fill the plots with the old
and young, dead of murder, disease,
rape, hatred, heartbreak and insanity
to make way for the new
and the cemeteries spread over the land
their white scab monuments.

Let us be friends, said Walt, and the graves
were opened and coffins laid on top
of one another for lack of space.
It was then the gravediggers slit
their throats, being alone in the world,
not a friend to bury.

DAVID IGNATOW

SUNDAY AT THE STATE HOSPITAL

I am sitting across the table
eating my visit sandwich.
The one I brought him stays suspended
near his mouth; his eyes focus
on the table and seem to think,
his shoulders hunched forward.
I chew methodically,
pretending to take him
as a matter of course.
The sandwich tastes mad
and I keep chewing.
My past is sitting in front of me
filled with itself
and trying with almost no success
to bring the present to its mouth.

MY PLACE

I have a place to come to.
It's my place. I come to it
morning, noon and night
and it is there. I expect it
to be there whether or not
it expects me—my place
where I start from and go
towards so that I know
where I am going and what
I am going from, making me
firm in my direction.

I am good to talk to,
you feel in my speech
a location, an expectation
and all said to me in reply
is to reinforce this feeling
because all said is towards
my place and the speaker
too grows his

from which he speaks to mine
having located himself
through my place.

THE INHERITANCE

I never thought your harsh voice would be silenced,
your contracted, vicious face relaxed and calm,
the big nose standing out magisterially,
and the once small, sharp, puckered mouth
lengthened into a soft, sad curve,
reminding me of your mother's photograph.
I kissed your cold forehead with my fingertips
first touched to my lips in farewell,
and as I lingered to study your face
the lid was slammed down by attendants
to get them on with their job. Later
I wept, and my wife too was impatient with me,
knowing you well. Nevertheless, I wept.
You gave me smiles and made me work
at your machines. It was you taught me
the necessity for freedom.
I am going to sell your shop,
you to be remembered in my lines.

EPITAPH

There were no hidden motives to his life,
he is remembered for his meanness.
Beyond that we may look into the sky
and lose ourselves in the blue air.

Reason with me,
I'll believe in reason
though my father is dead,
and when I die
remember of me
I sought for a reason.

DAVID IGNATOW

In the mirror the face I see
before me is my father's face,
as if I were thinking his thoughts
about me, in love
and disapproval.
I turn my face away.

Forgive me, father,
as I have forgiven you
my sins.

THE BAGEL

I stopped to pick up the bagel
rolling away in the wind,
annoyed with myself
for having dropped it
as it were a portent.
Faster and faster it rolled,
with me running after it
bent low, gritting my teeth,
and I found myself doubled over
and rolling down the street
head over heels, one complete somersault
after another like a bagel
and strangely happy with myself.

RESCUE THE DEAD

Finally, to forgo love is to kiss a leaf,
is to let rain fall nakedly upon your head,
is to respect fire,
is to study man's eyes and his gestures
as he talks,
is to set bread upon the table
and a knife discreetly by,
is to pass through crowds
like a crowd of oneself.
Not to love is to live.

DAVID IGNATOW

To love is to be led away
into a forest where the secret grave
is dug, singing, praising darkness
under the trees.

To live is to sign your name,
is to ignore the dead,
is to carry a wallet
and shake hands.

To love is to be a fish.
My boat wallows in the sea.
You who are free,
rescue the dead.

AGAINST THE EVIDENCE

As I reach to close each book
lying open on my desk, it leaps up
to snap at my fingers. My legs
won't hold me, I must sit down.
My fingers pain me
where the thick leaves snapped together
at my touch.

All my life
I've held books in my hands
like children, carefully turning
their pages and straightening out
their creases. I use books
almost apologetically. I believe
I often think their thoughts for them.
Reading, I never know where theirs leave off
and mine begin. I am so much alone
in the world, I can observe the stars
or study the breeze, I can count the steps
on a stair on the way up or down,
and I can look at another human being
and get a smile, knowing
it is for the sake of politeness.
Nothing must be said of estrangement

among the human race and yet
nothing is said at all
because of that.
But no book will help either.
I stroke my desk,
its wood so smooth, so patient and still.
I set a typewriter on its surface
and begin to type
to tell myself my troubles.
Against the evidence, I live by choice.

FIRST COFFIN POEM

I love you, my plain pine box,
because you also are a bench,
with the lid down. Can you see
my friends in a row seated
at ease with themselves?
I am in a coffin
and it has been set against the wall
of a living room. It is just before
dinner and several friends are standing
about with glasses in their hands,
drinking to the possibilities
that life offers.
    The coffin also
could be placed as a table
in front of a grand sofa, with food
and drinks served on it, and an ashtray.

It would be so much simpler, less gruesome
to use an actual coffee table, you say,
or a real bench, but ah, that would prove
how rigid we must be about ourselves
and cause us to languish, caught
in a limitation. We must make one thing
do for another.
    I am hope, in urging you
to use my pine box. Take me to your home
when I die imperceptibly. Without fuss

DAVID IGNATOW

place me against the wall in my coffin,
a conversation piece, an affirmation of change.
I am, sincerely, yours.

WAITING INSIDE

I protest my isolation
but protest is a mark of my defeat,
even as I write.
                    Being a victim,
I am an accuser. Being human,
others feel my fallen weight
upon their thoughts and are oppressed—
as I am, their guilt unlike mine
and unrelated and without hope in it
of change for me.
                    Guilty, my oppressor
and I go separate ways
though we could relieve each other
by going together, as Whitman wrote,
with our arms around each other's waists,
in support.

READING THE HEADLINES

I have a burial ground in me where I place the bodies
without fuss or emotion, hundreds of thousands at a
     glance.
I stow them in and as it happens I am eating dinner,
I continue to eat, feeding myself and the dead.

I walk around in this burial ground, examining it
with curiosity, find it dark but stroll with a sense
of safety, my own place. I want to lie down in it,
dissatisfied with it, true, but seeing no exit, I lie
down to rest and dream.

I am lost anyway, without horizon or recognizable
    features.
It's just to walk on. At least it's not necessary
to kill myself. I'll die of attrition of my energy to live.

I know my direction and have companions, after all.

WITH THE SUN'S FIRE

Are you a horror to yourself?
Do you have eyes peering at you
from within at the back of your skull
as you manage to stay calm, knowing
you are being watched by a stranger?

Be well, I am seated beside you,
planning a day's work. We are contending
with the stuff of stones and stars,
with water, air, with dirt, with food
and with the sun's fire.

THE QUESTION

I dream I am flying above the city
on the strength of my two outflung arms
and looking down upon the streets
where people are like so many
bacteria moving about upon a slide.
I am alone up here, with no one
to contradict me, free of the noise,
tumult and violence of the living.
Here is my true residence,
and if I say the people are bacteria
who will deny it? I declare
in my circumstances that the people
are what I say they are. The only
question now is whether I can
keep flying.

DAVID IGNATOW

from SUNLIGHT: A SEQUENCE FOR MY DAUGHTER

[I am proud of your soft, brown eyes]

I am proud of your soft, brown eyes
looking at me to understand my presence.
You have smiled and you have thrown your hands
and legs into the air in a rhapsody
of well being and I have followed
with laughter, awed to think it is possible
to be as small as you and yet human,
for I have confused love with size,
and you look at me steadily
when I cluck and coo.

I am proud of your brown eyes
I have not known could be so soft
and questioning, and I lift you
from the crib to carry you cheek to cheek
to see if I can rub your gentleness on me.

[My infinite child, hold me to sleep]

My infinite child, hold me to sleep
in your certitude where we play house
holding the doll for a baby being fed
the bottle. I am not the happiness
you find in me, nor is it in my love.
My sadness buoys you up,
as watching you asleep your childhood
slays my old age back into beginnings,
your lips parted in dream,
face softly strange
as with difficulty delighted in.

© Rollie McKenna

Randall Jarrell

THE BLACK SWAN

When the swans turned my sister into a swan
    I would go to the lake, at night, from milking:
The sun would look out through the reeds like a swan,
    A swan's red beak; and the beak would open
And inside there was darkness, the stars and the moon.

Out on the lake a girl would laugh.
    "Sister, here is your porridge, sister,"
I would call; and the reeds would whisper,
    "Go to sleep, go to sleep, little swan."
My legs were all hard and webbed, and the silky

Hairs of my wings sank away like stars
    In the ripples that ran in and out of the reeds:
I heard through the lap and hiss of water
    Someone's "Sister . . . sister," far away on the shore,
And then as I opened my beak to answer

I heard my harsh laugh go out to the shore
    And saw—saw at last, swimming up from the green
Low mounds of the lake, the white stone swans:
    The white, named swans . . . "It is all a dream,"
I whispered, and reached from the down of the pallet

To the lap and hiss of the floor.
    And "Sleep, little sister," the swans all sang
From the moon and stars and frogs of the floor.
    But the swan my sister called, "Sleep at last, little sister,"
And stroked all night, with a black wing, my wings.

RANDALL JARRELL

TO THE NEW WORLD

(For an emigrant of 1939)

In that bad year and city of your birth
They traded bread for bank-notes weight for weight,
And nothing but the statues kept the smile
The waltzers wore once: excluding, innocent,
The face of old and comfortable injustice.
And if you wept,
Dropped red into a city where the husbandless
And fatherless were weeping too, who cared
For one more cry or one more child? You grew,

Time put words into your mouth, and you put sugar
Upon your windowsill and waited for a brother—
The stork was greedy, ate, brought nothing in return.
But your life was thinking of you, took you back to Prague,
At school there, timid, boisterous, you spoke
The unaccustomed Czech—
The children laughed at you. For you were learning
New words and a new life, the old
City and its new country too were learning
An old wish: to be just; yes, to be free.

"I saw summer in my time." Summer is ending.
The storms plunge from the tree of winter, death
Moves like an impulse over Europe. Child,
What man is just or free?—but fortunate,
Warm in time's hand, turning and trusting to his face;
And that face changes.
Time is a man for men, and He is willing
For many a new life, for others death. Already
He buys His trench-coat, falls, writes His big book;

Points here, points here: to Jews, to wicked friends—
His words are the moments of a man's life . . .
And now the men march. One morning you awoke
And found Vienna gone, your father said:
"Us next!" And you were next.
Us next!
Cried map and mouth, oppressors and oppressed,
The appeasers as they gave you—but you were gone.

RANDALL JARRELL

"I had a speech, a city." *What is your name?*
"My name is what my name was." *You have no name.*

So the dream spoke to you: in Zurich, Paris,
In London on a lawn. The unbefriending sea
Cried to you, "Stranger!" Superb, inhospitable,
The towers of the island turned their gaze
Past the girl who looked to the great statue:
So green, so gay . . .
That is how you came. Your face shows white
Against the dark time, your words are indistinct,
One cry among so many, lost in the sound

Of degradation and of agony, the peoples dying.
The net was laid for you, and you are free.
Past the statue there is summer, and the summer smiles
The smile of justice or injustice: blind,
Comfortable, including. Here are the lives
And their old world;
Far off, inside you, a conclusive face
Watches in accusation, in acceptance. It is He.
You escaped from nothing: the westering soul
Finds Europe waiting for it over every sea.

90 NORTH

At home, in my flannel gown, like a bear to its floe,
I clambered to bed; up the globe's impossible sides
I sailed all night—till at last, with my black beard,
My furs and my dogs, I stood at the northern pole.

There in the childish night my companions lay frozen,
The stiff furs knocked at my starveling throat,
And I gave my great sigh: the flakes came huddling,
Were they really my end? In the darkness I turned to my rest.

—Here, the flag snaps in the glare and silence
Of the unbroken ice. I stand here,
The dogs bark, my beard is black, and I stare
At the North Pole . . .
                    And now what? Why, go back.

Turn as I please, my step is to the south.
The world—my world spins on this final point
Of cold and wretchedness: all lines, all winds
End in this whirlpool I at last discover.

And it is meaningless. In the child's bed
After the night's voyage, in that warm world
Where people work and suffer for the end
That crowns the pain—in that Cloud-Cuckoo-Land

I reached my North and it had meaning.
Here at the actual pole of my existence,
Where all that I have done is meaningless,
Where I die or live by accident alone—

Where, living or dying, I am still alone;
Here where North, the night, the berg of death
Crowd me out of the ignorant darkness,
I see at last that all the knowledge

I wrung from the darkness—that the darkness flung me—
Is worthless as ignorance: nothing comes from nothing,
The darkness from the darkness. Pain comes from the darkness
And we call it wisdom. It is pain.

THE SNOW-LEOPARD

His pads furring the scarp's rime,
Weightless in greys and ecru, gliding
Invisibly, incuriously
As the crystals of the cirri wandering
A mile below his absent eyes,
The leopard gazes at the caravan.
The yaks groaning with tea, the burlaps
Lapping and lapping each stunned universe
That gasps like a kettle for its thinning life
Are pools in the interminable abyss
That ranges up through ice, through air, to night.
Raiders of the unminding element,
The last cold capillaries of their kind,
They move so slowly they are motionless
To any eye less stubborn than a man's. . . .

RANDALL JARRELL

From the implacable jumble of the blocks
The grains dance icily, a scouring plume,
Into the breath, sustaining, unsustainable,
They trade to that last stillness for their death.
They sense with misunderstanding horror, with desire,
Behind the world their blood sets up in mist
The brute and geometrical necessity:
The leopard waving with a grating purr
His six-foot tail; the leopard, who looks sleepily—
Cold, fugitive, secure—at all that he knows,
At all that he is: the heart of heartlessness.

THE DEATH OF THE BALL TURRET GUNNER

From my mother's sleep I fell into the State,
And I hunched in its belly till my wet fur froze.
Six miles from earth, loosed from its dream of life,
I woke to black flak and the nightmare fighters.
When I died they washed me out of the turret with a hose.

EIGHTH AIR FORCE

If, in an odd angle of the hutment,
A puppy laps the water from a can
Of flowers, and the drunk sergeant shaving
Whistles O Paradiso!—shall I say that man
Is not as men have said: a wolf to man?

The other murderers troop in yawning;
Three of them play Pitch, one sleeps, and one
Lies counting missions, lies there sweating
Till even his heart beats: One; One; One.
O murderers! . . . Still, this is how it's done:

This is a war. . . . But since these play, before they die,
Like puppies with their puppy; since, a man,
I did as these have done, but did not die—
I will content the people as I can
And give up these to them: Behold the man!

I have suffered, in a dream, because of him,
Many things; for this last saviour, man,
I have lied as I lie now. But what is lying?
Men wash their hands, in blood, as best they can:
I find no fault in this just man.

A CAMP IN THE PRUSSIAN FOREST

I walk beside the prisoners to the road.
Load on puffed load,
Their corpses, stacked like sodden wood,
Lie barred or galled with blood

By the charred warehouse. No one comes today
In the old way
To knock the fillings from their teeth;
The dark, coned, common wreath

Is plaited for their grave—a kind of grief.
The living leaf
Clings to the planted profitable
Pine if it is able;

The boughs sigh, mile on green, calm, breathing mile,
From this dead file
The planners ruled for them. . . . One year
They sent a million here:

Here men were drunk like water, burnt like wood.
The fat of good
And evil, the breast's star of hope
Were rendered into soap.

I paint the star I sawed from yellow pine—
And plant the sign
In soil that does not yet refuse
Its usual Jews

Their first asylum. But the white, dwarfed star—
This dead white star—
Hides nothing, pays for nothing; smoke
Fouls it, a yellow joke,

The needles of the wreath are chalked with ash,
A filmy trash
Litters the black woods with the death
Of men; and one last breath

Curls from the monstrous chimney. . . . I laugh aloud
Again and again;
The star laughs from its rotting shroud
Of flesh. O star of men!

THE WOMAN AT THE WASHINGTON ZOO

The saris go by me from the embassies.

Cloth from the moon. Cloth from another planet.
They look back at the leopard like the leopard.

And I. . . .
              this print of mine, that has kept its color
Alive through so many cleanings; this dull null
Navy I wear to work, and wear from work, and so
To my bed, so to my grave, with no
Complaints, no comment: neither from my chief,
The Deputy Chief Assistant, nor his chief—
Only I complain. . . . this serviceable
Body that no sunlight dyes, no hand suffuses
But, dome-shadowed, withering among columns,
Wavy beneath fountains—small, far-off, shining
In the eyes of animals, these beings trapped
As I am trapped but not, themselves, the trap,
Aging, but without knowledge of their age,
Kept safe here, knowing not of death, for death—
Oh, bars of my own body, open, open!

The world goes by my cage and never sees me.
And there come not to me, as come to these,

The wild beasts, sparrows pecking the llamas' grain,
Pigeons settling on the bears' bread, buzzards
Tearing the meat the flies have clouded. . . .
                                        Vulture,
When you come for the white rat that the foxes left,
Take off the red helmet of your head, the black
Wings that have shadowed me, and step to me as man:
The wild brother at whose feet the white wolves fawn,
To whose hand of power the great lioness
Stalks, purring. . . .
                        You know what I was,
You see what I am: change me, change me!

THE BRONZE DAVID OF DONATELLO

A sword in his right hand, a stone in his left hand,
He is naked. Shod and naked. Hatted and naked.
The ribbons of his leaf-wreathed, bronze-brimmed bonnet
Are tasseled; crisped into the folds of frills,
Trills, graces, they lie in separation
Among the curls that lie in separation
Upon the shoulders.
                        Lightly, as if accustomed,
Loosely, as if indifferent,
The boy holds in grace
The stone moulded, somehow, by the fingers,
The sword alien, somehow, to the hand.
                                The boy David
Said of it: "There is none like *that*."
                                The boy David's
Body shines in freshness, still unhandled,
And thrusts its belly out a little in exact
Shamelessness. Small, close, complacent,
A labyrinth the gaze retraces,
The rib-case, navel, nipples are the features
Of a face that holds us like the whore Medusa's—
Of a face that, like the genitals, is sexless.
What sex has victory?
The mouth's cut Cupid's-bow, the chin's unwinning dimple
Are tightened, a little oily, take, use, notice:
Centering itself upon itself, the sleek

RANDALL JARRELL

Body with its too-large head, this green
Fruit now forever green, this offending
And efficient elegance draws subtly, supply,
Between the world and itself, a shining
Line of delimitation, demarcation.
The body mirrors itself.
                         Where the armpit becomes breast,
Becomes back, a great crow's-foot is slashed.
Yet who would gash
The sleek flesh so? the cast, filed, shining flesh?
The cuts are folds: these are the folds of flesh
That closes on itself as a knife closes.

The right foot is planted on a wing. Bent back in ease
Upon a supple knee—the toes curl a little, grasping
The crag upon which they are set in triumph—
The left leg glides toward, the left foot lies upon
A head. The head's other wing (the head is bearded
And winged and helmeted and bodiless)
Grows like a swan's wing up inside the leg;
Clothes, as the suit of a swan-maiden clothes,
The leg. The wing reaches, almost, to the rounded
Small childish buttocks. The dead wing warms the leg,
The dead wing, crushed beneath the foot, is swan's-down.
Pillowed upon the rock, Goliath's head
Lies under the foot of David.

Strong in defeat, in death rewarded,
The head dreams what has destroyed it
And is untouched by its destruction.
The stone sunk in the forehead, say the Scriptures;
There is no stone in the forehead. The head is helmed
Or else, unguarded, perfect still.
Borne high, borne long, borne in mastery,
The head is fallen.
                    The new light falls
As if in tenderness, upon the face—
Its masses shift for a moment, like an animal,
And settle, misshapen, into sleep: Goliath
Snores a little in satisfaction.
To so much strength, those overborne by it
Seemed girls, and death came to it like a girl,
Came to it, through the soft air, like a bird—

So that the boy is like a girl, is like a bird
Standing on something it has pecked to death.

The boy stands at ease, his hand upon his hip:
The truth of victory. A Victory
Angelic, almost, in indifference,
An angel sent with no message but this triumph
And alone, now, in his triumph,
He looks down at the head and does not see it.

Upon this head
As upon a spire, the boy David dances,
Dances, and is exalted.
                    Blessed are those brought low,
Blessed is defeat, sleep blessed, blessed death.

KIRILOV ON A SKYSCRAPER

Something gnaws inside my head
That changes everything I see:
An indolent and cloudy time,
The treasures of a barbarous scene,—

What use the crow's malignant look
Or joints as aching as a song
To show that aimless dignity
And ease that even an eye can own?—

The faces by the parapet,
Infected with their gazing, glare
As savagely as though they'd build
Another Eden, and a fruit

To reave from us the knowledge that we got.
What's good or evil to the man
So soon diminished to a doll,
Too rapid to catch a window's stare?—

His love, his mother, ranged at them—
Too fast! too fast! They gaze at, in their hour,
One instant in one instant's world—
Mortality distending like a flower.

© *Thomas Victor*

Galway Kinnell

FIRST SONG

Then it was dusk in Illinois, the small boy
After an afternoon of carting dung
Hung on the rail fence, a sapped thing
Weary to crying. Dark was growing tall
And he began to hear the pond frogs all
Calling on his ear with what seemed their joy.

Soon their sound was pleasant for a boy
Listening in the smoky dusk and the nightfall
Of Illinois, and from the fields two small
Boys came bearing cornstalk violins
And they rubbed the cornstalk bows with resins
And the three sat there scraping of their joy.

It was now fine music the frogs and the boys
Did in the towering Illinois twilight make
And into dark in spite of a shoulder's ache
A boy's hunched body loved out of a stalk
The first song of his happiness, and the song woke
His heart to the darkness and into the sadness of joy.

ON FROZEN FIELDS

1

We walk across the snow,
The stars can be faint,
The moon can be eating itself out,
There can be meteors flaring to death on earth,
The Northern Lights can be blooming and seething
And tearing themselves apart all night,
We walk arm in arm, and we are happy.

2

You in whose ultimate madness we live,
You flinging yourself out into the emptiness,
You—like us—great an instant,

O only universe we know, forgive us.

HOW MANY NIGHTS

How many nights
have I lain in terror,
O Creator Spirit, Maker of night and day,

only to walk out
the next morning over the frozen world
hearing under the creaking of snow
faint, peaceful breaths . . .
snake,
bear, earthworm, ant . . .

and above me
a wild crow crying 'yaw yaw yaw'
from a branch nothing cried from ever in my life.

ANOTHER NIGHT IN THE RUINS

1

In the evening
haze darkening on the hills,
purple
of the eternal, a last bird
crosses over, 'flop flop',
adoring
only the instant.

2

Nine years ago,
in a plane that rumbled all night
above the Atlantic,
I could see, lit up
by lightning bolts jumping out of it,
a thunderhead formed like the face
of my brother, looking nostalgically down
on blue,
lightning-flashed moments of the Atlantic.

3

He used to tell me,
"What good is the day?
On some hill of despair
the bonfire
you kindle can light the great sky—
though it's true, of course, to make it burn
you have to throw yourself in . . ."

4

Wind tears itself hollow
in the eaves of my ruins, ghost-flute
of snowdrifts
that build out there in the dark:
upside-down
ravines into which night sweeps
our torn wings, our ink-spattered feathers.

5

I listen.
I hear nothing. Only
the cow, the cow
of nothingness, mooing
down the bones.

6

Is that a
rooster? He
thrashes in the snow
for a grain. Finds
it. Rips
it into
flames. Flaps. Crows.
Flames
bursting out of his brow.

7

How many nights must it take
one such as me to learn
that we aren't, after all, made
from that bird which flies out of its ashes,
that for a man
as he goes up in flames, his one work
is
to open himself, to *be*
the flames?

VAPOR TRAIL REFLECTED IN THE FROG POND

1

The old watch: their
thick eyes
puff and foreclose by the moon. The young, heads
trailed by the beginnings of necks,
shiver,
in the guarantee they shall be bodies.

In the frog pond
the vapor trail of a SAC bomber creeps,

I hear its drone, drifting, high up
in immaculate ozone.

GALWAY KINNELL

2

And I hear,
coming over the hills, America singing,
her varied carols I hear:
crack of deputies' rifles practicing their aim on stray dogs
    at night,
sput of cattleprod,
TV groaning at the smells of the human body,
curses of the soldier as he poisons, burns, grinds, and stabs
the rice of the world,
with open mouth, crying strong, hysterical curses.

3

And by rice paddies in Asia
bones
wearing a few shadows
walk down a dirt road, smashed
bloodsuckers on their heel, knowing
the flesh a man throws down in the sunshine
dogs shall eat
and the flesh that is upthrown in the air
shall be seized by birds,
shoulder blades smooth, unmarked by old feather-holes,
hands rivered
by blue, erratic wanderings of the blood,
eyes crinkled up
as they gaze up at the drifting sun that gives us our lives,
seed dazzled over the footbattered blaze of the earth.

THE BEAR

1

In late winter
I sometimes glimpse bits of steam
coming up from
some fault in the old snow
and bend close and see it is lung-colored

and put down my nose
and know
the chilly, enduring odor of bear.

2

I take a wolf's rib and whittle
it sharp at both ends
and coil it up
and freeze it in blubber and place it out
on the fairway of the bears.

And when it has vanished
I move out on the bear tracks,
roaming in circles
until I come to the first, tentative, dark
splash on the earth.

And I set out
running, following the splashes
of blood wandering over the world.
At the cut, gashed resting places
I stop and rest,
at the crawl-marks
where he lay out on his belly
to overpass some stretch of bauchy ice
I lie out
dragging myself forward with bear-knives in my fists.

3

On the third day I begin to starve,
at nightfall I bend down as I knew I would
at a turd sopped in blood,
and hesitate, and pick it up,
and thrust it in my mouth, and gnash it down,
and rise
and go on running.

4

On the seventh day,
living by now on bear blood alone,
I can see his upturned carcass far out ahead, a scraggled,
steamy hulk,
the heavy fur riffling in the wind.

I come up to him
and stare at the narrow-spaced, petty eyes,
the dismayed
face laid back on the shoulder, the nostrils
flared, catching
perhaps the first taint of me as he
died.

I hack
a ravine in his thigh, and eat and drink,
and tear him down his whole length
and open him and climb in
and close him up after me, against the wind,
and sleep.

5

And dream
of lumbering flatfooted
over the tundra,
stabbed twice from within,
splattering a trail behind me,
splattering it out no matter which way I lurch,
no matter which parabola of bear-transcendence,
which dance of solitude I attempt,
which gravity-clutched leap,
which trudge, which groan.

6

Until one day I totter and fall—
fall on this
stomach that has tried so hard to keep up,
to digest the blood as it leaked in,

to break up
and digest the bone itself: and now the breeze
blows over me, blows off
the hideous belches of ill-digested bear blood
and rotted stomach
and the ordinary, wretched odor of bear,

blows across
my sore, lolled tongue a song
or screech, until I think I must rise up
and dance. And I lie still.

7

I awaken I think. Marshlights
reappear, geese
come trailing again up the flyway.
In her ravine under old snow the dam-bear
lies, licking
lumps of smeared fur
and drizzly eyes into shapes
with her tongue. And one
hairy-soled trudge stuck out before me,
the next groaned out,
the next,
the next,
the rest of my days I spend
wandering: wondering
what, anyway,
was that sticky infusion, that rank flavor of blood, that
    poetry, by which I lived?

UNDER THE MAUD MOON

1

On the path,
by this wet site
of old fires—

black ashes, black stones, where tramps
must have squatted down,
gnawing on stream water,
unhouseling themselves on cursed bread,
failing to get warm at a twigfire—

I stop,
gather wet wood,
cut dry shavings, and for her,
whose face
I held in my hands
a few hours, whom I gave back
only to keep holding the space where she was,

I light
a small fire in the rain.

The black
wood reddens, the deathwatches inside
begin running out of time, I can see
the dead, crossed limbs
longing again for the universe, I can hear
in the wet wood the snap
and re-snap of the same embrace being torn.

The raindrops trying
to put the fire out
fall into it and are
changed: the oath broken,
the oath sworn between earth and water, flesh and spirit, broken,
to be sworn again,
over and over, in the clouds, and to be broken again,
over and over, on earth.

2

I sit a moment
by the fire, in the rain, speak
a few words into its warmth—
stone   saint   smooth stone—and sing
one of the songs I used to croak
for my daughter, in her nightmares.

Somewhere out ahead of me
a black bear sits alone
on his hillside, nodding from side
to side. He sniffs
the blossom-smells, the rained earth,
finally he gets up,
eats a few flowers, trudges away,
his fur glistening
in the rain.

The singed grease streams
out of the words, the one
held note
remains—a love-note
twisting under my tongue, like the coyote's bark,
curving off, into a
howl.

3

A round-
cheeked girlchild comes awake
in her crib. The green
swaddlings tear open,
a filament or vestment
tears, the blue
flower opens.

And she who is born,
she who sings and cries,
she who begins the passage, her hair
sprouting out,
her gums budding for her first spring on earth,
the mist still clinging about
her face, puts
her hand
into her father's mouth, to take hold of
his song.

GALWAY KINNELL

4

It is all over,
little one, the flipping
and overleaping, the watery
somersaulting alone in the oneness
under the hill, under
the old, lonely bellybutton
pushing forth again
in remembrance,
the drifting there furled in the dark,
pressing a knee or elbow
along a slippery wall, sculpting
the world with each thrash—the stream
of omphalos blood humming all about you.

5

Her head
enters the headhold
which starts sucking her forth: being itself
closes down all over her, gives her
into the shuddering
grip of departure, the slow,
agonized clenches making
the last molds of her life in the dark.

6

The black eye
opens, the pupil
droozed with black hairs
stops, the chakra
on top of the brain throbs a long moment in world light,

and she skids out on her face into light,
this peck
of stunned flesh
clotted with celestial cheesiness, glowing
with the astral violet
of the underlife. And as they cut

her tie to the darkness
she dies
a moment, turns blue as a coal,
the limbs shaking
as the memories rush out of them. When

they hang her up
by the feet, she sucks
air, screams
her first song—and turns rose,
the slow,
beating, featherless arms
already clutching at the emptiness.

7

When it was cold
on our hillside, and you cried
in the crib rocking
through the darkness, on wood
knifed down to the curve of the smile, a sadness
stranger than ours, all of it
flowing from the other world,

I used to come to you
and sit by you
and sing to you. You did not know,
and yet you will remember,
in the silent zones
of the brain, a specter, descendant
of the ghostly forefathers, singing
to you in the nighttime—
not the songs
of light said to wave
through the bright hair of angels,
but a blacker
rasping flowering on that tongue.

For when the Maud moon
glimmered in those first nights,
and the Archer lay
sucking the icy biestings of the cosmos,
in his crib of stars,

I had crept down
to riverbanks, their long rustle
of being and perishing, down to marshes
where the earth oozes up
in cold streaks, touching the world
with the underglimmer
of the beginning,
and there learned my only song.

And in the days
when you find yourself orphaned,
emptied
of all wind-singing, of light,
the pieces of cursed bread on your tongue,

may there come back to you
a voice,
spectral, calling you
sister!
from everything that dies.

And then
you shall open
this book, even if it is the book of nightmares.

THE HEN FLOWER

1

Sprawled
on our faces in the spring
nights, teeth
biting down on hen feathers, bits of the hen
still stuck in the crevices—if only
we could let go
like her, throw ourselves
on the mercy of darkness, like the hen,

tuck our head
under a wing, hold ourselves still
a few moments, as she

falls out into her little trance in the witchgrass,
or turn over
and be stroked with a finger
down the throat feathers,
down the throat knuckles,
down over the hum
of the wishbone tuning its high D in thin blood,
down over
the breastbone risen up
out of breast flesh, until the fatted thing
woozes off, head
thrown back
on the chopping block, longing only
to die.

2

When the ax-
scented breeze flourishes
about her, her cheeks crush in,
her comb
grays, the gizzard
that turns the thousand acidic millstones of her fate
convulses: ready or not
the next egg, bobbling
its globe of golden earth,
skids forth, ridding her even
of the life to come.

3

Almost high
on subsided gravity, I remain afoot,
a hen flower
dangling from a hand,
wing
of my wing,
of my bones and veins,
of my flesh
hairs lifting all over me in the first ghostly breeze
after death,

wing
made only to fly—unable
to write out the sorrows of being unable
to hold another in one's arms—and unable
to fly,
and waiting, therefore,
for the sweet, eventual blaze in the genes,
that one day, according to gospel, shall carry it back
into pink skies, where geese
cross at twilight, honking
in tongues.

4

I have glimpsed
by corpse-light, in the opened cadaver
of hen, the mass of tiny,
unborn eggs, each getting
tinier and yellower as it reaches back toward
the icy pulp
of what is, I have felt the zero
freeze itself around the finger dipped slowly in.

5

When the Northern Lights
were opening across the black sky and vanishing,
lighting themselves up
so completely they were vanishing,
I put to my eye the lucent
section of the spealbone of a ram—

I thought suddenly
I could read the cosmos spelling itself,
the huge broken letters
shuddering across the black sky and vanishing,

and in a moment,
in the twinkling of an eye, it came to me
the mockingbird would sing all her nights the cry of the rifle,
the tree would hold the bones of the sniper who chose not to
    climb down,

the rose would bloom no one would see it,
the chameleon longing to be changed would remain the color
    of blood.

And I went up
to the henhouse, and took up
the hen killed by weasels, and lugged
the sucked
carcass into first light. And when I hoisted
her up among the young pines, a last
rubbery egg slipping out as I flung her high, didn't it happen
the dead
wings creaked open as she soared
across the arms of the Bear?

6

Sprawled face down, waiting
for the rooster to groan out
it is the empty morning, as he groaned out thrice
for the disciple
of stone,
he who crushed with his heel the brain out of the snake,

I remember long ago I sowed
my own first milk
tooth under hen feathers, I planted under hen feathers
the hook
of the wishbone,
which had broken itself so lovingly toward me.

For the future.

It has come to this.

7

Listen, Kinnell,
dumped alive
and dying into the old sway bed,
a layer of crushed feathers all that there is
between you

and the long shaft of darkness shaped as you,
let go.

Even this haunted room
all its materials photographed with tragedy,
even the tiny crucifix drifting face down at the center of the earth,
even these feathers freed from their wings forever
are afraid.

LAST SONGS

1

What do they sing, the last birds
coasting down the twilight,
banking
across woods filled with darkness, their
frayed wings
curved on the world like a lover's arms
which form, night after night, in sleep,
an irremediable absence?

2

Silence. Ashes
in the grate. Whatever it is
that keeps us from heaven,
sloth, wrath, greed, fear, could we only
reinvent it on earth
as song.

GALWAY KINNELL

SAINT FRANCIS AND THE SOW

The bud
stands for all things,
even for those things that don't flower,
because everything flowers from within, of self-blessing.
Though sometimes it's necessary
to reteach a thing its loveliness,
to put a hand on its brow
of the flower
and retell it in words and in touch
it is lovely
until it flowers again from within, of self-blessing.
As Saint Francis
put his hand on the creased forehead
of the sow, and told her in words and in touch
blessings of earth on the sow, and the sow
began remembering all down her thick length,
from the earthen snout all the way through the fodder and slops
to the spiritual curl of the tail,
from the hard spininess spiked out from the spine
down through the great, unbreakable heart
to the sheer blue milken dreaminess shuddering and squirting
from the fourteen teats into the fourteen mouths sucking and blowing
    beneath them:
the long, perfect loveliness of sow.

THE STILL TIME

I know there is still time—
time for the hands
to open, for the very bones of them
to be filled
by those failed harvests of want,
the bread imagined of the days of not having.

GALWAY KINNELL

Now that the fear
has been rummaged down to its husk,
and the wind blowing
the flesh away begins to translate itself
into flesh and the flesh
to stream itself in its reveries on the wind.

I remember those summer nights
when I was young and empty,
when I lay through the darkness
wanting, wanting,
knowing
I would have nothing of anything I wanted—
that total craving
that hollows the heart out irreversibly.

So it surprises me tonight to hear
the steps of my life following me—
so much of it gone
it returns, everything that drove me crazy
into the world
comes back, blessing the misery
of each step it took me into the world.

It is as if I had been praying a long time
and now that the prayer has ended,
the changed air between my palms goes free
to become the glitter
on ordinary things that inexplicably shine.

And all the old voices,
which once made broken-off, choked, parrot-incoherences
in the child's throat, sound again,
now in the heart's mouth, all of them
saying there is time, still time
for one able to groan
to sing, for whatever can sing
to heal itself almost into happiness, by singing.

© Thomas Victor

Kenneth Koch

FRESH AIR

1

At the Poem Society a black-haired man stands up to say
"You make me sick with all your talk about restraint and mature talent!
Haven't you ever looked out the window at a painting by Matisse,
Or did you always stay in hotels where there were too many spiders crawl-
  ing on your visages?
Did you ever glance inside a bottle of sparkling pop,
Or see a citizen split in two by the lightning?
I am afraid you have never smiled at the hibernation
Of bear cubs except that you saw in it some deep relation
To human suffering and wishes, oh what a bunch of crackpots!"
The black-haired man sits down, and the others shoot arrows at him.
A blond man stands up and says,
"He is right! Why should we be organized to defend the kingdom
Of dullness? There are so many slimy people connected with poetry,
Too, and people who know nothing about it!
I am not recommending that poets like each other and organize to fight
  them,
But simply that lightning should strike them."
Then the assembled mediocrities shot arrows at the blond-haired man.
The chairman stood up on the platform, oh he was physically ugly!
He was small-limbed and -boned and thought he was quite seductive,
But he was bald with certain hideous black hairs,
And his voice had the sound of water leaving a vaseline bathtub,
And he said, "The subject for this evening's discussion is poetry
On the subject of love between swans." And everyone threw candy hearts
At the disgusting man, and they stuck to his bib and tucker,
And he danced up and down on the platform in terrific glee
And recited the poetry of his little friends—but the blond man stuck his
  head
Out of a cloud and recited poems about the east and thunder,
And the black-haired man moved through the stratosphere chanting
Poems of the relationships between terrific prehistoric charcoal whales,
And the slimy man with candy hearts sticking all over him

237

Wilted away like a cigarette paper on which the bumblebees have urinated,
And all the professors left the room to go back to their duty,
And all that were left in the room were five or six poets
And together they sang the new poem of the twentieth century
Which, though influenced by Mallarmé, Shelley, Byron, and Whitman,
Plus a million other poets, is still entirely original
And is so exciting that it cannot be here repeated.
You must go to the Poem Society and wait for it to happen.
Once you have heard this poem you will not love any other,
Once you have dreamed this dream you will be inconsolable,
Once you have loved this dream you will be as one dead,
Once you have visited the passages of this time's great art!

2

"Oh to be seventeen years old
Once again," sang the red-haired man, "and not know that poetry
Is ruled with the sceptre of the dumb, the deaf, and the creepy!"
And the shouting persons battered his immortal body with stones
And threw his primitive comedy into the sea
From which it sang forth poems irrevocably blue.

Who are the great poets of our time, and what are their names?
Yeats of the baleful influence, Auden of the baleful influence, Eliot of
    the baleful influence
(Is Eliot a great poet? no one knows), Hardy, Stevens, Williams (is
    Hardy of our time?),
Hopkins (is Hopkins of our time?), Rilke (is Rilke of our time?), Lorca
    (is Lorca of our time?), who is still of our time?
Mallarmé, Valéry, Apollinaire, Eluard, Reverdy, French poets are still of
    our time,
Pasternak and Mayakovsky, is Jouve of our time?

Where are young poets in America, they are trembling in publishing
    houses and universities,
Above all they are trembling in universities, they are bathing the library
    steps with their spit,
They are gargling out innocuous (to whom?) poems about maple trees
    and their children,

Sometimes they brave a subject like the Villa d'Este or a lighthouse in
  Rhode Island,
Oh what worms they are! they wish to perfect their form.
Yet could not these young men, put in another profession,
Succeed admirably, say at sailing a ship? I do not doubt it, Sir, and I
  wish we could try them.
(A plane flies over the ship holding a bomb but perhaps it will not drop
  the bomb,
The young poets from the universities are staring anxiously at the skies,
Oh they are remembering their days on the campus when they looked up
  to watch birds excrete,
They are remembering the days they spent making their elegant poems.)

Is there no voice to cry out from the wind and say what it is like to be
  the wind,
To be roughed up by the trees and to bring music from the scattered
  houses
And the stones, and to be in such intimate relationship with the sea
That you cannot understand it? Is there no one who feels like a pair of
  pants?

3

Summer in the trees! "It is time to strangle several bad poets."
The yellow hobbyhorse rocks to and fro, and from the chimney
Drops the Strangler! The white and pink roses are slightly agitated by
  the struggle,
But afterwards beside the dead "poet" they cuddle up comfortingly
  against their vase. They are safer now, no one will compare them to
  the sea.

Here on the railroad train, one more time, is the Strangler.
He is going to get that one there, who is on his way to a poetry reading.
Agh! Biff! A body falls to the moving floor.

In the football stadium I also see him,
He leaps through the frosty air at the maker of comparisons
Between football and life and silently, silently strangles him!

Here is the Strangler dressed in a cowboy suit
Leaping from his horse to annihilate the students of myth!

The Strangler's ear is alert for the names of Orpheus,
Cuchulain, Gawain, and Odysseus,
And for poems addressed to Jane Austen, F. Scott Fitzgerald,
To Ezra Pound, and to personages no longer living
Even in anyone's thoughts—O Strangler the Strangler!

He lies on his back in the waves of the Pacific Ocean.

4

Supposing that one walks out into the air
On a fresh spring day and has the misfortune
To encounter an article on modern poetry
In *New World Writing*, or has the misfortune
To see some examples of some of the poetry
Written by the men with their eyes on the myth
And the Missus and the midterms, in the *Hudson Review*,
Or, if one is abroad, in *Botteghe Oscure*,
Or indeed in *Encounter*, what is one to do
With the rest of one's day that lies blasted to ruins
All bluely about one, what is one to do?
O surely one cannot complain to the President,
Nor even to the deans of Columbia College,
Nor to T. S. Eliot, nor to Ezra Pound,
And supposing one writes to the Princess Caetani,
"Your poets are awful!" what good would it do?
And supposing one goes to the *Hudson Review*
With a package of matches and sets fire to the building?
One ends up in prison with trial subscriptions
To the *Partisan, Sewanee,* and *Kenyon Review*!

5

Sun out! perhaps there is a reason for the lack of poetry
In these ill-contented souls, perhaps they need air!

KENNETH KOCH

Blue air, fresh air, come in, I welcome you, you are an art student,
Take off your cap and gown and sit down on the chair.
Together we shall paint the poets—but no, air! perhaps you should go to
    them, quickly,
Give them a little inspiration, they need it, perhaps they are out of
    breath,
Give them a little inhuman company before they freeze the English
    language to death!
(And rust their typewriters a little, be sea air! be noxious! kill them, if you
    must, but stop their poetry!
I remember I saw you dancing on the surf on the Côte d'Azur,
And I stopped, taking my hat off, but you did not remember me,
Then afterwards you came to my room bearing a handful of orange flowers
And we were together all through the summer night!)

That we might go away together, it is so beautiful on the sea, there are
    a few white clouds in the sky!

But no, air! you must go . . . Ah, stay!

But she has departed and . . . Ugh! what poisonous fumes and clouds!
    what a suffocating atmosphere!
Cough! whose are these hideous faces I see, what is this rigor
Infecting the mind? where are the green Azores,
Fond memories of childhood, and the pleasant orange trolleys,
A girl's face, red-white, and her breasts and calves, blue eyes, brown eyes,
    green eyes, fahrenheit
Temperatures, dandelions, and trains, O blue?!
Wind, wind, what is happening? Wind! I can't see any bird but the gull,
    and I feel it should symbolize . . .
Oh, pardon me, there's a swan, one two three swans, a great white swan,
    hahaha how pretty they are! Smack!
Oh! stop! help! yes, I see—disrespect of my superiors—forgive me, dear
    Zeus, nice Zeus, parabolic bird, O feathered excellence! white!
There is Achilles too, and there's Ulysses, I've always wanted to see them,
    hahaha!

And there is Helen of Troy, I suppose she is Zeus too, she's so terribly
pretty—hello, Zeus, my you are beautiful, Bang!

One more mistake and I get thrown out of the Modern Poetry Associa-
tion, help! Why aren't there any adjectives around?

Oh there are, there's practically nothing else—look, here's *grey, utter,
agonized, total, phenomenal, gracile, invidious, sundered,* and *fused,*

Elegant, absolute, pyramidal, and . . . Scream! but what can I describe
with these words? States!

States symbolized and divided by two, complex states, magic states, states
of consciousness governed by an aroused sincerity, cockadoodle doo!

Another bird! is it morning? Help! where am I? am I in the barnyard?
oink oink, scratch, moo! Splash!

My first lesson. "Look around you. What do you think and feel?"
Uhhh . . . "Quickly!" *This Connecticut landscape would have pleased
Vermeer.* Wham! A-Plus. "Congratulations!" I am promoted.

OOOhhhhh I wish I were dead, what a headache! My second lesson:
"Rewrite your first lesson line six hundred times. Try to make it into
a magnetic field." I can do it too. But my poor line! What a night-
mare! Here comes a tremendous horse,

Trojan, I presume. No, it's my third lesson. "Look, look! Watch him, see
what he's doing? That's what we want you to do. Of course it won't
be the same as his at first, but . . ." I demur. Is there no other way to
fertilize minds?

Bang! I give in . . . Already I see my name in two or three anthologies, a
serving girl comes into the barn bringing me the anthologies,

She is very pretty and I smile at her a little sadly, perhaps it is my last
smile! Perhaps she will hit me! But no, she smiles in return, and she
takes my hand.

My hand, my hand! what is this strange thing I feel in my hand, on my
arm, on my chest, my face—can it be . . . ? it is! AIR!

Air, air, you've come back! Did you have any success? "What do you
think?" I don't know, air. You are so strong, air.

And she breaks my chains of straw, and we walk down the road, behind
us the hideous fumes!

Soon we reach the seaside, she is a young art student who places her head
on my shoulder,

I kiss her warm red lips, and here is the Strangler, reading the *Kenyon
Review!* Good luck to you, Strangler!

Goodbye, Helen! goodbye, fumes! goodbye, abstracted dried-up boys!
goodbye, dead trees! goodbye, skunks!
Goodbye, manure! goodbye, critical manicure! goodbye, you big fat men
standing on the east coast as well as the west giving poems the test!
farewell, Valéry's stern dictum!
Until tomorrow, then, scum floating on the surface of poetry! goodbye for
a moment, refuse that happens to land in poetry's boundaries! adieu,
stale eggs teaching imbeciles poetry to bolster up your egos! adios,
boring anomalies of these same stale eggs!
Ah, but the scum is deep! Come, let me help you! and soon we pass into
the clear blue water. Oh GOODBYE, castrati of poetry! farewell, stale
pale skunky pentameters (the only honest English meter, gloop
gloop!) until tomorrow, horrors! oh, farewell!

Hello, sea! good morning, sea! hello, clarity and excitement, you great
expanse of green—

O green, beneath which all of them shall drown!

VARIATIONS ON A THEME BY
WILLIAM CARLOS WILLIAMS

1

I chopped down the house that you had been saving to live in next
summer.
I am sorry, but it was morning, and I had nothing to do
and its wooden beams were so inviting.

2

We laughed at the hollyhocks together
and then I sprayed them with lye.
Forgive me. I simply do not know what I am doing.

3

I gave away the money that you had been saving to live on for the next
　　ten years.
The man who asked for it was shabby
and the firm March wind on the porch was so juicy and cold.

4

Last evening we went dancing and I broke your leg.
Forgive me. I was clumsy, and
I wanted you here in the wards, where I am the doctor!

PERMANENTLY

One day the Nouns were clustered in the street.
An Adjective walked by, with her dark beauty.
The Nouns were struck, moved, changed.
The next day a Verb drove up, and created the Sentence.

Each Sentence says one thing—for example, "Although it was a dark
　　rainy day when the Adjective walked by, I shall remember the pure
　　and sweet expression on her face until the day I perish from the
　　green, effective earth."
Or, "Will you please close the window, Andrew?"
Or, for example, "Thank you, the pink pot of flowers on the window sill
　　has changed color recently to a light yellow, due to the heat from the
　　boiler factory which exists nearby."

In the springtime the Sentences and the Nouns lay silently on the grass.
A lonely Conjunction here and there would call, "And! But!"
But the Adjective did not emerge.

KENNETH KOCH

As the adjective is lost in the sentence,
So I am lost in your eyes, ears, nose, and throat—
You have enchanted me with a single kiss
Which can never be undone
Until the destruction of language.

TO YOU

I love you as a sheriff searches for a walnut
That will solve a murder case unsolved for years
Because the murderer left it in the snow beside a window
Through which he saw her head, connecting with
Her shoulders by a neck, and laid a red
Roof in her heart. For this we live a thousand years;
For this we love, and we live because we love, we are not
Inside a bottle, thank goodness! I love you as a
Kid searches for a goat; I am crazier than shirttails
In the wind, when you're near, a wind that blows from
The big blue sea, so shiny so deep and so unlike us;
I think I am bicycling across an Africa of green and white fields
Always, to be near you, even in my heart
When I'm awake, which swims, and also I believe that you
Are trustworthy as the sidewalk which leads me to
The place where I again think of you, a new
Harmony of thoughts! I love you as the sunlight leads the prow
Of a ship which sails
From Hartford to Miami, and I love you
Best at dawn, when even before I am awake the sun
Receives me in the questions which you always pose.

KENNETH KOCH

POEM

The thing
To do
Is organize
The sea
So boats will
Automatically float
To their destinations.
Ah, the Greeks
Thought of that!
Well, what if
They
Did? We have no
Gods
Of the winds!
And therefore
Must use
Science!

ALIVE FOR AN INSTANT

I have a bird in my head and a pig in my stomach
And a flower in my genitals and a tiger in my genitals
And a lion in my genitals and I am after you but I have a song in my
    heart
And my song is a dove
I have a man in my hands I have a woman in my shoes
I have a landmark decision in my reason
I have a death rattle in my nose I have summer in my brain water
I have dreams in my toes
This is the matter with me and the hammer of my mother and father
Who created me with everything
But I lack calm I lack rose
Though I do not lack extreme delicacy of rose petal
Who is it that I wish to astonish?
In the birdcall I found a reminder of you
But it was thin and brittle and gone in an instant
Has nature set out to be a great entertainer?
Obviously not A great reproducer? A great Nothing?

Well I will leave that up to you
I have a knocking woodpecker in my heart and I think I have three souls
One for love one for poetry and one for acting out my insane self
Not insane but boring but perpendicular but untrue but true
The three rarely sing together take my hand it's active
The active ingredient in it is a touch
I am Lord Byron I am Percy Shelley I am Ariosto
I eat the bacon I went down the slide I have a thunderstorm in my inside
    I will never hate you
But how can this maelstrom be appealing? do you like menageries? my
    god
Most people want a man! So here I am
I have a pheasant in my reminders I have a goshawk in my clouds
Whatever is it which has led all these animals to you?
A resurrection? or maybe an insurrection? an inspiration?
I have a baby in my landscape and I have a wild rat in my secrets from
    you.

© Thomas Victor

Maxine Kumin

MORNING SWIM

Into my empty head there come
a cotton beach, a dock wherefrom

I set out, oily and nude
through mist, in chilly solitude.

There was no line, no roof or floor
to tell the water from the air.

Night fog thick as terry cloth
closed me in its fuzzy growth.

I hung my bathrobe on two pegs.
I took the lake between my legs.

Invaded and invader, I
went overhand on that flat sky.

Fish twitched beneath me, quick and tame.
In their green zone they sang my name

and in the rhythm of the swim
I hummed a two-four-time slow hymn.

I hummed *Abide with Me*. The beat
rose in the fine thrash of my feet,

rose in the bubbles I put out
slantwise, trailing through my mouth.

My bones drank water; water fell
through all my doors. I was the well

that fed the lake that met my sea
in which I sang *Abide with Me*.

MAXINE KUMIN

STONES

The moving of stones, that sly jockeying thrust
takes place at night underground, shoulders first.

They bud in their bunkers like hydras. They puff
up head after head and allow them to drop off

on their own making quahogs, cow flops, eggs and knee
caps. In this way one stone can infuse a colony.

Eyeless and unsurprised they behave
in the manner of stones: swallow turnips, heave graves

rise up openmouthed into walls and from time
to time imitate oysters or mushrooms.

The doors of my house are held open by stones
and to see the tame herd of them hump their backbones

as cumbrous as bears across the pasture in
an allday rain is to believe for an afternoon

of objects that waver and blur
in some dark obedient order.

WOODCHUCKS

Gassing the woodchucks didn't turn out right.
The knockout bomb from the Feed and Grain Exchange
was featured as merciful, quick at the bone
and the case we had against them was airtight,
both exits shoehorned shut with puddingstone,
but they had a sub-sub-basement out of range.

Next morning they turned up again, no worse
for the cyanide than we for our cigarettes
and state-store Scotch, all of us up to scratch.
They brought down the marigolds as a matter of course
and then took over the vegetable patch
nipping the broccoli shoots, beheading the carrots.

MAXINE KUMIN

The food from our mouths, I said, righteously thrilling
to the feel of the .22, the bullets' neat noses.
I, a lapsed pacifist fallen from grace
puffed with Darwinian pieties for killing,
now drew a bead on the littlest woodchuck's face.
He died down in the everbearing roses.

Ten minutes later I dropped the mother. She
flipflopped in the air and fell, her needle teeth
still hooked in a leaf of early Swiss chard.
Another baby next. O one-two-three
the murderer inside me rose up hard,
the hawkeye killer came on stage forthwith.

There's one chuck left. Old wily fellow, he keeps
me cocked and ready day after day after day.
All night I hunt his humped-up form. I dream
I sight along the barrel in my sleep.
If only they'd all consented to die unseen
gassed underground the quiet Nazi way.

THINKING OF DEATH AND DOGFOOD

Amanda, you'll be going
to Alpo or to Gaines
when you run out of luck;
the flesh flensed from your bones
your mammoth rib cage rowing
away to the renderer's
a dry canoe on a truck

while I foresee my corpse
slid feet first into fire
light as the baker's loaf
to make of me at least
a pint of potash spoor.
I'm something to sweeten the crops
when the clock hand stops.

MAXINE KUMIN

Amanda, us in the woods
miles from home, the ground
upending in yellow flutes
that open but make no sound.
Ferns in the mouth of the brute,
chanterelles in the woman's sack . . .
what do I want for myself
dead center, bareback
on the intricate harp of your spine?
All that I name as mine

with the sure slow oxen of words:
feed sacks as grainy as boards
that air in the sun. A boy
who is wearing my mother's eyes.
Garlic to crush in the pan.
The family gathering in.
Already in the marsh
the yearling maples bleed
a rich onrush. Time slips
another abacus bead.

Let it not stick in the throat
or rattle a pane in the mind.
May I leave no notes behind
wishful, banal or occult
and you, small thinker in
the immensity of your frame
may you be caught and crammed
midmouthful of the best grain
when the slaughterer's bullet slams
sidelong into your brain.

THE ABSENT ONES

The two foals sleep back to back
in the sun like one butterfly.
Their mothers, the mares, have weaned them,
have bitten them loose like button thread.

The beavers have forced their kit
out of the stick house; he waddles
like a hairy beetle across the bottom land
in search of other arrangements.

My mother has begun to grow down,
tucking her head like a turtle.
She is pasting everyone's name
on the undersides of her silver tea service.

Our daughters and sons have burst
from the marionette show
leaving a tangle of strings
and gone into the unlit audience.

Alone I water the puffball patch.
I exhort the mushrooms to put up.
Alone I visit the hayfield.
I fork up last summer's horse-apples
to let the seeds back in the furrow.

Someone comes toward me—a shadow.
Two parts of a butterfly flicker
in false sun and knit together.
A thigh brushes my thigh.
The stones are talking in code.

I will braid up the absent ones like onions.
The missing I will wrap like green tomatoes.
I will split seventy logs for winter,
seven times seven times seven.

This is the life I came with.

SEEING THE BONES

This year again the bruised-colored oak
hangs on eating my heart out
with its slow change, the leaves at last

spiraling end over end like your
letters home that fall Fridays
in the box at the foot of the hill
saying the old news, keeping it neutral.
You ask about the dog, fourteen years
your hero, deaf now as a turnip,
thin as kindling.

In junior high your biology class
boiled a chicken down into its bones
four days at a simmer in my pot,
then wired joint by joint
the re-created hen
in an anatomy project
you stayed home from, sick.

Thus am I afflicted, seeing the bones.
How many seasons walking
on fallen apples like pebbles in
the shoes of the Canterbury faithful
have I kept the garden up
with leaven of wood ash, kitchen leavings
and the sure reciprocation of horse dung?

How many seasons have the foals
come right or breeched or in good time
turned yearlings, two-year-olds, and at three
clattered off in a ferment to the sales?

Your ponies, those dapple-gray kings
of the orchard, long gone to skeleton,
gallop across the landscape of my dreams.
I meet my father there, dead years before
you left us for a European career.
He is looping the loop on a roller coaster
called Mercy, he is calling his children in.

MAXINE KUMIN

I do the same things day by day.
They steady me against the wrong turn,
the closed-ward babel of anomie.
This Friday your letter in thinnest blue
script alarms me. Weekly you grow
more British with your *I shalls*
and now you're off to Africa
or Everest, daughter of the file drawer,
citizen of no return. I give
your britches, long outgrown, to the crows,
your boots with a summer visit's worth
of mud caked on them to the shrews
for nests if they will have them.

Working backward I reconstruct
you. Send me your baby teeth, some new
nail parings and a hank of hair
and let me do the rest. I'll
set the pot to boil.

HOW IT IS

Shall I say how it is in your clothes?
A month after your death I wear your blue jacket.
The dog at the center of my life recognizes
you've come to visit, he's ecstatic.
In the left pocket, a hole.
In the right, a parking ticket
delivered up last August on Bay State Road.
In my heart, a scatter like milkweed,
a flinging from the pods of the soul.
My skin presses your old outline.
It is hot and dry inside.

or culling the alfalfa-green ones, expelled
in a state of ooze, through the sawdust bed
to take a serviceable form, as putty does,
so as to lift out entire from the stall.

And wheeling to it, storming up the slope,
I think of the angle of repose the manure
pile assumes, how sparrows come to pick
the redelivered grain, how inky-cap

coprinus mushrooms spring up in a downpour.
I think of what drops from us and must then
be moved to make way for the next and next.
However much we stain the world, spatter

it with our leavings, make stenches, defile
the great formal oceans with what leaks down,
trundling off today's last barrowful,
I honor shit for saying: We go on.

THE GRACE OF GELDINGS IN RIPE PASTURES

Glutted, half asleep, browsing in
timothy grown so tall I see them
as through a pale-green stage scrim

they circle, nose to rump,
a trio of trained elephants.
It begins to rain, as promised.

Bit by bit they soak up drops
like laundry dampened to be ironed.
Runnels bedeck them. Their sides

MAXINE KUMIN

drip like the ribs of very broad
umbrellas. And still they graze
and grazing, one by one let down

their immense, indolent penises
to drench the everlasting grass
with the rich nitrogen

that repeats them.

© *Thomas Victor*

Stanley Kunitz

SINGLE VISION

Before I am completely shriven
I shall reject my inch of heaven.

Cancel my eyes, and, standing, sink
Into my deepest self; there drink

Memory down. The banner of
My blood, unfurled, will not be love,

Only the pity and the pride
Of it, pinned to my open side.

When I have utterly refined
The composition of my mind,

Shaped language of my marrow till
Its forms are instant to my will,

Suffered the leaf of my heart to fall
Under the wind, and, stripping all

The tender blanket from my bone,
Rise like a skeleton in the sun,

I shall have risen to disown
The good mortality I won.

Directly risen with the stain
Of life upon my crested brain,

Which I shall shake against my ghost
To frighten him, when I am lost.

Gladly, as any poison, yield
My halved conscience, brightly peeled;

Infect him, since we live but once,
With the unused evil in my bones.

I'll shed the tear of souls, the true
Sweat, Blake's intellectual dew,

Before I am resigned to slip
A dusty finger on my lip.

FATHER AND SON

Now in the suburbs and the falling light
I followed him, and now down sandy road
Whiter than bone-dust, through the sweet
Curdle of fields, where the plums
Dropped with their load of ripeness, one by one.
Mile after mile I followed, with skimming feet,
After the secret master of my blood,
Him, steeped in the odor of ponds, whose indomitable love
Kept me in chains. Strode years; stretched into bird;
Raced through the sleeping country where I was young,
The silence unrolling before me as I came,
The night nailed like an orange to my brow.

How should I tell him my fable and the fears,
How bridge the chasm in a casual tone,
Saying, "The house, the stucco one you built,
We lost. Sister married and went from home,
And nothing comes back, it's strange, from where she goes.
I lived on a hill that had too many rooms:
Light we could make, but not enough of warmth,
And when the light failed, I climbed under the hill.
The papers are delivered every day;
I am alone and never shed a tear."

At the water's edge, where the smothering ferns lifted
Their arms, "Father!" I cried, "Return! You know
The way. I'll wipe the mudstains from your clothes;

No trace, I promise, will remain. Instruct
Your son, whirling between two wars,
In the Gemara of your gentleness,
For I would be a child to those who mourn
And brother to the foundlings of the field
And friend of innocence and all bright eyes.
O teach me how to work and keep me kind."

Among the turtles and the lilies he turned to me
The white ignorant hollow of his face.

END OF SUMMER

An agitation of the air,
A perturbation of the light
Admonished me the unloved year
Would turn on its hinge that night.

I stood in the disenchanted field
Amid the stubble and the stones,
Amazed, while a small worm lisped to me
The song of my marrow-bones.

Blue poured into summer blue,
A hawk broke from his cloudless tower,
The roof of the silo blazed, and I knew
That part of my life was over.

Already the iron door of the north
Clangs open: birds, leaves, snows
Order their populations forth,
And a cruel wind blows.

THE WAR AGAINST THE TREES

The man who sold his lawn to standard oil
Joked with his neighbors come to watch the show
While the bulldozers, drunk with gasoline,

Tested the virtue of the soil
Under the branchy sky
By overthrowing first the privet-row.

Forsythia-forays and hydrangea-raids
Were but preliminaries to a war
Against the great-grandfathers of the town,
So freshly lopped and maimed.
They struck and struck again,
And with each elm a century went down.

All day the hireling engines charged the trees,
Subverting them by hacking underground
In grub-dominions, where dark summer's mole
Rampages through his halls,
Till a northern seizure shook
Those crowns, forcing the giants to their knees.

I saw the ghosts of children at their games
Racing beyond their childhood in the shade,
And while the green world turned its death-foxed page
And a red wagon wheeled,
I watched them disappear
Into the suburbs of their grievous age.

Ripped from the craters much too big for hearts
The club-roots bared their amputated coils,
Raw gorgons matted blind, whose pocks and scars
Cried Moon! on a corner lot
One witness-moment, caught
In the rear-view mirrors of the passing cars.

REFLECTION BY A MAILBOX

When I stand in the center of that man's madness,
Deep in his trauma, as in the crater of a wound,
My ancestors step from my American bones.
There's mother in a woven shawl, and that,
No doubt, is father picking up his pack
For the return voyage through those dreadful years
Into the winter of the raging eye.

STANLEY KUNITZ

One generation past, two days by plane away,
My house is dispossessed, my friends dispersed,
My teeth and pride knocked in, my people game
For the hunters of man-skins in the warrens of Europe,
The impossible creatures of an hysteriac's dream
Advancing with hatchets sunk into their skulls
To rip the god out of the machine.

Are these the citizens of the new estate
To which the continental shelves aspire;
Or the powerful get of a dying age, corrupt
And passion-smeared, with fluid on their lips,
As if a soul had been given to petroleum?

How shall we uncreate that lawless energy?

Now I wait under the hemlock by the road
For the red-haired postman with the smiling hand
To bring me my passport to the war.
Familiarly his car shifts into gear
Around the curve; he coasts up to my drive; the day
Strikes noon; I think of Pavlov and his dogs
And the motto carved on the broad lintel of his brain:
"Sequence, consequence, and again consequence."

INDIAN SUMMER AT LAND'S END

The season stalls, unseasonably fair,
blue-fair, serene, a stack of golden discs,
each disc a day, and the addition slow.
I wish you were here with me to walk the flats,
towards dusk especially when the tide is out
and the bay turns opal, filled with rolling fire
that washes on the mouldering wreck offshore,
our mussel-vineyard, strung with bearded grapes.
Last night I reached for you and shaped you there
lying beside me as we drifted past
the farthest seamarks and the watchdog bells,
and round Long Point throbbing its frosty light,
until we streamed into the open sea.
What did I know of voyaging till now?

STANLEY KUNITZ

Meanwhile I tend my flock, strange golden puffs
diminutive as wrens, with snipped-off tails,
who bounce down from the trees. High overhead,
on the trackless roads, skywriting V and yet
another V, the southbound Canada express
hoots of horizons and distances . . . .

THE ARTIST

His paintings grew darker every year.
They filled the walls, they filled the room;
eventually they filled his world—
all but the ravishment.
When voices faded, he would rush to hear
the scratched soul of Mozart
endlessly in gyre.
Back and forth, back and forth,
he paced the paint-smeared floor,
diminishing in size each time he turned,
trapped in his monumental void,
raving against his adversaries.
At last he took a knife in his hand
and slashed an exit for himself
between the frames of his tall scenery.
Through the holes of his tattered universe
the first innocence and the light
came pouring in.

THE PORTRAIT

My mother never forgave my father
for killing himself,
especially at such an awkward time
and in a public park,
that spring
when I was waiting to be born.

She locked his name
in her deepest cabinet
and would not let him out,
though I could hear him thumping.
When I came down from the attic
with the pastel portrait in my hand
of a long-lipped stranger
with a brave moustache
and deep brown level eyes,
she ripped it into shreds
without a single word
and slapped me hard.
In my sixty-fourth year
I can feel my cheek
still burning.

THE UNQUIET ONES

Years ago I lost
both my parents' addresses.
Father and mother lie
in their neglected cribs,
obscure as moles,
unvisited.
I do not need to summon them.
When I put out the light
I hear them stir, dissatisfied,
in their separate places,
in death as in life
remote from each other,
having no conversation
except in the common ground
of their son's mind.
They slip through narrow crevices
and, suddenly blown tall,
glide into my cave of phantoms,
unwelcome guests, but not
unloved, dark emissaries
of the two-faced god.

STANLEY KUNITZ

THE QUARREL

The word I spoke in anger
weighs less than a parsley seed,
but a road runs through it
that leads to my grave,
that bought-and-paid-for lot
on a salt-sprayed hill in Truro
where the scrub pines
overlook the bay.
Half-way I'm dead enough,
strayed from my own nature
and my fierce hold on life.
If I could cry, I'd cry,
but I'm too old to be
anybody's child.
Liebchen,
with whom should I quarrel
except in the hiss of love,
that harsh, irregular flame?

THE KNOT

I've tried to seal it in,
that cross-grained knot
on the opposite wall,
scored in the lintel of my door,
but it keeps bleeding through
into the world we share.
Mornings when I wake,
curled in my web,
I hear it come
with a rush of resin
out of the trauma
of its lopping-off.
Obstinate bud,
sticky with life,
mad for the rain again,
it racks itself with shoots

that crackle overhead,
dividing as they grow.
Let be! Let be!
I shake my wings
and fly into its boughs.

© *Arthur Furst*

Denise Levertov

THE JACOB'S LADDER

The stairway is not
a thing of gleaming strands
a radiant evanescence
for angels' feet that only glance in their tread, and need not
touch the stone.

It is of stone.
A rosy stone that takes
a glowing tone of softness
only because behind it the sky is a doubtful, a doubting
night gray.

A stairway of sharp
angles, solidly built.
One sees that the angels must spring
down from one step to the next, giving a little
lift of the wings:

and a man climbing
must scrape his knees, and bring
the grip of his hands into play. The cut stone
consoles his groping feet. Wings brush past him.
The poem ascends.

HYPOCRITE WOMEN

Hypocrite women, how seldom we speak
of our own doubts, while dubiously
we mother man in his doubt!

And if at Mill Valley perched in the trees
the sweet rain drifting through western air
a white sweating bull of a poet told us

our cunts are ugly—why didn't we
admit we have thought so too? (And
what shame? They are not for the eye!)

No, they are dark and wrinkled and hairy,
caves of the Moon . . .   And when a
dark humming fills us, a

coldness towards life,
we are too much women to
own to such unwomanliness.

Whorishly with the psychopomp
we play and plead—and say
nothing of this later.   And our dreams,

with what frivolity we have pared them
like toenails, clipped them like ends of
split hair.

A PSALM PRAISING THE HAIR OF MAN'S BODY

My great brother
         Lord of the Song
wears the ruff of
         forest bear.

Husband, thy fleece of silk is black,
         a black adornment;
lies so close to the turns of the flesh,
burns my palm-stroke.

My great brother
         Lord of the Song
wears the ruff of
         forest bear.

Strong legs of our son are dusted
         dark with hair.
Told of long roads,
we know his stride.

My great brother
      Lord of the Song
wears the ruff of
      forest bear.

Hair of man, man-hair, hair of
breast and groin, marking contour as
     silverpoint marks in cross-
     hatching, as river-
     grass on the woven current
     indicates ripple,
praise.

THE WINGS

Something hangs in back of me,
I can't see it, can't move it.

I know it's black,
a hump on my back.

It's heavy. You
can't see it.

What's in it? Don't tell me
you don't know. It's

what you told me about—
black

inimical power, cold
whirling out of it and

around me and
sweeping you flat.

But what if,
like a camel, it's

pure energy I store,
and carry humped and heavy?

Not black, not
that terror, stupidity

of cold rage; or black
only for being pent there?

What if released in air
it became a white

source of light, a fountain
of light? Could all that weight

be the power of flight?
Look inward: see me

with embryo wings, one
feathered in soot, the other

blazing ciliations of ember, pale
flare-pinions. Well—

could I go
on one wing,

the white one?

STEPPING WESTWARD

What is green in me
darkens, muscadine.

If woman is inconstant,
good, I am faithful to

ebb and flow, I fall
in season and now

is a time of ripening.
If her part

DENISE LEVERTOV

is to be true,
a north star,

good, I hold steady
in the black sky

and vanish by day,
yet burn there

in blue or above
quilts of cloud.

There is no savor
more sweet, more salt

than to be glad to be
what, woman,

and who, myself,
I am, a shadow

that grows longer as the sun
moves, drawn out

on a thread of wonder.
If I bear burdens

they begin to be remembered
as gifts, goods, a basket

of bread that hurts
my shoulders but closes me

in fragrance. I can
eat as I go.

DENISE LEVERTOV

THE ALTARS IN THE STREET

On June 17th, 1966, The New York Times reported that, as part of the Buddhist campaign of non-violent resistance, Viet-Namese children were building altars in the streets of Saigon and Hue, effectively jamming traffic.

Children begin at green dawn nimbly to build
topheavy altars, overweighted with prayers,
thronged each instant more densely

with almost-visible ancestors.
Where tanks have cracked the roadway
the frail altars shake; here a boy

with red stumps for hands steadies a corner,
here one adjusts with his crutch the holy base.
The vast silence of Buddha overtakes

and overrules the oncoming roar
of tragic life that fills alleys and avenues;
it blocks the way of pedicabs, police, convoys.

The hale and maimed together
hurry to construct for the Buddha
a dwelling at each intersection. Each altar

made from whatever stones, sticks, dreams, are at hand,
is a facet of one altar; by noon
the whole city in all its corruption,

all its shed blood the monsoon cannot wash away,
has become a temple,
fragile, insolent, absolute.

REVOLUTIONARY

When he said
'Your struggle is my struggle'
a curtain was pushed away.

DENISE LEVERTOV

A curtain was pushed away revealing
an open window
and beyond that

an open country.
For the first time I knew it was actual.
I was indoors still

but the air from fields
beyond me touched my face.

It was a country
of hilly fields, of many
shadows and rivers.

The thick heavy dark
curtain had hidden
a world from me;

curtain of sorrow, world
where far-off I see
people moving—

struggling to move, as I
towards my window
struggle, burdened but not

each alone. They move
out in that air together
where I too

will be moving,
not alone.

from ENTR'ACTE

"Let Us Sing Unto the Lord a New Song"

There's a pulse in Richard
that day and night says
revolution   revolution   revolution

and another
not always heard:

poetry   poetry

rippling through his sleep,
a river pulse.

Heart's fire
breaks the chest almost,
flame-pulse,
revolution:

and if its beat
falter
life itself
shall cease.

Heart's river,
living water,
poetry:

and if that pulse
grow faint
fever shall parch the soul, breath
choke upon ashes.

But when their rhythms
mesh
then though the pain of living
never lets up

the singing begins.

INTRUSION

After I had cut off my hands
and grown new ones

something my former hands had longed for
came and asked to be rocked.

After my plucked out eyes
had withered, and new ones grown

something my former eyes had wept for
came asking to be pitied.

August, 1969

THE POEM UNWRITTEN

For weeks the poem of your body,
of my hands upon your body
        stroking, sweeping, in the rite of
        worship, going
        their way of wonder down
        from neck-pulse to breast-hair to level
        belly to cock—
for weeks that poem, that prayer,
unwritten.
            The poem unwritten, the act
left in the mind, undone. The years
a forest of giant stones, of fossil stumps,
blocking the altar.

1970

MAN ALONE

When the sun goes down, it writes
a secret name in its own blood for remembrance,
the excess of light
an ardor slow to cool:
and man has time to seek shelter.

But when the moon
gains the horizon, though it tarries
a moment, it vanishes
without trace of silver

and he is left with the stars only,
fierce and remote, and not revealing
the stones of the dark roads.

So it is with the gods,
and with the halfgods,
and with the heroes.

WAYS OF CONQUEST

You invaded my country by accident,
not knowing you had crossed the border.
Vines that grew there touched you.
                              You ran past them,
shaking raindrops off the leaves—you or the wind.
It was toward the hills you ran,
inland—

I invaded your country with all my
'passionate intensity,'
pontoons and parachutes of my blindness.
But living now in the suburbs of the capital
incognito,
            my will to take the heart of the city
            has dwindled. I love
its unsuspecting life,
its adolescents who come to tell me their dreams in the dusty park
among the rocks and benches,
I the stranger who will listen.
I love
the wild herons who return each year to the marshy outskirts.
What I invaded has
invaded me.

DENISE LEVERTOV

WEDDING-RING

My wedding-ring lies in a basket
as if at the bottom of a well.
Nothing will come to fish it back up
and onto my finger again.
                         It lies
among keys to abandoned houses,
nails waiting to be needed and hammered
into some wall,
telephone numbers with no names attached,
idle paperclips.
                         It can't be given away
for fear of bringing ill-luck.
                         It can't be sold
for the marriage was good in its own
time, though that time is gone.
                         Could some artificer
beat into it bright stones, transform it
into a dazzling circlet no one could take
for solemn betrothal or to make promises
living will not let them keep? Change it
into a simple gift I could give in friendship?

© Thomas Victor

Philip Levine

ANIMALS ARE PASSING FROM OUR LIVES

It's wonderful how I jog
on four honed-down ivory toes
my massive buttocks slipping
like oiled parts with each light step.

I'm to market. I can smell
the sour, grooved block, I can smell
the blade that opens the hole
and the pudgy white fingers

that shake out the intestines
like a hankie. In my dreams
the snouts drool on the marble,
suffering children, suffering flies,

suffering the consumers
who won't meet their steady eyes
for fear they could see. The boy
who drives me along believes

that any moment I'll fall
on my side and drum my toes
like a typewriter or squeal
and shit like a new housewife

discovering television,
or that I'll turn like a beast
cleverly to hook his teeth
with my teeth. No. Not this pig.

TO A CHILD TRAPPED IN A BARBER SHOP

You've gotten in through the transom
    and you can't get out
till Monday morning or, worse,
    till the cops come.

That six-year-old red face
    calling for mama
is yours; it won't help you
    because your case

is closed forever, hopeless.
    So don't drink
the Lucky Tiger, don't
    fill up on grease

because that makes it a lot worse,
    that makes it a crime
against property and the state
    and that costs time.

We've all been here before,
    we took our turn
under the electric storm
    of the vibrator

and stiffened our wills to meet
    the close clippers
and heard the true blade mowing
    back and forth

on a strip of dead skin,
    and we stopped crying.
You think your life is over?
    It's just begun.

PHILIP LEVINE

COMING HOME

Detroit, 1968

A winter Tuesday, the city pouring fire,
Ford Rouge sulfurs the sun, Cadillac, Lincoln,
Chevy gray. The fat stacks
of breweries hold their tongues. Rags,
papers, hands, the stems of birches
dirtied with words.
                              Near the freeway
you stop and wonder what came off,
recall the snowstorm where you lost it all,
the wolverine, the northern bear, the wolf
caught out, ice and steel raining
from the foundries in a shower
of human breath. On sleds in the false sun
the new material rests. One brown child
stares and stares into your frozen eyes
until the lights change and you go
forward to work. The charred faces, the eyes
boarded up, the rubble of innards, the cry
of wet smoke hanging in your throat,
the twisted river stopped at the color of iron.
We burn this city every day.

ANGEL BUTCHER

At sun up I am up
hosing down the outdoor abattoir
getting ready. The water
steams and hisses on the white stones
and the air pales to a
thin blue.
                      Today it is
Christophe. I don't see him
come up the long climb or
know he's here until I hear
my breathing double
and he's beside me smiling
like a young girl.

PHILIP LEVINE

                                    He asks
me the names of all
the tools and all
their functions, he lifts
and weighs and
balances, and runs a long
forefinger down the tongue
of each blade.
                    He asks
me how I came to this place and
this work, and I tell him how
I began with animals, and
he tells me how
he began with animals. We
talk about growing up and losing
the strange things we never
understood and settling.
                              I help
him with his robes; he
has a kind of modesty and sits
on the stone table with
the ends of the gown crossed
in his lap.
                    He wants to die
like a rabbit, and he wants me
to help him. I hold
his wrist; it's small, like
the throat of a young hen, but
cool and dry. He holds
mine and I can feel the
blood thudding in the ring
his fingers make.
                        He helps me, he
guides my hand at first. I can
feel my shoulders settle and
the bones take the weight, I can
feel my lungs flower as the
swing begins. He smiles again
with only one side of his mouth
and looks down to the
dark valley where the cities
burn. When I hit
him he comes apart like a

perfect puzzle or an
old flower.
                    And my legs
dance and twitch for hours.

THEY FEED THEY LION

Out of burlap sacks, out of bearing butter,
Out of black bean and wet slate bread,
Out of the acids of rage, the candor of tar,
Out of creosote, gasoline, drive shafts, wooden dollies,
They Lion grow.
                    Out of the gray hills
Of industrial barns, out of rain, out of bus ride,
West Virginia to Kiss My Ass, out of buried aunties,
Mothers hardening like pounded stumps, out of stumps,
Out of the bones' need to sharpen and the muscles' to stretch,
They Lion grow.
                    Earth is eating trees, fence posts,
Gutted cars, earth is calling in her little ones,
"Come home, Come home!" From pig balls,
From the ferocity of pig driven to holiness,
From the furred ear and the full jowl come
The repose of the hung belly, from the purpose
They Lion grow.
                    From the sweet glues of the trotters
Come the sweet kinks of the fist, from the full flower
Of the hams the thorax of caves,
From "Bow Down" come "Rise Up,"
Come they Lion from the reeds of shovels,
The grained arm that pulls the hands,
They Lion grow.
                    From my five arms and all my hands,
From all my white sins forgiven, they feed,
From my car passing under the stars,
They Lion, from my children inherit,
From the oak turned to a wall, they Lion,
From they sack and they belly opened
And all that was hidden burning on the oil-stained earth
They feed they Lion and he comes.

PHILIP LEVINE

ZAYDEE

Why does the sea burn? Why do the hills cry?
My grandfather opens a fresh box
of English Ovals, lights up, and lets the smoke
drift like clouds from his lips.

Where did my father go in my fifth autumn?
In the blind night of Detroit
on the front porch, Grandfather points up
at a constellation shaped like a cock and balls.

A tiny man, at 13 I outgrew his shirts.
I then beheld a closet of stolen suits,
a hive of elevator shoes, crisp hankies,
new bills in the cupboard, old in the wash.

I held the spotted hands that passed over
the breasts of airlines stewardesses,
that moved in the fields like a wind
stirring the long hairs of grain.

Where is the ocean? the flying fish?
the God who speaks from a cloud?
He carries a card table out under the moon
and plays gin rummy and cheats.

He took me up in his arms
when I couldn't walk and carried me
into the grove where the bees sang
and the stream paused forever.

He laughs in the movies, cries in the streets,
the judges in their gowns are monkeys,
the lawyers mice, a cop is a fat hand.
He holds up a strawberry and bites it.

He sings a song of freestone peaches
all in a box,
in the street he sings out Idaho potatoes
California, California oranges.

PHILIP LEVINE

He sings the months in prison,
sings salt pouring down the sunlight,
shovelling all night in the stove factory
he sings the oven breathing fire.

Where did he go when his autumn came?
He sat before the steering wheel
of the black Packard, he turned the key,
pressed the starter, and he went.

The maples blazed golden and red
a moment and then were still,
the long streets were still and the snow
swirled where I lay down to rest.

STARLIGHT

My father stands in the warm evening
on the porch of my first house.
I am four years old and growing tired.
I see his head among the stars,
the glow of his cigarette, redder
than the summer moon riding
low over the old neighborhood. We
are alone, and he asks me if I am happy.
"Are you happy?" I cannot answer.
I do not really understand the word,
and the voice, my father's voice, is not
his voice, but somehow thick and choked,
a voice I have not heard before, but
heard often since. He bends and passes
a thumb beneath each of my eyes.
The cigarette is gone, but I can smell
the tiredness that hangs on his breath.
He has found nothing, and he smiles
and holds my head with both his hands.
Then he lifts me to his shoulder,
and now I too am there among the stars,
as tall as he. Are you happy? I say.

He nods in answer, Yes! oh yes! oh yes!
And in that new voice he says nothing,
holding my head tight against his head,
his eyes closed up against the starlight,
as though those tiny blinking eyes
of light might find a tall, gaunt child
holding his child against the promises
of autumn, until the boy slept
never to waken in that world again.

ASHES

Far off, from the burned fields
of cotton, smoke rises and scatters
on the last winds of afternoon.
The workers have come in hours ago,
and nothing stirs. The old bus creaked
by full of faces wide-eyed with hunger.
I sat wondering how long the earth
would let the same children die day
after day, let the same women curse
their precious hours, the same men bow
to earn our scraps. I only asked.
And now the answer batters the sky:
with fire there is smoke, and after, ashes.
You can howl your name into the wind
and it will blow it into dust, you
can pledge your single life, the earth
will eat it all, the way you eat
an apple, meat, skin, core, seeds.
Soon the darkness will fall on all
the tired bodies of those who have
torn our living from the silent earth,
and they can sleep and dream of sleep
without end, but before first light
bloodies the sky opening in the east
they will have risen one by one
and dressed in clothes still hot
and damp. Before I waken they are
already bruised by the first hours
of the new sun. The same men

PHILIP LEVINE

who were never boys, the same women
their faces gone gray with anger,
and the children who will say nothing.
Do you want the earth to be heaven?
Then pray, go down on your knees
as though a king stood before you,
and pray to become all you'll
never be, a drop of sea water,
a small hurtling flame across the sky,
a fine flake of dust that moves
at evening like smoke at great height
above the earth and sees it all.

YOU CAN HAVE IT

My brother comes home from work
and climbs the stairs to our room.
I can hear the bed groan and his shoes drop
one by one. You can have it, he says.

The moonlight streams in the window
and his unshaven face is whitened
like the face of the moon. He will sleep
long after noon and waken to find me gone.

Thirty years will pass before I remember
that moment when suddenly I knew each man
has one brother who dies when he sleeps
and sleeps when he rises to face this life,

and that together they are only one man
sharing a heart that always labors, hands
yellowed and cracked, a mouth that gasps
for breath and asks, Am I gonna make it?

All night at the ice plant he had fed
the chute its silvery blocks, and then I
stacked cases of orange soda for the children
of Kentucky, one gray box-car at a time

with always two more waiting. We were twenty
for such a short time and always in
the wrong clothes, crusted with dirt
and sweat. I think now we were never twenty.

In 1948 in the city of Detroit, founded
by de la Mothe Cadillac for the distant purposes
of Henry Ford, no one wakened or died,
no one walked the streets or stoked a furnace,

for there was no such year, and now
that year has fallen off all the old newspapers,
calendars, doctors' appointments, bonds,
wedding certificates, drivers licenses.

The city slept. The snow turned to ice.
The ice to standing pools or rivers
racing in the gutters. Then bright grass rose
between the thousands of cracked squares,

and that grass died. I give you back 1948.
I give you all the years from then
to the coming one. Give me back the moon
with its frail light falling across a face.

Give me back my young brother, hard
and furious, with wide shoulders and a curse
for God and burning eyes that look upon
all creation and say, You can have it.

LET ME BEGIN AGAIN

Let me begin again as a speck
of dust caught in the night winds
sweeping out to sea. Let me begin
this time knowing the world is
salt water and dark clouds, the world
is grinding and sighing all night, and dawn
comes slowly and changes nothing. Let
me go back to land after a lifetime
of going nowhere. This time lodged

PHILIP LEVINE

in the feathers of some scavenging gull
white above the black ship that docks
and broods upon the oily waters of
your harbor. This leaking freighter
has brought a hold full of hayforks
from Spain, great jeroboams of dark
Algerian wine and quill pens that can't
write English. The sailors have stumbled
off toward the bars or the bright houses.
The captain closes his log and falls asleep.
1/10'28. Tonight I shall enter my life
after being at sea for ages, quietly,
in a hospital named for an automobile.
The one child of millions of children
who has flown alone by the stars
above the black wastes of moonless waters
that stretched forever, who has turned
golden in the full sun of a new day.
A tiny wise child who this time will love
his life because it is like no other.

John Logan

THREE MOVES

Three moves in six months and I remain
the same.
Two homes made two friends.
The third leaves me with myself again.
(We hardly speak.)
Here I am with tame ducks
and my neighbors' boats,
only this electric heat
against the April damp.
I have a friend named Frank—
The only one who ever dares to call
and ask me, "How's your soul?"
I hadn't thought about it for a while,
and was ashamed to say I didn't know.
I have no priest for now.
Who
will forgive me then. Will you?
Tame birds and my neighbors' boats.
The ducks honk about the floats . . .
They walk dead drunk onto the land and grounds,
iridescent blue and black and green and brown.
They live on swill
our aged houseboats spill.
But still they are beautiful.
Look! The duck with its unlikely beak
has stopped to pick
and pull
at the potted daffodil.
Then again they sway home
to dream
bright gardens of fish in the early night.
Oh these ducks are all right.
They will survive.
But I am sorry I do not often see them climb.
Poor sons-a-bitching ducks.

JOHN LOGAN

You're all fucked up.
What do you do that for?
Why don't you hover near the sun anymore?
Afraid you'll melt?
These foolish ducks lack a sense of guilt,
and so all their multi-thousand-mile range
is too short for the hope of change.

Seattle, April 1965

TO A YOUNG POET WHO FLED

Your cries make us afraid, but we love your delicious music!

Kierkegaard

So you said you'd go home to work on your father's farm.
We've talked of how it is the poet alone can touch
with words, but I would touch you with my hand, my lost son,
to say good-bye again. You left some work, and have gone.
You don't know what you mean. Oh, not to me as a son,
for I have others. Perhaps too many. I cannot
answer all the letters. If I seem to brag, I add
I know how to shatter an image of the father
(twice have tried to end the yearning of an orphan son,
but opened up in him, and in me, another wound).
No—I say this: you don't know the reason of your gift.
It's not the suffering. Others have that. The gift of tears
is the hope of saints, Monica again and Austin.
I mean the gift of the structure of a poet's jaw,
which makes the mask that's cut out of the flesh of his face
a megaphone—as with the goat clad Greeks—to ampli-
fy the light gestures of his soul toward the high stone seats.
The magic of the mouth that can melt to tears the rock
of hearts. I mean the wand of tongues that charms the exile
of listeners into a bond of brothers, breaking
down the lines of lead that separate a man from a
man, and the husbands from their wives, in these old, burned glass
panels of our lives. The poet's jaw has its tongue ripped
as Philomel, its lips split (and kissed beside the grave),

the jawbone patched and cracked with fists and then with the salve
of his fellows. If they make him bellow, like a slave
cooked inside the ancient, brass bull, still that small machine
inside its throat makes music for an emperor's guest
out of his cries. Thus his curse: the poet cannot weep
but with a public and musical grief, and he laughs
with the joys of others. Yet, when the lean blessings come,
they are sweet, and great. My son, I could not make your choice.
Let me take your hand. I am too old or young to say,
"I'd rather be a swineherd in the hut, understood
by swine, than be a poet misunderstood by men."

SPRING OF THE THIEF

But if I look the ice is gone from the lake
and the altered air
no longer fills with the small
terrible bodies of the snow.
Only once these late winter weeks
the dying flakes
fell instead as manna or as wedding rice
blooming in the light
about the bronze Christ
and the thieves. There these three
still hang, more than man-
sized and heavier than life
on a hill over the lake
where I walk
this Third Sunday of Lent.
I come from Mass
melancholy at its ancient story
of the unclean ghost
a man thought he'd lost.
It came back into his well-swept house
and at the final state that man
was worse than he began.
Yet again today
there is the faintest edge of green
to trees about St. Joseph's Lake.

JOHN LOGAN

Ah God if our confessions show contempt
because we let them free us of our guilt
to sin again
forgive us still . . . before the leaves . . .
before the leaves have formed
you can glimpse the Christ and Thieves
on top of the hill. One of them was saved.
That day the snow had seemed to drop like grace
upon the four of us,
or like the peace of intercourse,
suddenly I wanted to confess—
or simply talk.
I paid a visit to the mammoth Sacred Heart
Church, and found it shut.
Who locked him out or in?
The name of God is changing in our time.
What is his winter name?
Where was his winter home.
Oh I've kept my love to myself before.
Even those ducks weave down the shore
together, drunk with hope
for the April water. One spring festival
near here I stripped and strolled
through a rain filled field.
Spread eagled on the soaking earth
I let the rain
move its audible little hands
gently on my skin . . . let the dark rain
raise up my love.
But why? I was alone
and no one saw how ardent I grew.
And when I rolled naked in the snow one night
as St. Francis with his Brother Ass
or a hard bodied Finn
I was alone. Underneath
the howling January moon
I knelt and dug my fist
full of the cold winter sand
and rubbed and
hid my manhood under it.
Washed up at some ancient or half-heroic shore
I was ashamed that I was naked there.
Before Nausicaä and the saints. Before myself.
But who took off my coat? Who put it on?

JOHN LOGAN

Who drove me home?
Blessed be sin if it teaches men shame.
Yet because of it we cannot talk
and I am separated from myself.
So what is all this reveling in snow and rain?
Or in the summer sun when the heavy gold
body weeps with joy or grief or love?
When we speak of God, is it God we speak of?
Perhaps his winter home
is in that field where I rolled or ran . . .
this hill where once the snow
fell serene as rain.
Oh I have walked around the lake
when I was not alone—
sometimes with my wife have seen these swans
dip down their necks
graceful as a girl, showering white and wet!
I've seen their heads delicately turn.
Have gone sailing with my quiet, older son.
And once on a morning walk
a student who had just come back
in fall found a perfect hickory shell
among the bronze and red
leaves and purple flowers of the time
and put its white bread into my hand.
Ekelöf said there is a freshness
nothing can destroy in us—
not even we ourselves.
Perhaps that
Freshness is the changed name of God.
Where all the monsters also hide
I bear him in the ocean of my blood
and in the pulp of my enormous head.
He lives beneath the unkempt potter's grass
of my belly and chest.
I feel his terrible, aged heart
moving under mine . . . can see the shadows
of the gorgeous light
that plays at the edges of his giant eye . . .
or tell the faint press and hum
of his eternal pool of sperm.
Like sandalwood! *Like sandalwood*
the righteous man
perfumes the axe that falls on him.

The cords of elm, of cedar oak and pine
will pile again in fall.
The ribs and pockets of the barns will swell.
Winds and fires in the field rage
and again burn out each
of the ancient roots.
Again at last the late November snow
will fill those fields, change this hill,
throw these figures in relief
and raining on them
will transform
the bronze Christ's brow and cheek,
the white face and thigh of the thief.

March–April, 1962

WHITE PASS SKI PATROL

His high-boned, young face is so brown
from the winter's sun,
the few brief lines in each green eye's
edge as of a leaf
that is not yet gone from the limb—
as of a nut which is gold or brown.

For he has become very strong
living on the slopes.
His belly and thighs are newly
lean from the thin skis.
Tough torso of the man, blue wooled.
Thin waist. White, tasseled cap of the child.

Beneath the fury of those great,
dark panes of glass, that
seem to take a man out of grace,
his gentle eyes wait.
(We feel their melancholy gaze
which is neither innocent nor wise.)

Like those knights of the winter snows—
with a healing pack
(sign of the cross on breast and back)—
serene, snow-lonely,
he patrols the beautiful peaks
and the pale wastes that slide like a beast.

Sometimes still blind from his patrol,
you'll see him pull down
from the dangerous Cascades his
heavy sledge of pain,
its odd, black-booted, canvas-laced
shape alive or dead, without a face.

Colors blooming in the sun, he
caroms down his own
path, speeds (bending knees), dances side
to side, balancing.
Under-skis glow golden in the
snow spume around his Christiana.

And as he lifts away from us,
skis dangle like the
outstretched limbs of a frog in spring.
He swings gently in
the air, vulnerable, so much
the "poor, bare, forked" human animal.

And now he slowly rises up
over trees and snow.
He begins to grow more thin, and then
vanishes in air!
as, high in the lithe boughs of pines,
the silver leaves flake silently down.

There are the shadow tracks he left
down the long, white hill
beside the lift. Wait! Look up! Cloud
trails in the bright sky!
Breathing a wake of snow ribbons,
something has just flown over the mountain!

Washington, February 19, 1966

SUZANNE

You make us want to stay alive, Suzanne,
the way you turn

your blonde head.
The way you curve your slim hand

toward your breast.
When you drew your legs

up, sitting by the fire,
and let your bronze hair

stream about your knees
I could see the grief

of the girl in your eyes.
It touched the high,

formal bones of your face.
Once I heard it in your lovely voice

when you sang—
the terrible time of being young.

Yet you bring us joy with your
self, Suzanne, wherever you are.

And once, although I wasn't here,
you left three roses on my stair.

One party night when you were high
you fled barefoot down the hall,

the fountain of your laughter
showering through the air.

"Chartreuse," you chanted
(the liqueur you always wanted),

JOHN LOGAN

"I have yellow chartreuse hair!"
Oh it was a great affair.

You were the most exciting person there.
Yesterday when I wasn't here

again,
you brought a blue, porcelain

egg to me—
colored beautifully

for the Russian Easter.
Since then, I have wanted to be your lover,

but I have only touched your shoulder
and let my fingers brush your hair,

because you left three roses on my stair.

LOVE POEM

Last night you would not come,
and you have been gone so long.
I yearn to find you in my aging, earthen arms
again (your alchemy can change my clay to skin).
I long to turn and watch again
from my half-hidden place
the lost, beautiful slopes and fallings of your face,
the black, rich leaf of each eyelash,
fresh, beach-brightened stones of your teeth.
I want to listen as you breathe yourself to sleep
(for by our human art we mime
the sleeper till we dream).
I want to smell the dark
herb gardens of your hair—touch the thin shock
that drifts over your high brow when
you rinse it clean,
for it is so fine.
I want to hear the light,
long wind of your sigh.

JOHN LOGAN

But again tonight I know you will not come.
I will never feel again
your gentle, sleeping calm
from which I took
so much strength, so much of my human heart.
Because the last time
I reached to you
as you sat upon the bed
and talked, you caught both my hands
in yours and crossed them gently on my breast.
I died mimicking the dead.

DAWN AND A WOMAN

The morning
        island light begins
to grow
    and now
the cocks cry
      at giving birth
to the colors
     of our day.
Their feathers make the dawn
blue and red and green
and they will strongly brighten up their combs,
as in the cold lodges
our women drop
naked to their haunches
         pok-
ing at the tepid fires.
Why, they will go out bare
to bring in another log
before coming back to bed!
The flames they build
as they squat
      and hug their chilling breasts
form halos in their pubic hair
           for
they are hunched in the ancient shape
of hope.

JOHN LOGAN

       The fire place
with
    its fine wisps
          of smoke
suddenly fills with peace
opening like
       the great, God-wide
             canyons of Kauai
that drop clean from the clouds into the sea,
their distant threads of waterfall
like darts of light playing on the wall
and on the
      body.
The woman will give us what she can.
We men will take what we are able.
(Painted blue
      the Sibyl
inside ourselves is also writhing there—
some kind of dance about the same, uncertain fire—
I do not know what for).
These early women, wives, lovers,
leave their dawning chores
and coming back needing to be held
            will hold

us too.
    They already see
we do not know our fathers
and cannot learn to love our brothers.
But they will do what they can
        once again
to warm our gut
     and heart
and also that secret, incomparable cold
that grows upward from the groin
when we learn
     we can lose a son.

JOHN LOGAN

POEM FOR MY BROTHER

Blue's my older brother's color. Mine is brown, you see.
So today I bought this ring
of gold and lapis lazuli flecked with a bright bronze.
His blue is the light hue of his eyes. Brown's the color
of our dead mother's long hair,
which fell so beautifully about her young shoulders
in the picture, and of my own eyes (I can't tell hers).
I loved my brother, but never quite knew what to think.
For example, he would beat
me up as soon as the folks
left the house, and I would cry big, loud feminine tears.
He was good at sports and played football, and so instead
I was in the marching band.
My brother stole rubbers from the store and smoked cigars
and pipes, which made me sick. But
once we swam together in
the Nishnabotna river
near home, naked, our blue overalls piled together
by the water, their copper
buttons like the bronze glints in my ring. I remember
once when I was very young
I looked deep into a pool
of blue water—we had no mirror—and I was so
amazed I looked over my shoulder, for I did not
imagine it was me, caught
in that cerulean sky.
Thinking it was someone other, I tell you I con-
fused myself with my brother!
Nothing goes with gold, but I can see in this rich blue
stone the meeting of our clothes like the touching of hands
when he taught me to hold my fishing pole well and wound
up the reel for me. You know
blue's the last of the primary colors to be named.
Why, some primitive societies still have no word
for it except "dark." It's associated with black:
in the night brother and I
would play at games that neither of us could understand.
But this is not a confession; it is a question.
We've moved apart and don't write,
and our children don't even know their own cousin!
So, I would have you know I

JOHN LOGAN

want this ring to *engage* us
in reconciliation.
Blue's the color of the heart.
I won't live forever. Is it too late now to be
a brother to my brother?
Let the golden snake bend round
again to touch itself and
all at once burst into azure!

from **POEM IN PROGRESS**

First Reunion in New Orleans: The Father as King of Revels

In New Orleans we part with cars.
We walk the blocks to Mardi Gras
and put on another mask to
catch the bright, luminescent beads
and gold doubloons flung from floats cruis-
ing the full streets in endless, fabulous parades
toward the Gulf. The tractors lugging floats for the Krewe
of great Zeus wish their way toward the engines of ships
because these floats move quite like "ships
passing in the night." Clown shapes piss behind parades,
for thousands are drinking beer in the streets from great, white
paper cups, or they arc red and light wine out of goat
skins into their mouths. Parades are plays before our own
audience. We watch the progress of King Proteus
who changes configurations in the dark like us.
There are floats for Thoth, Aphrodite and for Diane.
I think, well, Michael, here we go again—costumed with
painted faces like our thousand anonymous friends,
levels of beads about our necks,
wrists and the belt loops of our pants.
Why, we have so many beads we heave them back again
in an amiable exchange.
We shove and shout. We touch and dance
in the live New Orleans streets,
and the men and women both old and young *notice* us,
as we them. We are each other's dream within a dream.
After the parades and the great Cathedral of Saint
Louis, King of France, oldest in the land, on the same
site where its small predecessor

was blown apart two hundred and fifty years ago
by the greater King Tornado—
after the Cabildo where our ancient fathers signed
in lieu of us for the Louisiana Purchase,
we go for New Orleans jazz and hear Sweet Emma
singing and still playing a mean piano at age
eighty-nine, a garter of bells on one leg, red cap,
just as she had when jazz was born
in Preservation Hall (well named!)
just off Bourbon Street with its black
lace of delicate worked-iron balconies and the
old Absinthe House where King Faulkner
met and sipped double shots of Jack Daniels with his friend,
elder King Sherwood Anderson.
On Fat Tuesday night as the revels moved to their height
we leave and drive in the truck of a guy we had met
through the strange, moon-lighted Louisiana landscape
I had never seen by day, toward his sculptor's kiln
twelve miles out. Trees drop their gentle
debris of moss on us: we stop
only once to pick and give each other the newly
blooming, reaching azalea flowers which seem to glow
under the moon all in the same
color, although we know each fresh
pale cluster, like a feather plucked from a peacock's tail,
is radiantly different.
This seems an oracle of what we find just ahead:
a huge, monolithic concrete kiln glowing quiet
as the moon itself, all filled up
with white-hot lustrous ghosts of earth
our friend had made. We are not amazed to find they've reached
their peak of heat alone in the middle of a blue
field as Mardi Gras hits frenzy,
and consumed, burned up, everything falls away from us
under the white moon like revelers' masks and costumes
leaving us stark naked there as for making love or art.

JOHN LOGAN

THE BRIDGE OF CHANGE

(for Roger Aplon)

The bridge barely curved that connects the terrible with the tender.

Rilke

I

The children play at the Luxembourg fountain.
Their small ships catch wind and sail out and come round again.

II

Sometime between 250 and 200 B.C.
fishermen and boatmen of the tribe Parisii
discovered, and built their huts on, the largest island
in the River Seine. Celtic *Lutetia*, "Town surround-
ed by water,"
                thus was born there.
The island is shaped like a boat—
and this figure became a part
of the capital's coat-of-arms. So this was the start
of The City first named for its engulfing water
(on whose economy it depended), then after
the people themselves: members of the tribe of Paris.
We listen to these water folk and know they hear us,
for we are all born out of boats and out of water.
The first sound we hear is the heart
knocking quiet as a boat docks:
And we all dissolve to island, earth and tears later.

III

And into air and fire! Once in the Latin Quarter
in a space formed for him by waves of bright loiterers
near that shortest street named for the Cat Who Catches Fish—
or who (with slight inflection) "sins"—
I watched a dark young man, naked to his thin waist, push
long plumes of flame into the air
above our awed faces raised there.

From the sharp heat inside and out,
his head and chest glowed in the night
with an aura of oil or sweat.
Thirsting, he drank again from a sponge of kerosene
and breathed out long strings of fire and smoke into the Street
of The Harp.
Dark ash dropped back upon his face and cap,
which lay open on the cobbled road waiting for coins
from all who guessed at the mystery in what he'd done.
He built a vast pillar of fire as if to guide us,
then suddenly stopped, walked across
the space, and kissed a reaching child
(to bless and heal that amazed head),
waved gratefully to us who now filled his cap with alms,
and smiling and burned (I saw scars beneath his raised arm)
he sail-
ed up that narrowing street in a wildly bal-
looning white shirt we had watched him casually don
to cover his vestment of skin.

IV

For centuries that old City
ended its west boundary
in a small archipelago
separated from the main island by the Seine's two
arms. It was on one of these small islets that Phillip
the Fair about the year 1314 had raised up
a stake for the grand master, Order of Templars, whom
he condemned, then from the palace window watched him burn.
These little islands, quickened with their ghost victim's screams,
were joined in the sixteenth century by the decree
of Henry Third (and by a great engineering feat
Faust could envy) to the main island of The City.
This new western tip was given the name of a park,
"Vert Galant," nickname of Henry Fourth: "the Gay Old Spark."
Near there I watched in a loud street
a white haired man stand with one foot
on the curb, the other in the cobbled street, and play
an old mandolin. He was dressed in a black and frayed
tuxedo and played with intense passion, sadly, but
this desperate, dignified man transformed by his art
and by poverty (his case kept open for money)

JOHN LOGAN

could not play the mandolin—He
just strummed the same chord again
                                        and again and again . . .

V

It was also Phillip the Fair
who created an aristocratic prison air
by building the blocks-long Gothic Conciergerie.
The best view is from the Right Bank: The Slaughter House Quay
(which now is a market for pets).
You can see the four recently cleaned towers reflect-
ed in the Seine. (At the Seine in fall beneath the red
and gold leaves you see the rust, mahogany and beige
boats gently jostle together at the shore and wait.)
On the right: the crenelated Bonbec Tower stays.
Bonbec means "babbler," for this place
was used through the centuries as a torture chamber.
The right one of the twin towers, Argent, held treasure.
Still the gorgeous Horloge Tower on the left corner
of the ancient building across from The Bridge of Change
houses the giant clock which gave its name to that quay:
in its field of blue the many great gold fleurs de lys
and the two life-sized mythical
women, one with a fascicle
of wheat, one with a balanced scale raised high in the clock,
whose silver chime used to toll the hours for the monarch.
(This was melted down in those days when Terror struck.)
In this turreted place we have shaved the graceful neck
and head of Marie Antoinette, ripped her white, ruffled
collar wide and wrapped the cuff of
rope about her hands behind her back. We made her face
the casual knitting women and men making fists
sitting on steps in the "May Court"
(where a fresh tree was placed each spring by the lawyers' clerks!)
on her way to the guillotine. Its blade was heavy
as primeval stone: she, the chemist Lavoisier,
Charlotte Corday, poet and brother Andre Chenier,
Madame du Barry—all 2600 who died,
having said their last farewells in the Women's Courtyard,
twelve per day underneath the blade!
and some were disembowelled beside.
Was there sometimes an image of beauty in their minds

at the last? Perhaps on white sands
beside the blue black sea a matched pair of roan horses
galloping together in the bright spume, riderless.
Or a nude young man and woman lying together
touching in a field of flowers?

VI

Nearby on this Island the gargoyles of Notre Dame
gawk in ancient horror and some
forever gnaw on stone rabbits in the parapets
or wail in winged, formal misery outside the set
limits of the orthodox Church—
all glory happening within the walls where they squat:
so hunched, so beaked, so horrorstruck.

VII

A wing of the May Courtyard where the condemned waited
"Monsieur de Paris" as executioners were named
now adjoins the building of glass and light, with no walls,
it seems, jewel of Sainte Chapelle,
its windows of rose and blue, gold, green, yellow, purple,
rising fifty feet:
                   its spire piercing the foliate,
layered, manycolored egg of the vault of heaven,
showering all the primal hues and shadows given—
bright as the truth reflected in a drop of fresh blood
or the colors of the body's inner organs hid-
den before the sure explosion of light that hits them
at the moment of violent death—This is a time
like that of the sun that once a year just at the dawn
of winter solstice lights up an ancient Celtic stone
grave striking the bones spread on shelves
with all the colors of the flesh.

VIII

Who can stand these juxtapositions of person and place and time? I walk across the Bridge of Change where I have so often watched by the towers of the Conciergerie. Now, water laves a little higher up the stair from the River to the Quay, hiding some of the steps from me. Boats nudge at the edge. I walk along the Boulevard past the great gold and blue corner clock, the ornate wrought-iron gate and fence of the Palace of Justice (its name changed from the time of kings), past the shadow and spire of Sainte Chapelle. I cross the Bridge of Saint Michel into the Latin Quarter. But I do not look for the Street of the Cat Who Fishes or the Street of the Harp. I turn right, wandering a bit, and suddenly as if by chance find myself at *this* street, and here I will wait, for it is our street, Rue Gît le Coeur: Here Lies the Heart.

© *Thomas Victor*

Robert Lowell

COLLOQUY IN BLACK ROCK

Here the jack-hammer jabs into the ocean;
My heart, you race and stagger and demand
More blood-gangs for your nigger-brass percussions,
Till I, the stunned machine of your devotion,
Clanging upon this cymbal of a hand,
Am rattled screw and footloose. All discussions

End in the mud-flat detritus of death.
My heart, beat faster, faster. In Black Mud
Hungarian workmen give their blood
For the martyre Stephen, who was stoned to death.

Black Mud, a name to conjure with: O mud
For watermelons gutted to the crust,
Mud for the mole-tide harbor, mud for mouse,
Mud for the armored Diesel fishing tubs that thud
A year and a day to wind and tide; the dust
Is on this skipping heart that shakes my house,

House of our Savior who was hanged till death.
My heart, beat faster, faster. In Black Mud
Stephen the martyre was broken down to blood:
Our ransom is the rubble of his death.

Christ walks on the black water. In Black Mud
Darts the kingfisher. On Corpus Christi, heart,
Over the drum-beat of St. Stephen's choir
I hear him, *Stupor Mundi*, and the mud
Flies from his hunching wings and beak—my heart,
The blue kingfisher dives on you in fire.

ROBERT LOWELL

CHRISTMAS EVE UNDER HOOKER'S STATUE

Tonight a blackout. Twenty years ago
I hung my stocking on the tree, and hell's
Serpent entwined the apple in the toe
To sting the child with knowledge. Hooker's heels
Kicking at nothing in the shifting snow,
A cannon and a cairn of cannon balls
Rusting before the blackened Statehouse, know
How the long horn of plenty broke like glass
In Hooker's gauntlets. Once I came from Mass;

Now storm-clouds shelter Christmas, once again
Mars meets his fruitless star with open arms,
His heavy saber flashes with the rime,
The war-god's bronzed and empty forehead forms
Anonymous machinery from raw men;
The cannon on the Common cannot stun
The blundering butcher as he rides on Time—
The barrel clinks with holly. I am cold:
I ask for bread, my father gives me mould;

His stocking is full of stones. Santa in red
Is crowned with wizened berries. Man of war,
Where is the summer's garden? In its bed
The ancient speckled serpent will appear,
And black-eyed susan with her frizzled head.
When Chancellorsville mowed down the volunteer,
"All wars are boyish," Herman Melville said;
But we are old, our fields are running wild:
Till Christ again turn wanderer and child.

MR. EDWARDS AND THE SPIDER

I saw the spiders marching through the air,
Swimming from tree to tree that mildewed day
In latter August when the hay
Came creaking to the barn. But where
The wind is westerly,

ROBERT LOWELL

Where gnarled November makes the spiders fly
Into the apparitions of the sky,
They purpose nothing but their ease and die
Urgently beating east to sunrise and the sea;

What are we in the hands of the great God?
It was in vain you set up thorn and briar
   In battle array against the fire
   And treason crackling in your blood;
      For the wild thorns grow tame
And will do nothing to oppose the flame;
Your lacerations tell the losing game
You play against a sickness past your cure.
How will the hands be strong? How will the heart endure?

A very little thing, a little worm,
Or hourglass-blazoned spider, it is said,
   Can kill a tiger. Will the dead
   Hold up his mirror and affirm
      To the four winds the smell
And flash of his authority? It's well
If God who holds you to the pit of hell,
Much as one holds a spider, will destroy,
Baffle and dissipate your soul. As a small boy

On Windsor Marsh, I saw the spider die
When thrown into the bowels of fierce fire:
   There's no long struggle, no desire
   To get up on its feet and fly—
      It stretches out its feet
And dies. This is the sinner's last retreat;
Yes, and no strength exerted on the heat
Then sinews the abolished will, when sick
And full of burning, it will whistle on a brick.

But who can plumb the sinking of that soul?
Josiah Hawley, picture yourself cast
   Into a brick-kiln where the blast
   Fans your quick vitals to a coal—
      If measured by a glass,
How long would it seem burning! Let there pass
A minute, ten, ten trillion; but the blaze
Is infinite, eternal: this is death,
To die and know it. This is the Black Widow, death.

MEMORIES OF WEST STREET AND LEPKE

Only teaching on Tuesdays, book-worming
in pajamas fresh from the washer each morning,
I hog a whole house on Boston's
"hardly passionate Marlborough Street,"
where even the man
scavenging filth in the back alley trash cans,
has two children, a beach wagon, a helpmate,
and is a "young Republican."
I have a nine months' daughter,
young enough to be my granddaughter.
Like the sun she rises in her flame-flamingo infants' wear.

These are the tranquillized *Fifties*,
and I am forty. Ought I to regret my seedtime?
I was a fire-breathing Catholic C.O.,
and made my manic statement,
telling off the state and president, and then
sat waiting sentence in the bull pen
beside a Negro boy with curlicues
of marijuana in his hair.

Given a year,
I walked on the roof of the West Street Jail, a short
enclosure like my school soccer court,
and saw the Hudson River once a day
through sooty clothesline entanglements
and bleaching khaki tenements.
Strolling, I yammered metaphysics with Abramowitz,
a jaundice-yellow ("it's really tan")
and fly-weight pacifist,
so vegetarian,
he wore rope shoes and preferred fallen fruit.
He tried to convert Bioff and Brown,
the Hollywood pimps, to his diet.
Hairy, muscular, suburban,
wearing chocolate double-breasted suits,
they blew their tops and beat him black and blue.

ROBERT LOWELL

I was so out of things, I'd never heard
of the Jehovah's Witnesses.
"Are you a C.O.?" I asked a fellow jailbird.
"No," he answered, "I'm a J.W."
He taught me the "hospital tuck,"
and pointed out the T-shirted back
of *Murder Incorporated's* Czar Lepke,
there piling towels on a rack,
or dawdling off to his little segregated cell full
of things forbidden the common man:
a portable radio, a dresser, two toy American
flags tied together with a ribbon of Easter palm.
Flabby, bald, lobotomized,
he drifted in a sheepish calm,
where no agonizing reappraisal
jarred his concentration on the electric chair—
hanging like an oasis in his air
of lost connections. . . .

MAN AND WIFE

Tamed by *Miltown*, we lie on Mother's bed;
the rising sun in war paint dyes us red;
in broad daylight her gilded bed-posts shine,
abandoned, almost Dionysian.
At last the trees are green on Marlborough Street,
blossoms on our magnolia ignite
the morning with their murderous five days' white.
All night I've held your hand,
as if you had
a fourth time faced the kingdom of the mad—
its hackneyed speech, its homicidal eye—
and dragged me home alive. . . . Oh my *Petite*,
clearest of all God's creatures, still all air and nerve:
you were in your twenties, and I,
once hand on glass

and heart in mouth,
outdrank the Rahvs in the heat
of Greenwich Village, fainting at your feet—
too boiled and shy
and poker-faced to make a pass,
while the shrill verve
of your invective scorched the traditional South.

Now twelve years later, you turn your back.
Sleepless, you hold
your pillow to your hollows like a child;
your old-fashioned tirade—
loving, rapid, merciless—
breaks like the Atlantic Ocean on my head.

"TO SPEAK OF WOE THAT IS IN MARRIAGE"

"It is the future generation that presses into being by means of these exuberant feelings and supersensible soap bubbles of ours."

Schopenhauer

"The hot night makes us keep our bedroom windows open.
Our magnolia blossoms. Life begins to happen.
My hopped up husband drops his home disputes,
and hits the streets to cruise for prostitutes,
free-lancing out along the razor's edge.
This screwball might kill his wife, then take the pledge.
Oh the monotonous meanness of his lust. . . .
It's the injustice . . . he is so unjust—
whiskey-blind, swaggering home at five.
My only thought is how to keep alive.
What makes him tick? Each night now I tie
ten dollars and his car key to my thigh. . . .
Gored by the climacteric of his want,
he stalls above me like an elephant."

ROBERT LOWELL

SKUNK HOUR

(for Elizabeth Bishop)

Nautilus Island's hermit
heiress still lives through winter in her Spartan cottage;
her sheep still graze above the sea.
Her son's a bishop. Her farmer
is first selectman in our village;
she's in her dotage.

Thirsting for
the hierarchic privacy
of Queen Victoria's century,
she buys up all
the eyesores facing her shore,
and lets them fall.

The season's ill—
we've lost our summer millionaire,
who seemed to leap from an L. L. Bean
catalogue. His nine-knot yawl
was auctioned off to lobstermen.
A red fox stain covers Blue Hill.

And now our fairy
decorator brightens his shop for fall;
his fishnet's filled with orange cork,
orange, his cobbler's bench and awl;
there is no money in his work,
he'd rather marry.

One dark night,
my Tudor Ford climbed the hill's skull;
I watched for love-cars. Lights turned down,
they lay together, hull to hull,
where the graveyard shelves on the town. . . .
My mind's not right.

ROBERT LOWELL

A car radio bleats,
"Love, O careless Love. . . ." I hear
my ill-spirit sob in each blood cell,
as if my hand were at its throat. . . .
I myself am hell;
nobody's here—

only skunks, that search
in the moonlight for a bite to eat.
They march on their soles up Main Street:
white stripes, moonstruck eyes' red fire
under the chalk-dry and spar spire
of the Trinitarian Church.

I stand on top
of our back steps and breathe the rich air—
a mother skunk with her column of kittens swills the garbage pail.
She jabs her wedge-head in a cup
of sour cream, drops her ostrich tail,
and will not scare.

EYE AND TOOTH

My whole eye was sunset red,
the old cut cornea throbbed,
I saw things darkly,
as through an unwashed goldfish globe.

I lay all day on my bed.
I chain-smoked through the night,
learning to flinch
at the flash of the matchlight.

Outside, the summer rain,
a simmer of rot and renewal,
fell in pinpricks.
Even new life is fuel.

ROBERT LOWELL

My eyes throb.
Nothing can dislodge
the house with my first tooth
noosed in a knot to the doorknob.

Nothing can dislodge
the triangular blotch
of rot on the red roof,
a cedar hedge, or the shade of a hedge.

No ease from the eye
of the sharp-skinned hawk in the birdbook there,
with reddish-brown buffalo hair
on its shanks, one ascetic talon

clasping the abstract imperial sky.
It says:
an eye for an eye,
a tooth for a tooth.

No ease for the boy at the keyhole,
his telescope,
when the women's white bodies flashed
in the bathroom. Young, my eyes began to fail.

Nothing! No oil
for the eye, nothing to pour
on those waters or flames.
I am tired. Everyone's tired of my turmoil.

HISTORY

History has to live with what was here,
clutching and close to fumbling all we had—
it is so dull and gruesome how we die,
unlike writing, life never finishes.
Abel was finished; death is not remote,

ROBERT LOWELL

a flash-in-the-pan electrifies the skeptic,
his cows crowding like skulls against high-voltage wire,
his baby crying all night like a new machine.
As in our Bibles, white-faced, predatory,
the beautiful, mist-drunken hunter's moon ascends—
a child could give it a face: two holes, two holes,
my eyes, my mouth, between them a skull's no-nose—
O there's a terrifying innocence in my face
drenched with the silver salvage of the mornfrost.

from LONG SUMMER

[Everyone now is crowding everyone]

Everyone now is crowding everyone
to put off leaving till the Indian Summer;
and why? Because the others will be gone—
we too, dull drops in the decamping mass,
one in a million buying solitude. . . .
We asked to linger on past fall in Eden;
there must be good in man. Life fears us. Death
keeps our respect by keeping at a distance—
death we've never outdistanced as the Apostle boasted . . .
stream of heady, terrified poured stone,
suburban highway, rural superhighway,
foot of skunkweed, masts of scrub . . . the rich poor. . . .
We are loved by being distant; love-longing
mists the windshield, soothes the eye with milk.

READING MYSELF

Like millions, I took just pride and more than just,
first striking matches that brought my blood to boiling;
I memorized tricks to set the river on fire,
somehow never wrote something to go back to.
Even suppose I had finished with wax flowers
and earned a pass to the minor slopes of Parnassus . . .

ROBERT LOWELL

No honeycomb is built without a bee
adding circle to circle, cell to cell,
the wax and honey of a mausoleum—
this round dome proves its maker is alive,
the corpse of such insect lives preserved in honey,
prays that the perishable work live long
enough for the sweet-tooth bear to desecrate—
this open book . . . my open coffin.

HOMECOMING

What was is . . . since 1930;
the boys in my old gang
are senior partners. They start up
bald like baby birds
to embrace retirement.

At the altar of surrender,
I met you
in the hour of credulity.
How your misfortune came out clearly
to us at twenty.

At the gingerbread casino,
how innocent the nights we made it
on our *Vesuvio* martinis
with no vermouth but vodka
to sweeten the dry gin—

the lash across my face
that night we adored . . .
soon every night and all,
when your sweet, amorous
repetition changed.

ROBERT LOWELL

Fertility is not to the forward,
or beauty to the precipitous—
things gone wrong
clothe summer
with gold leaf.

Sometimes
I catch my mind
circling for you with glazed eye—
my lost love hunting
your lost face.

Summer to summer,
the poplars sere
in the glare—
it's a town for the young,
they break themselves against the surf.

No dog knows my smell.

EPILOGUE

Those blessèd structures, plot and rhyme—
why are they no help to me now
I want to make
something imagined, not recalled?
I hear the noise of my own voice:
The painter's vision is not a lens,
it trembles to caress the light.
But sometimes everything I write
with the threadbare art of my eye
seems a snapshot,
lurid, rapid, garish, grouped,
heightened from life,
yet paralyzed by fact.
All's misalliance.
Yet why not say what happened?
Pray for the grace of accuracy

ROBERT LOWELL

Vermeer gave to the sun's illumination
stealing like the tide across a map
to his girl solid with yearning.
We are poor passing facts,
warned by that to give
each figure in the photograph
his living name.

© Thomas Victor

James Merrill

Above my desk, whirring and self-important
(Though not much larger than a hummingbird)
In finely woven robes, school of Van Eyck,
Hovers an evidently angelic visitor.
He points one index finger out the window
At winter snatching to its heart,
To crystal vacancy, the misty
Exhalations of houses and of people running home
From the cold sun pounding on the sea;
While with the other hand
He indicates the piano
Where the Sarabande No. 1 lies open
At a passage I shall never master
But which has already, and effortlessly mastered me.
He drops his jaw as if to say, or sing,
'Between the world God made
And this music of Satie,
Each glimpsed through veils, but whole,
Radiant and willed,
Demanding praise, demanding surrender,
How can you sit there with your notebook?
What do you think you are doing?'
However he says nothing—wisely: I could mention
Flaws in God's world, or Satie's; and for that matter
How did he come by *his* taste for Satie?
Half to tease him, I turn back to my page,
Its phrases thus far clotted, unconnected.
The tiny angel shakes his head.
There is no smile on his round, hairless face.
He does not want even these few lines written.

JAMES MERRILL

AFTER GREECE

Light into the olive entered
And was oil. Rain made the huge pale stones
Shine from within. The moon turned his hair white
Who next stepped from between the columns,
Shielding his eyes. All through
The countryside were old ideas
Found lying open to the elements.
Of the gods' houses only
A minor premise here and there
Would be balancing the heaven of fixed stars
Upon a Doric capital. The rest
Lay spilled, their fluted drums half sunk in cyclamen
Or deep in water's biting clarity
Which just barely upheld me
The next week, when I sailed for home.
But where is home—these walls?
These limbs? The very spaniel underfoot
Races in sleep, toward what?
It is autumn. I did not invite
Those guests, windy and brittle, who drink my liquor.
Returning from a walk I find
The bottles filled with spleen, my room itself
Smeared by reflection on to the far hemlocks.
I some days flee in dream
Back to the exposed porch of the maidens
Only to find my great-great-grandmothers
Erect there, peering
Into a globe of red Bohemian glass.
As it swells and sinks, I call up
Graces, Furies, Fates, removed
To my country's warm, lit halls, with rivets forced
Through draper, and nothing left to bear.
They seem anxious to know
What holds up heaven nowadays.
I start explaining how in that vast fire
Were other irons—well, Art, Public Spirit,
Ignorance, Economics, Love of Self,
Hatred of Self, a hundred more,
Each burning to be felt, each dedicated
To sparing us the worst; how I distrust them
As I should have done those ladies; how I want

JAMES MERRILL

Essentials: salt, wine, olive, the light, the scream—
No! I have scarcely named you,
And look, in a flash you stand full-grown before me,
Row upon row, Essentials,
Dressed like your sister caryatids
Or tombstone angels jealous of their dead,
With undulant coiffures, lips weathered, cracked by grime,
And faultless eyes gone blank beneath the immense
Zinc and gunmetal northern sky. . . .
Stay then. Perhaps the system
Calls for spirits. This first glass I down
To the last time
I ate and drank in that old world. May I
Also survive its meanings, and my own.

A DEDICATION

Hans, there are moments when the whole mind
Resolves into a pair of brimming eyes, or lips
Parting to drink from the deep spring of a death
That freshness they do not yet need to understand.
These are the moments, if ever, an angel steps
Into the mind, as kings into the dress
Of a poor goatherd, for their acts of charity.
There are moments when speech is but a mouth pressed
Lightly and humbly against the angel's hand.

THE OCTOPUS

There are many monsters that a glassen surface
Restrains. And none more sinister
Than vision asleep in the eye's tight translucence.
Rarely it seeks now to unloose
Its diamonds. Having divined how drab a prison
The purest mortal tissue is,
Rarely it wakes. Unless, coaxed out by lusters
Extraordinary, like the octopus
From the gloom of its tank half-swimming half-drifting

JAMES MERRILL

Toward anything fair, a handkerchief
Or child's face dreaming near the glass, the writher
Advances in a godlike wreath
Of its own wrath. Chilled by such fragile reeling
A hundred blows of a boot-heel
Shall not quell, the dreamer wakes and hungers.
Percussive pulses, drum or gong,
Build in his skull their loud entrancement,
Volutions of a Hindu dance.
His hands move clumsily in the first conventional
Gestures of assent.
He is willing to undergo the volition and fervor
Of many fleshlike arms, observe
These in their holiness of indirection
Destroy, adore, evolve, reject—
Till on glass rigid with his own seizure
At length the sucking jewels freeze.

LABORATORY POEM

Charles used to watch Naomi, taking heart
And a steel saw, open up turtles, live.
While she swore they felt nothing, he would gag
At blood, at the blind twitching, even after
The murky dawn of entrails cleared, revealing
Contours he knew, egg-yellows like lamps paling.

Well then. She carried off the beating heart
To the kymograph and rigged it there, a rag
In fitful wind, now made to strain, now stopped
By her solutions tonic or malign
Alternately in which it would be steeped.
What the heart bore, she noted on a chart,

For work did not stop only with the heart.
He thought of certain human hearts, their climb
Through violence into exquisite disciplines
Of which, as it now appeared, they all expired.
Soon she would fetch another and start over,
Easy in the presence of her lover.

JAMES MERRILL

CHARLES ON FIRE

Another evening we sprawled about discussing
Appearances. And it was the consensus
That while uncommon physical good looks
Continued to launch one, as before, in life
(Among its vaporous eddies and false calms),
Still, as one of us said into his beard,
"Without your intellectual and spiritual
Values, man, you are sunk." No one but squared
The shoulders of his own unloveliness.
Long-suffering Charles, having cooked and served the meal,
Now brought out little tumblers finely etched
He filled with amber liquor and then passed.
"Say," said the same young man, "in Paris, France,
They do it this way"—bounding to his feet
And touching a lit match to our host's full glass.
A blue flame, gentle, beautiful, came, went
Above the surface. In a hush that fell
We heard the vessel crack. The contents drained
As who should step down from a crystal coach.
Steward of spirits, Charles's glistening hand
All at once gloved itself in eeriness.
The moment passed. He made two quick sweeps and
Was flesh again. "It couldn't matter less,"
He said, but with a shocked, unconscious glance
Into the mirror. Finding nothing changed,
He filled a fresh glass and sank down among us.

NIKE

The lie shone in her face before she spoke it.
Moon-battered, cloud-torn peaks, mills, multitudes
Implied. A floating sphere
Her casuist had at most to suck his pen,
Write of *Unrivalled by truth's own*
For it to dawn upon me. Near the gate
A lone iris was panting, purple-tongued.
I thought of my village, of tonight's *Nabucco*
She would attend, according to the lie,

Bemedalled at the royal right elbow. High
Already on entr'acte kümmel, hearing as always
Through her ears the sad waltz of the slaves,
I held my breath in pity for the lie
Which nobody would believe unless I did.
Mines (unexploded from the last one) lent
Drama to its rainbow surface tension.
Noon struck. Far off, a cataract's white thread
Kept measuring the slow drop into the gorge.
I thought of his forge and crutch who hobbled
At her prayer earthward. What he touched bloomed.
Fire-golds, oil-blacks. The pond people
Seemed victims rather, bobbing belly-up,
Of constitutional vulnerability
Than dynamite colluding with a fast buck.
Everywhere soldiers were falling, reassembling,
As we unpacked our picnic, she and I.
No wiser than the ant. Prepared to die
For all we knew. And even at the end,
Faced with a transcript bound in sunset
Of muffled depositions underground,
She offered wine and cookies first. She asked,
Before the eyes were bandaged, the bubble burst
And what she uttered with what I held back
Ran in red spittle down the chin,
Asked why I could not have lived the lie.
Flicking a crumb off, diffident, asked why
I thought my loved ones had been left to dream
Whole nights unbridled in the bed's brass jail
Beneath a ceiling washed by her reflected snows.

from UP AND DOWN

The Emerald

Hearing that on Sunday I would leave,
My mother asked if we might drive downtown.
Why certainly—off with my dressing gown!
The weather had turned fair. *We* were alive.

JAMES MERRILL

Only the gentle General she married
Late, for both an old way out of harm's,
Fought for breath, surrendered in her arms,
With military honors now lay buried.

That week the arcana of his medicine chest
Had been disposed of, and his clothes. Gold belt
Buckle and the letter from President Roosevelt
Went to an unknown grandchild in the West.

Downtown, his widow raised her parasol
Against the Lenten sun's not yet detectable
Malignant atomies which an electric needle
Unfreckles from her soft white skin each fall.

Hence too her chiffon scarf, pale violet,
And spangle-paste dark glasses. Each spring we number
The new dead. Above ground, who can remember
Her as she once was? Even I forget,

Fail to attend her, seem impervious . . .
Meanwhile we have made through a dense shimmy
Of parked cars burnished by the midday chamois
For Mutual Trust. Here cool gloom welcomes us,

And all, director, guard, quite palpably
Adore her. Spinster tellers one by one
Darting from cages, sniffling to meet her son,
Think of her having a son—! She holds the key

Whereby palatial bronze gates shut like jaws
On our descent into this inmost vault.
The keeper bends his baldness to consult,
Brings a tin box painted mud-brown, withdraws.

She opens it. Security. Will. Deed.
Rummages further. Rustle of tissue, a sprung
Lid. Her face gone queerly lit, fair, young,
Like faces of our dear ones who have died.

No rhinestone now, no dilute amethyst,
But of the first water, linking star to pang,
Teardrop to fire, my father's kisses hang
In lipless concentration round her wrist.

JAMES MERRILL

Gray are these temple-drummers who once more
Would rouse her, girl-bride jeweled in his grave.
Instead, she next picks out a ring. "He gave
Me this when you were born. Here, take it for—

For when you marry. For your bride. It's yours."
A den of greenest light, it grows, shrinks, glows,
Hermetic stanza bedded in the prose
Of the last thirty semiprecious years.

I do not tell her, it would sound theatrical,
Indeed this green room's mine, my very life.
We are each other's; there will be no wife;
The little feet that patter here are metrical.

But onto her worn knuckle slip the ring.
Wear it for me, I silently entreat,
Until—until the time comes. Our eyes meet.
The world beneath the world is brightening.

THE VICTOR DOG

for Elizabeth Bishop

Bix to Buxtehude to Boulez,
The little white dog on the Victor label
Listens long and hard as he is able.
It's all in a day's work, whatever plays.

From judgment, it would seem, he has refrained.
He even listens earnestly to Bloch,
Then builds a church upon our acid rock.
He's man's—no—he's the Leiermann's best friend,

Or would be if hearing and listening were the same.
Does he hear? I fancy he rather smells
Those lemon-gold arpeggios in Ravel's
'Les jets d'eau du palais de ceux qui s'aiment.'

JAMES MERRILL

He ponders the Schumann Concerto's tall willow hit
By lightning, and stays put. When he surmises
Through one of Bach's eternal boxwood mazes
The oboe pungent as a bitch in heat,

Or when the calypso decants its raw bay rum
Or the moon in *Wozzeck* reddens ripe for murder,
He doesn't sneeze or howl; just listens harder.
Adamant needles bear down on him from

Whirling of outer space, too black, too near—
But he was taught as a puppy not to flinch,
Much less to imitate his bête noire Blanche
Who barked, fat foolish creature, at King Lear.

Still others fought in the road's filth over Jezebel,
Slavered on hearths of horned and pelted barons.
His forebears lacked, to say the least, forbearance.
Can nature change in him? Nothing's impossible.

The last chord fades. The night is cold and fine.
His master's voice rasps through the grooves' bare groves.
Obediently, in silence like the grave's
He sleeps there on the still-warm gramophone

Only to dream he is at the première of a Handel
Opera long thought lost—*Il Cane Minore.*
Its allegorical subject is his story!
A little dog revolving round a spindle

Gives rise to harmonies beyond belief,
A cast of stars. . . . Is there in Victor's heart
No honey for the vanquished? Art is art.
The life it asks of us is a dog's life.

© Thomas Victor

W. S. Merwin

THE DRUNK IN THE FURNACE

For a good decade
The furnace stood in the naked gully, fireless
And vacant as any hat. Then when it was
No more to them than a hulking black fossil
To erode unnoticed with the rest of the junk-hill
By the poisonous creek, and rapidly to be added
        To their ignorance,

        They were afterwards astonished
To confirm, one morning, a twist of smoke like a pale
Resurrection, staggering out of its chewed hole,
And to remark then other tokens that someone,
Cosily bolted behind the eye-holed iron
Door of the drafty burner, had there established
        His bad castle.

        Where he gets his spirits
It's a mystery. But the stuff keeps him musical:
Hammer-and-anvilling with poker and bottle
To his jugged bellowings, till the last groaning clang
As he collapses onto the rioting
Springs of a litter of car-seats ranged on the grates,
        To sleep like an iron pig.

        In their tar-paper church
On a text about stoke-holes that are sated never
Their Reverend lingers. They nod and hate trespassers.
When the furnace wakes, though, all afternoon
Their witless offspring flock like piped rats to its siren
Crescendo, and agape on the crumbling ridge
        Stand in a row and learn.

W. S. MERWIN

LEMUEL'S BLESSING

Let Lemuel bless with the wolf, which is a dog without a master, but the Lord hears his cries and feeds him in the desert.

Christopher Smart: Jubilate Agno

You that know the way,
Spirit,
I bless your ears which are like cypruses on a mountain
With their roots in wisdom. Let me approach.
I bless your paws and their twenty nails which tell their own prayer
And are like dice in command of their own combinations.
Let me not be lost.
I bless your eyes for which I know no comparison.
Run with me like the horizon, for without you
I am nothing but a dog lost and hungry,
Ill-natured, untrustworthy, useless.

My bones together bless you like an orchestra of flutes.
Divert the weapons of the settlements and lead their dogs a dance.
Where a dog is shameless and wears servility
In his tail like a banner,
Let me wear the opprobrium of possessed and possessors
As a thick tail properly used
To warm my worst and my best parts. My tail and my laugh bless you.
Lead me past the error at the fork of hesitation.
Deliver me

From the ruth of the lair, which clings to me in the morning,
Painful when I move, like a trap;
Even debris has its favorite positions but they are not yours;
From the ruth of kindness, with its licked hands;
I have sniffed baited fingers and followed
Toward necessities which were not my own: it would make me
An habitué of back steps, faithful custodian of fat sheep;

From the ruth of prepared comforts, with its
Habitual dishes sporting my name and its collars and leashes of vanity;

From the ruth of approval, with its nets, kennels, and taxidermists;
It would use my guts for its own rackets and instruments, to play its own
    games and music;
Teach me to recognize its platforms, which are constructed like scaffolds;

From the ruth of known paths, which would use my feet, tail, and ears
    as curios,
My head as a nest for tame ants,
My fate as a warning.

I have hidden at wrong times for wrong reasons.
I have been brought to bay. More than once.
Another time, if I need it,
Create a little wind like a cold finger between my shoulders, then
Let my nails pour out a torrent of aces like grain from a threshing machine;
Let fatigue, weather, habitation, the old bones, finally,
Be nothing to me,
Let all lights but yours be nothing to me.
Let the memory of tongues not unnerve me so that I stumble or quake.

But lead me at times beside the still waters;
There when I crouch to drink let me catch a glimpse of your image
Before it is obscured with my own.

Preserve my eyes, which are irreplaceable.
Preserve my heart, veins, bones,
Against the slow death building in them like hornets until the place is
    entirely theirs.
Preserve my tongue and I will bless you again and again.

Let my ignorance and my failings
Remain far behind me like tracks made in a wet season,
At the end of which I have vanished,
So that those who track me for their own twisted ends
May be rewarded only with ignorance and failings.
But let me leave my cry stretched out behind me like a road
On which I have followed you.
And sustain me for my time in the desert
On what is essential to me.

DEAD HAND

Temptations still nest in it like basilisks.
Hang it up till the rings fall.

AIR

Naturally it is night.
Under the overturned lute with its
One string I am going my way
Which has a strange sound.

This way the dust, that way the dust.
I listen to both sides
But I keep right on.
I remember the leaves sitting in judgment
And then winter.

I remember the rain with its bundle of roads.
The rain taking all its roads.
Nowhere.

Young as I am, old as I am,

I forget tomorrow, the blind man.
I forget the life among the buried windows.
The eyes in the curtains.
The wall
Growing through the immortelles.
I forget silence
The owner of the smile.

This must be what I wanted to be doing,
Walking at night between the two deserts,
Singing.

W. S. MERWIN

WE CONTINUE

for Galway Kinnell

The rust, a little pile of western color, lies
At the end of its travels,
Our instrument no longer.

Those who believe
In death have their worship cut out for them.
As for myself, we
Continue,

An old
Scar of light our trumpet,

Pilgrims with thorns
To the eye of the cold
Under flags made by the blind,
In one fist

This letter that vanishes
If the hand opens:

Charity, come home,
Begin.

SOME LAST QUESTIONS

What is the head
      A. Ash
What are the eyes
      A. The wells have fallen in and have
         Inhabitants
What are the feet
      A. Thumbs left after the auction
No what are the feet
      A. Under them the impossible road is moving
         Down which the broken necked mice push
         Balls of blood with their noses

What is the tongue
    A. The black coat that fell off the wall
       With sleeves trying to say something
What are the hands
    A. Paid
No what are the hands
    A. Climbing back down the museum wall
       To their ancestors the extinct shrews that will
       Have left a message
What is the silence
    A. As though it had a right to more
Who are the compatriots
    A. They make the stars of bone

DECEMBER NIGHT

The cold slope is standing in darkness
But the south of the trees is dry to the touch

The heavy limbs climb into the moonlight bearing feathers
I came to watch these
White plants older at night
The oldest
Come first to the ruins

And I hear magpies kept awake by the moon
The water flows through its
Own fingers without end

Tonight once more
I find a single prayer and it is not for men

FOR THE ANNIVERSARY OF MY DEATH

Every year without knowing it I have passed the day
When the last fires will wave to me
And the silence will set out
Tireless traveller
Like the beam of a lightless star

Then I will no longer
Find myself in life as in a strange garment
Surprised at the earth
And the love of one woman
And then shamelessness of men
As today writing after three days of rain
Hearing the wren sing and the falling cease
And bowing not knowing to what

TERGVINDER'S STONE

One time my friend Tergvinder brought a large round boulder into his living room. He rolled it up the steps with the help of some two-by-fours, and when he got it out into the middle of the room, where some people have coffee tables (though he had never had one there himself) he left it. He said that was where it belonged.

It is really a plain-looking stone. Not as large as Plymouth Rock by a great deal, but then it does not have all the claims of a big shaky promotion campaign to support. That was one of the things Tergvinder said about it. He made no claims at all for it, he said. It was other people who called it Tergvinder's Stone. All he said was that according to him it belonged there.

His dog took to peeing on it, which created a problem (Tergvinder had not moved the carpet before he got the stone to where he said it belonged). Their tomcat took to squirting it, too. His wife fell over it quite often at first and it did not help their already strained marriage. Tergvinder said there was nothing to be done about it. It was in the order of things. That was a phrase he seldom employed, and never when he conceived that there was any room left for doubt.

He confided in me that he often woke in the middle of the night, troubled by the ancient, nameless ills of the planet, and got up quietly not to wake his wife, and walked through the house naked, without turning on any lights. He said that at such times he found himself listening, listening, aware of how some shapes in the darkness emitted low sounds like breathing, as they never did by day. He said he had become aware of a hole in the darkness in the middle of the living room, and out of that hole a breathing, a mournful dissatisfied sound of an absence waiting for what belonged to it, for something it had never seen and could not conceive of, but without which it could not rest. It was a sound, Tergvinder said, that touched him with fellow-feeling, and he had undertaken—oh, without saying anything to anybody—to assuage, if he could, that wordless longing that seemed always on the verge of despair. How to do it was another matter, and for months he had circled the problem, night and day, without apparently coming any closer to a solution. Then one day he had seen the stone. It had been there all the time at the bottom of his drive, he said, and he had never really seen it. Never recognized it for what it was. The nearer to the house he had got it, the more certain he had become. The stone had rolled into its present place like a lost loved one falling into arms that had long ached for it.

Tergvinder says that now on nights when he walks through the dark house he comes and stands in the living room doorway and listens to the peace in the middle of the floor. He knows its size, its weight, the touch of it, something of what is thought of it. He knows that it is peace. As he listens, some hint of that peace touches him too. Often, after a while, he steps down into the living room and goes and kneels beside the stone and they converse for hours in silence—a silence broken only by the sound of his own breathing.

THE HANDS

. . . Ma non è cosa in terra
Che ti somigli . . .

Leopardi

I have seen them when there was
nothing else
small swollen flames lighting my way at
corners
where they have waited for
me

cut off from
everything they have made their way to me
one more day one more night leading
their blood and I wake
to find them lying at home
with my own

like a bird lying in its wings
a stunned
bird till they stir and
break
open cradling a heart not theirs
not mine
and I bend to hear who is beating

W. S. MERWIN

DO NOT DIE

In each world they may put us
farther apart
do not die
as this world is made I might
live forever

ANIMULA

Look soul
soul
barefoot presence
through whom blood falls as through
a water clock
and tears rise before they wake
I will take you

at last to
where the wind stops
by the river we
know
by that same water
and the nights are not separate
remember

EYES OF SUMMER

All the stones have been us
and will be again
as the sun touches them you can feel
sun
and remember waking with no face
knowing that it was summer
still
when the witnesses
day after day are blinded
so that they will forget nothing

W. S. MERWIN

HABITS

Even in the middle of the night
they go on handing me around
but it's dark and they drop more of me
and for longer

then they hang onto my memory
thinking it's theirs

even when I'm asleep they take
one or two of my eyes for their sockets
and they look around believing
that the place is home

when I wake and can feel the black lungs
flying deeper into the century
carrying me
even then they borrow
most of my tongues to tell me
that they're me
and they lend me most of my ears to hear them

A DOOR

This is a place where a door might be
here where I am standing
in the light outside all the walls

there would be a shadow here
all day long
and a door into it
where now there is me

and somebody would come and knock
on this air
long after I have gone
and there in front of me a life
would open

W. S. MERWIN

THE FALCONS

There were years when I knew
the flowers in the red stone walls

now in the courtyard where I have returned with you
we drink the wine of visitors
the temperature of the cellars

dusk is welling
out of the dried blood of the masonry
no hour remains on the sundial
by now the owls of the tower corners
are waking on their keepers' fists
but it is still day
out in the air
and three falcons appear there
over the courtyard

no feathers on heads or breasts
and they fly down to us
to our wrists and between them
then hover and perch just above us
keeping us in sight
waiting
they are waiting for us

this time they will come with us
when we leave the island
tonight for the rest of our lives

© Kenward Elmslie

Frank O'Hara

AUTOBIOGRAPHIA LITERARIA

When I was a child
I played by myself in a
corner of the schoolyard
all alone.

I hated dolls and I
hated games, animals were
not friendly and birds
flew away.

If anyone was looking
for me I hid behind a
tree and cried out "I am
an orphan."

And here I am, the
center of all beauty!
writing these poems!
Imagine!

POEM

The eager note on my door said "Call me,
call when you get in!" so I quickly threw
a few tangerines into my overnight bag,
straightened my eyelids and shoulders, and

headed straight for the door. It was autumn
by the time I got around the corner, oh all
unwilling to be either pertinent or bemused, but
the leaves were brighter than grass on the sidewalk!

Funny, I thought, that the lights are on this late
and the hall door open; still up at this hour, a
champion jai-alai player like himself? Oh fie!
for shame! What a host, so zealous! And he was

there in the hall, flat on a sheet of blood that
ran down the stairs. I did appreciate it. There are few
hosts who so thoroughly prepare to greet a guest
only casually invited, and that several months ago.

POEM

All the mirrors in the world
don't help, nor am I moved

by the calm emergence of my
image in the rain, it is not

I who appears or imagines. See,
if you can, if you can make

the unpleasant trip, the
house where shadows of my own

childhood are watered and forced
like overgrown bludgeons, you

must look, for I cannot. I
cannot face that fearful usage,

and my eyes in, say, the glass
of a public bar, become a

depraved hunt for other re-
flections. And what a blessed

relief! when it is some
disgusting sight, anything

but the old shadowy bruising,
anything but my private haunts.

When I am fifty shall my
face drift into those elongations

of innocence and confront me?
Oh rain, melt me! mirror, kill!

TO MY DEAD FATHER

Don't call to me father
wherever you are I'm
still your little son
running through the dark

I couldn't do what you
say even if I could hear
your roses no longer grow
my heart's black as their

bed their dainty thorns
have become my face's
troublesome stubble you
must not think of flowers

And do not frighten my
blue eyes with hazel flecks
or thicken my lips when
I face my mirror don't ask

that I be other than your
strange son understanding
minor miracles not death
father I am alive! father

forgive the roses and me

MEDITATIONS IN AN EMERGENCY

Am I to become profligate as if I were a blonde? Or religious as if I were French?

Each time my heart is broken it makes me feel more adventurous (and how the same names keep recurring on that interminable list!), but one of these days there'll be nothing left with which to venture forth.

Why should I share you? Why don't you get rid of someone else for a change?

I am the least difficult of men. All I want is boundless love.

Even trees understand me! Good heavens, I lie under them, too, don't I? I'm just like a pile of leaves.

However, I have never clogged myself with the praises of pastoral life, nor with nostalgia for an innocent past of perverted acts in pastures. No. One need never leave the confines of New York to get all the greenery one wishes—I can't even enjoy a blade of grass unless I know there's a subway handy, or a record store or some other sign that people do not totally *regret* life. It is more important to affirm the least sincere; the clouds get enough attention as it is and even they continue to pass. Do they know what they're missing? Uh huh.

My eyes are vague blue, like the sky, and change all the time; they are indiscriminate but fleeting, entirely specific and disloyal, so that no one trusts me. I am always looking away. Or again at something after it has given me up. It makes me restless and that makes me unhappy, but I cannot keep them still. If only I had grey, green, black, brown, yellow eyes; I would stay at home and do something. It's not that I'm curious. On the contrary, I am bored but it's my duty to be attentive, I am needed by things as the sky must be above the earth. And lately, so great has *their* anxiety become, I can spare myself little sleep.

Now there is only one man I love to kiss when he is unshaven. Heterosexuality! you are inexorably approaching. (How discourage her?)

St. Serapion, I wrap myself in the robes of your whiteness which is like midnight in Dostoevsky. How am I to become a legend, my dear? I've tried love, but that hides you in the bosom of another and I am always springing forth from it like the lotus—the ecstasy of always bursting forth! (but one must not be distracted by it!) or like a hyacinth, "to keep the filth of life away," yes, there, even in the heart, where the filth is pumped in and slanders and pollutes and determines. I will my will, though I may become famous for a mysterious vacancy in that department, that greenhouse.

Destroy yourself, if you don't know!

It is easy to be beautiful; it is difficult to appear so. I admire you, beloved, for the trap you've set. It's like a final chapter no one reads because the plot is over.

"Fanny Brown is run away—scampered off with a Cornet of Horse; I do love that little Minx, & hope She may be happy, tho' She has vexed me by this Exploit a little too. —Poor silly Cecchina! or F: B: as we used to call her. —I wish She had a good Whipping and 10,000 pounds." —Mrs. Thrale.

I've got to get out of here. I choose a piece of shawl and my dirtiest suntans. I'll be back, I'll re-emerge, defeated, from the valley; you don't want me to go where you go, so I go where you don't want me to. It's only afternoon, there's a lot ahead. There won't be any mail downstairs. Turning, I spit in the lock and the knob turns.

TO JOHN ASHBERY

I can't believe there's not
another world where we will sit
and read new poems to each other
high on a mountain in the wind.
You can be Tu Fu, I'll be Po Chü-i
and the Monkey Lady'll be in the moon,
smiling at our ill-fitting heads
as we watch snow settle on a twig.
Or shall we be really gone? this
is not the grass I saw in my youth!
and if the moon, when it rises
tonight, is empty—a bad sign,
meaning "You go, like the blossoms."

FRANK O'HARA

WHY I AM NOT A PAINTER

I am not a painter, I am a poet.
Why? I think I would rather be
a painter, but I am not. Well,

for instance, Mike Goldberg
is starting a painting. I drop in.
"Sit down and have a drink" he
says. I drink; we drink. I look
up. "You have SARDINES in it."
"Yes, it needed something there."

"Oh." I go and the days go by
and I drop in again. The painting
is going on, and I go, and the days
go by. I drop in. The painting is
finished. "Where's SARDINES?"
All that's left is just
letters, "It was too much," Mike says.

But me? One day I am thinking of
a color: orange. I write a line
about orange. Pretty soon it is a
whole page of words, not lines.
Then another page. There should be
so much more, not of orange, of
words, of how terrible orange is
and life. Days go by. It is even in
prose, I am a real poet. My poem
is finished and I haven't mentioned
orange yet. It's twelve poems, I call
it ORANGES. And one day in a gallery
I see Mike's painting, called SARDINES.

THE DAY LADY DIED

It is 12:20 in New York a Friday
three days after Bastille day, yes
it is 1959 and I go get a shoeshine

because I will get off the 4:19 in Easthampton
at 7:15 and then go straight to dinner
and I don't know the people who will feed me

I walk up the muggy street beginning to sun
and have a hamburger and a malted and buy
an ugly NEW WORLD WRITING to see what the poets
in Ghana are doing these days
                              I go on to the bank
and Miss Stillwagon (first name Linda I once heard)
doesn't even look up my balance for once in her life
and in the GOLDEN GRIFFIN I get a little Verlaine
for Patsy with drawings by Bonnard although I do
think of Hesiod, trans. Richmond Lattimore or
Brendan Behan's new play or *Le Balcon* or *Les Nègres*
of Genet, but I don't, I stick with Verlaine
after practically going to sleep with quandariness

and for Mike I just stroll into the PARK LANE
Liquor Store and ask for a bottle of Strega and
then I go back where I came from to 6th Avenue
and the tobacconist in the Ziegfeld Theatre and
casually ask for a carton of Gauloises and a carton
of Picayunes, and a NEW YORK POST with her face on it

and I am sweating a lot by now and thinking of
leaning on the john door in the 5 SPOT
while she whispered a song along the keyboard
to Mal Waldron and everyone and I stopped breathing

STEPS

How funny you are today New York
like Ginger Rogers in *Swingtime*
and St. Bridget's steeple leaning a little to the left

here I have just jumped out of a bed full of V-days
(I got tired of D-days) and blue you there still
accepts me foolish and free
all I want is a room up there
and you in it

and even the traffic halt so thick is a way
for people to rub up against each other
and when their surgical appliances lock
they stay together
for the rest of the day (what a day)
I go by to check a slide and I say
that painting's not so blue

where's Lana Turner
she's out eating
and Garbo's backstage at the Met
everyone's taking their coat off
so they can show a rib-cage to the rib-watchers
and the park's full of dancers with their tights and shoes
in little bags
who are often mistaken for worker-outers at the West Side Y
why not
the Pittsburgh Pirates shout because they won
and in a sense we're all winning
we're alive

the apartment was vacated by a gay couple
who moved to the country for fun
they moved a day too soon
even the stabbings are helping the population explosion
though in the wrong country
and all those liars have left the U N
the Seagram Building's no longer rivalled in interest
not that we need liquor (we just like it)

and the little box is out on the sidewalk
next to the delicatessen
so the old man can sit on it and drink beer
and get knocked off it by his wife later in the day
while the sun is still shining

oh god it's wonderful
to get out of bed
and drink too much coffee
and smoke too many cigarettes
and love you so much

FRANK O'HARA

YESTERDAY DOWN AT THE CANAL

You say that everything is very simple and interesting
it makes me feel very wistful, like reading a great Russian novel
does
I am terribly bored
sometimes it is like seeing a bad movie
other days, more often, it's like having an acute disease of the
kidney
god knows it has nothing to do with the heart
nothing to do with people more interesting than myself
yak yak
that's an amusing thought
how can anyone be more amusing than oneself
how can anyone fail to be
can I borrow your forty-five
I only need one bullet preferably silver
if you can't be interesting at least you can be a legend
(but I hate all that crap)

POEM

Lana Turner has collapsed!
I was trotting along and suddenly
it started raining and snowing
and you said it was hailing
but hailing hits you on the head
hard so it was really snowing and
raining and I was in such a hurry
to meet you but the traffic
was acting exactly like the sky
and suddenly I see a headline
LANA TURNER HAS COLLAPSED!
there is no snow in Hollywood
there is no rain in California
I have been to lots of parties
and acted perfectly disgraceful
but I never actually collapsed
oh Lana Turner we love you get up

© Gerard Malanga

Charles Olson

MAXIMUS, TO HIMSELF

I have had to learn the simplest things
last. Which made for difficulties.
Even at sea I was slow, to get the hand out, or to cross
a wet deck.
                The sea was not, finally, my trade.
But even my trade, at it, I stood estranged
from that which was most familiar. Was delayed,
and not content with the man's argument
that such postponement
is now the nature of
obedience,

                that we are all late
                in a slow time,
                that we grow up many
                And the single
                is not easily
                known

It could be, though the sharpness (the *achiote*)
I note in others,
makes more sense
than my own distances. The agilities

                they show daily
                who do the world's
                businesses
                And who do nature's
                as I have no sense
                I have done either

I have made dialogues,
have discussed ancient texts,
have thrown what light I could, offered
what pleasures
doceat allows

But the known?
This, I have had to be given,
a life, love, and from one man
the world.

Tokens.
But sitting here
I look out as a wind
and water man, testing
And missing
some proof

I know the quarters
of the weather, where it comes from,
where it goes. But the stem of me,
this I took from their welcome,
or their rejection, of me

And my arrogance
was neither diminished
nor increased,
by the communication

2

It is undone business
I speak of, this morning,
with the sea
stretching out
from my feet

I, MAXIMUS OF GLOUCESTER, TO YOU

Off-shore, by islands hidden in the blood
jewels & miracles, I, Maximus
a metal hot from boiling water, tell you
what is a lance, who obeys the figures of
the present dance

CHARLES OLSON

1

the thing you're after
may lie around the bend
of the nest (second, time slain, the bird! the bird!

And there! (strong) thrust, the mast! flight
                              (of the bird
                              o kylix, o
                              Antony of Padua
                              sweep low, o bless

the roofs, the old ones, the gentle steep ones
on whose ridge-poles the gulls sit, from which they depart,

                                   And the flake-racks
of my city!

2

love is form, and cannot be without
important substance (the weight
say, 58 carats each one of us, perforce
our goldsmith's scale

                    feather to feather added
                    (and what is mineral, what
                    is curling hair, the string
                    you carry in your nervous beak, these

                    make bulk, these, in the end, are
                    the sum

                    (o my lady of good voyage
                    in whose arm, whose left arm rests
no boy but a carefully carved wood, a painted face, a schooner!
a delicate mast, as bow-sprit for

                    forwarding

3

the underpart is, though stemmed, uncertain
is, as sex is, as moneys are, facts!
facts, to be dealt with, as the sea is, the demand
that they be played by, that they only can be, that they must
be played by, said he, coldly, the
ear!

By ear, he sd.
But that which matters, that which insists, that which will last,
that! o my people, where shall you find it, how, where, where shall you
    listen
when all is become billboards, when, all, even silence, is spray-gunned?

when even our bird, my roofs,
cannot be heard

when even you, when sound itself is neoned in?

when, on the hill, over the water
where she who used to sing,
when the water glowed,
black, gold, the tide
outward, at evening

when bells came like boats
over the oil-slicks, milkweed
hulls

And a man slumped,
attentionless,
against pink shingles

o sea city)

4

one loves only form,
and form only comes
into existence when
the thing is born

born of yourself, born
of hay and cotton struts,
of street-pickings, wharves, weeds
you carry in, my bird

                    of a bone of a fish
                    of a straw, or will
                    of a color, of a bell
                    of yourself, torn

5

love is not easy
but how shall you know,
New England, now
that pejorocracy is here, how
that street-cars, o Oregon, twitter
in the afternoon, offend
a black-gold loin?

                    how shall you strike,
                    o swordsman, the blue-red back
                    when, last night, your aim
                    was mu-sick, mu-sick, mu-sick
                    And not the cribbage game?

                                        (o Gloucester-man,
                                        weave
                                        your birds and fingers
                                        new, your roof-tops,
                                        clean shit upon racks
                                        sunned on
                                        American
                                        braid
                                        with others like you, such
                                        extricable surface
                                        as faun and oral,
                                        satyr lesbos vase

                                        o kill kill kill kill kill
                                        those
                                        who advertise you
                                        out)

6

in! in! the bow-sprit, bird, the beak
in, the bend is, in, goes in, the form
that which you make, what holds, which is
the law of object, strut after strut, what you are, what you must be, what
the force can throw up, can, right now hereinafter erect,
the mast, the mast, the tender
mast!

        The nest, I say, to you, I Maximus, say
        under the hand, as I see it, over the waters
        from this place where I am, where I hear,
        can still hear

        from where I carry you a feather
        as though, sharp, I picked up,
        in the afternoon delivered you
        a jewel,
                it flashing more than a wing,
        than any old romantic thing,
        than memory, than place,
        than anything other than that which you carry

        than that which is,
        call it a nest, around the head of, call it
        the next second

        than that which you
        can do!

MAXIMUS, TO GLOUCESTER, LETTER 19
(A PASTORAL LETTER

    relating
    to the care of souls,
    it says)

He had smiled at us,
each time we were in town, inquired
how the baby was, had two cents
for the weather, wore
(besides his automobile)
good clothes.
                    And a pink face.

It was yesterday
it all came out. The gambit
(as he crossed the street,
after us) : "I don't believe
I know your name." Given.
How do you do,
how do you do. And then:
"Pardon me, but
what church
do you belong to,
may I ask?"

And the whole street, the town, the cities, the nation
blinked, in the afternoon sun, at the gun
was held at them. And I wavered
in the thought.

            I sd, you may, sir.
            He sd, what, sir.
            I sd, none,
            sir.

And the light was back.

For I am no merchant.
Nor so young I need to take a stance
to a loaded
smile.

            I have known the face
            of God.
            And turned away,
            turned,
            as He did,
            his backside

2

And now it is noon
of a cloudy sunday.
And a bird sings
loudly

And my daughter, naked
on the porch, sings
as best she can, and loudly,
back

>   She wears her own face
>   as we do not,
>   until we cease to wear
>   the clouds
>   of all confusion,

>   of all confusers
>   who wear the false face
>   He never wore, Whose
>   is terrible. Is
>   perfection

THE LIBRARIAN

The landscape (the landscape!) again: Gloucester,
the shore one of me is (duplicates), and from which
(from offshore, I, Maximus) am removed, observe.

In this night I moved on the territory with combinations
(new mixtures) of old and known personages: the leader,
my father, in an old guise, here selling books and manuscripts.

My thought was, as I looked in the window of his shop,
there should be materials here for Maximus, when, then,
I saw he was the young musician has been there (been before me)

before. It turned out it wasn't a shop, it was a loft (wharf-
house) in which, as he walked me around, a year ago
came back (I had been there before, with my wife and son,

CHARLES OLSON

I didn't remember, he presented me insinuations via
himself and his girl) both of whom I had known for years.
But never in Gloucester. I had moved them in, to my country.

His previous appearance had been in my parents' bedroom where I
found him intimate with my former wife: this boy
was now the Librarian of Gloucester, Massachusetts!

> Black space,
> old fish-house.
> Motions
> of ghosts.
> I,
> dogging
> his steps.
>
> He
> (not my father,
> by name himself
> with his face
> twisted
> at birth)
> possessed of knowledge
> pretentious
> giving me
> what in the instant
> I knew better of.
>
> But the somber
> place, the flooring
> crude like a wharf's
> and a barn's
> space

I was struck by the fact I was in Gloucester, and that my daughter
was there—that I would see her! She was over the Cut. I
hadn't even connected her with my being there, that she was

here. That she was there (in the Promised Land—the Cut!
But there was this business, of poets,that all my Jews
were in the fish-house too, that the Librarian had made a party

I was to read. They were. There were many of them, slumped
around. It was not for me. I was outside. It was the Fort.
The Fort was in East Gloucester—old Gorton's Wharf, where the Library

was. It was a region of coal houses, bins. In one a gang
was beating someone to death, in a corner of the labyrinth
of fences. I could see their arms and shoulders whacking

down. But not the victim. I got out of there. But cops
tailed me along the Fort beach toward the Tavern

The places still
half-dark, mud,
coal-dust.

There is no light
east
of the Bridge

Only on the headland
toward the harbor
from Cressy's

have I seen it (once
when my daughter ran
out on a spit of sand

isn't even there.) Where
is Bristow? when does I-A
get me home? I am caught

in Gloucester. (What's buried
behind Lufkin's
Diner? Who is

Frank Moore?

CHARLES OLSON

MAXIMUS TO GLOUCESTER, LETTER 27 [WITHHELD]

I come back to the geography of it,
the land falling off to the left
where my father shot his scabby golf
and the rest of us played baseball
into the summer darkness until no flies
could be seen and we came home
to our various piazzas where the women
buzzed

To the left the land fell to the city,
to the right, it fell to the sea

I was so young my first memory
is of a tent spread to feed lobsters
to Rexall conventioneers, and my father,
a man for kicks, came out of the tent roaring
with a bread-knife in his teeth to take care of
a druggist they'd told him had made a pass at
my mother, she laughing, so sure, as round
as her face, Hines pink and apple,
under one of those frame hats women then

This, is no bare incoming
of novel abstract form, this

is no welter or the forms
of those events, this,

Greeks, is the stopping
of the battle

              It is the imposing
of all those antecedent predecessions, the precessions

of me, the generation of those facts
which are my words, it is coming

from all that I no longer am, yet am,
the slow westward motion of

more than I am

There is no strict personal order

for my inheritance.

   No Greek will be able

to discriminate my body.

   An American

is a complex of occasions,

themselves a geometry

of spatial nature.

   I have this sense,

that I am one

with my skin

   Plus this—plus this:

that forever the geography

which leans in

on me I compell

backwards I compell Gloucester

to yield, to

change

   Polis

is this

A LATER NOTE ON
LETTER #15

In English the poetics became meubles—furniture—
thereafter (after 1630

& Descartes was the value

until Whitehead, who cleared out the gunk
by getting the universe in (as against man alone

& that concept of history (not Herodotus's,
which was a verb, to find out for yourself:
'istorin, which makes any one's acts a finding out for him or her
self, in other words restores the traum: that we act somewhere

at least by seizure, that the objective (example Thucidides, or
the latest finest tape-recorder, or any form of record on the spot

—live television or what—is a lie

as against what we know went on, the dream: the dream being
self-action with Whitehead's important corollary: that no event

is not penetrated, in intersection or collision with, an eternal
event

      The poetics of such a situation
are yet to be found out

MOONSET, GLOUCESTER,
DECEMBER 1, 1957, 1:58 AM

Goodbye red moon
In that color you set
west of the Cut I should imagine
forever Mother

After 47 years this month
a Monday at 9 AM
you set I rise I hope
a free thing as probably
what you more were Not
the suffering one you sold
sowed me on Rise
Mother from off me
God damn you God damn me my
misunderstanding of you

I can die now I just begun to live

© Rollie McKenna

Sylvia Plath

THE COLOSSUS

I shall never get you put together entirely,
Pieced, glued, and properly jointed.
Mule-bray, pig-grunt and bawdy cackles
Proceed from your great lips.
It's worse than a barnyard.

Perhaps you consider yourself an oracle,
Mouthpiece of the dead, or of some god or other.
Thirty years now I have labored
To dredge the silt from your throat.
I am none the wiser.

Scaling little ladders with gluepots and pails of lysol
I crawl like an ant in mourning
Over the weedy acres of your brow
To mend the immense skull plates and clear
The bald, white tumuli of your eyes.

A blue sky out of the Oresteia
Arches above us. O father, all by yourself
You are pithy and historical as the Roman Forum.
I open my lunch on a hill of black cypress.
Your fluted bones and acanthine hair are littered

In their old anarchy to the horizon-line.
It would take more than a lightning-stroke
To create such a ruin.
Nights, I squat in the cornucopia
Of your left ear, out of the wind,

Counting the red stars and those of plum-color.
The sun rises under the pillar of your tongue.
My hours are married to shadow.
No longer do I listen for the scrape of a keel
On the blank stones of the landing.

DADDY

You do not do, you do not do
Any more, black shoe
In which I have lived like a foot
For thirty years, poor and white,
Barely daring to breathe or Achoo.

Daddy, I have had to kill you.
You died before I had time——
Marble-heavy, a bag full of God,
Ghastly statue with one grey toe
Big as a Frisco seal

And a head in the freakish Atlantic
Where it pours bean green over blue
In the waters off beautiful Nauset.
I used to pray to recover you.
Ach, du.

In the German tongue, in the Polish town
Scraped flat by the roller
Of wars, wars, wars.
But the name of the town is common.
My Polack friend

Says there are a dozen or two.
So I never could tell where you
Put your foot, your root,
I never could talk to you.
The tongue stuck in my jaw.

It stuck in a barb wire snare.
Ich, ich, ich, ich,
I could hardly speak.
I thought every German was you.
And the language obscene

An engine, an engine
Chuffing me off like a Jew.
A Jew to Dachau, Auschwitz, Belsen.
I began to talk like a Jew.
I think I may well be a Jew.

The snows of the Tyrol, the clear beer of Vienna
Are not very pure or true.
With my gypsy ancestress and my weird luck
And my Taroc pack and my Taroc pack
I may be a bit of a Jew.

I have always been scared of *you*,
With your Luftwaffe, your gobbledygoo.
And your neat moustache
And your Aryan eye, bright blue.
Panzer-man, panzer-man, O You——

Not God but a swastika
So black no sky could squeak through.
Every woman adores a Fascist,
The boot in the face, the brute
Brute heart of a brute like you.

You stand at the blackboard, daddy,
In the picture I have of you,
A cleft in your chin instead of your foot
But no less a devil for that, no not
Any less the black man who

Bit my pretty red heart in two.
I was ten when they buried you.
At twenty I tried to die
And get back, back, back to you.
I thought even the bones would do.

But they pulled me out of the sack,
And they stuck me together with glue.
And then I knew what to do.
I made a model of you,
A man in black with a Meinkampf look

And a love of the rack and the screw.
And I said I do, I do.
So daddy, I'm finally through.
The black telephone's off at the root,
The voices just can't worm through.

If I've killed one man, I've killed two——
The vampire who said he was you
And drank my blood for a year,
Seven years, if you want to know.
Daddy, you can lie back now.

There's a stake in your fat black heart
And the villagers never liked you.
They are dancing and stamping on you.
They always *knew* it was you.
Daddy, daddy, you bastard, I'm through.

THE MUNICH MANNEQUINS

Perfection is terrible, it cannot have children.
Cold as snow breath, it tamps the womb

Where the yew trees blow like hydras,
The tree of life and the tree of life

Unloosing their moons, month after month, to no purpose.
The blood flood is the flood of love,

The absolute sacrifice.
It means: no more idols but me,

Me and you.
So, in their sulphur loveliness, in their smiles

These mannequins lean tonight
In Munich, morgue between Paris and Rome,

Naked and bald in their furs,
Orange lollies on silver sticks,

Intolerable, without mind.
The snow drops its pieces of darkness,

Nobody's about. In the hotels
Hands will be opening doors and setting

Down shoes for a polish of carbon
Into which broad toes will go tomorrow.

O the domesticity of these windows,
The baby lace, the green-leaved confectionery,

The thick Germans slumbering in their bottomless Stolz.
And the black phones on hooks

Glittering
Glittering and digesting

Voicelessness. The snow has no voice.

MARY'S SONG

The Sunday lamb cracks in its fat.
The fat
Sacrifices its opacity. . . .

A window, holy gold.
The fire makes it precious,
The same fire

Melting the tallow heretics,
Ousting the Jews.
Their thick palls float

Over the cicatrix of Poland, burnt-out
Germany.
They do not die.

Grey birds obsess my heart,
Mouth-ash, ash of eye.
They settle. On the high

Precipice
That emptied one man into space
The ovens glowed like heavens, incandescent.

It is a heart,
This holocaust I walk in,
O golden child the world will kill and eat.

NICK AND THE CANDLESTICK

I am a miner. The light burns blue.
Waxy stalactites
Drip and thicken, tears

The earthen womb
Exudes from its dead boredom.
Black bat airs

Wrap me, raggy shawls,
Cold homicides.
They weld to me like plums.

Old cave of calcium
Icicles, old echoer.
Even the newts are white,

Those holy Joes.
And the fish, the fish——
Christ! They are panes of ice,

A vice of knives,
A piranha
Religion, drinking

Its first communion out of my live toes.
The candle
Gulps and recovers its small altitude,

Its yellows hearten.
O love, how did you get here?
O embryo

Remembering, even in sleep,
Your crossed position.
The blood blooms clean

In you, ruby.
The pain
You wake to is not yours.

Love, love,
I have hung our cave with roses.
With soft rugs——

The last of Victoriana.
Let the stars
Plummet to their dark address,

Let the mercuric
Atoms that cripple drip
Into the terrible well,

You are the one
Solid the spaces lean on, envious.
You are the baby in the barn.

LADY LAZARUS

I have done it again.
One year in every ten
I manage it——

A sort of walking miracle, my skin
Bright as a Nazi lampshade,
My right foot

A paperweight,
My face a featureless, fine
Jew linen.

Peel off the napkin
O my enemy.
Do I terrify?——

The nose, the eye pits, the full set of teeth?
The sour breath
Will vanish in a day.

Soon, soon the flesh
The grave cave ate will be
At home on me

And I a smiling woman.
I am only thirty.
And like the cat I have nine times to die.

This is Number Three.
What a trash
To annihilate each decade.

What a million filaments.
The peanut-crunching crowd
Shoves in to see

Them unwrap me hand and foot——
The big strip tease.
Gentleman, ladies,

These are my hands,
My knees.
I may be skin and bone,

Nevertheless, I am the same, identical woman.
The first time it happened I was ten.
It was an accident.

The second time I meant
To last it out and not come back at all.
I rocked shut

As a seashell.
They had to call and call
And pick the worms off me like sticky pearls.

Dying
Is an art, like everything else.
I do it exceptionally well.

I do it so it feels like hell.
I do it so it feels real.
I guess you could say I've a call.

It's easy enough to do it in a cell.
It's easy enough to do it and stay put.
It's the theatrical

Comeback in broad day
To the same place, the same face, the same brute
Amused shout:

"A miracle!"
That knocks me out.
There is a charge

For the eyeing of my scars, there is a charge
For the hearing of my heart——
It really goes.

And there is a charge, a very large charge,
For a word or a touch
Or a bit of blood

Or a piece of my hair or my clothes.
So, so, Herr Doktor.
So, Herr Enemy.

I am your opus,
I am your valuable,
The pure gold baby

That melts to a shriek.
I turn and burn.
Do not think I underestimate your great concern.

Ash, ash—
You poke and stir.
Flesh, bone, there is nothing there——

A cake of soap,
A wedding ring,
A gold filling.

Herr God, Herr Lucifer,
Beware
Beware.

Out of the ash
I rise with my red hair
And I eat men like air.

CUT

for Susan O'Neill Roe

What a thrill——
My thumb instead of an onion.
The top quite gone
Except for a sort of a hinge

Of skin,
A flap like a hat,
Dead white.
Then that red plush.

Little pilgrim,
The Indian's axed your scalp.
Your turkey wattle
Carpet rolls

Straight from the heart.
I step on it,
Clutching my bottle
Of pink fizz.

A celebration, this is.
Out of a gap
A million soldiers run,
Redcoats, every one.

Whose side are they on?
O my
Homunculus, I am ill.
I have taken a pill to kill

The thin
Papery feeling.
Saboteur,
Kamikaze man——

The stain on your
Gauze Ku Klux Klan
Babushka
Darkens and tarnishes and when

The balled
Pulp of your heart
Confronts its small
Mill of silence

How you jump——
Trepanned veteran,
Dirty girl,
Thumb stump.

WINTER TREES

The wet dawn inks are doing their blue dissolve.
On their blotter of fog the trees
Seem a botanical drawing.
Memories growing, ring on ring,
A series of weddings.

Knowing neither abortions nor bitchery,
Truer than women,
They seed so effortlessly!
Tasting the winds, that are footless,
Waist-deep in history.

Full of wings, otherworldliness.
In this, they are Ledas.
O mother of leaves and sweetness
Who are these pietas?
The shadows of ringdoves chanting, but easing nothing.

CROSSING THE WATER

Black lake, black boat, two black, cut-paper people.
Where do the black trees go that drink here?
Their shadows must cover Canada.

A little light is filtering from the water flowers.
Their leaves do not wish us to hurry:
They are round and flat and full of dark advice.

Cold worlds shake from the oar.
The spirit of blackness is in us, it is in the fishes.
A snag is lifting a valedictory, pale hand;

Stars open among the lilies.
Are you not blinded by such expressionless sirens?
This is the silence of astounded souls.

WITCH BURNING

In the marketplace they are piling the dry sticks.
A thicket of shadows is a poor coat. I inhabit
The wax image of myself, a doll's body.
Sickness begins here: I am a dartboard for witches.
Only the devil can eat the devil out.
In the month of red leaves I climb to a bed of fire.

It is easy to blame the dark: the mouth of a door,
The cellar's belly. They've blown my sparkler out.
A black-sharded lady keeps me in a parrot cage.
What large eyes the dead have!
I am intimate with a hairy spirit.
Smoke wheels from the beak of this empty jar.

If I am a little one, I can do no harm.
If I don't move about, I'll knock nothing over. So I said,
Sitting under a potlid, tiny and inert as a rice grain.
They are turning the burners up, ring after ring.
We are full of starch, my small white fellows. We grow.
It hurts at first. The red tongues will teach the truth.

Mother of beetles, only unclench your hand:
I'll fly through the candle's mouth like a singeless moth.
Give me back my shape. I am ready to construe the days
I coupled with dust in the shadow of a stone.
My ankles brighten. Brightness ascends my thighs.
I am lost, I am lost, in the robes of all this light.

BRASÍLIA

Will they occur,
These people with torsos of steel
Winged elbows and eyeholes

Awaiting masses
Of cloud to give them expression,
These super-people!—

And my baby a nail
Driven in, driven in.
He shrieks in his grease,

Bones nosing for distances.
And I, nearly extinct,
His three teeth cutting

Themselves on my thumb—
And the star,
The old story.

In the lane I meet sheep and wagons,
Red earth, motherly blood.
O You who eat

People like light rays, leave
This one
Mirror safe, unredeemed

By the dove's annihilation,
The glory
The power, the glory.

© Thomas Victor

Adrienne Rich

AUNT JENNIFER'S TIGERS

Aunt Jennifer's tigers prance across a screen,
Bright topaz denizens of a world of green.
They do not fear the men beneath the tree;
They pace in sleek chivalric certainty.

Aunt Jennifer's fingers fluttering through her wool
Find even the ivory needle hard to pull.
The massive weight of Uncle's wedding band
Sits heavily upon Aunt Jennifer's hand.

When Aunt is dead, her terrified hands will lie
Still ringed with ordeals she was mastered by.
The tigers in the panel that she made
Will go on prancing, proud and unafraid.

THE KNOT

In the heart of the queen anne's lace, a knot of blood.
For years I never saw it,

years of metallic vision,
spears glancing off a bright eyeball,

suns off a Swiss lake.
A foaming meadow; the Milky Way;

and there, all along, the tiny dark-red spider
sitting in the whiteness of the bridal web,

waiting to plunge his crimson knifepoint
into the white apparencies.

Little wonder the eye, healing, sees
for a long time through a mist of blood.

1965

NOVEMBER 1968

Stripped
you're beginning to float free
up through the smoke of brushfires
and incinerators
the unleafed branches won't hold you
nor the radar aerials

You're what the autumn knew would happen
after the last collapse
of primary color
once the last absolutes were torn to pieces
you could begin

How you broke open, what sheathed you
until this moment
I know nothing about it
my ignorance of you amazes me
now that I watch you
starting to give yourself away
to the wind

1968

PLANETARIUM

Thinking of Caroline Herschel (1750–1848)
astronomer, sister of William; and others.

A woman in the shape of a monster
a monster in the shape of a woman
the skies are full of them

ADRIENNE RICH

a woman   'in the snow
among the Clocks and instruments
or measuring the ground with poles'

in her 98 years to discover
8 comets

she whom the moon ruled
like us
levitating into the night sky
riding the polished lenses

Galaxies of women, there
doing penance for impetuousness
ribs chilled
in those spaces   of the mind

An eye,

        'virile, precise and absolutely certain'
        from the mad webs of Uranusborg

                                    encountering the NOVA

every impulse of light exploding
from the core
as life flies out of us

        Tycho whispering at last
        'Let me not seem to have lived in vain'

What we see, we see
and seeing is changing

the light that shrivels a mountain
and leaves a man alive

Heartbeat of the pulsar
heart sweating through my body

The radio impulse
pouring in from Taurus

        I am bombarded yet   I stand

I have been standing all my life in the
direct path of a battery of signals
the most accurately transmitted most
untranslatable language in the universe
I am a galactic cloud so deep   so invo-
luted that a light wave could take 15
years to travel through me   And has
taken   I am an instrument in the shape
of a woman trying to translate pulsations
into images   for the relief of the body
and the reconstruction of the mind.

1968

DIVING INTO THE WRECK

First having read the book of myths,
and loaded the camera,
and checked the edge of the knife-blade,
I put on
the body-armor of black rubber
the absurd flippers
the grave and awkward mask.
I am having to do this
not like Cousteau with his
assiduous team
aboard the sun-flooded schooner
but here alone.

There is a ladder.
The ladder is always there
hanging innocently
close to the side of the schooner.
We know what it is for,
we who have used it.
Otherwise
it's a piece of maritime floss
some sundry equipment.

I go down.
Rung after rung and still
the oxygen immerses me

ADRIENNE RICH

the blue light
the clear atoms
of our human air.
I go down.
My flippers cripple me,
I crawl like an insect down the ladder
and there is no one
to tell me when the ocean
will begin.

First the air is blue and then
it is bluer and then green and then
black I am blacking out and yet
my mask is powerful
it pumps my blood with power
the sea is another story
the sea is not a question of power
I have to learn alone
to turn my body without force
in the deep element.

And now: it is easy to forget
what I came for
among so many who have always
lived here
swaying their crenellated fans
between the reefs
and besides
you breathe differently down here.

I came to explore the wreck.
The words are purposes.
The words are maps.
I came to see the damage that was done
and the treasures that prevail.
I stroke the beam of my lamp
slowly along the flank
of something more permanent
than fish or weed

the thing I came for:
the wreck and not the story of the wreck
the thing itself and not the myth
the drowned face always staring

toward the sun
the evidence of damage
worn by salt and sway into this threadbare beauty
the ribs of the disaster
curving their assertion
among the tentative haunters.

This is the place.
And I am here, the mermaid whose dark hair
streams black, the merman in his armored body
We circle silently
about the wreck
we dive into the hold.
I am she: I am he

whose drowned face sleeps with open eyes
whose breasts still bear the stress
whose silver, copper, vermeil cargo lies
obscurely inside barrels
half-wedged and left to rot
we are the half-destroyed instruments
that once held to a course
the water-eaten log
the fouled compass

We are, I am, you are
by cowardice or courage
the one who find our way
back to this scene
carrying a knife, a camera
a book of myths
in which
our names do not appear.

1972

FROM A SURVIVOR

The pact that we made was the ordinary pact
of men & women in those days

ADRIENNE RICH

I don't know who we thought we were
that our personalities
could resist the failures of the race

Lucky or unlucky, we didn't know
the race had failures of that order
and that we were going to share them

Like everybody else, we thought of ourselves as special

Your body is as vivid to me
as it ever was: even more

since my feeling for it is clearer:
I know what it could and could not do

it is no longer
the body of a god
or anything with power over my life

Next year it would have been 20 years
and you are wastefully dead
who might have made the leap
we talked, too late, of making

which I live now
not as a leap
but a succession of brief, amazing movements

each one making possible the next

1972

AUGUST

Two horses in yellow light
eating windfall apples under a tree

as summer tears apart   milkweeds stagger
and grasses grow more ragged

They say there are ions in the sun
neutralizing magnetic fields on earth

Some way to explain
what this week has been, and the one before it!

If I am flesh sunning on rock
if I am brain burning in fluorescent light

if I am dream like a wire with fire
throbbing along it

if I am death to man
I have to know it

His mind is too simple, I cannot go on
sharing his nightmares

My own are becoming clearer, they open
into prehistory

which looks like a village lit with blood
where all the fathers are crying: *My son is mine!*

1972

RE-FORMING THE CRYSTAL

I am trying to imagine
how it feels to you
to want a woman

trying to hallucinate
desire
centered in a cock
focused like a burning-glass

desire without discrimination:
to want a woman like a fix

Desire: yes: the sudden knowledge, like coming out of 'flu, that the
body is sexual. Walking in the streets with that knowledge. That evening

ADRIENNE RICH

in the plane from Pittsburgh, fantasizing going to meet you. Walking through the airport blazing with energy and joy. But knowing all along that you were not the source of that energy and joy; you were a man, a stranger, a name, a voice on the telephone, a friend; this desire was mine, this energy my energy; it could be used a hundred ways, and going to meet you could be one of them.

Tonight is a different kind of night.
I sit in the car, racing the engine,
calculating the thinness of the ice.
In my head I am already threading the beltways
that rim this city,
all the old roads that used to wander the country
having been lost.

Tonight I understand
my photo on the license is not me,
my
name on the marriage-contract was not mine.
If I remind you of my father's favorite daughter,
look again. The woman
I needed to call my mother
was silenced before I was born.

Tonight if the battery charges I want to take the car out on sheet-ice; I want to understand my fear both of the machine and of the accidents of nature. My desire for you is not trivial; I can compare it with the greatest of those accidents. But the energy it draws on might lead to racing a cold engine, cracking the frozen spiderweb, parachuting into the field of a poem wired with danger, or to a trip through gorges and canyons, into the cratered night of female memory, where delicately and with intense care the chieftainess inscribes upon the ribs of the volcano the name of the one she has chosen.

1973

RAPE

There is a cop who is both prowler and father:
he comes from your block, grew up with your brothers,
had certain ideals.

You hardly know him in his boots and silver badge,
on horseback, one hand touching his gun.

You hardly know him but you have to get to know him:
he has access to machinery that could kill you.
He and his stallion clop like warlords among the trash,
his ideals stand in the air, a frozen cloud
from between his unsmiling lips.

And so, when the time comes, you have to turn to him,
the maniac's sperm still greasing your thighs,
your mind whirling like crazy. You have to confess
to him, you are guilty of the crime
of having been forced.

And you see his blue eyes, the blue eyes of all the family
whom you used to know, grow narrow and glisten,
his hand types out the details
and he wants them all
but the hysteria in your voice pleases him best.

You hardly know him but now he thinks he knows you:
he has taken down your worst moment
on a machine and filed it in a file.
He knows, or thinks he knows, how much you imagined;
he knows, or thinks he knows, what you secretly wanted.

He has access to machinery that could get you put away;
and if, in the sickening light of the precinct,
and if, in the sickening light of the precinct,
your details sound like a portrait of your confessor,
will you swallow, will you deny them, will you lie your way home?

1972

SPLITTINGS

1

My body opens over San Francisco like the day-
light raining down   each pore crying the change of light
I am not with her   I have been waking off and on

ADRIENNE RICH

all night to that pain   not simply absence but
the presence of the past   destructive
to living here and now   Yet if I could instruct
myself, if we could learn to learn from pain
even as it grasps us   if the mind, the mind that lives
in this body could refuse   to let itself be crushed
in that grasp   it would loosen   Pain would have to stand
off from me and listen   its dark breath still on me
but the mind could begin to speak to pain
and pain would have to answer:

                         We are older now
we have met before   these are my hands before your eyes
my figure blotting out   all that is not mine
I am the pain of division   creator of divisions
it is I who blot your lover from you
and not the time-zones nor the miles
It is not separation calls me forth   but I
who am separation   And remember
I have no existence   apart from you

2

I believe I am choosing something new
not to suffer uselessly   yet still to feel
Does the infant memorize the body of the mother
and create her in absence?   or simply cry
primordial loneliness?   does the bed of the stream
once diverted   mourning   remember wetness?

But we, we live so much in these
configurations of the past   I choose
to separate her   from my past we have not shared
I choose not to suffer uselessly
to detect primordial pain as it stalks toward me
flashing its bleak torch in my eyes   blotting out
her particular being   the details of her love
I will not be divided   from her or from myself
by myths of separation
while her mind and body in Manhattan are more with me
than the smell of eucalyptus coolly burning   on these hills

ADRIENNE RICH

3

The world tells me I am its creature
I am raked by eyes   brushed by hands
I want to crawl into her for refuge   lay my head
in the space   between her breast and shoulder
abnegating power for love
as women have done   or hiding
from power in her love   like a man
I refuse these givens   the splitting
between love and action   I am choosing
not to suffer uselessly   and not to use her
I choose to love   this time   for once
with all my intelligence

1974

UPPER BROADWAY

The leafbud straggles forth
toward the frigid light of the airshaft   this is faith
this pale extension of a day
when looking up   you know   something is changing
winter has turned   though the wind is colder
Three streets away   a roof collapses   onto people
who thought they still had time   Time out of mind

I have written so many words
wanting to live inside you
to be of use to you

Now I must write for myself   for this blind
woman scratching the pavement   with her wand of thought
this slippered crone   inching on icy streets
reaching into wire trashbaskets   pulling out
what was thrown away   and infinitely precious

I look at my hands and see   they are still unfinished
I look at the vine and see the leafbud
inching towards life

I look at my face in the glass   and see
a halfborn woman

1975

© Mary Randlett 1980

Theodore Roethke

THE PREMONITION

Walking this field I remember
Days of another summer.
Oh that was long ago! I kept
Close to the heels of my father,
Matching his stride with half-steps
Until we came to a river.
He dipped his hand in the shallow:
Water ran over and under
Hair on a narrow wrist bone;
His image kept following after,—
Flashed with the sun in the ripple.
But when he stood up, that face
Was lost in a maze of water.

CUTTINGS

(later)

This urge, wrestle, resurrection of dry sticks,
Cut stems struggling to put down feet,
What saint strained so much,
Rose on such lopped limbs to a new life?

I can hear, underground, that sucking and sobbing,
In my veins, in my bones I feel it,—
The small waters seeping upward,
The tight grains parting at last.
When sprouts break out,
Slippery as fish,
I quail, lean to beginnings, sheath-wet.

FORCING HOUSE

Vines tougher than wrists
And rubbery shoots,
Scums, mildews, smuts along stems,
Great cannas or delicate cyclamen tips,—
All pulse with the knocking pipes
That drip and sweat,
Sweat and drip,
Swelling the roots with steam and stench,
Shooting up lime and dung and ground bones,—
Fifty summers in motion at once,
As the live heat billows from pipes and pots.

MY PAPA'S WALTZ

The whiskey on your breath
Could make a small boy dizzy;
But I hung on like death:
Such waltzing was not easy.

We romped until the pans
Slid from the kitchen shelf;
My mother's countenance
Could not unfrown itself.

The hand that held my wrist
Was battered on one knuckle;
At every step you missed
My right ear scraped a buckle.

You beat time on my head
With a palm caked hard by dirt,
Then waltzed me off to bed
Still clinging to your shirt.

THE LOST SON

1   The Flight

At Woodlawn I heard the dead cry:
I was lulled by the slamming of iron,
A slow drip over stones,

Toads brooding in wells.
All the leaves stuck out their tongues;
I shook the softening chalk of my bones,
Saying,
Snail, snail, glister me forward,
Bird, soft-sigh me home,
Worm, be with me.
This is my hard time.

Fished in an old wound,
The soft pond of repose;
Nothing nibbled my line,
Not even the minnows came.

Sat in an empty house
Watching shadows crawl,
Scratching.
There was one fly.

Voice, come out of the silence.
Say something.
Appear in the form of a spider
Or a moth beating the curtain.

Tell me:
Which is the way I take;
Out of what door do I go,
Where and to whom?

  Dark hollows said, lee to the wind,
  The moon said, back of an eel,
  The salt said, look by the sea,
  Your tears are not enough praise,
  You will find no comfort here,
  In the kingdom of bang and blab.

  Running lightly over spongy ground,
  Past the pasture of flat stones,
  The three elms,
  The sheep strewn on a field,
  Over a rickety bridge
  Toward the quick-water, wrinkling and rippling.

  Hunting along the river,
  Down among the rubbish, the bug-riddled foliage,

By the muddy pond-edge, by the bog-holes,
By the shrunken lake, hunting, in the heat of summer.

The shape of a rat?
      It's bigger than that.
      It's less than a leg
      And more than a nose,
      Just under the water
      It usually goes.

Is it soft like a mouse?
Can it wrinkle its nose?
Could it come in the house
On the tips of its toes?

      Take the skin of a cat
      And the back of an eel,
      Then roll them in grease,—
      That's the way it would feel.

      It's sleek as an otter
      With wide webby toes
      Just under the water
      It usually goes.

2   *The Pit*

Where do the roots go?
    Look down under the leaves.
Who put the moss there?
    These stones have been here too long.
Who stunned the dirt into noise?
    Ask the mole, he knows.
I feel the slime of a wet nest.
    Beware Mother Mildew.
Nibble again, fish nerves.

3   *The Gibber*

At the wood's mouth,
By the cave's door,
I listened to something
I had heard before.

THEODORE ROETHKE

Dogs of the groin
Barked and howled,
The sun was against me,
The moon would not have me.

The weeds whined,
The snakes cried,
The cows and briars
Said to me: Die.

What a small song. What slow clouds. What dark water.
Hath the rain a father? All the caves are ice. Only the snow's here.
I'm cold. I'm cold all over. Rub me in father and mother.
Fear was my father, Father Fear.
His look drained the stones.

What gliding shape
Beckoning through halls,
Stood poised on the stair,
Fell dreamily down?

From the mouths of jugs
Perched on many shelves,
I saw substance flowing
That cold morning.

Like a slither of eels
That watery cheek
As my own tongue kissed
My lips awake.

Is this the storm's heart? The ground is unstilling itself.
My veins are running nowhere. Do the bones cast out their fire?
Is the seed leaving the old bed? These buds are live as birds.
Where, where are the tears of the world?
Let the kisses resound, flat like a butcher's palm;
Let the gestures freeze; our doom is already decided.
All the windows are burning! What's left of my life?
I want the old rage, the lash of primordial milk!
Goodbye, goodbye, old stones, the time-order is going,
I have married my hands to perpetual agitation,
I run, I run to the whistle of money.

Money money money
Water water water

How cool the grass is.
Has the bird left?
The stalk still sways.
Has the worm a shadow?
What do the clouds say?

These sweeps of light undo me.
Look, look, the ditch is running white!
I've more veins than a tree!
Kiss me, ashes, I'm falling through a dark swirl.

4   *The Return*

The way to the boiler was dark,
Dark all the way,
Over slippery cinders
Through the long greenhouse.

The roses kept breathing in the dark.
They had many mouths to breathe with.
My knees made little winds underneath
Where the weeds slept.

There was always a single light
Swinging by the fire-pit,
Where the fireman pulled out roses,
The big roses, the big bloody clinkers.

Once I stayed all night.
The light in the morning came slowly over the white
Snow.
There were many kinds of cool
Air.
Then came steam.

Pipe-knock.

Scurry of warm over small plants.
Ordnung! ordnung!
Papa is coming!

A fine haze moved off the leaves;
Frost melted on far panes;

The rose, the chrysanthemum turned toward the light.
Even the hushed forms, the bent yellowy weeds
Moved in a slow up-sway.

5   *"It was beginning winter"*

It was beginning winter,
An in-between time,
The landscape still partly brown:
The bones of weeds kept swinging in the wind,
Above the blue snow.

It was beginning winter,
The light moved slowly over the frozen field,
Over the dry seed-crowns,
The beautiful surviving bones
Swinging in the wind.

Light traveled over the wide field;
Stayed.
The weeds stopped swinging.
The mind moved, not alone,
Through the clear air, in the silence.

Was it light?
Was it light within?
Was it light within light?
Stillness becoming alive,
Yet still?

A lively understandable spirit
Once entertained you.
It will come again.
Be still.
Wait.

ELEGY FOR JANE

My Student, Thrown by a Horse

I remember the neckcurls, limp and damp as tendrils;
And her quick look, a sidelong pickerel smile;
And how, once startled into talk, the light syllables leaped for her,

And she balanced in the delight of her thought,
A wren, happy, tail into the wind,
Her song trembling the twigs and small branches.
The shade sang with her;
The leaves, their whispers turned to kissing;
And the mold sang in the bleached valleys under the rose.

Oh, when she was sad, she cast herself down into such a pure depth,
Even a father could not find her:
Scraping her cheek against straw;
Stirring the clearest water.

My sparrow, you are not here,
Waiting like a fern, making a spiny shadow.
The sides of wet stones cannot console me,
Nor the moss, wound with the last light.

If only I could nudge you from this sleep,
My maimed darling, my skittery pigeon.
Over this damp grave I speak the words of my love:
I, with no rights in this matter,
Neither father nor lover.

THE WAKING

I wake to sleep, and take my waking slow.
I feel my fate in what I cannot fear.
I learn by going where I have to go.

We think by feeling. What is there to know?
I hear my being dance from ear to ear.
I wake to sleep, and take my waking slow.

Of those so close beside me, which are you?
God bless the Ground! I shall walk softly there,
And learn by going where I have to go.

Light takes the Tree; but who can tell us how?
The lowly worm climbs up a winding stair;
I wake to sleep, and take my waking slow.

Great Nature has another thing to do
To you and me; so take the lively air,
And, lovely, learn by going where to go.

This shaking keeps me steady. I should know.
What falls away is always. And is near.
I wake to sleep, and take my waking slow.
I learn by going where I have to go.

I KNEW A WOMAN

I knew a woman, lovely in her bones,
When small birds sighed, she would sigh back at them;
Ah, when she moved, she moved more ways than one:
The shapes a bright container can contain!
Of her choice virtues only gods should speak,
Or English poets who grew up on Greek
(I'd have them sing in chorus, cheek to cheek).

How well her wishes went! She stroked my chin,
She taught me Turn, and Counter-turn, and Stand;
She taught me Touch, that undulant white skin;
I nibbled meekly from her proffered hand;
She was the sickle; I, poor I, the rake,
Coming behind her for her pretty sake
(But what prodigious mowing we did make).

Love likes a gander, and adores a goose:
Her full lips pursed, the errant note to seize;
She played it quick, she played it light and loose;
My eyes, they dazzled at her flowing knees;
Her several parts could keep a pure repose,
Or one hip quiver with a mobile nose
(She moved in circles, and those circles moved).

Let seed be grass, and grass turn into hay:
I'm martyr to a motion not my own;
What's freedom for? To know eternity.
I swear she cast a shadow white as stone.
But who would count eternity in days?
These old bones live to learn her wanton ways:
(I measure time by how a body sways).

THEODORE ROETHKE

MEDITATION AT OYSTER RIVER

1

Over the low, barnacled, elephant-colored rocks,
Come the first tide-ripples, moving, almost without sound, toward me,
Running along the narrow furrows of the shore, the rows of dead clam
    shells;
Then a runnel behind me, creeping closer,
Alive with tiny striped fish, and young crabs climbing in and out of the
    water.

No sound from the bay. No violence.
Even the gulls quiet on the far rocks,
Silent, in the deepening light,
Their cat-mewing over,
Their child-whimpering.

At last one long undulant ripple,
Blue-black from where I am sitting,
Makes almost a wave over a barrier of small stones,
Slapping lightly against a sunken log.
I dabble my toes in the brackish foam sliding forward,
Then retire to a rock higher up on the cliff-side.
The wind slackens, light as a moth fanning a stone:
A twilight wind, light as a child's breath
Turning not a leaf, not a ripple.
The dew revives on the beach-grass;
The salt-soaked wood of a fire crackles;
A fish raven turns on its perch (a dead tree in the rivermouth),
Its wings catching a last glint of the reflected sunlight.

2

The self persists like a dying star,
In sleep, afraid. Death's face rises afresh,
Among the shy beasts, the deer at the salt-lick,
The doe with its sloped shoulders loping across the highway,
The young snake, poised in green leaves, waiting for its fly,
The hummingbird, whirring from quince-blossom to morning-glory—
With these I would be.
And with water: the waves coming forward, without cessation,

The waves, altered by sand-bars, beds of kelp, miscellaneous driftwood,
Topped by cross-winds, tugged at by sinuous undercurrents
The tide rustling in, sliding between the ridges of stone,
The tongues of water, creeping in, quietly.

3

In this hour,
In this first heaven of knowing,
The flesh takes on the pure poise of the spirit,
Acquires, for a time, the sandpiper's insouciance,
The hummingbird's surety, the kingfisher's cunning—
I shift on my rock, and I think:
Of the first trembling of a Michigan brook in April,
Over a lip of stone, the tiny rivulet;
And that wrist-thick cascade tumbling from a cleft rock,
Its spray holding a double rain-bow in early morning,
Small enough to be taken in, embraced, by two arms,—
Or the Tittebawasee, in the time between winter and spring,
When the ice melts along the edges in early afternoon.
And the midchannel begins cracking and heaving from the pressure
    beneath,
The ice piling high against the iron-bound spiles,
Gleaming, freezing hard again, creaking at midnight—
And I long for the blast of dynamite,
The sudden sucking roar as the culvert loosens its debris of branches and
    sticks,
Welter of tin cans, pails, old bird nests, a child's shoe riding a log,
As the piled ice breaks away from the battered spiles,
And the whole river begins to move forward, its bridges shaking.

4

Now, in this waning of light,
I rock with the motion of morning;
In the cradle of all that is,
I'm lulled into half-sleep
By the lapping of water,
Cries of the sandpiper.
Water's my will, and my way,
And the spirit runs, intermittently,
In and out of the small waves,

Runs with the intrepid shorebirds—
How graceful the small before danger!

In the first of the moon,
All's a scattering,
A shining.

IN A DARK TIME

In a dark time, the eye begins to see,
I meet my shadow in the deepening shade;
I hear my echo in the echoing wood—
A lord of nature weeping to a tree.
I live between the heron and the wren,
Beasts of the hill and serpents of the den.

What's madness but nobility of soul
At odds with circumstance? The day's on fire!
I know the purity of pure despair,
My shadow pinned against a sweating wall.
That place among the rocks—is it a cave,
Or winding path? The edge is what I have.

A steady storm of correspondences!
A night flowing with birds, a ragged moon,
And in broad day the midnight come again!
A man goes far to find out what he is—
Death of the self in a long, tearless night,
All natural shapes blazing unnatural light.

Dark, dark my light, and darker my desire.
My soul, like some heat-maddened summer fly,
Keeps buzzing at the sill. Which I is I?
A fallen man, I climb out of my fear.
The mind enters itself, and God the mind,
And one is One, free in the tearing wind.

THEODORE ROETHKE

IN EVENING AIR

1

A dark theme keeps me here,
Though summer blazes in the vireo's eye.
Who would be half possessed
By his own nakedness?
Waking's my care—
I'll make a broken music, or I'll die.

2

Ye littles, lie more close!
Make me, O Lord, a last, a simple thing
Time cannot overwhelm.
Once I transcended time:
A bud broke to a rose,
And I rose from a last diminishing.

3

I look down the far light
And I behold the dark side of a tree
Far down a billowing plain,
And when I look again,
It's lost upon the night—
Night I embrace, a dear proximity.

4

I stand by a low fire
Counting the wisps of flame, and I watch how
Light shifts upon the wall.
I bid stillness be still.
I see, in evening air,
How slowly dark comes down on what we do.

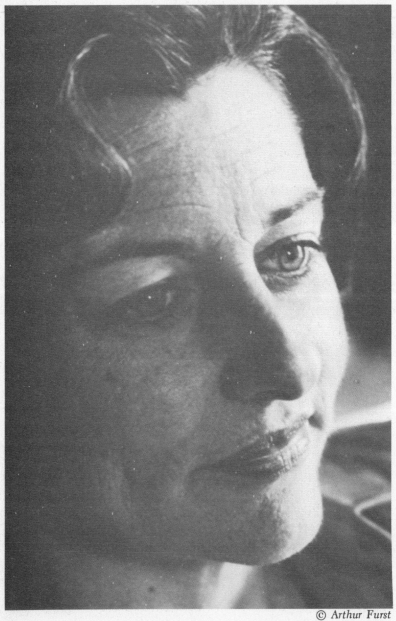

© *Arthur Furst*

Anne Sexton

HER KIND

I have gone out, a possessed witch,
haunting the black air, braver at night;
dreaming evil, I have done my hitch
over the plain houses, light by light:
lonely thing, twelve-fingered, out of mind.
A woman like that is not a woman, quite.
I have been her kind.

I have found the warm caves in the woods,
filled them with skillets, carvings, shelves,
closets, silks, innumerable goods;
fixed the suppers for the worms and the elves:
whining, rearranging the disaligned.
A woman like that is misunderstood.
I have been her kind.

I have ridden in your cart, driver,
waved my nude arms at villages going by,
learning the last bright routes, survivor
where your flames still bite my thigh
and my ribs crack where your wheels wind.
A woman like that is not ashamed to die.
I have been her kind.

WITH MERCY FOR THE GREEDY

*For my friend, Ruth, who urges me to make an
appointment for the Sacrament of Confession*

Concerning your letter in which you ask
me to call a priest and in which you ask
me to wear The Cross that you enclose;
your own cross,
your dog-bitten cross,

no larger than a thumb,
small and wooden, no thorns, this rose—

I pray to its shadow,
that gray place
where it lies on your letter . . . deep, deep.
I detest my sins and I try to believe
in The Cross. I touch its tender hips, its dark jawed face,
its solid neck, its brown sleep.

True. There is
a beautiful Jesus.
He is frozen to his bones like a chunk of beef.
How desperately he wanted to pull his arms in!
How desperately I touch his vertical and horizontal axes!
But I can't. Need is not quite belief.

All morning long
I have worn
your cross, hung with package string around my throat.
It tapped me lightly as a child's heart might,
tapping secondhand, softly waiting to be born.
Ruth, I cherish the letter you wrote.

My friend, my friend, I was born
doing reference work in sin, and born
confessing it. This is what poems are:
with mercy
for the greedy,
they are the tongue's wrangle,
the world's pottage, the rat's star.

THE ABORTION

Somebody who should have been born
is gone.

Just as the earth puckered its mouth,
each bud puffing out from its knot,
I changed my shoes, and then drove south.

ANNE SEXTON

Up past the Blue Mountains, where
Pennsylvania humps on endlessly,
wearing, like a crayoned cat, its green hair,

its roads sunken in like a gray washboard;
where, in truth, the ground cracks evilly,
a dark socket from which the coal has poured,

Somebody who should have been born
is gone.

the grass as bristly and stout as chives,
and me wondering when the ground would break,
and me wondering how anything fragile survives;

up in Pennsylvania, I met a little man,
not Rumpelstiltskin, at all, at all . . .
he took the fullness that love began.

Returning north, even the sky grew thin
like a high window looking nowhere.
The road was as flat as a sheet of tin.

Somebody who should have been born
is gone.

Yes, woman, such logic will lead
to loss without death. Or say what you meant,
you coward . . . this baby that I bleed.

MAN AND WIFE

To speke of wo
    that is in mariage . . .

      We are not lovers.
      We do not even know each other.
      We look alike
      but we have nothing to say.
      We are like pigeons . . .

that pair who came to the suburbs
by mistake,
forsaking Boston where they bumped
their small heads against a blind wall,
having worn out the fruit stalls in the North End,
the amethyst windows of Louisburg Square,
the seats on the Common
And the traffic that kept stamping
and stamping.

Now there is green rain for everyone
as common as eyewash.
Now they are together
like strangers in a two-seater outhouse,
eating and squatting together.
They have teeth and knees
but they do not speak.
A soldier is forced to stay with a soldier
because they share the same dirt
and the same blows.

They are exiles
soiled by the same sweat and the drunkard's dream.
As it is they can only hang on,
their red claws wound like bracelets
around the same limb.
Even their song is not a sure thing.
It is not a language;
it is a kind of breathing.
They are two asthmatics
whose breath sobs in and out
through a small fuzzy pipe.

Like them
we neither talk nor clear our throats.
Oh darling,
we gasp in unison beside our window pane,
drunk on the drunkard's dream.
Like them
we can only hang on.

But they would pierce our heart
if they could only fly the distance.

ANNE SEXTON

IN CELEBRATION OF MY UTERUS

Everyone in me is a bird.
I am beating all my wings.
They wanted to cut you out
but they will not.
They said you were immeasurably empty
but you are not.
They said you were sick unto dying
but they were wrong.
You are singing like a school girl.
You are not torn.

Sweet weight,
in celebration of the woman I am
and of the soul of the woman I am
and of the central creature and its delight
I sing for you. I dare to live.

Hello, spirit. Hello, cup.
Fasten, cover. Cover that does contain.
Hello to the soil of the fields.
Welcome, roots.

Each cell has a life.
There is enough here to please a nation.
It is enough that the populace own these goods.
Any person, any commonwealth would say of it,
"It is good this year that we may plant again
and think forward to a harvest.
A blight had been forecast and has been cast out."
Many women are singing together of this:
one is in a shoe factory cursing the machine,
one is at the aquarium tending a seal,
one is dull at the wheel of her Ford,
one is at the toll gate collecting,
one is tying the cord of a calf in Arizona,
one is straddling a cello in Russia,
one is shifting pots on the stove in Egypt,
one is painting her bedroom walls moon color,
one is dying but remembering a breakfast,
one is stretching on her mat in Thailand,
one is wiping the ass of her child,

one is staring out the window of a train
in the middle of Wyoming and one is
anywhere and some are everywhere and all
seem to be singing, although some can not
sing a note.

Sweet weight,
in celebration of the woman I am
let me carry a ten-foot scarf,
let me drum for the nineteen-year-olds,
let me carry bowls for the offering
(if that is my part).
Let me study the cardiovascular tissue,
let me examine the angular distance of meteors,
let me suck on the stems of flowers
(if that is my part).
Let me make certain tribal figures
(if that is my part).
For this thing the body needs
let me sing
for the supper,
for the kissing,
for the correct
yes.

US

I was wrapped in black
fur and white fur and
you undid me and then
you placed me in gold light
and then you crowned me,
while snow fell outside
the door in diagonal darts.
While a ten-inch snow
came down like stars
in small calcium fragments,
we were in our own bodies
(that room that will bury us)

and you were in my body
(that room that will outlive us)
and at first I rubbed your
feet dry with a towel
because I was your slave
and then you called me princess.
Princess!

Oh then
I stood up in my gold skin
and I beat down the psalms
and I beat down the clothes
and you undid the bridle
and you undid the reins
and I undid the buttons,
the bones, the confusions,
the New England postcards,
the January ten o'clock night,
and we rose up like wheat,
acre after acre of gold,
and we harvested,
we harvested.

GODS

Mrs. Sexton went out looking for the gods.
She began looking in the sky—
expecting a large white angel with a blue crotch.

No one.

She looked next in all the learned books
and the print spat back at her.

No one.

She made a pilgrimage to the great poet
and he belched in her face.

No one.

She prayed in all the churches of the world
and learned a great deal about culture.

No one.

She went to the Atlantic, the Pacific, for surely God . . .

No one.

She went to the Buddha, the Brahma, the Pyramids
and found immense postcards.

No one.

Then she journeyed back to her own house
and the gods of the world were shut in the lavatory.

At last!
she cried out,
and locked the door

THE FURY OF COCKS

There they are
drooping over the breakfast plates,
angel-like,
folding in their sad wing,
animal sad,
and only the night before
there they were
playing the banjo.
Once more the day's light comes
with its immense sun,
its mother trucks,
its engines of amputation.
Whereas last night
the cock knew its way home,
as stiff as a hammer,

battering in with all
its awful power.
That theater.
Today it is tender,
a small bird,
as soft as a baby's hand.
She is the house.
He is the steeple.
When they fuck they are God.
When they break away they are God.
When they snore they are God.
In the morning they butter the toast.
They don't say much.
They are still God.
All the cocks of the world are God,
blooming, blooming, blooming
into the sweet blood of woman.

from O YE TONGUES

Second Psalm

Let Noah build an ark out of the old lady's shoe and fill it with the creatures of the Lord.

Let the ark of salvation have many windows so the creatures of the Lord will marry mouthfuls of oxygen.

Let the ark of salvation do homage to the Lord and notch his belt repeatedly.

Let Anne and Christopher kneel with a buzzard whose mouth will bite her toe so that she may offer it up.

Let Anne and Christopher appear with two robins whose worms are sweet and pink as lipstick.

Let them present a bee, cupped in their palms, zinging the electricity of the Lord out into little yellow Z's.

Let them give praise with a bull whose horns are yellow with history.

Praise the Lord with an ox who grows sweet in heaven and ties the hair ribbons of little girls.

Humble themselves with the fly buzzing like the mother of the engine.

Serve with the ape who tore down the Empire State Building and won the maid.

Dedicate an ant who will crawl toward the Lord like the print of this page.

Bless with a sable who bleeds ink across the dresses of ladies of the court.

Bless with a rabbit who comes with a whole sackful of sperm.

Bless with the locust who dances a curtain over the sky and makes the field blind.

Bless with the kingfish who melts down dimes into slim silver beside Frisco.

Rejoice with the day lily for it is born for a day to live by the mailbox and glorify the roadside.

Rejoice with the olive for it gives forth a faithful oil and eaten alone it will grease the mouth and bury the teeth.

Rejoice with a French angelfish which floats by like a jewel glowing like a blue iceberg in the Caribbean.

Rejoice with a cottonbush which grows stars and seeds to clothe the multitudes of America.

Rejoice with the sea horse who lives in amusement parks and poems.

Let Anne and Christopher rejoice with the worm who moves into the light like a doll's penis.

ANNE SEXTON

ROWING

A story, a story!
(Let it go. Let it come.)
I was stamped out like a Plymouth fender
into this world.
First came the crib
with its glacial bars.
Then dolls
and the devotion to their plastic mouths.
Then there was school,
the little straight rows of chairs,
blotting my name over and over,
but undersea all the time,
a stranger whose elbows wouldn't work.
Then there was life
with its cruel houses
and people who seldom touched—
though touch is all—
but I grew,
like a pig in a trenchcoat I grew,
and then there were many strange apparitions,
the nagging rain, the sun turning into poison
and all of that, saws working through my heart,
but I grew, I grew,
and God was there like an island I had not rowed to,
still ignorant of Him, my arms and my legs worked,
and I grew, I grew,
I wore rubies and bought tomatoes
and now, in my middle age,
about nineteen in the head I'd say,
I am rowing, I am rowing
though the oarlocks stick and are rusty
and the sea blinks and rolls
like a worried eyeball,
but I am rowing, I am rowing,
though the wind pushes me back
and I know that that island will not be perfect,

it will have the flaws of life,
the absurdities of the dinner table,
but there will be a door
and I will open it
and I will get rid of the rat inside of me,
the gnawing pestilential rat.
God will take it with his two hands
and embrace it.

As the African says:
This is my tale which I have told,
if it be sweet, if it be not sweet,
take somewhere else and let some return to me.
This story ends with me still rowing.

TWO HANDS

From the sea came a hand,
ignorant as a penny,
troubled with the salt of its mother,
mute with the silence of the fishes,
quick with the altars of the tides,
and God reached out of His mouth
and called it man.
Up came the other hand
and God called it woman.
The hands applauded.
And this was no sin.
It was as it was meant to be.

I see them roaming the streets:
Levi complaining about his mattress,
Sarah studying a beetle,
Mandrake holding his coffee mug,
Sally playing the drum at a football game,
John closing the eyes of the dying woman,
and some who are in prison,
even the prison of their bodies,
as Christ was prisoned in His body
until the triumph came.

ANNE SEXTON

Unwind, hands,
you angel webs,
unwind like the coil of a jumping jack,
cup together and let yourselves fill up with sun
and applaud, world,
applaud.

Louis Simpson

TO THE WESTERN WORLD

A siren sang, and Europe turned away
From the high castle and the shepherd's crook.
Three caravels went sailing to Cathay
On the strange ocean, and the captains shook
Their banners out across the Mexique Bay.

And in our early days we did the same.
Remembering our fathers in their wreck
We crossed the sea from Palos where they came
And saw, enormous to the little deck,
A shore in silence waiting for a name.

The treasures of Cathay were never found.
In this America, this wilderness
Where the axe echoes with a lonely sound,
The generations labor to possess
And grave by grave we civilize the ground.

HOT NIGHT ON WATER STREET

A hot midsummer night on Water Street—
The boys in jeans were combing their blond hair,
Watching the girls go by on tired feet;
And an old woman with a witch's stare
Cried "Praise the Lord!" She vanished on a bus
With hissing air brakes, like an incubus.

Three hardware stores, a barbershop, a bar,
A movie playing Westerns—where I went
To see a dream of horses called *The Star.* . . .
Some day, when this uncertain continent
Is marble, and men ask what was the good
We lived by, dust may whisper "Hollywood."

Then back along the river bank on foot
By moonlight. . . . On the West Virginia side
An owlish train began to huff and hoot;
It seemed to know of something that had died.
I didn't linger—sometimes when I travel
I think I'm being followed by the Devil.

At the newsstand in the lobby, a cigar
Was talkative: "Since I've been in this town
I've seen one likely woman, and a car
As she was crossing Main Street knocked her down."
I was a stranger here myself, I said,
And bought the *New York Times*, and went to bed.

THE SILENT GENERATION

When Hitler was the Devil
He did as he had sworn
With such enthusiasm
That even, *donnerwetter*,
The Germans say, "Far better
Had he been never born!"

It was my generation
That put the Devil down
With great enthusiasm.
But now our occupation
Is gone. Our education
Is wasted on the town.

We lack enthusiasm.
Life seems a mystery;
It's like the play a lady
Told me about: "It's not . . .
It doesn't *have* a plot,"
She said, "it's history."

LOUIS SIMPSON

IN THE SUBURBS

There's no way out.
You were born to waste your life.
You were born to this middleclass life

As others before you
Were born to walk in procession
To the temple, singing.

LOVE, MY MACHINE

Love, my machine,
We rise by this escape,
We travel on the shocks we make.

For every man and woman
Is an immortal spirit
Trapped and dazed on a star shoot.

Tokyo, come in!
Yuzuru Karagiri, do you read me?
San Francisco, darkest of cities, do you read me?

Here is eternal space,
Here is eternal solitude.
Is it any different with you on earth?

There are so many here!
Here's Gandhi, here's Jesus,
Moses, and all the other practical people.

By the light of the stars
This night is serious.
I am going into the night to find a world of my own.

LOUIS SIMPSON

WALT WHITMAN AT BEAR MOUNTAIN

"... *life which does not give the preference to any other life, of any previous*
period, which therefore prefers its own existence ..."

Ortega Y Gasset

Neither on horseback nor seated,
But like himself, squarely on two feet,
The poet of death and lilacs
Loafs by the footpath. Even the bronze looks alive
Where it is folded like cloth. And he seems friendly.

"Where is the Mississippi panorama
And the girl who played the piano?
Where are you, Walt?
The Open Road goes to the used-car lot.

"Where is the nation you promised?
These houses built of wood sustain
Colossal snows,
And the light above the street is sick to death.

"As for the people—see how they neglect you!
Only a poet pauses to read the inscription."

"I am here," he answered.
"It seems you have found me out.
Yet, did I not warn you that it was Myself
I advertised? Were my words not sufficiently plain?

"I gave no prescriptions,
And those who have taken my moods for prophecies
Mistake the matter."
Then, vastly amused—"Why do you reproach me?
I freely confess I am wholly disreputable.
Yet I am happy, because you have found me out."

A crocodile in wrinkled metal loafing ...

Then all the realtors,
Pickpockets, salesmen, and the actors performing
Official scenarios,
Turned a deaf ear, for they had contracted
American dreams.

But the man who keeps a store on a lonely road,
And the housewife who knows she's dumb,
And the earth, are relieved.

All that grave weight of America
Cancelled! Like Greece and Rome.
The future in ruins!
The castles, the prisons, the cathedrals
Unbuilding, and roses
Blossoming from the stones that are not there . . .

The clouds are lifting from the high Sierras,
The Bay mists clearing.
And the angel in the gate, the flowering plum,
Dances like Italy, imagining red.

AFTER MIDNIGHT

The dark streets are deserted,
With only a drugstore glowing
Softly, like a sleeping body;

With one white, naked bulb
In the back, that shines
On suicides and abortions.

Who lives in these dark houses?
I am suddenly aware
I might live here myself.

The garage man returns
And puts the change in my hand,
Counting the singles carefully.

LUMINOUS NIGHT

I love the dark race of poets,
And yet there is also happiness.
Happiness . . .

If I can stand it, I can stand anything.
Luminous night, let fall your pearls!
Wind, toss the sodden boughs!

Then let the birch trees shine
Like crystal. Light the boughs!
We can live here, Cristina,

We can live here,
In this house, among these trees,
This world so many have left.

AMERICAN DREAMS

In dreams my life came toward me,
my loves that were slender as gazelles.
But America also dreams. . . .
Dream, you are flying over Russia,
dream, you are falling in Asia.

As I look down the street
on a typical sunny day in California
it is my house that is burning
and my dear ones that lie in the gutter
as the American army enters.

Every day I wake far away
from my life, in a foreign country.
These people are speaking a strange language.
It is strange to me
and strange, I think, even to themselves.

LOUIS SIMPSON

PORT JEFFERSON

My whole life coming to this place,
and understanding it better
maybe for having been born
offshore, and at an early age
left to my own support . . .

I have come where sea and wind,
wave and leaf, are one sighing,
where the house strains at an anchor
and the salt-rose clings and clambers
on the humorous grave.

This is the place, Camerado,
that hides the sea-bird's nest.
Listening to the distant voices
in summer, a murmur of the sea,
I seem to remember everything.

THE SILENT PIANO

We have lived like civilized people.
O ruins, traditions!

And we have seen the barbarians,
breakers of sculpture and glass.

And now we talk of 'the inner life',
and I ask myself, where is it?

Not here, in these streets and houses,
so I think it must be found

in indolence, pure indolence,
an ocean of darkness,

in silence, an arm of the moon,
a hand that enters slowly.

*

I am reminded of a story
Camus tells, of a man in prison camp.

He had carved a piano keyboard
with a nail on a piece of wood.

And sat there playing the piano.
This music was made entirely of silence.

SACRED OBJECTS

I am taking part in a great experiment—
whether writers can live peacefully in the suburbs
and not be bored to death.

As Whitman said, an American muse
installed amid the kitchen ware.
And we have wonderful household appliances . . .
now tell me about the poets.

Where are your children, Lucina?
Since Eliot died and Pound
has become . . . an authority,
chef d'école au lieu d'être tout de go,

I have been listening to the whispers
of U.S. Steel and Anaconda:
'In a little while it will stiffen . . .
blown into the road,

drifting with the foam of chemicals.'

2

The light that shines through the *Leaves*
is clear: 'to form individuals.'

A swamp where the seabirds brood.
When the psyche is still and the soul does nothing,
a Sound, with shining tidal pools and channels.

And the kingdom is within you . . .
the hills and all the streams
running west to the Mississippi.
There the roads are lined with timothy
and the clouds are tangled with the haystacks.

Your loves are a line of birch trees.
When the wind flattens the grass, it
shines, and a butterfly
writes dark lines on the air.

There are your sacred objects,
the wings and gazing eyes
of the life you really have.

3

Where then shall we meet?

                         Where you left me.

At the drive-in restaurant . . .
the fields on either side covered with stubble,
an odor of gasoline and burning asphalt,
glare on tinted glass, chrome-plated hubcaps and bumpers.

I came out, wiping my hands
on my apron, to take your orders.
Thin hands, streaked with mustard,
give us a hot-dog,
give us a Pepsi-Cola.

Listening to the monotonous grasshoppers
for years I have concentrated on the moment.

And at night when the passing headlights hurl
shadows flitting across the wall,
I sit in a window, combing my hair
day in day out.

THE MANNEQUINS

Whenever I passed Saks Fifth Avenue
I would stop at a certain window.
They didn't acknowledge my presence—they just stared.

He was sitting in his favorite chair,
smoking a pipe and reading a best seller.
She was standing in front of an easel.

She was finding it easy to paint
by filling in the numbered spaces
with colors. $5.98.

The artificial logs glowed in the fireplace.
Soon it would be Christmas. Santa would come down the chimney,
and they'd give each other presents.

She would give him skis and cuff links.
He would give her a watch with its works exposed,
and a fur coat, and perfume.

Though I knew it was "neurasthenic"
I couldn't help listening to the words
that they said without moving their lips.

LOUIS SIMPSON

THE STREET

Here comes the subway grating fisher
letting down his line through the sidewalk.

Yesterday there was the running man
who sobbed and wept as he ran.

Today there is the subway grating fisher.
Standing as if in thought . . .

He fishes a while. Then winds up the line
and continues to walk, looking down.

© Arthur Furst

W. D. Snodgrass

APRIL INVENTORY

The green catalpa tree has turned
All white; the cherry blooms once more.
In one whole year I haven't learned
A blessed thing they pay you for.
The blossoms snow down in my hair;
The trees and I will soon be bare.

The trees have more than I to spare.
The sleek, expensive girls I teach,
Younger and pinker every year,
Bloom gradually out of reach.
The pear tree lets its petals drop
Like dandruff on a tabletop.

The girls have grown so young by now
I have to nudge myself to stare.
This year they smile and mind me how
My teeth are falling with my hair.
In thirty years I may not get
Younger, shrewder, or out of debt.

The tenth time, just a year ago,
I made myself a little list
Of all the things I'd ought to know,
Then told my parents, analyst,
And everyone who's trusted me
I'd be substantial, presently.

I haven't read one book about
A book or memorized one plot.
Or found a mind I did not doubt.
I learned one date. And then forgot.
And one by one the solid scholars
Get the degrees, the jobs, the dollars.

And smile above their starchy collars.
I taught my classes Whitehead's notions;
One lovely girl, a song of Mahler's.
Lacking a source-book or promotions,
I showed one child the colors of
A luna moth and how to love.

I taught myself to name my name,
To bark back, loosen love and crying;
To ease my woman so she came,
To ease an old man who was dying.
I have not learned how often I
Can win, can love, but choose to die.

I have not learned there is a lie
Love shall be blonder, slimmer, younger;
That my equivocating eye
Loves only by my body's hunger;
That I have forces, true to feel,
Or that the lovely world is real.

While scholars speak authority
And wear their ulcers on their sleeves,
My eyes in spectacles shall see
These trees procure and spend their leaves.
There is a value underneath
The gold and silver in my teeth.

Though trees turn bare and girls turn wives,
We shall afford our costly seasons;
There is a gentleness survives
That will outspeak and has its reasons.
There is a loveliness exists,
Preserves us, not for specialists.

W. D. SNODGRASS

HEART'S NEEDLE

For Cynthia

" 'Your father is dead.' 'That grieves me,' said he. 'Your mother is dead,' said the lad. 'Now all pity for me is at an end,' said he. 'Your brother is dead,' said Loingsechan. 'I am sorely wounded by that,' said Suibne. 'Your daughter is dead,' said Loingsechan. 'And an only daughter is the needle of the heart,' said Suibne. 'Dead is your son who used to call you "Father," ' said Loingsechan. 'Indeed,' said he, 'that is the drop that brings a man to the ground.' "

From an old Irish story, The Frenzy of Suibne,
As translated by Myles Dillon

1

Child of my winter, born
When the new fallen soldiers froze
In Asia's steep ravines and fouled the snows,
When I was torn

By love I could not still,
By fear that silenced my cramped mind
To that cold war where, lost, I could not find
My peace in my will,

All those days we could keep
Your mind a landscape of new snow
Where the chilled tenant-farmer finds, below,
His fields asleep

In their smooth covering, white
As quilts to warm the resting bed
Of birth or pain, spotless as paper spread
For me to write,

And thinks: Here lies my land
Unmarked by agony, the lean foot
Of the weasel tracking, the thick trapper's boot;
And I have planned

My chances to restrain
The torments of demented summer or
Increase the deepening harvest here before
It snows again.

2

Late April and you are three; today
   We dug your garden in the yard.
To curb the damage of your play,
Strange dogs at night and the moles tunneling,
   Four slender sticks of lath stand guard
      Uplifting their thin string.

So you were the first to tramp it down.
   And after the earth was sifted close
You brought your watering can to drown
All earth *and* us. But these mixed seeds are pressed
   With light loam in their steadfast rows.
      Child, we've done our best.

Someone will have to weed and spread
   The young sprouts. Sprinkle them in the hour
When shadow falls across their bed.
You should try to look at them every day
   Because when they come to full flower
      I will be away.

3

The child between them on the street
Comes to a puddle, lifts his feet
   And hangs on their hands. They start
At the live weight and lurch together,
Recoil to swing him through the weather,
   Stiffen and pull apart.

We read of cold war soldiers that
Never gained ground, gave none, but sat
   Tight in their chill trenches.
Pain seeps up from some cavity
Through the ranked teeth in sympathy;
   The whole jaw grinds and clenches

Till something somewhere has to give.
It's better the poor soldiers live
   In someone else's hands
Than drop where helpless powers fall

On crops and barns, on towns where all
    Will burn. And no man stands.

For good, they sever and divide
Their won and lost land. On each side
    Prisoners are returned
Excepting a few unknown names.
The peasant plods back and reclaims
    His fields that strangers burned

And nobody seems very pleased.
It's best. Still, what must not be seized
    Clenches the empty fist.
I tugged your hand, once, when I hated
Things less: a mere game dislocated
    The radius of your wrist.

Love's wishbone, child, although I've gone
As men must and let you be drawn
    Off to appease another,
It may help that a Chinese play
Or Solomon himself might say
    I am your real mother.

       4

      No one can tell you why
      the season will not wait;
      the night I told you I
   must leave, you wept a fearful rate
      to stay up late.

      Now that it's turning Fall,
     we go to take our walk
      among municipal
  flowers, to steal one off its stalk,
      to try and talk.

     We huff like windy giants
    scattering with our breath
     gray-headed dandelions;
Spring is the cold wind's aftermath.
      The poet saith.

But the asters, too, are gray,
ghost-gray. Last night's cold
is sending on their way
petunias and dwarf marigold,
hunched sick and old.

Like nerves caught in a graph,
the morning-glory vines
frost has erased by half
still scrawl across their rigid twines.
Like broken lines

of verses I can't make.
In its unraveling loom
we find a flower to take,
with some late buds that might still bloom,
back to your room.

Night comes and the stiff dew.
I'm told a friend's child cried
because a cricket, who
had minstreled every night outside
her window, died.

5

Winter again and it is snowing;
Although you are still three,
You are already growing
Strange to me.

You chatter about new playmates, sing
Strange songs; you do not know
Hey ding-a-ding-a-ding
Or where I go

Or when I sang for bedtime, *Fox*
Went out on a chilly night,
Before I went for walks
And did not write;

You never mind the squalls and storms
That are renewed long since;
Outside, the thick snow swarms
Into my prints

And swirls out by warehouses, sealed,
Dark cowbarns, huddled, still,
Beyond to the blank field,
The fox's hill

Where he backtracks and sees the paw,
Gnawed off, he cannot feel;
Conceded to the jaw
Of toothed, blue steel.

6

Easter has come around
again; the river is rising
over the thawed ground
and the banksides. When you come you bring
an egg dyed lavender.
We shout along our bank to hear
our voices returning from the hills to meet us.
We need the landscape to repeat us.

You lived on this bank first.
While nine months filled your term, we knew
how your lungs, immersed
in the womb, miraculously grew
their useless folds till
the fierce, cold air rushed in to fill
them out like bushes thick with leaves. You took your hour,
caught breath, and cried with your full lung power.

Over the stagnant bight
we see the hungry bank swallow
flaunting his free flight
still; we sink in mud to follow
the killdeer from the grass
that hides her nest. That March there was
rain; the rivers rose; you could hear killdeers flying
all night over the mudflats crying.

W. D. SNODGRASS

You bring back how the red-
winged blackbird shrieked, slapping frail wings,
    diving at my head—
I saw where her tough nest, cradled, swings
    in tall reeds that must sway
with the winds blowing every way.
If you recall much, you recall this place. You still
    live nearby—on the opposite hill.

    After the sharp windstorm
of July Fourth, all that summer
    through the gentle, warm
afternoons, we heard great chain saws chirr
    like iron locusts. Crews
of roughneck boys swarmed to cut loose
branches wrenched in the shattering wind, to hack free
    all the torn limbs that could sap the tree.

    In the debris lay
starlings, dead. Near the park's birdrun
    we surprised one day
a proud, tan-spatted, buff-brown pigeon.
    In my hands she flapped so
fearfully that I let her go.
Her keeper came. And we helped snarl her in a net.
    You bring things I'd as soon forget.

    You raise into my head
a Fall night that I came once more
    to sit on your bed;
sweat beads stood out on your arms and fore-
    head and you wheezed for breath,
for help, like some child caught beneath
its comfortable woolly blankets, drowning there.
    Your lungs caught and would not take the air.

    Of all things, only we
have power to choose that we should die;
    nothing else is free
in this world to refuse it. Yet I,
    who say this, could not raise
myself from bed how many days
to the thieving world. Child, I have another wife,
    another child. We try to choose our life.

W. D. SNODGRASS

7

Here in the scuffled dust
    is our ground of play.
I lift you on your swing and must
    shove you away,
see you return again,
    drive you off again, then

stand quiet till you come.
    You, though you climb
higher, farther from me, longer,
    will fall back to me stronger.
Bad penny, pendulum,
    you keep my constant time

to bob in blue July
    where fat goldfinches fly
over the glittering, fecund
    reach of our growing lands.
Once more now, this second,
    I hold you in my hands.

8

I thumped on you the best I could
    which was no use;
you would not tolerate your food
until the sweet, fresh milk was soured
    with lemon juice.

That puffed you up like a fine yeast.
    The first June in your yard
like some squat Nero at a feast
you sat and chewed on white, sweet clover.
    That is over.

When you were old enough to walk
    we went to feed
the rabbits in the park milkweed;
saw the paired monkeys, under lock,
    consume each other's salt.

W. D. SNODGRASS

Going home we watched the slow
stars follow us down Heaven's vault.
You said, let's catch one that comes low,
        pull off its skin
    and cook it for our dinner.

    As absentee bread-winner,
I seldom got you such cuisine;
we ate in local restaurants
or bought what lunches we could pack
        in a brown sack

with stale, dry bread to toss for ducks
    on the green-scummed lagoons,
crackers for porcupine and fox,
life-savers for the footpad coons
        to scour and rinse,

snatch after in their muddy pail
    and stare into their paws.
When I moved next door to the jail
        I learned to fry
omelettes and griddlecakes so I

could set you supper at my table.
As I built back from helplessness,
        when I grew able,
the only possible answer was
    you had to come here less.

This Hallowe'en you come one week.
        You masquerade
    as a vermilion, sleek,
fat, crosseyed fox in the parade
or, where grim jackolanterns leer,

go with your bag from door to door
foraging for treats. How queer:
    when you take off your mask
my neighbors must forget and ask
        whose child you are.

Of course you lose your appetite,
   whine and won't touch your plate;
      as local law
I set your place on an orange crate
in your own room for days. At night

you lie asleep there on the bed
      and grate your jaw.
Assuredly your father's crimes
      are visited
on you. You visit me sometimes.

The time's up. Now our pumpkin sees
   me bringing your suitcase.
      He holds his grin;
the forehead shrivels, sinking in.
You break this year's first crust of snow

off the runningboard to eat.
   We manage, though for days
I crave sweets when you leave and know
they rot my teeth. Indeed our sweet
      foods leave us cavities.

9

   I get numb and go in
though the dry ground will not hold
   the few dry swirls of snow
and it must not be very cold.
A friend asks how you've been
      and I don't know

   or see much right to ask.
Or what use it could be to know.
   In three months since you came
the leaves have fallen and the snow;
your pictures pinned above my desk
      seem much the same.

Somehow I come to find
myself upstairs in the third floor
    museum's halls,
walking to kill my time once more
among the enduring and resigned
        stuffed animals,

    where, through a century's
caprice, displacement and
    known treachery between
its wars, they hear some old command
and in their peaceable kingdoms freeze
        to this still scene,

    Nature Morte. Here
by the door, its guardian,
    the patchwork dodo stands
where you and your stepsister ran
laughing and pointing. Here, last year,
        you pulled my hands

    and had your first, worst quarrel,
so toys were put up on your shelves.
    Here in the first glass cage
the little bobcats arch themselves,
still practicing their snarl
        of constant rage.

    The bison, here, immense,
shoves at his calf, brow to brow,
    and looks it in the eye
to see what is it thinking now.
I forced you to obedience;
        I don't know why.

    Still the lean lioness
beyond them, on her jutting ledge
    of shale and desert shrub,
stands watching always at the edge,
stands hard and tanned and envious
        above her cub;

with horns locked in tall heather,
two great Olympian Elk stand bound,
    fixed in their lasting hate
till hunger brings them both to ground.
Whom equal weakness binds together
    none shall separate.

Yet separate in the ocean
of broken ice, the white bear reels
    beyond the leathery groups
of scattered, drab Arctic seals
arrested here in violent motion
    like Napoleon's troops.

Our states have stood so long
At war, shaken with hate and dread,
    they are paralyzed at bay;
once we were out of reach, we said,
we would grow reasonable and strong.
    Some other day.

Like the cold men of Rome,
we have won costly fields to sow
    in salt, our only seed.
Nothing but injury will grow.
I write you only the bitter poems
    that you can't read.

Onan who would not breed
a child to take his brother's bread
    and be his brother's birth,
rose up and left his lawful bed,
went out and spilled his seed
    in the cold earth.

I stand by the unborn,
by putty-colored children curled
    in jars of alcohol,
that waken to no other world,
unchanging where no eye shall mourn.
    I see the caul

that wrapped a kitten, dead.
I see the branching, doubled throat
of a two-headed foal;
I see the hydrocephalic goat;
here is the curled and swollen head,
there, the burst skull;

skin of a limbless calf;
a horse's foetus, mummified;
mounted and joined forever,
the Siamese twin dogs that ride
belly to belly, half and half,
that none shall sever.

I walk among the growths,
by gangrenous tissue, goitre, cysts,
by fistulas and cancers,
where the malignancy man loathes
is held suspended and persists.
And I don't know the answers.

The window's turning white.
The world moves like a diseased heart
packed with ice and snow.
Three months now we have been apart
less than a mile. I cannot fight
or let you go.

10

The vicious winter finally yields
the green winter wheat;
the farmer, tired in the tired fields
he dare not leave will eat.

Once more the runs come fresh; prevailing
piglets, stout as jugs,
harry their old sow to the railing
to ease her swollen dugs

and game colts trail the herded mares
   that circle the pasture courses;
our seasons bring us back once more
   like merry-go-round horses.

With crocus mouths, perennial hungers,
   into the park Spring comes;
we roast hot dogs on old coat hangers
   and feed the swan bread crumbs,

pay our respects to the peacocks, rabbits,
   and leathery Canada goose
who took, last Fall, our tame white habits
   and now will not turn loose.

In full regalia, the pheasant cocks
   march past their dubious hens;
the porcupine and the lean, red fox
   trot around bachelor pens

and the miniature painted train
   wails on its oval track:
you said, I'm going to Pennsylvania!
   and waved. And you've come back.

If I loved you, they said, I'd leave
   and find my own affairs.
Well, once again this April, we've
   come around to the bears;

punished and cared for, behind bars,
   the coons on bread and water
stretch thin black fingers after ours.
   And you are still my daughter.

A FLAT ONE

Old Fritz, on this rotating bed
For seven wasted months you lay
Unfit to move, shrunken, gray,
No good to yourself or anyone

W. D. SNODGRASS

But to be babied—changed and bathed and fed.
        At long last, that's all done.

    Before each meal, twice every night,
    We set pads on your bedsores, shut
    Your catheter tube off, then brought
    The second canvas-and-black-iron
Bedframe and clamped you in between them, tight,
        Scared, so we could turn

    You over. We washed you, covered you,
    Cut up each bite of meat you ate;
    We watched your lean jaws masticate
    As ravenously your useless food
As thieves at hard labor in their chains chew
        Or insects in the wood.

    Such pious sacrifice to give
    You all you could demand of pain:
    Receive this haddock's body, slain
    For you, old tyrant; take this blood
Of a tomato, shed that you might live.
        You had that costly food.

    You seem to be all finished, so
    We'll plug your old recalcitrant anus
    And tie up your discouraged penis
    In a great, snow-white bow of gauze.
We wrap you, pin you, and cart you down below,
        Below, below, because

    Your credit has finally run out.
    On our steel table, trussed and carved,
    You'll find this world's hardworking, starved
    Teeth working in your precious skin.
The earth turns, in the end, by turn about
        And opens to take you in.

    Seven months gone down the drain; thank God
    That's through. Throw out the four-by-fours,
    Swabsticks, the thick salve for bedsores,
    Throw out the diaper pads and drug
Containers, pile the bedclothes in a wad,
        And rinse the cider jug

Half-filled with the last urine. Then
Empty out the cotton cans,
Autoclave the bowls and spit pans,
Unhook the pumps and all the red
Tubes—catheter, suction, oxygen;
        Next, wash the empty bed.

—All this Dark Age machinery
On which we had tormented you
To life. Last, we collect the few
Belongings: snapshots, some odd bills,
Your mail, and half a pack of Luckies we
        Won't light you after meals.

Old man, these seven months you've lain
Determined—not that you would live—
Just to not die. No one would give
You one chance you could ever wake
From that first night, much less go well again,
        Much less go home and make

Your living; how could you hope to find
A place for yourself in all creation?—
Pain was your only occupation.
And pain that should content and will
A man to give it up, nerved you to grind
        Your clenched teeth, breathing, till

Your skin broke down, your calves went flat
And your legs lost all sensation. Still,
You took enough morphine to kill
A strong man. Finally, nitrogen
Mustard: you could last two months after that;
        It would kill you then.

Even then you wouldn't quit.
Old soldier, yet you must have known
Inside the animal had grown
Sick of the world, made up its mind
To stop. Your mind ground on its separate
        Way, merciless and blind,

Into these last weeks when the breath
Would only come in fits and starts
That puffed out your sections like the parts
Of some enormous, damaged bug.
You waited, not for life, not for your death,
        Just for the deadening drug

That made your life seem bearable.
You still whispered you would not die.
Yet in the nights I heard you cry
Like a whipped child; in fierce old age
You whimpered, tears stood on your gun-metal
        Blue cheeks shaking with rage

And terror. So much pain would fill
Your room that when I left I'd pray
That if I came back the next day
I'd find you gone. You stayed for me—
Nailed to your own rapacious, stiff self-will.
        You've shook loose, finally.

They'd say this was a worthwhile job
Unless they tried it. It is mad
To throw our good lives after bad;
Waste time, drugs, and our minds, while strong
Men starve. How many young men did we rob
        To keep you hanging on?

I can't think we did *you* much good.
Well, when you died, none of us wept.
You killed for us, and so we kept
You, because we need to earn our pay.
No. We'd still have to help you try. We would
        Have killed for you today.

"AFTER EXPERIENCE TAUGHT ME..."

After experience taught me that all the ordinary
Surroundings of social life are futile and vain;

W. D. SNODGRASS

I'm going to show you something very
Ugly: someday, it might save your life.

Seeing that none of the things I feared contain
In themselves anything either good or bad

What if you get caught without a knife;
Nothing—even a loop of piano wire;

Excepting only in the effect they had
Upon my mind, I resolved to inquire

Take the first two fingers of this hand;
Fork them out—kind of a "V for Victory"—

Whether there might be something whose discovery
Would grant me supreme, unending happiness.

And jam them into the eyes of your enemy.
You have to do this hard. Very hard. Then press

No virtue can be thought to have priority
Over this endeavor to preserve one's being.

Both fingers down around the cheekbone
And setting your foot high into the chest

No man can desire to act rightly, to be blessed,
To live rightly, without simultaneously

You must call up every strength you own
And you can rip off the whole facial mask.

Wishing to be, to act, to live. He must ask
First, in other words, to actually exist.

And you, whiner, who wastes your time
Dawdling over the remorseless earth,
What evil, what unspeakable crime
Have you made your life worth?

W. D. SNODGRASS

EVA BRAUN

—22 April, 1945.

(*Hitler's mistress received no public recognition and often felt badly neglected. Her small revenges included singing American songs, her favorite being "Tea for Two." Having chosen to die with him in the bunker, she appeared quite serene during the last days.*)

Tea for two
And two for tea

                    I ought to feel ashamed
Feeling such joy. Behaving like a spoiled child!
So fulfilled. This is a very serious matter.
All of them have come here to die. And they grieve.
I have come here to die. If this is dying,
Why else did I ever live?

Me for you
And you for me

We ought never to flaunt our good luck
In the face of anyone less fortunate—
These live fools mourning already
For their own deaths; these dead fools
Who believe they can go on living . . .

And you for me
   Alone.

Who out of all of them, officers, ministers,
These liars that despise me, these empty
Women that envy me—so they hate me—
Who else of them dares to disobey Him
As I dared? I have defied Him to His face
And He has honored me.

> *We will raise*
> *A family*

They sneer at me—at my worrying about
Frau Goebbels' children, that I make fairytales
For them, that we play at war. Is our war
More lost if I console these poor trapped rabbits?
These children He would not give me . . .

A boy for you
A girl for me

They sneer that I should bring
Fine furniture down this dank hole. Speer
Built this bed for me. Where I have slept
Beside our Chief. Who else should have it?
My furs, my best dress to my little sister—
They would sneer even at this; yet
What else can I give her?

> *Can't you see*
> *How happy we would be?*

Or to the baby
She will bear Fegelein? Lechering dolt!
Well, I have given her her wedding
As if it was my own. And she will have
My diamonds, my watch. The little things you
Count on, things that see you through your
Missing life, the life that stood you up.

Nobody near us
To see us or hear us

I have it all. They are all gone, the others—
The Valkyrie; and the old rich bitch Bechstein;
Geli above all. No, the screaming mobs above all.
They are all gone now; He has left them all.
No one but me and the love-struck secretaries—
Traudl, Daran—who gave up years ago.

No friends or relations
On weekend vacations

That I, I above all, am chosen—even I
Must find that strange. I who was always
Disobedient, rebellious—smoked in the dining car,
Wore rouge whenever he said I shouldn't.
When he ordered that poor Chancellor Schussnig
Was to starve, I sent in food.

We won't have it known, dear,
That we own a telephone, dear.

I who joined the Party, I who took Him
For my lover just to spite my old stiff father—
Den Alten Fritz!—and those stupid nuns.
I ran my teachers crazy, and my mother—I
Held out even when she stuck my head in water.
He shall have none but me.

Day will break
And you will wake

We cannot make it through another month;
We follow the battles now on a subway map.
Even if the Russians pulled back—
His hand trembles, the whole left side
Staggers. His marvellous eyes are failing.
We go out to the sunlight less each day. We live
Like flies sucked up in a sweeper bag.

And start to bake
  A sugar cake

He forbade me to leave Berchtesgaden,
Forbade me to come here. I tricked
My keepers, stole my own car, my driver Jung.
He tried to scold me; He was too
Proud of me. Today He ordered me to leave,
To go back to the mountain. I refused.
I have refused to save my own life and He,
In public, He kissed me on the mouth.

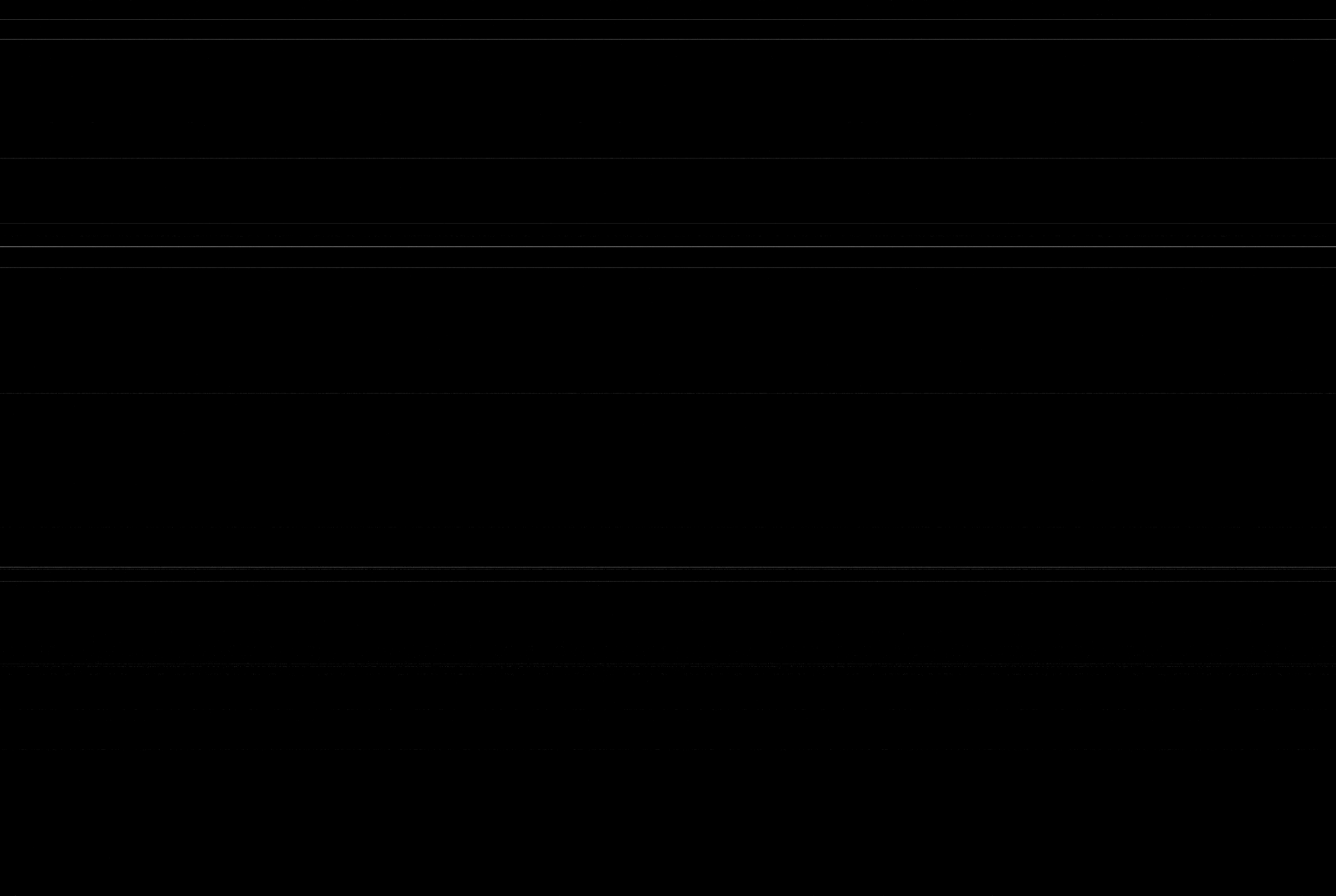

When every friend proved false, in the
Delirium of treachery
On every hand, when even He
    Had turned His face aside.
He shut himself in with His whore;
Then, though I screamed outside His door,
Said He'd not see me anymore.
    They both took cyanide.

Open wide, now, little bird;
I who sang you your first word
Soothe away every sound you've heard
    Except your Leader's voice.
Close your eyes, now; take your death.
Once we slapped you to take breath.
Vengeance is mine, the Lord God saith
    And cancels each last choice.

Once, my first words marked out your mind;
Just as our Leader's phrases bind
All hearts to Him, building a blind
    Loyalty through the nation,
We shape you into a pure form.
Trapped, our best soldiers tricked the storm,
The Reds: those last hours, they felt warm
    Who stood fast to their station.

You needn't fear what your life meant;
You won't curse how your hours were spent;
You'll grow like your own monument
    To all things sure and good,
Fixed like a frieze in high relief
Of granite figures that our Chief
Accepts into His true belief,
    His true blood-brotherhood.

> You'll never bite the hand that fed you,
> Won't turn away from those that bred you,
> Comforted your nights and led you
>   Into the thought of virtue;
> You won't be turned from your own bed;
> Won't turn into that thing you dread;
> No new betrayal lies ahead;
>   Now no one else can hurt you.

DR. JOSEPH GOEBBELS

—1 May, 1945; 1800 hours.

(The day after Hitler's death, Goebbels and his wife climbed the steps into the garden where both committed suicide.)

> Say goodbye to the help, the ranks
> Of Stalin-bait. Give too much thanks
> To Naumann—Magda's lover: we
> Thank him for *all* his loyalty.
> Schwaegermann; Rach. After a while
> Turn back to them with a sad smile:
> We'll save them trouble—no one cares
> Just now to carry us upstairs.
>
> Turn away; check your manicure;
> Pull on your gloves. Take time; make sure
> The hat brim curves though the hat's straight.
> Give her your arm. Let the fools wait;
> They act like they've someplace to go.
> Take the stairs, now. Self-control. Slow.
> A slight limp; just enough to see,
> Pass on, and infect history.

W. D. SNODGRASS

The rest is silence. Left like sperm
In a stranger's gut, waiting its term,
Each thought, each step lies; the roots spread.
They'll believe in us when we're dead.
When we took "Red Berlin" we found
We always worked best underground.
So; the vile body turns to spirit
That speaks soundlessly. They'll hear it.

© *Thomas Victor*

Gary Snyder

RIPRAP

Lay down these words
Before your mind like rocks.
           placed solid, by hands
In choice of place, set
Before the body of the mind
           in space and time:
Solidity of bark, leaf, or wall
           riprap of things:
Cobble of milky way,
           straying planets,
These poems, people,
           lost ponies with
Dragging saddles—
           and rocky sure-foot trails.
The worlds like an endless
           four-dimensional
Game of Go.
           ants and pebbles
In the thin loam, each rock a word
           a creek-washed stone
Granite: ingrained
           with torment of fire and weight
Crystal and sediment linked hot
           all change, in thoughts,
As well as things.

MILTON BY FIRELIGHT

"O hell, what do mine eyes
           with grief behold?"
Working with an old
Singlejack miner, who can sense

The vein and cleavage
In the very guts of rock, can
Blast granite, build
Switchbacks that last for years
Under the beat of snow, thaw, mule-hooves.
What use, Milton, a silly story
Of our lost general parents,
    eaters of fruit?

The Indian, the chainsaw boy,
And a string of six mules
Came riding down to camp
Hungry for tomatoes and green apples.
Sleeping in saddle-blankets
Under a bright night-sky
Han River slantwise by morning.
Jays squall
Coffee boils

In ten thousand years the Sierras
Will be dry and dead, home of the scorpion.
Ice-scratched slabs and bent trees.

No paradise, no fall,
Only the weathering land
The wheeling sky,
Man, with his Satan
Scouring the chaos of the mind.
Oh Hell!

Fire down
Too dark to read, miles from a road
The bell-mare clangs in the meadow
That packed dirt for a fill-in
Scrambling through loose rocks
On an old trail
All of a summer's day.

Piute Creek, August 1955

GARY SNYDER

from HUNTING

16

How rare to be born a human being!
Wash him off with cedar-bark and milkweed
                   send the damned doctors home.
Baby, baby, noble baby
Noble-hearted baby

One hand up, one hand down
"I alone am the honored one"
Birth of the Buddha.
And the whole world-system trembled.
"If that baby really said that,
I'd cut him up and throw him to the dogs!"
said Chao-chou the Zen Master. But
Chipmunks, gray squirrels, and
Golden-mantled ground squirrels
                   brought him each a nut.
Truth being the sweetest of flavors.

Girls would have in their arms
A wild gazelle or wild wolf-cubs
And give them their white milk,
                   those who had new-born infants home
Breasts still full.
Wearing a spotted fawnskin
                   sleeping under trees
                   bacchantes, drunk
On wine or truth, what you will,
Meaning: compassion.
Agents: man and beast, beasts
Got the buddha-nature
All but
Coyote.

VAPOR TRAILS

Twin streaks twice higher than cumulus,
Precise plane icetracks in the vertical blue
Cloud-flaked light-shot shadow-arcing
Field of all future war, edging off to space.

Young expert U.S. pilots waiting
The day of criss-cross rockets
And white blossoming smoke of bomb,
The air world torn and staggered for these
Specks of brushy land and ant-hill towns—

I stumble on the cobble rockpath,
Passing through temples,
Watching for two-leaf pine
        —spotting that design.

SONG OF THE TASTE

Eating the living germs of grasses
Eating the ova of large birds

    the fleshy sweetness packed
    around the sperm of swaying trees

The muscles of the flanks and thighs of
            soft-voiced cows
        the bounce in the lamb's leap
        the swish in the ox's tail

Eating roots grown swoll
            inside the soil

Drawing on life of living
    clustered points of light spun
            out of space
hidden in the grape.

Eating each other's seed
eating
ah, each other.

Kissing the lover in the mouth of bread:
lip to lip.

LONG HAIR

Hunting season:

Once every year, the Deer catch human beings. They
do various things which irresistibly draw men near them:
each one selects a certain man. The Deer shoots the man,
who is then compelled to skin it and carry its meat home
and eat it. Then the Deer is inside the man. He waits
and hides in there, but the man doesn't know it. When
enough Deer have occupied enough men, they will strike
all at once. The men who don't have Deer in them will
also be taken by surprise, and everything will change
some. This is called "takeover from inside."

Deer trails:

Deer trails run on the side hills
        cross county access roads
        dirt ruts to bone-white
        board house ranches,
        tumbled down.

Waist high through manzanita,
Through sticky, prickly, crackling
        gold dry summer grass.

Deer trails lead to water,
Lead sidewise all ways
Narrowing down to one best path—
And split—
And fade away to nowhere.

Deer trails slide under freeways
    slip into cities
      swing back and forth in crops and orchards
      run up the sides of schools!

Deer spoor and crisscross dusty tracks
Are in the house: and coming out the walls:

And deer bound through my hair.

I WENT INTO THE MAVERICK BAR

I went into the Maverick Bar
In Farmington, New Mexico.
And drank double shots of bourbon
        backed with beer.
My long hair was tucked up under a cap
I'd left the earring in the car.

Two cowboys did horseplay
      by the pool tables,
A waitress asked us
      where are you from?
a country-and-western band began to play
"We don't smoke Marijuana in Muskokie"
And with the next song,
      a couple began to dance.

They held each other like in High School dances
      in the fifties;
I recalled when I worked in the woods
      and the bars of Madras, Oregon.
That short-haired joy and roughness—
      America—your stupidity.
I could almost love you again.

We left—onto the freeway shoulders—
      under the tough old stars—
In the shadow of bluffs
      I came back to myself,
To the real work, to
      "What is to be done."

GARY SNYDER

THE BATH

Washing Kai in the sauna,
The kerosene lantern set on a box
    outside the ground-level window,
Lights up the edge of the iron stove and the
    washtub down on the slab
Steaming air and crackle of waterdrops
    brushed by on the pile of rocks on top
He stands in warm water
Soap all over the smooth of his thigh and stomach
    "Gary don't soap my hair!"
    —his eye-sting fear—
    the soapy hand feeling
    through and around the globes and curves of his body
    up in the crotch,
And washing-tickling out the scrotum, little anus,
    his penis curving up and getting hard
    as I pull back skin and try to wash it
Laughing and jumping, flinging arms around,
    I squat all naked too,
                  is this our body?

Sweating and panting in the stove-steam hot-stone
    cedar-planking wooden bucket water-splashing
    kerosene lantern-flicker wind-in-the-pines-out
    sierra forest ridges night—
Masa comes in, letting fresh cool air
    sweep down from the door
    a deep sweet breath
And she tips him over gripping neatly, one knee down
    her hair falling hiding one whole side of
    shoulder, breast, and belly,
Washes deftly Kai's head-hair
    as he gets mad and yells—
The body of my lady, the winding valley spine,
    the space between the thighs I reach through,
    cup her curving vulva arch and hold it from behind,
    a soapy tickle   a hand of grail
The gates of Awe
That open back a turning double-mirror world of
    wombs in wombs, in rings,
    that start in music,

The hidden place of seed
The veins net flow across the ribs, that gathers
    milk and peaks up in a nipple—fits
    our mouth—
The sucking milk from this our body sends through
    jolts of light; the son, the father,
    sharing mother's joy
That brings a softness to the flower of the awesome
    open curling lotus gate I cup and kiss
As Kai laughs at his mother's breast he now is weaned
    from, we
    wash each other,
                this our body

Kai's little scrotum up close to his groin,
    the seed still tucked away, that moved from us to him
In flows that lifted with the same joys forces
    as his nursing Masa later,
    playing with her breast,
Or me within her,
Or him emerging,
                this is our body:

Clean, and rinsed, and sweating more, we stretch
    out on the redwood benches hearts all beating
Quiet to the simmer of the stove,
    the scent of cedar
And then turn over,
    murmuring gossip of the grasses,
    talking firewood,
Wondering how Gen's napping, how to bring him in
    soon wash him too—
These boys who love their mother
    who loves men, who passes on
    her sons to other women;

The cloud across the sky. The windy pines.
    the trickle gurgle in the swampy meadow

    this is our body.

Fire inside and boiling water on the stove
We sigh and slide ourselves down from the benches
    wrap the babies, step outside,

black night & all the stars.

Pour cold water on the back and thighs
Go in the house—stand steaming by the center fire
Kai scampers on the sheepskin
Gen standing hanging on and shouting,

"Bao! bao! bao! bao! bao!"

This is our body. Drawn up crosslegged by the flames
      drinking icy water
      hugging babies, kissing bellies,

Laughing on the Great Earth

Come out from the bath.

BEDROCK

for Masa

Snowmelt pond   warm granite
we make camp,
no thought of finding more.
and nap
and leave our minds to the wind.

on the bedrock, gently tilting,
sky and stone,

teach me to be tender.

the touch that nearly misses—
brush of glances—
tiny steps—
that finally cover worlds
        of hard terrain.
cloud wisps and mists
gathered into slate blue
bolts of summer rain.

tea together in the purple starry eve;
new moon soon to set;
why does it take so
long to learn to
love,
     we laugh
         and grieve.

AS FOR POETS

As for poets
The Earth Poets
Who write small poems,
Need help from no man.

The Air Poets
Play out the swiftest gales
And sometimes loll in the eddies.
Poem after poem,
Curling back on the same thrust.

At fifty below
Fuel oil won't flow
And propane stays in the tank.
Fire Poets
Burn at absolute zero
Fossil love pumped back up.

The first
Water Poet
Stayed down six years.
He was covered with seaweed.
The life in his poem
Left millions of tiny
Different tracks
Criss-crossing through the mud.

GARY SNYDER

With the Sun and Moon
In his belly,
The Space Poet
Sleeps.
No end to the sky—
But his poems,
Like wild geese,
Fly off the edge.

A Mind Poet
Stays in the house.
The house is empty
And it has no walls.
The poem
Is seen from all sides,
Everywhere,
At once.

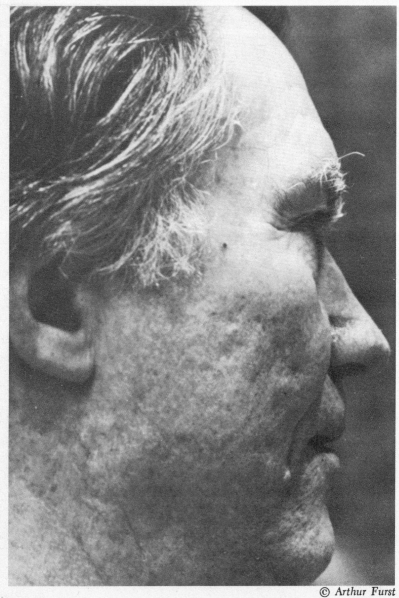

© Arthur Furst

William Stafford

AT THE BOMB TESTING SITE

At noon in the desert a panting lizard
waited for history, its elbows tense,
watching the curve of a particular road
as if something might happen.

It was looking at something farther off
than people could see, an important scene
acted in stone for little selves
at the flute end of consequences.

There was just a continent without much on it
under a sky that never cared less.
Ready for a change, the elbows waited.
The hands gripped hard on the desert.

TRAVELING THROUGH THE DARK

Traveling through the dark I found a deer
dead on the edge of the Wilson River road.
It is usually best to roll them into the canyon:
that road is narrow; to swerve might make more dead.

By glow of the tail-light I stumbled back of the car
and stood by the heap, a doe, a recent killing;
she had stiffened already, almost cold.
I dragged her off; she was large in the belly.

My fingers touching her side brought me the reason—
her side was warm; her fawn lay there waiting,
alive, still, never to be born.
Beside that mountain road I hesitated.

The car aimed ahead its lowered parking lights;
under the hood purred the steady engine.
I stood in the glare of the warm exhaust turning red;
around our group I could hear the wilderness listen.

I thought hard for us all—my only swerving—,
then pushed her over the edge into the river.

VOCATION

This dream the world is having about itself
includes a trace on the plains of the Oregon trail,
a groove in the grass my father showed us all
one day while meadowlarks were trying to tell
something better about to happen.

I dreamed the trace to the mountains, over the hills,
and there a girl who belonged wherever she was.
But then my mother called us back to the car:
she was afraid; she always blamed the place,
the time, anything my father planned.

Now both of my parents, the long line through the plain,
the meadowlarks, the sky, the world's whole dream
remain, and I hear him say while I stand between the two,
helpless, both of them part of me:
"Your job is to find what the world is trying to be."

MY FATHER: OCTOBER 1942

He picks up what he thinks is
a road map, and it is
his death: he holds it easily, and
nothing can take it from his firm hand.
The pulse in his thumb on the map
says, "1:19 P.M. next Tuesday, at
this intersection." And an ambulance
begins to throb while his face looks tired.

Any time anyone may pick up something
so right that he can't put it down:
that is the problem for all who travel—they
fatally own whatever is really theirs,
and that is the inner thread, the lock,
what can hold. If it is to be, nothing breaks
it. Millions of observers guess all the
time, but each person, once, can say, "Sure."

Then he's no longer an observer. He isn't right,
or wrong. He just wins or loses.

ACROSS KANSAS

My family slept those level miles
but like a bell rung deep till dawn
I drove down an aisle of sound,
nothing real but in the bell,
past the town where I was born.

Once you cross a land like that
you own your face more: what the light
struck told a self; every rock
denied all the rest of the world.
We stopped at Sharon Springs and ate—

My state still dark, my dream too long to tell.

A FAMILY TURN

All her Kamikaze friends admired my aunt,
their leader, charmed in vinegar,
a woman who could blaze with such white blasts
as Lawrence's that lit Arabia.
Her mean opinions bent her hatpins.

We'd take a ride in her old car
that ripped like Sherman through society:
Main Street's oases sheltered no one
when she pulled up at Thirty-first
and whirled that Ford for another charge.

We swept headlines from under rugs, names
all over town, which I learned her way, by heart,
and blazed with love that burns because it's real.
With a turn that's our family's own,
she'd say, "Our town is not the same"—

Pause—"And it's never been."

AN INTRODUCTION TO SOME POEMS

Look: no one ever promised for sure
that we would sing. We have decided
to moan. In a strange dance that
we don't understand till we do it, we
have to carry on.

Just as in sleep you have to dream
the exact dream to round out your life,
so we have to live that dream into stories
and hold them close at you, close at the
edge we share, to be right.

We find it an awful thing to meet people,
serious or not, who have turned into vacant
effective people, so far lost that they
won't believe their own feelings
enough to follow them out.

The authentic is a line from one thing
along to the next; it interests us.
Strangely, it relates to what works,
but is not quite the same. It never
swerves for revenge,

WILLIAM STAFFORD

Or profit, or fame: it holds
together something more than the world,
this line. And we are your wavery
efforts at following it. Are you coming?
Good: now it is time.

FOR A CHILD GONE TO LIVE IN A COMMUNE

Outside our ways you found
a way, no name for your home,
no number, not even words.

I thought your voice held onto curves
over cliffs when you said, "We let the animals
have whatever they wanted."

I forgot to tell you: this house too
is a wanderer. Under its paint it is
orbiting all I ever thought it would find—

Those empty spaces. It has found them.

TOUCHES

Late, you can hear the stars. And beyond them
some kind of quiet other than silence, a deepness
the miles make, the way canyons
hold their miles back: you are in the earth and
it guides you; out where the sun comes
it is the precious world.

There are stones too quiet for these days,
old ones that belong in the earlier mountains.
You put a hand out in the dark of a cave and
the wall waits for your fingers. Cold, that stone
tells you all of the years that passed without knowing.
You think of caves held in the earth, no mouth,

no light. Down there the years have lost their way.
Under your hand it all steadies,
is the world under your hand.

REPORT FROM A FAR PLACE

Making these word things to
step on across the world, I
could call them snowshoes.

They creak, sag, bend, but
hold, over the great deep cold,
and they turn up at the toes.

In war or city or camp
they could save your life;
you can muse them by the fire.

Be careful, though: they
burn, or don't burn, in their own
strange way, when you say them.

THE STICK IN THE FOREST

A stick in the forest that pointed
where the center of the universe is
broke in the wind that started
its exact note of mourning
when Buddha's mother died.

Around us then a new crystal
began to form itself, and men—
awakened by what happened—
held precious whatever breathed:
we are all gestures that the world makes.

"Be, be," Buddha said.

FINDING OUT

for Willa Cather

'*I am that poor Marie, the sinner who died in the cave.*'
                                                                    —*Shadows on the Rock*

No, not dark. Even at night a glow from a shaft
spread near me. But hardly a breath, and the sound
only of stones becoming themselves, or denying it.

Now I am seeking the reason my life was in the world:
all up and down these roads I am turning the leaves,
moving the grass, turning on my tongue the secret words.

At the last I will be able to say, 'Forgive me,'
and be quiet. Almost saved now, I wander, brought back
by the American woman with the wide hat, the cave-looking eyes.

I will go now. Think about me, my
story, how I was in the world—
maybe to help you—a long time ago.

ASSURANCE

You will never be alone, you hear so deep
a sound when autumn comes. Yellow
pulls across the hills and thrums,
or the silence after lightning before it says
its names—and then the clouds' wide-mouthed
apologies. You were aimed from birth:
you will never be alone. Rain
will come, a gutter filled, an Amazon,
long aisles—you never heard so deep a sound,
moss on rock, and years. You turn your head—
that's what the silence meant: *you're not alone.*
The whole wide world pours down.

A CERTAIN BEND

A certain bend in the road, swayed willows
beyond a fence, and a flat farmyard
waiting—we come around and that instant
freezes: years later I remember.
Why? Why did a lifetime pass, two wars,
a family move and scatter, the country
skid where it is—and only now
that scene return? I put my teacup
down here to hold it all steady. Was that
the day I became the person I am?
Father, you should have held my face
in your hands and stared into my eyes. That farmyard
or one like it could be ours, in Kansas, or
Alaska, or anywhere. You would be there
now, I would hold out my hand
for whatever came, and the willows would bend
still in that picture we saw that day.

ANSWERERS

There are songs too wide for sound. There are quiet
places where something stopped a long time
ago and the days began to open
their mouths toward nothing but the sky. We live
in place of the many who stir only
if we listen, only because the living
live and call out. I am ready
as all of us are who wake at night:
we become rooms for whatever almost
is. It speaks in us, trying. And even if
only by a note like this, we answer.

WILLIAM STAFFORD

THINGS THAT HAPPEN
WHERE THERE AREN'T ANY PEOPLE

It's cold on Lakeside Road
with no one traveling. At its turn
on the hill an old sign sags and
finally goes down. The traveler rain
walks back and forth over its victim
flat on the mud.

You don't have to have any people when
sunlight stands on the rocks or gloom
comes following the great dragged clouds
over a huddle of hills. Plenty of
things happen in deserted places, maybe
dust counting millions of its little worlds
or the slow arrival of deep dark.

And out there in the country a rock has been
waiting to be mentioned for thousands of years.
Every day its shadow leans, crouches,
then walks away eastward in one measured stride
exactly right for its way of being. To reach
for that rock we have the same reasons
that explorers always have for their journeys:
because it is far, because there aren't any people.

© Clemens Kalischer/Photographer

Richard Wilbur

ADVICE TO A PROPHET

When you come, as you soon must, to the streets of our city,
Mad-eyed from stating the obvious,
Not proclaiming our fall but begging us
In God's name to have self-pity,

Spare us all word of the weapons, their force and range,
The long numbers that rocket the mind;
Our slow, unreckoning hearts will be left behind,
Unable to fear what is too strange.

Nor shall you scare us with talk of the death of the race.
How should we dream of this place without us?—
The sun mere fire, the leaves untroubled about us,
A stone look on the stone's face?

Speak of the world's own change. Though we cannot conceive
Of an undreamt thing, we know to our cost
How the dreamt cloud crumbles, the vines are blackened by frost,
How the view alters. We could believe,

If you told us so, that the white-tailed deer will slip
Into perfect shade, grown perfectly shy,
The lark avoid the reaches of our eye,
The jack-pine lose its knuckled grip

On the cold ledge, and every torrent burn
As Xanthus once, its gliding trout
Stunned in a twinkling. What should we be without
The dolphin's arc, the dove's return,

These things in which we have seen ourselves and spoken?
Ask us, prophet, how we shall call
Our natures forth when that live tongue is all
Dispelled, that glass obscured or broken

In which we have said the rose of our love and the clean
Horse of our courage, in which beheld
The singing locust of the soul unshelled,
And all we mean or wish to mean.

Ask us, ask us whether with the worldless rose
Our hearts shall fail us; come demanding
Whether there shall be lofty or long standing
When the bronze annals of the oak-tree close.

LOVE CALLS US TO THE THINGS OF THIS WORLD

The eyes open to a cry of pulleys,
And spirited from sleep, the astounded soul
Hangs for a moment bodiless and simple
As false dawn.
                Outside the open window
The morning air is all awash with angels.

Some are in bed-sheets, some are in blouses,
Some are in smocks: but truly there they are.
Now they are rising together in calm swells
Of halcyon feeling, filling whatever they wear
With the deep joy of their impersonal breathing;

Now they are flying in place, conveying
The terrible speed of their omnipresence, moving
And staying like white water; and now of a sudden
They swoon down into so rapt a quiet
That nobody seems to be there.
                        The soul shrinks

From all that it is about to remember,
From the punctual rape of every blessèd day,
And cries,
           "Oh, let there be nothing on earth but laundry,
Nothing but rosy hands in the rising steam
And clear dances done in the sight of heaven."

RICHARD WILBUR

Yet, as the sun acknowledges
With a warm look the world's hunks and colors,
The soul descends once more in bitter love
To accept the waking body, saying now
In a changed voice as the man yawns and rises,

"Bring them down from their ruddy gallows.
Let there be clean linen for the backs of thieves;
Let lovers go fresh and sweet to be undone,
And the heaviest nuns walk in a pure floating
Of dark habits,
               keeping their difficult balance."

ON THE EYES OF AN SS OFFICER

I think of Amundsen, enormously bit
By arch-dark flurries on the ice plateaus,
An amorist of violent virgin snows
At the cold end of the world's spit.

Or a Bombay saint asquat in the market place,
Eyes gone from staring the sun over the sky,
Who still dead-reckons that acetylene eye,
An eclipsed mind in a blind face.

But this one's iced or ashen eyes devise,
Foul purities, in flesh their wilderness,
Their fire; I ask my makeshift God of this
My opulent bric-a-brac earth to damn his eyes.

YEAR'S END

Now winter downs the dying of the year,
And night is all a settlement of snow;
From the soft street the rooms of houses show
A gathered light, a shapen atmosphere,
Like frozen-over lakes whose ice is thin
And still allows some stirring down within.

I've known the wind by water banks to shake
The late leaves down, which frozen where they fell
And held in ice as dancers in a spell
Fluttered all winter long into a lake;
Graved on the dark in gestures of descent,
They seemed their own most perfect monument.

There was perfection in the death of ferns
Which laid their fragile cheeks against the stone
A million years. Great mammoths overthrown
Composedly have made their long sojourns,
Like palaces of patience, in the gray
And changeless lands of ice. And at Pompeii

The little dog lay curled and did not rise
But slept the deeper as the ashes rose
And found the people incomplete, and froze
The random hands, the loose unready eyes
Of men expecting yet another sun
To do the shapely thing they had not done.

These sudden ends of time must give us pause.
We fray into the future, rarely wrought
Save in the tapestries of afterthought.
More time, more time. Barrages of applause
Come muffled from a buried radio.
The New-year bells are wrangling with the snow.

A BAROQUE WALL-FOUNTAIN
IN THE VILLA SCIARRA

for Dore and Adja

Under the bronze crown
Too big for the head of the stone cherub whose feet
    A serpent has begun to eat,
Sweet water brims a cockle and braids down

RICHARD WILBUR

Past spattered mosses, breaks
On the tipped edge of a second shell, and fills
   The massive third below. It spills
In threads then from the scalloped rim, and makes

   A scrim or summery tent
For a faun-ménage and their familiar goose.
   Happy in all that ragged, loose
Collapse of water, its effortless descent

   And flatteries of spray,
The stocky god upholds the shell with ease,
   Watching, about his shaggy knees,
The goatish innocence of his babes at play;

   His fauness all the while
Leans forward, slightly, into a clambering mesh
   Of water-lights, her sparkling flesh
In a saecular ecstasy, her blinded smile

   Bent on the sand floor
Of the trefoil pool, where ripple-shadows come
   And go in swift reticulum,
More addling to the eye than wine, and more

   Interminable to thought
Than pleasure's calculus. Yet since this all
   Is pleasure, flash, and waterfall,
Must it not be too simple? Are we not

   More intricately expressed
In the plain fountains that Maderna set
   Before St. Peter's—the main jet
Struggling aloft until it seems at rest

   In the act of rising, until
The very wish of water is reversed,
   That heaviness borne up to burst
In a clear, high, cavorting head, to fill

With blaze, and then in gauze
Delays, in a gnatlike shimmering, in a fine
    Illumined version of itself, decline,
And patter on the stones its own applause?

    If that is what men are
Or should be, if those water-saints display
    The pattern of our areté,
What of these showered fauns in their bizarre,

    Spangled, and plunging house?
They are at rest in fulness of desire
    For what is given, they do not tire
Of the smart of the sun, the pleasant water-douse

    And riddled pool below,
Reproving our disgust and our ennui
    With humble insatiety.
Francis, perhaps, who lay in sister snow

    Before the wealthy gate
Freezing and praising, might have seen in this
    No trifle, but a shade of bliss—
That land of tolerable flowers, that state

    As near and far as grass
Where eyes become the sunlight, and the hand
    Is worthy of water: the dreamt land
Toward which all hungers leap, all pleasures pass.

POTATO

for André du Bouchet

An underground grower, blind and a common brown;
Got a misshapen look, it's nudged where it could;
Simple as soil yet crowded as earth with all.

RICHARD WILBUR

Cut open raw, it looses a cool clean stench,
Mineral acid seeping from pores of prest meal;
It is like breaching a strangely refreshing tomb:

Therein the taste of first stones, the hands of dead slaves,
Waters men drank in the earliest frightful woods,
Flint chips, and peat, and the cinders of buried camps.

Scrubbed under faucet water the planet skin
Polishes yellow, but tears to the plain insides;
Parching, the white's blue-hearted like hungry hands.

All of the cold dark kitchens, and war-frozen gray
Evening at window; I remember so many
Peeling potatoes quietly into chipt pails.

"It was potatoes saved us, they kept us alive."
Then they had something to say akin to praise
For the mean earth-apples, too common to cherish or steal.

Times being hard, the Sikh and the Senegalese,
Hobo and Okie, the body of Jesus the Jew,
Vestigial virtues, are eaten; we shall survive.

What has not lost its savor shall hold us up,
And we are praising what saves us, what fills the need.
(Soon there'll be packets again, with Algerian fruits.)

Oh, it will not bear polish, the ancient potato,
Needn't be nourished by Caesars, will blow anywhere,
Hidden by nature, counted-on, stubborn and blind.

You may have noticed the bush that it pushes to air,
Comical-delicate, sometimes with second-rate flowers
Awkward and milky and beautiful only to hunger.

RICHARD WILBUR

A DUBIOUS NIGHT

A bell diphthonging in an atmosphere
Of shying night air summons some to prayer
Down in the town, two deep lone miles from here,

Yet wallows faint or sudden everywhere,
In every ear, as if the twist wind wrung
Some ten years' tangled echoes from the air.

What kyries it says are mauled among
The queer elisions of the mist and murk,
Of lights and shapes; the senses were unstrung,

Except that one star's synecdochic smirk
Burns steadily to me, that nothing's odd
And firm as ever is the masterwork.

I weary of the confidence of God.

PRAISE IN SUMMER

Obscurely yet most surely called to praise,
As sometimes summer calls us all, I said
The hills are heavens full of branching ways
Where star-nosed moles fly overhead the dead;
I said the trees are mines in air, I said
See how the sparrow burrows in the sky!
And then I wondered why this mad *instead*
Perverts our praise to uncreation, why
Such savor's in this wrenching things awry.
Does sense so stale that it must needs derange
The world to know it? To a praiseful eye
Should it not be enough of fresh and strange
That trees grow green, and moles can course in clay,
And sparrows sweep the ceiling of our day?

RICHARD WILBUR

ON THE MARGINAL WAY

for J. C. P.

Another cove of shale,
But the beach here is rubbled with strange rock
   That is sleek, fluent, and taffy-pale.
I stare, reminded with a little shock
How, by a shore in Spain, George Borrow saw
A hundred women basking in the raw.

   They must have looked like this,
That catch of bodies on the sand, that strew
   Of rondure, crease, and orifice,
Lap, flank, and knee—a too abundant view
Which, though he'd had the lenses of a fly,
Could not have waked desire in Borrow's eye.

   Has the light altered now?
The rocks flush rose and have the melting shape
   Of bodies fallen anyhow.
It is a Géricault of blood and rape,
Some desert town despoiled, some caravan
Pillaged, its people murdered to a man,

   And those who murdered them
Galloping off, a rumpling line of dust
   Like the wave's white, withdrawing hem.
But now the vision of a colder lust
Clears, as the wind goes chill and all is greyed
By a swift cloud that drags a carrion shade.

   If these are bodies still,
Theirs is a death too dead to look asleep,
   Like that of Auschwitz' final kill,
Poor slaty flesh abandoned in a heap
And then, like sea-rocks buried by a wave,
Bulldozed at last into a common grave.

RICHARD WILBUR

It is not tricks of sense
But the time's fright within me which distracts
　　Least fancies into violence
And makes my thought take cover in the facts,
As now it does, remembering how the bed
Of layered rock two miles above my head

　　Hove ages up and broke
Soundless asunder, when the shrinking skin
　　Of Earth, blacked out by steam and smoke,
Gave passage to the muddled fire within,
Its crannies flooding with a sweat of quartz,
And lathered magmas out of deep retorts

　　Welled up, as here, to fill
With tumbled rockmeal, stone-fume, lithic spray,
　　The dike's brief chasm and the sill.
Weathered until the sixth and human day
By sanding winds and water, scuffed and brayed
By the slow glacier's heel, these forms were made

　　That now recline and burn
Comely as Eve and Adam, near a sea
　　Transfigured by the sun's return.
And now three girls lie golden in the lee
Of a great arm or thigh, and are as young
As the bright boulders that they lie among.

　　Though, high above the shore
On someone's porch, spread wings of newsprint flap
　　The tidings of some dirty war,
It is a perfect day: the waters clap
Their hands and kindle, and the gull in flight
Loses himself at moments, white in white,

　　And like a breaking thought
Joy for a moment floods into the mind,
　　Blurting that all things shall be brought
To the full state and stature of their kind,
By what has found the manhood of this stone.
May that vast motive wash and wash our own.

RICHARD WILBUR

COTTAGE STREET, 1953

Framed in her phoenix fire-screen, Edna Ward
Bends to the tray of Canton, pouring tea
For frightened Mrs. Plath; then, turning toward
The pale, slumped daughter, and my wife, and me,

Asks if we would prefer it weak or strong.
Will we have milk or lemon, she enquires?
The visit seems already strained and long.
Each in his turn, we tell her our desires.

It is my office to exemplify
The published poet in his happiness,
Thus cheering Sylvia, who has wished to die;
But half-ashamed, and impotent to bless,

I am a stupid life-guard who has found,
Swept to his shallows by the tide, a girl
Who, far from shore, has been immensely drowned,
And stares through water now with eyes of pearl.

How large is her refusal; and how slight
The genteel chat whereby we recommend
Life, of a summer afternoon, despite
The brewing dusk which hints that it may end.

And Edna Ward shall die in fifteen years,
After her eight-and-eighty summers of
Such grace and courage as permit no tears,
The thin hand reaching out, the last word *love*,

Outliving Sylvia who, condemned to live,
Shall study for a decade, as she must,
To state at last her brilliant negative
In poems free and helpless and unjust.

RICHARD WILBUR

THE WRITER

In her room at the prow of the house
Where light breaks, and the windows are tossed with linden,
My daughter is writing a story.

I pause in the stairwell, hearing
From her shut door a commotion of typewriter-keys
Like a chain hauled over a gunwale.

Young as she is, the stuff
Of her life is a great cargo, and some of it heavy:
I wish her a lucky passage.

But now it is she who pauses,
As if to reject my thought and its easy figure.
A stillness greatens, in which

The whole house seems to be thinking,
And then she is at it again with a bunched clamor
Of strokes, and again is silent.

I remember the dazed starling
Which was trapped in that very room, two years ago;
How we stole in, lifted a sash

And retreated, not to affright it;
And how for a helpless hour, through the crack of the door,
We watched the sleek, wild, dark

And iridescent creature
Batter against the brilliance, drop like a glove
To the hard floor, or the desk-top,

And wait then, humped and bloody,
For the wits to try it again; and how our spirits
Rose when, suddenly sure,

RICHARD WILBUR

It lifted off from a chair-back,
Beating a smooth course for the right window
And clearing the sill of the world.

It is always a matter, my darling,
Of life or death, as I had forgotten. I wish
What I wished you before, but harder.

© Gerard Malanga

James Wright

GOODBYE TO THE POETRY OF CALCIUM

Dark cypresses—
The world is uneasily happy:
It will all be forgotten.

Theodor Storm

Mother of roots, you have not seeded
The tall ashes of loneliness
For me. Therefore,
Now I go.
If I knew the name,
Your name, all trellises of vineyards and old fire
Would quicken to shake terribly my
Earth, mother of spiralling searches, terrible
Fable of calcium, girl. I crept this afternoon
In weeds once more,
Casual, daydreaming you might not strike
Me down. Mother of window sills and journeys,
Hallower of scratching hands,
The sight of my blind man makes me want to weep.
Tiller of waves or whatever, woman or man,
Mother of roots or father of diamonds,
Look: I am nothing.
I do not even have ashes to rub into my eyes.

AS I STEP OVER A PUDDLE AT THE END OF WINTER, I THINK OF AN ANCIENT CHINESE GOVERNOR

And how can I, born in evil days
And fresh from failure, ask a kindness
of Fate?

Written A.D. *819*

Po Chu-i, balding old politician,
What's the use?
I think of you,

Uneasily entering the gorges of the Yang-Tze,
When you were being towed up the rapids
Toward some political job or other
In the city of Chungshou.
You made it, I guess,
By dark.

But it is 1960, it is almost spring again,
And the tall rocks of Minneapolis
Build me my own black twilight
Of bamboo ropes and waters.
Where is Yuan Chen, the friend you loved?
Where is the sea, that once solved the whole loneliness
Of the Midwest? Where is Minneapolis? I can see nothing
But the great terrible oak tree darkening with winter.
Did you find the city of isolated men beyond mountains?
Or have you been holding the end of a frayed rope
For a thousand years?

AUTUMN BEGINS IN MARTINS FERRY, OHIO

In the Shreve High football stadium,
I think of Polacks nursing long beers in Tiltonsville,
And gray faces of Negroes in the blast furnace at Benwood,
And the ruptured night watchman of Wheeling Steel,
Dreaming of heroes.

All the proud fathers are ashamed to go home.
Their women cluck like starved pullets,
Dying for love.

Therefore,
Their sons grow suicidally beautiful
At the beginning of October,
And gallop terribly against each other's bodies.

JAMES WRIGHT

LYING IN A HAMMOCK AT WILLIAM DUFFY'S FARM IN PINE ISLAND, MINNESOTA

Over my head, I see the bronze butterfly,
Asleep on the black trunk,
Blowing like a leaf in green shadow.
Down the ravine behind the empty house,
The cowbells follow one another
Into the distances of the afternoon.
To my right,
In a field of sunlight between two pines,
The droppings of last year's horses
Blaze up into golden stones.
I lean back, as the evening darkens and comes on.
A chicken hawk floats over, looking for home.
I have wasted my life.

THE JEWEL

There is this cave
In the air behind my body
That nobody is going to touch:
A cloister, a silence
Closing around a blossom of fire.
When I stand upright in the wind,
My bones turn to dark emeralds.

FEAR IS WHAT QUICKENS ME

1

Many animals that our fathers killed in America
Had quick eyes.
They stared about wildly,
When the moon went dark.
The new moon falls into the freight yards
Of cities in the south,

But the loss of the moon to the dark hands of Chicago
Does not matter to the deer
In this northern field.

2

What is that tall woman doing
There, in the trees?
I can hear rabbits and mourning doves whispering together
In the dark grass, there
Under the trees.

3

I look about wildly.

EISENHOWER'S VISIT TO FRANCO, 1959

"... we die of cold, and not of darkness."

Unamuno

The American hero must triumph over
The forces of darkness.
He has flown through the very light of heaven
And come down in the slow dusk
Of Spain.

Franco stands in a shining circle of police.
His arms open in welcome.
He promises all dark things
Will be hunted down.

State police yawn in the prisons.
Antonio Machado follows the moon
Down a road of white dust,
To a cave of silent children
Under the Pyrenees.
Wine darkens in stone jars in villages.
Wine sleeps in the mouths of old men, it is a dark red color.

Smiles glitter in Madrid.
Eisenhower has touched hands with Franco, embracing
In a glare of photographers.
Clean new bombers from America muffle their engines
And glide down now.
Their wings shine in the searchlights
Of bare fields,
In Spain.

A BLESSING

Just off the highway to Rochester, Minnesota,
Twilight bounds softly forth on the grass.
And the eyes of those two Indian ponies
Darken with kindness.
They have come gladly out of the willows
To welcome my friend and me.
We step over the barbed wire into the pasture
Where they have been grazing all day, alone.
They ripple tensely, they can hardly contain their happiness
That we have come.
They bow shyly as wet swans. They love each other.
There is no loneliness like theirs.
At home once more,
They begin munching the young tufts of spring in the darkness.
I would like to hold the slenderer one in my arms,
For she has walked over to me
And nuzzled my left hand.
She is black and white,
Her mane falls wild on her forehead,
And the light breeze moves me to caress her long ear
That is delicate as the skin over a girl's wrist.
Suddenly I realize
That if I stepped out of my body I would break
Into blossom.

JAMES WRIGHT

LATE NOVEMBER IN A FIELD

Today I am walking alone in a bare place,
And winter is here.
Two squirrels near a fence post
Are helping each other drag a branch
Toward a hiding place; it must be somewhere
Behind those ash trees.
They are still alive, they ought to save acorns
Against the cold.
Frail paws rifle the troughs between cornstalks when the moon
Is looking away.
The earth is hard now,
The soles of my shoes need repairs.
I have nothing to ask a blessing for,
Except these words.
I wish they were
Grass.

THE LIGHTS IN THE HALLWAY

The lights in the hallway
Have been out a long time.
I clasp her,
Terrified by the roundness of the earth
And its apples and the voluptuous rings
Of poplar trees, the secret Africas,
The children they give us.
She is slim enough.
Her knee feels like the face
Of a surprised lioness
Nursing the lost children
Of a gazelle by pure accident.
In that body I long for,
The Gabon poets gaze for hours
Between boughs toward heaven, their noble faces
Too secret to weep.
How do I know what color her hair is? I float among
Lonely animals, longing
For the red spider who is God.

JAMES WRIGHT

IN RESPONSE TO A RUMOR THAT THE OLDEST WHOREHOUSE IN WHEELING, WEST VIRGINIA, HAS BEEN CONDEMNED

I will grieve alone,
As I strolled alone, years ago, down along
The Ohio shore.
I hid in the hobo jungle weeds
Upstream from the sewer main,
Pondering, gazing.

I saw, down river,
At Twenty-third and Water Streets
By the vinegar works,
The doors open in early evening.
Swinging their purses, the women
Poured down the long street to the river
And into the river.

I do not know how it was
They could drown every evening.
What time near dawn did they climb up the other shore,
Drying their wings?
For the river at Wheeling, West Virginia,
Has only two shores:
The one in hell, the other
In Bridgeport, Ohio.

And nobody would commit suicide, only
To find beyond death
Bridgeport, Ohio.

A MORAL POEM FREELY ACCEPTED FROM SAPPHO

(For the marriage of Frances Seltzer and Philip Mendlow)

I would like to sleep with deer.
Then she emerges.
I sleep with both.
This poem is a deer with a dream in it.
I have stepped across its rock.

The three wings coiling out of that black stone in my breast
Jut up slashing the other two
Sides of the sky.
Let the dead rise.
Let us two die
Down with the two deer.
I believe that love among us
And those two animals
Has its place in the
Brilliance of the sun that is
More gold than gold,
And in virtue.

A POEM OF TOWERS

I am becoming one
Of the old men.
I wonder about them,
And how they became
So happy. Tonight
The trees in the Carl Schurz
Park by the East River
Had no need of electricity
To light their boughs, for the moon
And my love were enough.
More than enough the garbage
Scow plunging, the front hoof
Of a mule gone so wild through the water,
No need to flee. Who pities
You tonight, white-haired
Lu Yu? Wise and foolish
Both are gone, and my love
Leans on my shoulder precise
As the flute notes
Of the snow, with songs
And poems scattered
Over Shu, over the East River
That loves them and drowns them.

JAMES WRIGHT

TO A BLOSSOMING PEAR TREE

Beautiful natural blossoms,
Pure delicate body,
You stand without trembling.
Little mist of fallen starlight,
Perfect, beyond my reach,
How I envy you.
For if you could only listen,
I would tell you something,
Something human.

An old man
Appeared to me once
In the unendurable snow.
He had a singe of white
Beard on his face.
He paused on a street in Minneapolis
And stroked my face.
Give it to me, he begged.
I'll pay you anything.

I flinched. Both terrified,
We slunk away,
Each in his own way dodging
The cruel darts of the cold.

Beautiful natural blossoms,
How could you possibly
Worry or bother or care
About the ashamed, hopeless
Old man? He was so near death
He was willing to take
Any love he could get,
Even at the risk
Of some mocking policeman
Or some cute young wiseacre
Smashing his dentures,
Perhaps leading him on
To a dark place and there
Kicking him in his dead groin
Just for the fun of it.

Young tree, unburdened
By anything but your beautiful natural blossoms
And dew, the dark
Blood in my body drags me
Down with my brother.

BEAUTIFUL OHIO

Those old Winnebago men
Knew what they were singing.
All summer long and all alone,
I had found a way
To sit on a railroad tie
Above the sewer main.
It spilled a shining waterfall out of a pipe
Somebody had gouged through the slanted earth.
Sixteen thousand and five hundred more or less people
In Martins Ferry, my home, my native country,
Quickened the river
With the speed of light.
And the light caught there
The solid speed of their lives
In the instant of that waterfall.
I know what we call it
Most of the time.
But I have my own song for it,
And sometimes, even today,
I call it beauty.

Notes on the Poets

A. R. AMMONS (1926)

Born in Whiteville, North Carolina, A. R. Ammons was educated at Wake Forest College and the University of California at Berkeley. From 1952 to 1962, he was an executive of a biological glass company; since 1964 he has taught at Cornell University where he is presently Goldwin Smith Professor of Poetry. The recipient of fellowships from the Guggenheim Foundation and the American Academy of Arts and Letters, Ammons also was awarded the National Book Award in 1973 and the Bollingen Prize in 1975.

A. R. Ammons has been called an American Romantic. So he is—in more ways than one. To begin with, the surface of his poems bristles and blooms primarily with the flora of the natural world observed by a well-trained and informed sensibility. At times one senses that this poet has observed the ever-shifting vagaries of the natural world with the zeal of a professional bird watcher. At the same time, the world that Ammons perceives seems remarkably devoid of other humans and—perhaps as a consequence—devoid of that darker, painful, and seamier side of human life we've come to expect in the work of contemporary poets. Even when he turns his attention to an urban existence quite removed from nature, as in "The City Limits," or to the possibility of "the explosion or cataclysm," as in "The Eternal City," Ammons has a distinctive capacity for reaffirming the "gold skeined wings of flies swarming . . . / the coiled shit" and the manner in which even ruinage must "accept . . . into itself . . . all the old / perfect human visions, all the old perfect loves."

At the heart of Ammons's poetry and vision seems to be a profound philosophical belief that the radiant energy at the heart of the natural world—as perceived by the seer-poet—becomes the inward and organic energy of the poem itself, which in turn is transformed from within into an emblematic and musical affirmation of the cosmic energy at the heart of all life. In the presence of this radiance, even "fear lit by the breadth of such calmly turns to praise." And the more we hear Ammons's philosophical music, the more we see those "hues, shadings, rises, flowing bends and blends"; as we move further into the world of Ammons's poetry, the better we can understand his moral and aesthetic conviction: "I understand / and won't give assertion up."

517

Poetry

Ommateum, with Doxology. Philadelphia: Dorrance, 1955.   *Expressions of Sea Level*. Columbus: Ohio State University, 1964.   *Corsons Inlet*. Ithaca, N.Y.: Cornell University, 1965.   *Tape for the Turn of the Year*. Ithaca, N.Y.: Cornell University, 1965.   *Northfield Poems*. Ithaca, N.Y.: Cornell University, 1966.   *Selected Poems*. Ithaca, N.Y.: Cornell University, 1968. *Uplands*. New York: Norton, 1970.   *Briefings: Poems Small and Easy*. New York: Norton, 1971.   *Collected Poems 1951–1971*. New York: Norton, 1972. *Sphere: The Form of a Motion*. New York: Norton, 1974.   *Diversifications*. New York: Norton, 1975.   *The Snow Poems*. New York: Norton, 1977. *The Selected Poems 1951–1977*. New York: Norton, 1977.

JOHN ASHBERY (1927)

John Ashbery was born in Rochester, New York. A graduate of Harvard and Columbia, he was executive editor of *Art News* from 1965 to 1972; he currently teaches at Brooklyn College. His many honors include Fulbright Fellowships, grants from the Ingram Merrill and Guggenheim Foundations, and a National Institute of Arts and Letters award. In 1975 Ashbery's *Self-Portrait in a Convex Mirror* received the Pulitzer Prize, the National Book Award, and the National Book Critics Circle Award.

With the publication of *The Tennis Court Oath*, Ashbery was recognized as one of the most experimental and as, at times, one of the most exasperating poets of his generation: montages of words and unrelated, juxtaposed images threatened the reader to attention, but then these fragments slipped away like verbal hallucinations, leaving the atmosphere charged with an emotional haze. Critics recognized the possible influences of Wallace Stevens, the French symbolists, and New York action painters; however, even the most unorthodox tools of criticism were blunted by this enigmatic poetry whose syntax refused to yield a recognizable sense of development or sustained meaning. While Ashbery's recent poems have become ostensibly more accessible and translucent, most critics continue to be baffled and to venture complex interpretations that, by comparison, make Ashbery's poems sound utterly transparent.

One critic has observed that Ashbery's largest aesthetic principle is the discovery that the world consents, every day, to being shaped into a poem. Ashbery himself has modified this view by asserting that there are no traditional subjects or themes in his poetry: "Most of my poems," he has said in an interview, "are about the experience of experience . . . and the particular experience is of lesser interest to me than the way it filters through to me. I believe this is the way in which it happens with most people, and I'm trying to record a kind of generalized transcript of what's really going on in our minds all day long."

Before the publication of *Three Poems*—long prose poems that may be viewed, at least in part, as an extended statement of poetics—Ashbery offered a somewhat minimal key to his enigmatic poetics when he wrote: "the carnivorous / Way of these lines is to devour their own nature, leaving / Nothing but a bitter impression of absence, which as we know involves presence, but still. / Nevertheless these are fundamental absences, struggling to get up and be off themselves." And the more one reads Ashbery's work, the more it is clear that these "absences" in his poetry—as in the work of Rilke—are the consequences of the innocent eye confronting experience: the lingering pain of loss.

Poetry

Turandot and Other Poems. New York: Tibor de Nagy, 1953.   *Some Trees.* New Haven: Yale University, 1956; reprint, New York: Corinth, 1970.   *The Tennis Court Oath.* Middletown: Wesleyan, 1962.   *Rivers and Mountains.* New York: Holt, Rinehart and Winston, 1966; reprint, New York: Ecco, 1977. *Sunrise in Suburbia.* New York: Phoenix Book Shop, 1968.   *Fragment.* Los Angeles: Black Sparrow, 1969.   *The Double Dream of Spring.* New York: Dutton, 1970; reprint, New York: Ecco, 1976.   *Three Poems.* New York: Viking, 1972; reprint, New York: Penguin, 1977.   *The Vermont Journal.* Los Angeles: Black Sparrow, 1975.   *Self-Portrait in a Convex Mirror.* New York: Viking, 1975; reprint, New York: Penguin, 1976.   *Houseboat Days.* New York: Viking/Penguin, 1977.   *As We Know.* New York: Viking/Penguin, 1979.

Fiction and Drama

A Nest of Ninnies (novel, with James Schuyler). New York: Dutton, 1969; reprint, Calais, Vt.: Z Press, 1975.   *Three Plays.* Calais, Vt.: Z Press, 1978.

Bibliography

Kermani, David. *John Ashbery: A Comprehensive Bibliography.* New York: Garland, 1976.

Critical Study

Shapiro, David. *John Ashbery: An Introduction to the Poetry.* New York: Columbia, 1979.

IMAMU AMIRI BARAKA (LEROI JONES) (1934)

Born in Newark as LeRoi Jones, Amiri Baraka was educated at Rutgers, Howard, the New School of Social Research, and Columbia. He has taught at the New School, Columbia, Yale, and the State University of

New York at Buffalo. He was the founder of *Yugen* magazine, Totem Press, and the Black Arts Repertory Theatre. His political commitment, meanwhile, has led him to serve as a member of the Congress of Afrikan Peoples, as chairman of the Congress of Afrikan Peoples, and as secretary-general of the National Black Political Assembly. His awards as a poet, dramatist, and essayist include an Obie Award for drama, a Guggenheim Fellowship, a grant from the National Endowment for the Arts, and the Dakar Festival Prize.

In Donald M. Allen's *The New American Poetry*, Jones has said: "MY POETRY is whatever I think I am . . . I CAN BE ANYTHING I CAN. I make poetry with what I feel is useful and can be saved out of all the garbage of our lives. What I see, am touched by (CAN HEAR) . . . wives, gardens, jobs, cement yards where cats pee, all my interminable artifacts . . . ALL are poetry. . . ." Some of his early poems reflect Jones's affiliation with Frank O'Hara and other New York poets—as well as the influence of Pound, Williams, and Charles Olson.

Baraka has also said: "I have always thought of writing as a moral art; that is, basically, I think of the artist as a moralist, as demanding a moral construct of the world, as asking for a cleaner vision of society. . . ." Since his participation in the Black Nationalist movement—at which time he assumed the name Imamu Amiri Baraka—and since his more recent affiliation with Marxism, his vision and poetics have remained unmistakably moral but perhaps have become increasingly didactic. In his introduction to *Black Magic*, Baraka wrote: "We are spiritual, and we must force this issue, we must see our selves again, as black men, as the strength of the planet, and rise to rebuild what is actually spiritual, what is actually good." As he makes eminently clear in a poem like "Black Art," the function of poetry in this vision is not aesthetic but rather social—a political gesture, a medium for revolution: "we want 'poems that kill.' / Assassin poems, Poems that shoot / guns."

Like much of the political and antiwar poetry written during the sixties and much of the Black poetry published to date, Baraka's later verse, often powerful and moving, challenges many basic assumptions about the nature and function of poetry—and thus of all art. Many of his poems are as much aesthetic and critical challenges as they are social and moral ones. And yet at the heart of many are also clustering sparks of human passion for beauty that transcends revolution.

Poetry

Preface to a Twenty Volume Suicide Note. New York: Totem-Corinth Books, 1961. *The Dead Lecturer*. New York: Grove, 1964. *Black Art*. Newark, N.J.: Jihad, 1966. *A Poem for Black Hearts*. Detroit: Broadside, 1967. *Black Magic: Poetry 1961–1967*. Indianapolis: Bobbs-Merrill, 1969. *It's Nation Time*. Chicago: Third World, 1970. *Spirit Reach*. Newark, N.J.: Jihad, 1972. *Hard Facts*. Newark, N.J.: People's War, 1975.

Fiction

The System of Dante's Hell. New York: Grove, 1965.   *Tales*. New York: Grove, 1967.

Drama

Dutchman and The Slave. New York: Morrow, 1964.   *Jello*, Chicago: Third World, 1970.   *The Baptism and The Toilet*. New York: Grove, 1967.   *Arm Yrself and Harm Yrself*. Newark, N.J.: Jihad, 1967.   *Slave Ship: A Historical Pageant*. Newark, N.J.: Jihad, 1969.   *Four Black Revolutionary Plays*. Indianapolis: Bobbs-Merrill, 1969.

Essays and Other Prose

Blues People: Negro Music in White America. New York: Morrow, 1963. *Home: Social Essays*. New York: Morrow, 1966.   *Black Music*. New York: Morrow, 1967.   *In Our Terribleness: Some Elements and Meaning in Black Style*. Indianapolis: Bobbs-Merrill, 1970.   *A Black Value System*. Newark, N.J.: Jihad, 1970.   *Raise Race Rays Raze: Essays Since 1965*. New York: Random House, 1971.

Critical Study

Sollors, Werner. *Amiri Baraka/LeRoi Jones: The Quest for a Populist Modernism*. New York: Columbia, 1979.

JOHN BERRYMAN (1914–1972)

John Berryman graduated from Columbia and Clare College (Cambridge). He taught at Brown, Harvard, Princeton, and was, at the time of his death, professor of humanities at the University of Minnesota. A recipient of Rockefeller and Guggenheim fellowships and of a special grant from the National Arts Council, he also won the Pulitzer Prize (1965) and the National Book Award (1969). On January 7, 1972, John Berryman committed suicide.

In the course of his career, Berryman wrote not only a distinguished long poem in homage to Anne Bradstreet but also an equally notable sonnet sequence. However, his major work is his sequence of 385 "Dream Songs," for which he may well be recognized as one of the truly great poets of the century. The scope, depth, daring, and craftsmanship of these poems have caused critics to compare Berryman with Homer, Dante, and Whitman.

The Dream Songs constitute a loose narrative about a multidimensional figure most often called Henry Pussycat. Berryman wrote that Henry is "an imaginary character (not the poet . . .), a white American in early middle age sometimes in blackface, who has suffered an irreversible loss and talks to himself sometimes in the first person, sometimes in the third, sometimes even in the second; he has a friend, never named, who addresses him as Mr Bones and variants thereof." There are moments in the Dream Songs when Henry, Mr Bones, and the poet are barely distinguishable from one another—and are not meant to be distinguishable. Thus Berryman attempts and achieves a linear-multidimensional vision—maneuvered by a dazzling shift of pronouns—which is a verbal equivalent to what Picasso achieved in his cubist period.

Like Odysseus, Henry Pussycat undergoes a fantastic range of experience. He even dies and comes back to life. His emotions shift from incredible panic, horror, and self-pity to sheer joy and self-deprecating slapstick. If Henry gets out of hand, his friend and conscience, his sidekick and minstrel chorus are always there either to cut him down to size or to support him through despair. At the end of his journey, which takes him across spiritual as well as spatial and historical boundaries, Henry, the schizophrenic Odysseus of the atomic age, returns to his wife and child, scarred but bearing that most ancient and essential knowledge: to be human is to suffer.

Poetry

Poems. Norfolk, Conn.: New Directions, 1942.   *The Dispossessed*. New York: William Sloane, 1948.   *Homage to Mistress Bradstreet*. New York: Farrar, Straus & Giroux, 1956.   *His Thoughts Made Pockets & The Plane Buckt*. Pawlet, Vt.: C. Fredericks, 1958.   *77 Dream Songs*. New York: Farrar, Straus & Giroux, 1967.   *Short Poems*. New York: Farrar, Straus & Giroux, 1967.   *His Toy, His Dream, His Rest*. New York: Farrar, Straus & Giroux, 1968.   *The Dream Songs*. New York: Farrar, Straus & Giroux, 1969.   *Love & Fame*. New York: Farrar, Straus & Giroux, 1970; revised edition, 1972.   *Delusions, Etc*. New York: Farrar, Straus & Giroux, 1972.   *Henry's Fate & Other Poems, 1967–1972*. New York: Farrar, Straus & Giroux, 1977.

Fiction and Criticism

Stephen Crane (biography). New York: William Sloane, 1950; reprint, Cleveland: World, 1962.   *Recovery* (novel). New York: Farrar, Straus & Giroux, 1973.   *The Freedom of the Poet* (essays and stories). Farrar, Straus & Giroux, 1976.

Bibliographies

Arpin, Gary Q. *John Berryman: A Reference Guide*. Boston: G. K. Hall, 1976.   Kelly, Richard J. *John Berryman: A Checklist*. Metuchen, N.J.: Scarecrow, 1972.   Stefanik, Ernest C., Jr. *John Berryman: A Descriptive Bibliography*. Pittsburgh: University of Pittsburgh, 1972.

Critical Studies

Linebarger, J. M. *John Berryman*. New York: Twayne, 1974.   Martz, William J. *John Berryman*. Minneapolis: University of Minnesota, 1969.

ELIZABETH BISHOP (1911–1979)

A native of Worcester, Massachusetts, Elizabeth Bishop received her formal education at Vassar. She lived in Brazil for the better part of sixteen years; she taught at the University of Washington and at Harvard. She was Consultant in Poetry at the Library of Congress from 1949 to 1950 and was subsequently elected a chancellor of the Academy of American Poets and a member of the National Institute of Arts and Letters. Her many other honors include grants from the Guggenheim and Ingram Merrill Foundations, the Pulitzer Prize (1956), the National Book Award (1970), and the Order of Rio Branco (Brazil, 1971).

Although Elizabeth Bishop was far less prolific than most poets of her generation, she was one of the few poets about whom it could be said that each new book—indeed each new poem—was an "event." One reason may be that she was far less predictable than many of her contemporaries; that is, readers of poetry did not come to expect a particular kind of poem from Bishop the way that they had come to expect a certain kind of poem from Anne Sexton or Robert Lowell.

Another reason why Bishop's poems are rare moments of delight and epiphany stems from her stunning perceptions and reconstruction of the details of physical reality. As Randall Jarrell says in *Poetry and the Age*: "all her poems have written underneath, *I have seen it.*" Whether the matter at hand is the exotic rainbow glow of a tremendous fish or the commonplace sheen of oil in a dingy filling station, Bishop knows that poetry and vision are rooted, first of all, in what Archibald MacLeish has called "the shine of the world." In her better poems, Bishop amply demonstrates that the perception of sensible objects and moral vision, for the poet, may be one and the same experience.

Ralph J. Mills, Jr., has rightfully noted another, more ambitious dimension of Bishop's achievement. In addition to her graceful use of fairly strict forms—and the unmistakable presence of a formalist approach even in the freer verse—Elizabeth Bishop's poems are distinguished by what Mills calls a "total accomplishment of language, technique, music, and imagery working simultaneously, or (in Eliot's phrase) 'the complete consort of dancing together.' "

Poetry

North and South. Boston: Houghton Mifflin, 1946.   *Poems: North and South—A Cold Spring*. Boston: Houghton Mifflin, 1955.   *Questions of Travel*. New York: Farrar, Straus & Giroux, 1965.   *The Ballad of the Burglar of Babylon*. New York: Farrar, Straus & Giroux, 1968.   *The Complete Poems*. New York: Farrar, Straus & Giroux, 1969; reprint, 1979.   *Geography III*. New York: Farrar, Straus & Giroux, 1976.

Translations: Prose and Poetry

The Diary of Helena Morley. New York: Farrar, Straus & Giroux, 1957.
Anthology of Contemporary Brazilian Poetry (editor and translator with others).
Middletown: Wesleyan, 1972.

Critical Study

Stevenson, Ann. *Elizabeth Bishop*. New York: Twayne, 1966.

ROBERT BLY (1923)

Robert Bly lives in rural Minnesota where he edits *The Eighties* (formerly *The Seventies, The Sixties, The Fifties*) and manages The Eighties Press (formerly The Seventies Press and The Sixties Press). For the 1975 edition of *Contemporary Poets*, Bly wrote: "I earn my living giving readings at American colleges and universities, and by translating." He graduated from Harvard and—though he hates to admit it—later did graduate work at the University of Iowa's Writers' Workshop. He has received Fulbright, Guggenheim, and Rockefeller fellowships; a grant from the National Institute of Arts and Letters; and the National Book Award in 1968.

In addition to his many books of poetry and of translations, Robert Bly also has translated Scandinavian fiction and has edited a number of small but vital anthologies such as *The Sea and the Honeycomb: A Book of Tiny Poems* (1966), *Forty Poems Touching on Recent American History* (1970), and *Leaping Poetry: An Idea with Poems and Translations* (1975). Among his contemporaries, Bly is one of the few poets who has consistently written a rather substantial amount of theoretical criticism as well as critical essays on the work of other poets.

Influenced by the thought of the seventeenth-century German theosophist, Jacob Boehme, and the techniques of such twentieth-century Spanish surrealists as Lorca and Neruda, Bly's poems tend to be almost purely phenomenological. Revolting against the rationalism and empiricism of his century, Boehme emphasized an intuitive perception of the outer tangible world of humans and things as a symbol of the corresponding and truer inner spiritual world. The outward man is asleep, Boehme wrote; he is only the husk of the real inner man. Like the American Romantic Transcendentalist Emerson, Boehme insisted that men neither see nor respond to that inner spiritual world: "the wise of this world . . . have shut and locked us up in their art and rationality, so that we have had to see with their eyes."

Bly himself has written that American poetry took a wrong turn, moving in "a destructive motion outward" rather than a "plunge inward, trying for a great (spiritual and imaginative) intensity." In his revolt against Eliot's theory of the "objective correlative" and against Pound's practice in the *Cantos* of "eating up more and more of the outer world, with less and less life at the center," Bly has fashioned his poems after the works of twentieth-century Spanish surrealists. In them, he seems to have found a poetics that corresponds to Boehme's mysticism, enabling him to plunge beneath the phenomenology of surfaces and find images and words to suggest the inner reality and spiritual intensity of experience. Moreover, many of Bly's poems continue to be implicit reaffirmations of a statement that appeared on the flyleaf of *The Lion's Tail and Eyes* (1962) in which he suggests that his poems come from "the part of the personality which is nourished by notice of things that are growing" and simultaneously that they "resist the Puritan insistence on being busy, the need to think of everything in terms of work."

Poetry

The Lion's Tail and Eyes: Poems Written Out of Laziness and Silence (with James Wright and William Duffy). Madison, Minn.: Sixties Press, 1962. *Silence in the Snowy Fields*. Middletown: Wesleyan, 1962. *The Light Around the Body*. New York: Harper & Row, 1967. *The Morning Glory*. San Francisco: Kayak, 1969; expanded edition, New York: Harper & Row, 1975. *The Teeth Mother Naked at Last*. San Francisco: City Lights, 1970. *Jumping Out of Bed*. Barre, Mass.: Barre, 1973. *Sleepers Joining Hands*. New York: Harper & Row, 1973. *Point Reyes Poems*. Half Moon Bay, Calif.: Mudra, 1974. *Old Man Rubbing His Eyes*. Greensboro, N.C.: Unicorn, 1975. *This Body Is Made of Camphor and Gopherwood*. New York: Harper & Row, 1977. *This Tree Will Be Here for a Thousand Years*. New York: Harper & Row, 1979.

Translations and Versions: Poetry

Twenty Poems of Georg Trakl (with James Wright). Madison, Minn.: Sixties Press, 1961. *Twenty Poems of Cesar Vallejo* (with John Knoepfle and James Wright). Madison, Minn.: Sixties Press, 1962. *Juan Ramón Jiménez: Forty Poems*. Madison, Minn.: Sixties Press, 1967. *Pablo Neruda: Twenty Poems* (with James Wright). Madison, Minn.: Sixties Press, 1967. *Tomas Transtromer: Twenty Poems*. Madison, Minn.: Seventies Press, 1970. *Neruda and Vallejo: Selected Poems* (with John Knoepfle and James Wright). Boston: Beacon, 1971. *Night Vision* [Thomas Transtromer]. Northwood Narrows, N.H.: Lillabulero Press, 1971. *Basho*. San Francisco: Mudra, 1972. *Lorca and Jiménez: Selected Poems*. Boston: Beacon, 1973. *Friends, You Drank Some Darkness: Three Swedish Poets, Martinson, Ekelof and Transtromer*. Boston: Beacon, 1976. *The Kabir Book: Forty-Four of the Ecstatic Poems of Kabir*. Boston: Beacon, 1977. *Vicente Aleixandre: Twenty Poems* (with Lewis Hyde). Madison, Minn.: Seventies Press, 1977. *Rolf Jacobsen: Twenty Poems*. Madison, Minn.: Seventies Press, 1977. *Rainer Maria Rilke: Selected Poems*. New York: Harper & Row, 1979.

Criticism

Leaping Poetry: An Idea with Poems and Translations. Boston: Beacon, 1975. *Talking All Morning: Collected Interviews and Conversations.* Ann Arbor: University of Michigan, 1979.

GWENDOLYN BROOKS (1917)

A graduate of Wilson Junior College in Chicago, Gwendolyn Brooks began her professional career in 1941 with Inez Stark Boulton's poetry workshop at the South Side Community Art Center in Chicago. She was awarded two Guggenheim Fellowships, a grant from the National Institute of Arts and Letters, and the Pulitzer Prize for her second book of poems in 1950. In 1969 Gwendolyn Brooks was named "Poet Laureate of the State of Illinois," an honor formerly held by Carl Sandburg.

Gwendolyn Brooks's poems are often marked by direct and bold social observation and by language which precedes—indeed foreshadows—much of the Black poetry written by younger poets today and the later poetry of Amiri Baraka. Her Black hero's assertion, "I helped to save them . . . / Even if I had to kick their law into their teeth in order to do that for them," might well have been written in the sixties or seventies rather than in the forties. In those poems addressed specifically to the horror of the Black experience in America, she is also capable of a range of emotions: brutal anger, wry satire, and visionary serenity.

Informed by the spectrum of the Black experience and her own emotional objectivity, some of her poems are also marked by the simplicity, quiet, and gentility of a woman's sensibilities. Yet in a poem like "The Mother," she also demonstrates the kind of fierce emotion that other women poets like Anne Sexton and Adrienne Rich have displayed in more consciously personal or political poems. But gentle or fierce, personal or social, her poems consistently affirm the common denominator of human experience in poetry and in the human community.

Poetry

A Street in Bronzeville. New York: Harper & Brothers, 1945.   *Annie Allen.* New York: Harper & Brothers, 1949.   *Bronzeville Boys and Girls.* New York: Harper & Brothers, 1956.   *Selected Poems.* New York: Harper & Row, 1963.   *In the Mecca: Poems.* New York: Harper & Row, 1968. *Riot.* Detroit: Broadside, 1969.   *The Wall.* Detroit: Broadside, n.d. *Family Pictures.* Detroit: Broadside, 1970.   *Aloneness.* Detroit: Broadside, 1971.

Prose and Poetry

Maud Martha (novel). New York: Harper & Brothers, 1953.   *Report from*
Part One: An Autobiography. Detroit: Broadside, 1972.   *The World of*
Gwendolyn Brooks. New York: Harper & Row, 1972.

ROBERT CREELEY (1926)

A New Englander by birth and sensibility, Robert Creeley was born in
Arlington, Massachusetts, and was educated at Harvard, Black Mountain
College, and the University of New Mexico. He has traveled widely and
has taught at the University of New Mexico and at Black Mountain
College where he also edited the influential journal *Black Mountain
Review.* In addition to his many books of poetry, fiction, and criticism,
Creeley has edited a variety of other collections, including Charles
Olson's letters. He is currently a professor of English at the State Univer-
sity of New York at Buffalo.

Generally associated with the "Projectivists" and poets of the Black
Mountain School, Creeley nevertheless is a Puritan at heart—Emily
Dickinson's cool, hip, one-eyed, and unvirginal nephew. Like all good
Puritans, Creeley is "hung up": "I think I grow tensions / like flow-
ers . . ." Pain is central to his work—a sharp, stinging pain evoked in
such images as "I can / feel my eye breaking." In more recent poems,
like "Moment" and "On Vacation," a Puritan sensibility surfaces more
explicitly, as it does in the very structure and substance of collections
like *A Day Book* and *Hello*—sustained attempts at recording and dis-
covering the "meaning" of diurnal events, an implicit quest for signs of
salvation, especially love. "I love you. / Do you love me. / What to
say / when you see me . . ." might be a summary of one of Creeley's
central concerns.

No critical essay or explanatory statement reveals Creeley's poetics
as precisely as his own poems, especially "The Language" and "The
Window." In the former, he states simply: "Locate *I* . . ."; in the latter,
he writes: "Position is where you / put it, where it is . . ." The position
of the I—as locus, as viewer, and as speaker—largely determines the
form and the direction of the poem. The position of words on the page
results from the location of this I, who, by arranging the poem as it is,
speaks not only in grammatical units but also in linear units. In other
words, Creeley's poems evolve on both a sequential grammatical level
and on a cumulative linear level, with each individual line reaffirming or
modifying the sense of the sentence and of the poem. And such con-
trapuntal tension in the very structure of Creeley's poems—perhaps

more than the sparse, occasionally hesitant language—reflects the contemporary struggle with those forces that would make us all inarticulate.

Poetry

Le Fou. Columbus, Ohio: Golden Goose, 1952.   *The Kind of Act Of.* Majorca: Divers, 1953.   *The Immoral Proposition.* Highlands, N.C.: Jonathan Williams, 1953.   *All That Is Lovely in Men.* Highlands, N.C.: Jargon, 1955.   *A Form of Women.* New York: Jargon-Corinth, 1959. *For Love: Poems 1950–1960.* New York: Scribner's, 1962.   *Words.* New York: Scribner's, 1967.   *The Charm: Early and Uncollected Poems.* Madison, Wis.: Perishable Press, 1967; reprint, San Francisco: Four Seasons, 1969. *The Finger* (with Bobbie Creeley). Los Angeles: Black Sparrow, 1968. *Pieces.* Los Angeles: Black Sparrow, 1968.   *St. Martin's* (with Bobbie Creeley). Los Angeles: Black Sparrow, 1971.   *1–2–3–4–5–6–7–8–9–0* (with Arthur Okamura). Berkeley: Mudra, 1971.   *A Day Book.* New York: Scribner's, 1972.   *Thirty Things* (with Bobbie Creeley). Los Angeles: Black Sparrow, 1974.   *Away* (with Bobbie Creeley). Santa Barbara: Black Sparrow, 1976.   *Presences* (with Marisol). Santa Barbara: Black Sparrow, 1976.   *Selected Poems.* New York: Scribner's, 1976.   *Hello.* New York: New Directions, 1978.   *Later.* New York: New Directions, 1979.

Fiction and Criticism

The Island (novel). New York: Scribner's, 1963.   *The Gold Diggers and Other Stories.* New York: Scribner's, 1965.   *A Quick Graph: Collected Notes and Essays.* San Francisco: Four Seasons, 1970.   *Contexts of Poetry: Interviews 1961–1971.* Edited by Donald M. Allen. Bolinas, Calif.: Four Seasons, 1973.

Bibliography

Novik, Mary. *Robert Creeley: An Inventory, 1945–1970.* Kent, Ohio: Kent State University, 1973.

JAMES DICKEY (1923)

James Dickey received his bachelor's and master's degree from Vanderbilt University. He was a night fighter pilot during both World War II and the Korean War; as a civilian, he has worked as an advertising executive in Atlanta and New York; and he has taught at a variety of colleges and universities, including the University of South Carolina where he is presently poet-in-residence. In 1966 James Dickey received the National Book Award for poetry; from 1966 to 1968, he served as Consultant in Poetry at the Library of Congress.

One of the less ostensibly "academic" poets of his generation, Dickey's poems are often disarmingly frank in subject matter and in "moral tone."

He has refused to assume those moral postures often expected of today's poets: during Vietnam, he did not write antiwar poetry but rather, in a poem like "The Firebombing," he confronted his own understanding of and sympathy with the pilot whose mission was to drop napalm on enemy villages without the luxury of questioning the morality of such an act. In several other poems, he has explored varieties of sexual experiences, including implicit and explicit sexual encounters between humans and animals, as in "The Sheep Child."

Dickey's poems are marked by an exuberant language and by a primal energy, passion, and ritual. Probing the most elemental in humankind, his poems often trace a human's mythic subconscious and paradoxical evolution to a primitive level where humans and animals become companions and mates in the same irrational but holy species. Moreover, in much of Dickey's work, poetry is the tongue articulating the consciousness of all creation on this planet, from the mute stone up the earthly chain of being to humankind. And in this way, his poems often recall Whitman's poetry and vision.

Simultaneously, many of Dickey's poems are also marked by a Southern Puritanism. His characters are grotesque—physically and spiritually wounded. They are violent creatures; their brutal sexuality is immersed in pain and death. And they move about in a world churning with violence and profound evil that is as much inherent in the human condition as it is man-made. Dickey's vision, then, includes the polarities of light and grace, darkness and sin. The total impact of his poems is often the drama of Adam, shimmering with primal light, awakening to guilt, and finding it magical.

Poetry

Into the Stone and Other Poems. In *Poets of Today VII*. New York: Scribner's, 1960.   *Drowning with Others*. Middletown: Wesleyan, 1962.   *Helmets*. Middletown: Wesleyan, 1964.   *Buckdancer's Choice*. Middletown: Wesleyan, 1965.   *Poems 1957–1967*. Middletown: Wesleyan, 1967; paper edition, New York: Collier, 1968; second paper edition, Middletown: Wesleyan, 1978.   *The Eye-Beaters, Blood, Victory, Madness, Buckhead and Mercy*. New York: Doubleday, 1970.   *Exchanges*. Bloomfield Hills, Mich.: Bruccoli-Clark, 1971.   *The Zodiac*. New York: Doubleday, 1976.   *The Strength of Fields* (for the Inauguration of Jimmy Carter). Bloomfield Hills, Mich.: Bruccoli-Clark, 1977.   *The Enemy from Eden* (prose poems). Northridge, Calif.: Lord John, 1978.   *The Strength of Fields*. New York: Doubleday, 1979.

Criticism

The Suspect in Poetry. Madison, Minn.: Sixties Press, 1964.   *Babel to Byzantium: Poets & Poetry Now*. New York: Farrar, Straus & Giroux, 1968. *Self-Interviews*. Edited by Barbara and James Reiss. New York: Doubleday, 1970. *Sorties: Journals and New Essays*. New York: Doubleday, 1971.

NOTES ON THE POETS

Fiction and Other Prose

Deliverance (novel). Boston: Houghton Mifflin, 1970.   *Jericho: The South Beheld* (with paintings by Hubert Shuptrine). Birmingham, Ala.: Oxmoor, 1974. *God's Images* (with photographs by Marvin Hayes). Birmingham, Ala.: Oxmoor, 1974.   *In Pursuit of the Grey Soul*. Bloomfield Hills, Mich.: Bruccoli-Clark, 1979.

Bibliographies

Ashley, Franklin. *James Dickey: A Checklist*. Detroit: Bruccoli-Clark/Gale Research, 1972.   Glancy, Eileen. *James Dickey, the Critic as Poet: An Annotated Bibliography with an Introductory Essay*. Troy, N.Y.: Whitston, 1971.

Critical Studies

Calhoun, Richard J., ed. *James Dickey: The Expansive Imagination*. Deland, Fla.: Everett Edwards, 1973.   Lieberman, Laurence. *The Achievement of James Dickey*. Glenview, Ill.: Scott, Foresman, 1968.

ALAN DUGAN (1923)

Born in Brooklyn and a graduate of Mexico City College, Alan Dugan's first book of poems won the Yale Series of Younger Poets award, the Pulitzer Prize, and the National Book Award.

Although Dugan's most effective poems can be humorous, lyrical, or cerebral, his work also can be tough, brutal, and ugly. For William J. Martz's *The Distinctive Voice*, Dugan wrote about his voice as a poet: "I am trying to say what is hardest to say; that is, words wrung out of intense experience and not constructed." Moreover, as Richard Howard has observed, in Dugan's poetry one senses that "the act of writing poetry is, precisely, an invocation of destruction, a luring of language to its wreck... He is too honest... for the consolation of some visionary transcendence of language...."

In many of his poems, Dugan talks about the least public of experiences in a language still generally considered the least public—perhaps "unpoetic." Moreover, he refuses to burden his subject and language with any obviously stated mystical, magical, or "great social" impact. He tells it "like it is" and, rather than being offensive—as one might vaguely and uneasily wish they were—his poems emerge as the product of a fierce and fully American honesty and of a craftsmanship generating words that burn through all pretense like acid.

Poetry

Poems. New Haven: Yale University, 1961.   *Poems 2*. New Haven: Yale University, 1963.   *Poems 3*. New Haven: Yale University, 1967.   *Col-*

lected Poems. New Haven: Yale University, 1969.   Poems 4. Boston: Atlantic-Little, Brown, 1974.   Sequence. Cambridge, Mass.: Dolphin Editions, 1976.

ROBERT DUNCAN (1919)

A native of California, Robert Duncan was educated at the University of California, Berkeley. He has traveled extensively and has taught at San Francisco State, the University of British Columbia, and at Black Mountain College with Charles Olson. He has served as editor of *The Experimental Review* and *The Berkeley Miscellany*; in addition to poetry and criticism, he has been writing an extended study of H. D., parts of which have appeared in various journals. His awards include the Harriet Monroe Memorial Prize, two grants from the National Endowment for the Arts, and a Guggenheim Fellowship.

In *The Truth & Life of Myth*, Robert Duncan wrote: "The meaning and intent of what it is to be a man and, among men, to be a poet, I owe to the working of myth in my spirit, both the increment and associations gathered in my continuing study of mythological lore and my own apprehension of what my life is at work here." And in his statement reprinted in Donald Allen's anthology, *The New American Poetry* (1960), Duncan stated that "every moment of life is an attempt to come to life. Poetry is a 'participation,' a oneness." It is "the very life of the soul: the body's dreaming that it can dream. And perish into its own imagination." A poem, according to Duncan, is "a ritual referring to divine orders."

If not so much through his seemingly anachronistic use of classical and medieval mythology, then surely in his fundamental attitude toward his art, Duncan attempts to return poetry to its most profound roots in the rituals of the divine orders. Erudite, orphic, at times homoerotic (long before sexual preference was a political and aesthetic issue), lyrical, and often profoundly religious, the poems of Robert Duncan gather a momentum that is more, much more, than the "passages of moonlight upon the floor." Rather, they are human clues to what might conceivably be "the meaning of the music of the spheres."

Poetry

Heavenly City, Earthly City. Berkeley: Bern Porter, 1947.   *Poems 1948–1949*. Berkeley: Berkeley Miscellany Editions, 1950.   *Medieval Scenes*. San Francisco: Centaur, 1950; reprint, Kent, Ohio: Kent State University Libraries, 1978.   *Caesar's Gate: Poems 1949–1950*. Palma, Mallorca: Divers, 1955; reprint, Albany, Calif.: Sand Dollar, 1972.   *Letters: Poems 1953–1956*.

Highlands, N.C.: Jargon, 1958. *Selected Poems*. San Francisco: City Lights, 1959. *The Opening of the Field*. New York: Grove, 1960; reprint, New York: New Directions, 1973. *Roots and Branches*. New York: Scribner's, 1964. *Of the War: Passages 22–27*. Berkeley: Oyez, 1966. *The Years As Catches: First Poems 1939–1946*. Berkeley: Oyez, 1966. *Epilogos*. Los Angeles: Black Sparrow, 1967. *Bending the Bow*. New York: New Directions, 1968. *Names of People*. Los Angeles: Black Sparrow, 1968. *Poetic Disturbances*. San Francisco: Maya, 1970. *Bring It Up from the Dark*. Berkeley: Cody's Books, 1970. *Tribunals: Passages 31–35*. Los Angeles: Black Sparrow, 1970. *The Truth and Life of Myrtle*. Fremont, Mich.: Sumac, 1972.

Criticism and Other Prose

As Testimony: The Poem and the Scene. San Francisco: White Rabbit, 1964. *Six Prose Pieces*. Rochester, Mich.: Perishable Press, 1966. *The Truth and Life of Myth: An Essay in Essential Autobiography*. New York: House of Books, 1968; reprint, Fremont, Mich.: Sumac, 1968. *Notes on Grossinger's "Solar Journal: Oecological Sections."* Los Angeles: Black Sparrow, 1970. *Fictive Certainties: Five Essays in Essential Autobiography*. New York: New Directions, 1979.

Critical Study

Bertholf, Robert J., and Ian W. Reid, eds. *Robert Duncan: Scales of the Marvellous*. New York: New Directions, 1979.

LAWRENCE FERLINGHETTI (1919)

Born in Yonkers, New York, Lawrence Ferlinghetti received an A.B. from the University of North Carolina, an M.A. from Columbia, and a Doctorat de l'Université from the Sorbonne. He was a lieutenant-commander in the Naval Reserve during World War II and worked for *Time* magazine in the forties. He was cofounder of City Lights Books in 1952 and has been both owner and editor-in-chief since 1953. He is also generally recognized as having been one of the leading figures of what is known as the San Francisco Renaissance and the Beat Generation.

In a "Note on Poetry in San Francisco" (1955), Ferlinghetti wrote: "the kind of poetry which has been making the most noise here . . . is what should be called street poetry. For it amounts to getting the poet out of the inner esthetic sanctum where he has too long been contemplating his complicated navel. It amounts to getting poetry back into the street where it once was, out of the classroom, out of the speech department, and—in fact—off the printed page. The printed word has made poetry so silent."

Ferlinghetti's own poems, often conceived as "oral messages," are designed primarily for their oral impact and often share the characteristics of popular songs. In fact, Ferlinghetti's experiments with poetry and jazz in the early sixties may well have foreshadowed the later successful fusion of music and lyrics by such popular poets as Bob Dylan. Intended to be understood by the ear, not primarily by the eye, Ferlinghetti's poems often lack the density and complexity of the printed poem. For the same reason, they often depend on the literary cliché, which serves much the same function as the formula in ancient oral poetry.

Like Hart Crane, Ferlinghetti sees the poet as "a charleychaplin man," and with a measure of self-directed irony that Crane never could quite muster, he admits that the poet is "constantly risking absurdity." Thus in his poems, while engaging in slapstick and often corny humor aimed at sociocultural evils and absurdities, he pokes fun at the world and at himself, seeks moments of tenderness, sometimes succumbs to sentimentality, and occasionally discovers moments of terror.

Poetry

Pictures of the Gone World. San Francisco: City Lights, 1955.   *A Coney Island of the Mind*. New York: New Directions, 1958.   *Tentative Description of a Dinner Given to Promote the Impeachment of President Eisenhower*. San Francisco: Golden Mountain, 1958.   *One Thousand Fearful Words for Fidel Castro*. San Francisco: City Lights, 1961.   *Berlin*. San Francisco: Golden Mountain, 1961.   *Starting from San Francisco*. New York: New Directions, 1961; revised edition, 1967.   *Where Is Vietnam?* San Francisco: City Lights, 1965.   *The Secret Meaning of Things*. New York: New Directions, 1969.   *Tyrannus Nix?* New York: New Directions, 1969.   *Back Roads to Far Places*. New York: New Directions, 1971: *Open Eye, Open Heart*. New York: New Directions, 1973.   *Who Are We Now?* New York: New Directions, 1976.   *Northwest Ecolog*. San Francisco: City Lights, 1978.   *Landscapes of Living & Dying*. New York: New Directions, 1979.

Translations: Poetry

Selections from Paroles by Jacques Prévert. San Francisco: City Lights, 1963.

Drama and Prose

Her (fiction). New York: New Directions, 1960.   *Unfair Arguments with Existence* (drama). New York: New Directions, 1963.   *Routines* (drama). New York: New Directions, 1964.   *The Mexican Night: Travel Journal*. New York: New Directions, 1970.

ALLEN GINSBERG (1926)

Born in Newark, New Jersey, Allen Ginsberg attended Columbia University, was dismissed, but returned later to receive his B.A. in 1948. A leader of the Beat Movement and the San Francisco Renaissance, in 1954 he married Peter Orlovsky. He is the recipient of grants from the Guggenheim Foundation, the National Endowment for the Arts, and the National Institute of Arts and Letters of which he is a member. In 1974 he was cowinner of the National Book Award with Adrienne Rich.

In his relatively recent poem, "Ego Confession," Allen Ginsberg asserts: "I want to be known as the most brilliant man in America . . . / I want to be the spectacle of Poesy triumphant over trickery of the world . . ." Poet, guru, world traveler, prophet, and visionary Uncle Sam of the Flower-Acid-Rock Generation, Ginsberg may well be the planet's most renowned poet. And if Ginsberg's notoriety as a sociocultural *enfant terrible* has obscured his power as a poet, he is nevertheless recognized by his contemporaries as one of the most influential post-1945 poets. His first major poem, "Howl," is a milestone of the generation, perhaps as significant a poem and document as Eliot's "Waste Land"; moreover, Ginsberg's entire work eventually may achieve the stature of *Leaves of Grass*.

At once intimate and prophetic, hilarious and terrifying, profoundly religious and, at times, commensurately outrageous, Ginsberg's poetry encompasses a myriad of experiences, ranges over the full spectrum of human life on this planet, and—like the poetry of Whitman—is a combination of incredible power and drivel. Clearly in technique, scope, and intent, Whitman is Ginsberg's model and mentor; like him, Ginsberg is attempting to recreate not only the world but also the full dimensions of a human's physical and spiritual odyssey through a given moment in history—with the crucial difference that Whitman's poems were hefty songs and Ginsberg's are often reverberating lamentations.

Part of Ginsberg's impact results from his prophetic stance as a man and as a poet, sustained by the vital spirit of William Blake and the prophets of the Old Testament. A modern-day Isaiah, whose public personality often betrays the range and depth of his erudition, Ginsberg is the public conscience of the nation—if not of the species—lamenting the imponderable evil humankind has perpetrated against life. But like Isaiah, Blake, and Whitman, he is also moved by a profound belief in the holiness of life and by a vision of a new Jerusalem, a new world.

Poetry

Howl and Other Poems. San Francisco: City Lights, 1956.   *Empty Mirror: Early Poems.* New York: Totem-Corinth, 1961.   *Kaddish and Other Poems.*

San Francisco: City Lights, 1961.   *Reality Sandwiches.* San Francisco: City Lights, 1963.   *T. V. Baby Poems.* London: Cape Goliard, 1967; New York: Grossman, 1968.   *Airplane Dreams: Compositions from Journals.* Toronto: House of Anansi, 1968; San Francisco: City Lights, 1969.   *Ankor-Wat.* London: Fulcrum, 1968.   *Planet News, 1961–1967.* San Francisco: City Lights, 1968.   *Bixby Canyon Ocean Path Word Breeze.* New York: Gotham Book Mart, 1972.   *The Gates of Wrath: Rhymed Poems, 1948–1952.* Bolinas, Calif.: Four Seasons, 1972.   *The Fall of America: Poems of These States, 1965–1971.* San Francisco: *City Lights,* 1973.   *Iron Horse.* Toronto: Coach House; San Francisco: City Lights, 1974.   *First Blues.* New York: Full Court, 1975.   *Sad Dust Glories.* Berkeley: Workingman's Press, 1975.   *Mind Breaths: Poems 1972–1977.* San Francisco: City Lights, 1977. *Poems All Over the Place, Mostly 'Seventies.* Cherry Valley, N.Y.: Cherry Valley Editions, 1978.   *Mostly Sitting Haiku.* Patterson, N.J.: From Here Press, 1979.

Criticism and Other Prose

The Yage Letters (with William Burroughs). San Francisco: City Lights, 1963. *Indian Journals.* San Francisco: Dave Haselwood, 1970.   *Improvised Poetics.* Edited with an introduction by Mark Robinson. San Francisco: Anonym Books, 1971.   *Gay Sunshine Interview.* Bolinas, Calif.: Grey Fox, 1974.   *Allen Verbatim: Lectures on Poetry, Politics, Consciousness.* Edited by Gordon Ball. New York: McGraw-Hill, 1974.   *The Visions of the Great Rememberer.* Amherst, Mass.: Mulch, 1974.   *Chicago Trial Testimony.* San Francisco: City Lights, 1975.   *To Eberhart from Ginsberg: A Letter About Howl 1956.* Lincoln, Mass.: Penmaen, 1976.   *As Ever: The Collected Correspondence of Allen Ginsberg & Neal Cassady.* Edited with an introduction by Barry Gifford. Berkeley: Creative Arts, 1977.   *Journals: Early Fifties Early Sixties.* Edited by Gordon Ball. New York: Grove, 1977.

Bibliography

Dowden, George and Lawrence McGilvery. A *Bibliography of the Works of Allen Ginsberg.* San Francisco: City Lights, 1971.

Biographical and Critical Studies

Ehrlich, J. W. E. *Howl of the Censor.* San Francisco: Nourse, 1956. Kramer, Jane. *Allen Ginsberg in America.* New York: Random House, 1969. Merrill, Thomas F. *Allen Ginsberg.* New York: Twayne, 1969.   Portuges, Paul. *The Visionary Poetics of Allen Ginsberg.* Santa Barbara: Ross-Erikson, 1979.   Simpson, Louis. A *Revolution in Taste: Studies in Dylan Thomas, Allen Ginsberg, Sylvia Plath and Robert Lowell.* New York: Morrow, 1978.

DONALD HALL (1928)

Born in New Haven, Connecticut, Donald Hall is a graduate of Phillips Exeter Academy, Harvard University, Oxford University, and Stanford University. In a way, he is also a "graduate" of the University of Michigan: he taught there for some ten years before resigning to return to his family's farm in Danbury, New Hampshire, where he currently lives. Hall has been poetry editor for *The Paris Review*, a member of the editorial board for Wesleyan's Poetry Series, and literary consultant for Harper & Row. He is the recipient of the Lamont Award for Poetry and of Guggenheim Fellowships.

Donald Hall's many other accomplishments include monographs on Marianne Moore and Henry Moore and such noted textbooks as *Writing Well* (1973) and *The Pleasures of Poetry* (1971). He also has edited some thirteen anthologies, including *New Poets of England and America* (with Robert Pack and Louis Simpson, 1957; revised with Robert Pack, 1962) and, of course, *Contemporary American Poetry* (Penguin, 1962; revised, 1971), the introduction to which offers this editor a major point of contention for his essay "The Radical Tradition" on page 577.

In a variety of statements—and especially in his dazzling essay "Goatfoot, Milktongue, Twinbird: The Psychic Origins of Poetic Form"—Donald Hall has repeatedly affirmed that the essential beauty of poetry lies in the sensual body of the poem—the sheer physical pleasure that a poem offers. That physical pleasure, Hall observes, "reaches us through our mouths (Milktongue) . . . in the muscles of our legs (Goatfoot) . . . in the resolution of dance and noise (Twinbird)." Hall's quest for the sensual body of his own poems was originally in more traditional forms; later, his poems became less formal, more expansive, and more sensual—without losing the control and discipline learned in the atelier of formalism.

Moreover, Hall's quest for the sensual body of poetry hasn't been the aesthete's pursuit of pleasure found in the notions of Walter Pater or in the work of some of Hall's own contemporaries. For Hall knows all too well: "Milktongue also remembers hunger, and the cry without answer. Goatfoot remembers falling, and the ache that bent the night. Twinbird remembers the loss of the brother, so long he believed in abandonment forever." At the heart of Hall's own poetry are the ever-present ache and modulated cry of abandonment, of grief over loss that is also at the heart of human experience: the baby son who documents his father's bodily decay; the emblematic skeleton of the pilot in the lost airplane; the town buried under water.

More recently the acute sense of loss in Hall's poems has been complemented by a commensurate measure of a joyous reconciliation with personal history, a discovery of the redemptive power inherent in all cycles of existence. Thus twenty-five years after the grandfather's body has slid into the ground like snow melting on the roof of the saphouse, his grandchildren dip their fingers in the maple syrup the dead man preserved in his cellar. Thus Hall himself can exclaim: "Oh, this delicious falling into the arms of leaves / into the soft laps of leaves! . . . /

Now I leap and fall, exultant, recovering / from death, on account of death, in accord with the dead ..." And thus he evokes still another ancient image of the sensual pleasure of poetry in the myth of Philomel, magically transformed into a nightingale whose torn tongue makes song, makes music, out of grief.

Poetry

(*Poems*). Oxford, England: Fantasy, 1952.   *To the Loud Wind and Other Poems*. Cambridge, Mass.: Harvard Advocate, 1955.   *Exiles and Marriages*. New York: Viking, 1955.   *The Dark Houses*. New York: Viking, 1958. *A Roof of Tiger Lilies: Poems*. New York: Viking, 1964.   *The Alligator Bride: Poems New and Selected*. New York: Harper & Row, 1969.   *The Yellow Room: Love Poems*. New York: Harper & Row, 1971.   *The Town of Hill*. Boston: David R. Godine, 1975.   *Kicking the Leaves*. New York: Harper & Row, 1978.   *The Toy Bone*. Brockport, N.Y.: BOA Editions, 1979.

Prose and Criticism

String Too Short To Be Saved: Childhood Reminiscences. New York: Viking, 1961; reprint, Boston: Godine, 1979.   *Henry Moore: The Life and Work of a Great Sculptor*. New York: Harper & Row, 1966.   *Dock Ellis: In The Country of Baseball*. New York: Coward, McCann & Geoghegan, 1976. *Goatfoot Milktongue Twinbird: Interviews, Essays, and Notes on Poetry, 1970–76*. Ann Arbor: University of Michigan, 1978.   *Remembering Poets: Reminiscences and Opinions*. New York: Harper & Row, 1978.

ROBERT HAYDEN (1913)

A native of Detroit, Robert Hayden received a B.A. from Wayne State University and an M.A. from the University of Michigan. He has taught at Fisk, Louisville, and Washington, and is presently professor of English at the University of Michigan. He has been a staff member of the Bread-loaf Writers Conference, and from 1976 to 1978 he served as Consultant in Poetry at the Library of Congress. Hayden is the editor of the anthology *Kaleidoscope: Poems by American Negro Poets* (Harcourt Brace, 1967) and one of the editors of *Afro-American Literature: An Introduction* (Harcourt Brace, 1971). His honors and awards include a Rosenwald Fellowship, a Ford Foundation grant, and the First World Festival of Negro Arts Prize for Poetry, Dakar, Senegal, in 1966.

Since the publication of his first book in 1940, Robert Hayden's poetry has consistently reflected a sensibility informed by a vital awareness of and participation in the broad spectrum of the Black experience. He has explored dimensions of his own childhood and personal life; he has focused on central historical and cultural figures and events; and he has recreated such immeasurable horrors as a Black man's castration at the hands of the Ku Klux Klan. No less important, while eschewing political rhetoric, he has recognized that much the same moral poison infected the air of both Selma and Saigon, that the ashes in the pits at Dachau resulted from a fire not unlike that which burned on lawns in innumerable American towns.

Hayden's moral vision is all the more powerful because his work reveals that he is equally conscious of the broader aesthetic traditions in the art of poetry and of the obvious—but often overlooked—fact that the wellsprings of poetry run more deeply and serendipitously than even the most active pools of political or racial experience. The impact of a poem like "Monet's 'Waterlilies' " emerges out of the fact that Hayden's vision is rooted specifically in such a seemingly apolitical and nonmoral work of art. The depths of horror in "Night, Death, Mississippi" are intensified by the delicate and exquisite lyrical qualities of "The Night-Blooming Cereus."

In short, whether writing about Frederick Douglass or Rilke or a diver, Robert Hayden's poems are themselves vibrant "lives grown out of his life, the lives / fleshing his dream of *the beautiful, needful thing.*"

Poetry

Heart-Shape in the Dust. Detroit: Falcon, 1940.   *The Lion and the Archer* (with Myron O'Higgins). Nashville: Counterpoise, 1948.   *Figures of Time: Poems*. Nashville: Hemphill, 1955.   *A Ballad of Remembrance*. London: Paul Breman, 1962.   *Selected Poems*. New York: October House, 1966. *Words in the Mourning Time*. New York: October House, 1970.   *The Night-Blooming Cereus*. London: Paul Breman, 1972.   *Angle of Ascent: New and Selected Poems*. New York: Liveright, 1975.   *American Journal*. Taunton, Mass.: Effendi, 1978; expanded edition, New York: Liveright, 1980.

RICHARD HUGO (1923)

Richard Hugo was born in Seattle and educated at the University of Washington. He was a bombardier in the U.S. Army Air Corps during World War II and subsequently worked for the Boeing Company for twelve years. Since 1964 he has been a member of the English Department at the University of Montana (Missoula), where he is presently professor of English and director of the creative writing program. His awards include the Theodore Roethke Memorial Poetry Prize, a Rockefeller Fellowship, and a Guggenheim Fellowship. At the present time he is also serving as the editor of the Yale Younger Poets series.

Perhaps more than the work of any other poet of his generation, Richard Hugo's poetry is rooted in and mines a specific, identifiable landscape—the American far West. However, Hugo's landscape isn't the breathtaking panorama of a Grand Canyon or spectacular hills and plains against a blazing sunset of romantic American western movies. The landscape in his poetry is suggested in Hugo's comment: "Usually I find a poem is triggered by something, a small town or an abandoned house, that I feel others would ignore." Thus the geographic, human, and moral landscape in Hugo's poems is a bleak and threatening panorama in which one finds those small, dry, and blistered towns where all life and human constructs decay too soon—and where perhaps nothing dies soon enough.

If, like Wallace Stevens, Richard Hugo understands the extent to which "the soil is man's intelligence," he nevertheless does not succumb to easy fatalism. In poems whose language and texture assert their own organic shapes and rhythms, as if in defiance of the odds of lunar dust, Hugo affirms the things of this earth and of his poetic landscape. Just as Rilke could assert: "Maybe we're here only to say: *house, / bridge, well, gate, jug, olive tree, window*— / at most, *pillar, tower* . . . but to say them, remember, / oh, to say them in a way that the things themselves / never dreamed of existing so intensely," so Hugo can assert: "To live good, keep your life and the scene. / Cow, brook, hay: these are names of coins."

"A part of the West belongs to Hugo," William Stafford has written. "By telling over and over again its places and people, he reclaims it from the very bleakness he confronts; and it all begins to loom as a great intense abode that we can't neglect, that we can't bear to let go." Thus Richard Hugo's intense love of the things of *his* earth keeps them and us alive at a level of intensity and joy we could not know without the melancholy and redemptive beauty of his poems.

Poetry

A *Run of Jacks*. Minneapolis: University of Minnesota, 1961.   *Death of the Kapowsin Tavern*. New York: Harcourt Brace, 1965.   *Good Luck in Cracked Italian*. Cleveland: World, 1969.   *The Lady in Kicking Horse Reservoir*. New York: Norton, 1973.   *What Thou Lovest Well, Remains American*. New York: Norton, 1975.   *31 Letters and 13 Dreams*. New York: Norton, 1977.   *Road Ends at Tahola*. Pittsburgh: Slow Loris, 1978. *Selected Poems*. New York: Norton, 1979.

Criticism

The Triggering Town: Lectures and Essays on Poetry and Writing. New York: Norton, 1979.

DAVID IGNATOW (1914)

A native of Brooklyn, David Ignatow has worked as a salesman, public relations writer, shipyard handyman—and treasurer and president of a bindery firm. He has taught at the New School for Social Research, Vassar, and Columbia; since 1969 he has been poet-in-residence at York College. Coeditor of *Beloit Poetry Journal* from 1950 to 1959, he has also served as poetry editor for *The Nation* and as an associate editor of *American Poetry Review*. In addition to awards from the National Institute of Arts and Letters and the National Endowment for the Arts, he has received a Rockefeller Fellowship and two Guggenheim Fellowships. In 1975 he was awarded the Bollingen Prize in poetry.

An avowed disciple of William Carlos Williams, who focuses primarily on the urban experience, Ignatow has written in his *Notebooks* that his role is to remind other poets—and, by implication, all readers of poetry—that "there is a world outside, the more decisive world that yet must be treated tragically by us in the highest intensity and sensuousness, though while it ignores us we must not run off into separate worlds of our own." Admitting that he is "antipoetic," he affirms that experience must be looked at and accepted just as it is and that "nothing should be taken for more than it says to you on its surface."

Ranging from comedy, through rage, to tragedy—and addressing himself to both his personal experiences as well as to our communal life—Ignatow constantly attempts to see life as it really is, without illusion or self-deception of any kind. And in so doing, he views himself as being at the opposite pole of Whitman's affirmative optimism. "My idea of being a moral leader," he writes, "is to point out the terrible deficiencies in man. Whitman spent his life boosting the good side. My life will be spent pointing out the bad." But he adds a most crucial phrase: if he is intent on pointing to human deficiencies, he says that he will do so "from the standpoint of forgiveness and peace."

A singular and powerful voice in contemporary poetry, eschewing all current modes of language to be himself first of all, David Ignatow's poetry is marked by a certain nontheatrical directness and is also charged with a unique strength of spirit, humanity, and wisdom.

Poetry

Poems. Prairie City, Ill.: Decker Press, 1948. *The Gentle Weight Lifter*. New York: Morris Gallery, 1955. *Say Pardon*. Middletown: Wesleyan, 1962. *Figures of the Human*. Middletown: Wesleyan, 1964. *Rescue the Dead*. Middletown: Wesleyan, 1968. *Poems: 1934–1969*. Middletown: Wesleyan, 1970. *Facing the Tree: New Poems*. Boston: Atlantic-Little, Brown, 1975. *Selected Poems*. Chosen with introductory notes and an afterword by Robert Bly. Middletown: Wesleyan, 1975. *The Animal in the Bush: Poems on Poetry*. Edited by Patrick Carey. Pittsburgh: Slow Loris,

1978.   *Tread the Dark: New Poems.* Boston: Atlantic-Little, Brown, 1978.
Sunlight: A Sequence for My Daughter. Brockport, N.Y.: BOA Editions, 1979.

Criticism and Other Prose

The Notebooks of David Ignatow. Edited with an introduction by Ralph J.
Mills, Jr. Chicago: Swallow, 1973.   *Open Between Us: Essays, Reviews and
Interviews.* Edited by Ralph J. Mills, Jr. Ann Arbor: University of Michigan,
1980.

RANDALL JARRELL (1914–1965)

Randall Jarrell was born in Nashville and educated at Vanderbilt University where he received degrees in psychology and English. He served as a control tower operator in the U.S. Air Corps during World War II. Before and after the war, he taught at several colleges and universities, including Sarah Lawrence, Kenyon, the University of North Carolina, and Princeton. In addition, he was literary editor for *The Nation* and poetry critic for the *Partisan Review* and *Yale Review.* In 1956 he was appointed Consultant in Poetry at the Library of Congress and was elected a member of the National Institute of Arts and Letters and a chancellor of the Academy of American Poets. His many awards included a Guggenheim Fellowship, grants from the National Institute of Arts and Letters and from the Ingram Merrill Foundation, and the National Book Award.

Heralded for his translations, his criticism, and his poetry, Randall Jarrell seemed destined to be one of his generation's authentic men of letters before his untimely and enigmatic death. However, a measure of controversy continues to hound Jarrell's reputation as a poet. Some would argue that he was too much of a formalist, and yet a poem like "The Black Swan" certainly compares well to other formal poems written by someone like Richard Wilbur, while simultaneously calling to mind a coupling of Yeats's romantic and mythic concerns. Others would argue that too many of his poems succumbed to an excessive conversational and prosaic style, and yet Jarrell's successful nonformalist poems seem to presage the structural and lyrical quality of Robert Lowell's later work, especially the poems in *Day by Day.*

At the heart of Randall Jarrell's vision as a poet is an intense, Rilkean pursuit of transformation, if not transcendence. Jarrell was obsessed by the need to discover the possibility of *more* in the world around him and especially in himself. Like the speaker in "The Woman at the Washington Zoo," Jarrell repeatedly insists: "You know what I was, / You see what I am: change me, change me!" But the magnificent snow-leopard is "the heart of heartlessness"; the soul of the European emigrant to the new world "finds Europe waiting for it over every sea"; the ball turret gunner who dies for his country and topples from the sky like a modern-day Icarus isn't immortalized, rather his body is washed out of the turret with a hose. In short, "nothing comes from nothing . . . / Pain comes from the darkness / And we call it wisdom. It is pain." Given such evidence, no wonder Robert Lowell said that Jarrell was "the most heartbreaking . . . poet of his generation."

Poetry

Five Young American Poets (with others). New York: New Directions, 1940. *Blood for a Stranger.* New York: Harcourt Brace, 1942.   *Little Friend, Little Friend.* New York: Dial, 1945.   *Losses.* New York: Harcourt Brace, 1948.   *The Seven-League Crutches.* New York: Harcourt Brace, 1951. *Selected Poems.* New York: Knopf, 1955.   *The Woman at the Washington Zoo: Poems and Translations.* New York: Atheneum, 1960.   *Selected Poems.* New York: Atheneum, 1964.   *The Lost World: New Poems.* New York: Macmillan, 1965.   *The Complete Poems.* New York: Farrar, Straus & Giroux, 1969.

Translations: Prose and Poetic Drama

The Ghetto and the Jews of Rome [Ferdinand Gregorovius] (with Moses Hadas). New York: Schocken, 1948.   *The Rabbit Catcher and Other Fairy Tales of Ludwig Bechstein.* New York: Macmillan, 1962.   *The Golden Bird and Other Fairy Tales by the Brothers Grimm.* New York: Macmillan, 1962. *Snow White and the Seven Dwarfs: A Tale from the Brothers Grimm.* New York: Farrar, Straus & Giroux, 1972.   *The Juniper Tree and Other Tales by the Brothers Grimm.* New York: Farrar, Straus & Giroux, 1973.   *Goethe's Faust: Part One.* New York: Farrar, Straus & Giroux, 1974.

Criticism and Fiction

Poetry and the Age (essays). New York: Knopf, 1953.   *Pictures from an Institution: A Comedy* (novel). New York: Knopf, 1954.   *A Sad Heart at the Supermarket: Essays and Fables.* New York: Atheneum, 1962.   *The Third Book of Criticism* (essays). New York: Farrar, Straus & Giroux, 1969. *Kipling, Auden & Co.* New York: Farrar, Straus & Giroux, 1979.

Bibliography

Adams, Charles M. *Randall Jarrell: A Bibliography.* Chapel Hill: University of North Carolina, 1958.

Critical Studies

Ferguson, Suzanne. *The Poetry of Randall Jarrell.* Baton Rouge: Louisiana State, 1971.   Lowell, Robert, Peter Taylor, and Robert Penn Warren, eds. *Randall Jarrell 1914–1965.* New York: Farrar, Straus & Giroux, 1967.

GALWAY KINNELL (1927)

Galway Kinnell received an A.B. from Princeton and an M.A. from the University of Rochester. He was a Fulbright Fellow in Paris, served in the U.S. Navy and as a field worker for the Congress of Racial Equality, and has traveled widely in the Middle East and Europe. Kinnell has taught at the universities of Grenoble and Nice (France), California (Irvine), and Pittsburgh—and at Sarah Lawrence. He has received the Brandeis University Creative Arts Award and awards from the Rockefeller and Guggenheim Foundations and from the National Institute of Arts and Letters.

Galway Kinnell's earlier poems were both traditionally formal and informed by a traditional Christian sensibility. However, while retaining an essentially religious and sacramental dimension, his later work—as he has said in an interview—has become an increasing "struggle against the desire for heaven," as well as a movement away from competent, pleasing poetry that risks being ornamental and toward a freer verse that takes more risks and in which "there is the chance of finding that great thing you might be after, of finding glory."

Confronted by a constant threat of extinction, in his poetry Kinnell accepts all forms of death as part of the rhythm that produces life, but he is capable of witnessing even the most elemental energy as an affirmation of life. Perhaps human life is a participation in the ultimate madness of a universe flinging itself into emptiness; the image of fire often reappearing in his poems may not be the flame of the phoenix. Thus Kinnell insists that for man, "as he goes up in flames, his own work / is / to open himself, to *be* / the flames."

In their language and substance, Kinnell's poems achieve that rhythm and solemnity often found in a shaman's chant. And yet his poems are also intensely personal, reflecting an attempt to strip away personality, to go deeper into the self "until," he says, "you're just a person. If you could keep going deeper and deeper, you'd finally not be a person either; you'd be an animal; and if you kept going deeper and deeper, you'd be a blade of grass or ultimately perhaps a stone. And if a stone could read, [poetry] would speak for it." For Kinnell, then, poetry is primal experience and myth, the most elemental kind of prayer, or a "paradigm of what people might wish to say in addressing the cosmos."

Poetry

What a Kingdom It Was. Boston. Houghton Mifflin, 1960.　　*Flower Herding on Mount Monadnock*. Boston: Houghton Mifflin, 1964.　　*Body Rags*. Boston: Houghton Mifflin, 1968.　　*First Poems: 1946–54*. Mt. Horeb, Wis.: Perishable Press, 1970.　　*The Book of Nightmares*. Boston: Houghton Mifflin, 1971.　　*The Shoes of Wandering*. Mt. Horeb, Wis.: Perishable Press, 1971.　　*The Avenue Bearing the Initial of Christ into the New World: Poems 1946–64*. Boston: Houghton Mifflin, 1974.　　*Three Poems*. New York: Phoenix Book Shop, 1976.　　*Mortal Acts, Mortal Words*. Boston: Houghton Mifflin, 1980.

Translations: Poetry and Prose

Bitter Victory [a novel by René Hardy]. New York: Doubleday, 1956.　　*The Poems of François Villon*. New York: New American Library, 1965; revised edition, Boston: Houghton Mifflin, 1977.   *On the Motion and Immobility of Douve* [poems by Yves Bonnefoy]. Athens, Ohio: Ohio University, 1968. *Lackawanna Elegy* [poems by Yvan Goll]. Fremont, Michigan: Sumac, 1970.

Criticism and Fiction

Black Light (novel). Boston: Houghton Mifflin, 1965.   *Walking Down the Stairs: Selections from Interviews.* Ann Arbor: University of Michigan, 1978.

KENNETH KOCH (1925)

Born in Cincinnati, Ohio, Kenneth Koch was educated at Harvard and Columbia. He served in the U.S. Army during World War II and has taught at the New School for Social Research, Brooklyn College, Rutgers, and Columbia where he is currently professor of English. He has received Fulbright, Guggenheim, and Ingram Merrill fellowships as well as a grant from the National Endowment for the Arts and the Harbison Award for teaching. Moreover, since 1970 Koch has been recognized for his trail-blazing work in teaching the writing and study of poetry to children and to the elderly.

Generally associated with the New York School (whose other major representatives are John Ashbery and Frank O'Hara), Kenneth Koch also was recognized early in his career as one of his generation's fine comic poets. Although Koch's comic effect is often at the expense of literary subjects—as Paul Carroll has rightfully observed—his humor is certainly not a cerebral, metaphysical wit à la Auden. For Donald M. Allen's *The New American Poetry*, Koch wrote that while in France he became very excited by French poetry: "I began to try to get the same incomprehensible excitement into my own work . . . to recreate the excitement I had felt." That excitement is present in the humor of his poems, which are also marked by a genuine spontaneity and exuberance.

The incomprehensible is equally central to Koch's poems. Although funny, they are also often macabre, as in the last stanza of his spoof on William Carlos Williams' poem: "I was clumsy and / I wanted you here in the wards, where I am the doctor!" Moreover, one senses that the poet is trapped in an absurd situation, the victim of "an absolute and total misunderstanding (but not fatal)." Koch's poems, then, often sound like the kind Kafka might have written if he'd had a galloping and slapstick sense of humor, and thereby they risk collapsing into frivolity under the weight of their own energy.

In recent poems Kenneth Koch seems to have moved away from more obvious comic situations, but the spontaneity, the linguistic excitement, and the rambunctious rhythms generated remain—edged with a

verbal grin that may leave readers wondering whether it is mildly playful
or deadly grim.

Poetry

Poems. New York: Tibor de Nagy Gallery, 1953.   *Ko; or, A Season on
Earth*. New York: Grove, 1960.   *Permanently*. New York: Tiber Press,
1960.   *Thank You and Other Poems*. New York: Grove, 1962.   *Poems
from 1952 and 1953*. Los Angeles: Black Sparrow, 1968.   *When the Sun
Tries to Go On*. Los Angeles: Black Sparrow, 1969.   *Sleeping with Women*.
Los Angeles: Black Sparrow, 1969.   *The Pleasures of Peace*. New York:
Grove, 1969.   *The Art of Love*. New York: Random House, 1975.   *The
Duplications*. New York: Random House, 1977.   *The Burning Mystery of
Anna in 1951*. New York: Random House, 1979.

Prose and Drama

Bertha and Other Plays. New York: Grove, 1966.   *Wishes, Lies and
Dreams: Teaching Children to Write Poetry*. New York: Random House, 1970.
A Change of Hearts: Plays, Films, and Other Dramatic Works 1951–1971. New
York: Random House, 1973.   *Rose, Where Did You Get That Red?
Teaching Great Poetry to Children*. New York: Random House, 1973.

MAXINE KUMIN (1925)

Born in Philadelphia, Maxine Kumin received a bachelor's and master's
degree from Radcliffe. The author of some twenty books for children
(three of which she wrote with Anne Sexton), Maxine Kumin has served
as a consultant for the Central Atlantic Regional Educational Laboratory
and the Board of Coordinated Educational Services (Nassau County,
New York). She also has taught at Tufts, the University of Massachu-
setts, Centre College (Kentucky), and at Princeton. An officer of the
Radcliffe Institute's Society of Fellows and former chairperson of the
Literature Panel of the National Endowment for the Arts, Maxine
Kumin was awarded the Pulitzer Prize in 1973.

One of Maxine Kumin's critics has faulted her work for often being
"the poetry of a special world, unmistakably upper middle-class, comfor-
table, urbane, safe in its place at the center of things." To suggest that
such arenas of experience may not be legitimate or "worthy" concerns
of poetry in this century and country is blatant nonsense, of course.
Besides, when Eliot posited his dictum, "Redeem the time," he didn't
specify that it had to be an urban and industrial time fraught with its
unique sets of psychic and physical terrors. Moreover, if Kumin's poetry
does focus on the middle-class experience, like Louis Simpson she too
is "taking part in a great experiment— / whether writers can live peace-
fully in the suburbs / and not be bored to death."

Kumin's personal experiment as a poet also has an edge of intensity that goes considerably beyond mere survival of boredom. Because of her powerful sense of observation and her masterful handling of technique, the objects and experiences of suburban life in Kumin's poetry assume a greater hum and buzz of emblematic implication of the direction of the human soul.

Consequently, the ordinary task of ridding one's garden of woodchucks suggests a greater kind of historical extermination. Beneath the ostensible safety of suburban life lies the nightmare of a cleansing fire all inhabitants must pass through. No less important, one senses in Kumin's poetry a conscious urgency to discover in the natural world not only emblems of endurance, survival, and continuity but also momentary symbols of that more human longing for the possibility of transcendence. With remarkable grace and wit, the poems of Maxine Kumin do indeed redeem the time in which she lives and in which most of us measure the worth of our lives.

Poetry

Halfway. New York: Holt, Rinehart and Winston, 1961.   *The Privilege*. New York: Harper & Row, 1965.   *The Nightmare Factory*. New York: Harper & Row, 1970.   *Up Country*. New York: Harper & Row, 1972. *House, Bridge, Fountain, Gate*. New York: Viking, 1975.   *The Retrieval System*. New York: Viking, 1978.

Fiction

Through Dooms of Love. New York: Harper & Row, 1965.   *The Passions of Uxport*. New York: Harper & Row, 1968.   *The Abduction*. New York: Harper & Row, 1971.   *The Designated Heir*. New York: Viking, 1974.

STANLEY KUNITZ (1905)

Born in Worcester, Massachusetts, and educated at Harvard, Stanley Kunitz has taught at Bennington, Brandeis, Columbia, and Yale. He also has been a Cultural Exchange Scholar in Russia and Poland. From 1969 to 1976, he was editor of the Yale Series of Younger Poets; from 1974 to 1976, he served as Consultant in Poetry at the Library of Congress. The recipient of grants from the Guggenheim and Ford Foundations, the Academy of American Poets, and the National Institute of Arts and Letters, he was also awarded the Pulitzer Prize in 1959 and elected a chancellor of the Academy of American Poets in 1970.

In addition to his moving translations of the poetry of Anna Akhmatova, Stanley Kunitz has been a major contributor to the many collections of translations of the poetry of Andrei Voznesensky and Yevgeny Yevtushenko that have appeared in this country. Moreover, since 1931, he has been one of the editors of eight major dictionaries of literary biographies.

After the publication of *The Testing-Tree* in 1971, Stanley Kunitz wrote: "I am no more reconciled than I ever was to the world's wrongs and the injustice of time." Among the wrongs and injustices present in Kunitz's poetry are: the memories of a painful childhood that seemingly cannot be redeemed or reshaped; inevitable participation in the outrageous scientific and technological violence against the human spirit; and—despite the moments of beauty's hope—the inescapable promise of "a dusty finger on my lip."

Throughout his career, Kunitz's measure of emotional and moral energy has been further intensified by his equally passionate reverence for and use of form. In his poems, more than in the work of most poets of his generation, one senses that any experience or vision—regardless of how intense it might have been in itself—has consistently been forged by the white heat of a metaphysical sensibility. Thus Kunitz's poems have a physical presence and quality that are verbal equivalents of graceful sculptures forged out of the toughest metal—just as the works of a contemporary metalsmith like Albert Paley are intricate sculptures of iron and steel that seem to be leaping toward pure sound.

Poetry

Intellectual Things. New York: Doubleday, 1930.   *Passport to the War: A Selection of Poems.* New York: Holt, Rinehart and Winston, 1944.   *Selected Poems 1928–1958.* Boston: Little, Brown, 1958.   *The Testing-Tree: Poems.* Boston: Atlantic-Little, Brown, 1971.   *The Lincoln Relics: A Poem.* Port Townsend, Wash.: Graywolf, 1978.   *The Poems of Stanley Kunitz 1928–1978.* Boston: Atlantic-Little, Brown, 1979.

Translations

Poems of Akhmatova (with Max Hayward). Boston: Atlantic-Little, Brown, 1973.

Criticism

A Kind of Order, A Kind of Folly: Essays and Conversations. Boston: Atlantic-Little, Brown, 1975.

DENISE LEVERTOV (1923)

Born in Essex, England, Denise Levertov was privately educated, served as a nurse during World War II, and emigrated to the United States in 1948. She has taught at Vassar, Drew, City College of New York, M.I.T., and has recently retired from Tufts where she was a full professor. A scholar at the Radcliffe Institute for Independent Study, Levertov also has received the Morton Dauwen Zabel Prize for poetry, a Guggenheim Fellowship, and a grant from the National Institute of Arts and Letters.

Influenced by William Carlos Williams and the Black Mountain School—or simply their natural aesthetic compatriot—Denise Levertov's poems are nevertheless charged by an unmistakably distinctive voice. The following is a difficult statement to make these days, but clearly hers is also a woman's voice, capable of ranging from a tough to a tender lyricism that is proportionately intense. But her poems are not simply spoken by a woman; they fully explore and—with assurance, pleasure, or grief—celebrate the multifaceted experience of the contemporary woman. By so doing, they invite all of us into a celebration of the full range of human experience.

In an early interview Denise Levertov said: "I believe in writing about what lies under the hand, in a sense. . . . Not necessarily in the visual world—the external world—it can be an inner experience—but it must be something true." And in one of her poems Levertov writes: "The best work is made / from hard, strong materials, / obstinately precise. . . ." Her own poems repeatedly assert that the most obstinate and hard materials—even in that kind of natural lyrical poem she has mastered— are not onyx and steel, but rather the small, at times elusive, materials of daily human life.

An antiwar poem like "The Altars in the Street" affirms the inestimable power of the simple but sacred human gesture over "the frenzy of weapons, their impudent power." But so much of her work also reminds us that each new poem is that difficult and laborious Jacob's ladder between the facts of the diurnal and the bid for the eternal; each poem carves the physical details and quality of our daily communal experience in the unyielding onyx and steel of a cosmic history that would obliterate us.

Poetry

The Double Image. London: Cresset Books, 1946.   *Here and Now.* San Francisco: City Lights, 1957.   *Overland to the Islands.* Highlands, N.C.: Jargon, 1958.   *With Eyes at the Back of Our Heads.* New York: New Directions, 1959.   *The Jacob's Ladder.* New York: New Directions, 1961. *O Taste and See: New Poems.* New York: New Directions, 1964.   *City Psalm.* Berkeley: Oyez, 1964.   *The Sorrow Dance.* New York: New Directions, 1966.   *Three Poems.* Mt. Horeb, Wis.: Perishable Press, 1968. *A Tree Telling of Orpheus.* Los Angeles: Black Sparrow, 1968.   *Embroideries.* Los Angeles: Black Sparrow, 1969.   *Summer Poems / 1969.* Berkeley: Oyez, 1970.   *Relearning the Alphabet.* New York: New Directions, 1970.   *To Stay Alive.* New York: New Directions, 1971.   *Footprints.* New York: New Directions, 1972.   *The Freeing of the Dust.* New York: New Directions, 1975.   *Life in the Forest.* New York: New Directions, 1978.   *Collected Earlier Poems 1940–1960.* New York: New Directions, 1979.

NOTES ON THE POETS

Translations: Poetry

In Praise of Krishna: Songs from the Bengali (with Edward C. Dimmock, Jr.). New York: Doubleday, 1968. *Selected Poems of Guillevic*. New York: New Directions, 1969.

Bibliography

Wilson, Robert. A *Bibliography of Denise Levertov*. New York: Phoenix Book Shop, 1972.

Critical Studies

Wagner, Linda Welshimer. *Denise Levertov*. New York: Twayne, 1967. Wagner, Linda Welshimer, ed. *Denise Levertov: In Her Own Province*. New York: New Directions, 1979.

PHILIP LEVINE (1928)

Philip Levine was born in Detroit. He received a B.A. and an M.A. from Wayne State University and an M.F.A. from the University of Iowa. Subsequently, he held a fellowship in poetry at Stanford University. Since 1958 he has taught at California State University, Fresno. He has received grants from the National Endowment for the Arts and the National Institute of Arts and Letters, as well as a Guggenheim Fellowship.

Critics can't seem to agree on what Philip Levine's central theme is. One says it's a "rogue's gallery" of drunks, draft-dodgers, boxers, Hell's Angels, midgets, poor neighbors." Another asserts that his themes include "Hiroshima, the torture of Algerian prisoners, soldiers in eye-to-eye combat, generalized and brutal bigotry . . . man's cruelty to man." Still another critic argues that Levine's "fields of exploration" include "experiences which manifest themselves in irrational, dreamlike, fantastic or visionary forms." In fact, all of these observations are true, for what is consistently striking about Levine's poetry is specifically his wide range of themes.

Levine himself has written: "I try to pay homage to the people who taught me my life was a holy thing, who convinced me that my formal education was a lie. . . . These people, both Black and white, were mainly rural people, and the horror of the modern world was clearer to them than to me, and the beauty and value of the world was something they knew in a way I did not, first hand." No less important in his poetry is the vital role of Levine's own sense of place—especially the bleak, dirty, and threatening industrial cityscape of Levine's childhood in Detroit; more recently one notes references to Levine's own personal life and background, especially members of his family.

Equally striking—although not immediately noticeable to the more casual reader—is Levine's mastery of a range of forms, from the most ostensible manipulation of tighter forms, through the freer lyric, to the more surrealistic and incantatory poems. One is also struck by Levine's seemingly contradictory range of emotional, moral, and often profoundly religious responses to the horror and beauty in the world around him and around us—as well as inside us all.

Reading the body of Philip Levine's work, one senses a fiercely honest exploration of the totality of a complex human life and a particular personality moving about the crucial arenas of our common experience. One also senses a complex, intense, and disciplined sensibility's response—in pity and in condemnation, in anger and in awe, in lamentation and in song—to the conflicting phenomena of contemporary life that offer us these choices: to sit on the father's shoulders and awaken in another world, to pray to become all we'll never be, or to offer ourselves as sacrificial animals in the slaughterhouse of a blasphemous industrial liturgy of annihilation. Philip Levine's answer to the last alternative continues to be a resounding, "No. Not this pig."

Poetry

On the Edge. Iowa City: Stone Wall Press, 1963.   Silent in America: Vivas for Those Who Failed. Iowa City: Shaw Avenue Press, 1965.   Not This Pig. Middletown: Wesleyan, 1968.   Five Detroits. Santa Barbara: Unicorn, 1970.   Pili's Wall. Santa Barbara: Unicorn, 1971.   Red Dust. Santa Cruz, Calif.: Kayak, 1971.   They Feed They Lion. New York: Atheneum, 1972.   1933. New York: Atheneum, 1974.   The Names of the Lost. New York: Atheneum, 1978.   Ashes: Poems Old and New. New York: Atheneum, 1979.   7 Years from Somewhere. New York: Atheneum, 1979.

JOHN LOGAN (1923)

Born in Red Oak, Iowa, John Logan received a B.A. in zoology from Coe College, an M.A. in English from the University of Iowa, and did graduate work in philosophy at Georgetown, Notre Dame, and Berkeley. He has taught at Notre Dame, San Francisco State, the University of Hawaii, and the State University of New York at Buffalo where he is a professor of English. Logan served as poetry editor for The Nation; he also founded and, with Aaron Siskind, edited Choice—a magazine of poetry and photography. He has been the recipient of a Rockefeller grant, a Morton Dauwen Zabel award for poetry from the National Institute of Arts and Letters, and a Guggenheim Fellowship.

Perhaps because he began his career as a scientist, John Logan's poems are constructed out of the most minute details observed from the world around him. Such lines as "I let the rain / move its audible little hands / gently on my skin" suggest the sensuousness of his language in response to the physical world. He lingers on things and the words for things, delighting in their sound and texture. In Logan's poetry suffering neither negates the fact of beauty nor the possibility of celebration. Pain and guilt do not negate the alternatives of joy and grace. His poems repeatedly affirm that "there is a freshness / nothing can destroy in us / not even we ourselves."

Moreover, what distinguishes the work of Logan from that of most personal-confessional poets is that his poems are far less confessional and less self-flagellating. He spares us the leprous details of individual incidents of failure, deterioration, and guilt. If he asks his readers to be confessors, as he openly does in "Three Moves," he doesn't seek absolution for any given act of general Manichean sense of sin. Rather, he offers an exchange of that more human and grace-giving embrace of an accepting forgiveness of the guilt that is in each of us. And thus each of us readers, as it were, becomes Logan's anonymous lover.

The full organic development and structure of his poems, as well as the careful orchestration of tone, further distinguish Logan's work. At his best, his poems are utterly personal and natural, determined neither by structural, thematic, nor tonal formula. His poems succeed in sounding as natural as breathing; they begin simply and grow in intensity out of their own emotional necessity, as the breath of a man in battle or in love. Through a harmonious counterpoint of tones that reflect the varied inner strains of a total personality, these poems rise to discoveries of—and are themselves—epiphanies. Rich mosaics of an integrated personality's experience of the human, illuminations of that range of music rising from the total self, the poems of John Logan are at once "unpredictable as grace" and "a ballet for the ear."

Poetry

Cycle for Mother Cabrini. New York: Grove, 1955; reprint, Berkeley: Cloud Marauder, 1972.   Ghosts of the Heart. Chicago: University of Chicago, 1960.   Spring of the Thief: Poems 1960–1962. New York: Knopf, 1963. The Zig-Zag Walk: Poems 1963–1968. New York: Dutton, 1969.   The Anonymous Lover. New York: Liveright, 1973.   Poem in Progress. Washington, D.C.: Dryad, 1975.   John Logan / Poems Aaron Siskind / Photographs. Rochester, N.Y.: Visual Studies Workshop, 1976.   The Bridge of Change: Poems 1974–1979. Brockport, N.Y.: BOA Editions, 1980.

Fiction and Criticism

The House That Jack Built; or, A Portrait of the Artist as a Sad Sensualist.
Omaha: Abbatoir, 1974.　　　*A Ballet for the Ear: Essays, Interviews, Fore-
words and Reviews.* Edited by A. Poulin, Jr. Ann Arbor: University of Michigan,
1980.

ROBERT LOWELL (1917–1978)

Born in Boston in 1917, Robert Lowell attended Harvard and graduated
from Kenyon College in 1940. A conscientious objector during World
War II, he spent several months in prison. During his career, he taught
at various universities, including Harvard, the University of Iowa, and
Boston University; in 1947–48, he served as Consultant in Poetry at the
Library of Congress. His many awards include the Pulitzer Prize (1947),
the National Book Award (1960), the Bollingen Poetry Translation
Award (1964), the Copernicus Award (1974), and the National Book
Critics Circle Award (posthumously, 1978).

Lowell's career seems to have evolved in three stages. His early poems,
written under the tutelage of John Crowe Ransom and Allen Tate, were
intricately wrought and complex, clearly reflecting the dictates of the
New Criticism. Emerging out of a Christian spiritual tradition, an English
poetic tradition influenced by the French symbolists, and a New England
historical and ethical tradition, they were poems written by a young man
whose sensibilities and talent began to mature at a time when T. S. Eliot
was an overpowering presence in American poetry.

In *Life Studies*, perhaps his most brilliant and significant book—the
result of an encounter with W. D. Snodgrass—Lowell implicitly re-
nounced many of the New Critics' formal demands and Eliot's cultural
and spiritual vision. His poems were less consciously wrought and ex-
tremely intimate. As M. L. Rosenthal has observed, the orchestration of
Life Studies traced the deterioration of Western civilization, the United
States republic, Lowell's own family, and his very self. In the powerful
concluding poem, "Skunk Hour," Lowell asserted: "The season's ill . . . /
My mind's not right." And in this cultural and personal wasteland, he
found no kingfisher, no Christ diving in fire.

"I am tired. Everyone's tired of my turmoil," Lowell wrote in *For the
Union Dead*, and this realization marked the start of a third phase in
his career. The poems grew more serenely formal, less intricate, and surely
less hysterical. In *Near the Ocean*, he turned to muted couplets; his

Notebook and *History*, though tracing intimate aspects of his life, were sonnet sequences. Although their central theme of the desolation and deterioration of humans and their world remained, Lowell was able to view that drama with a measure of objectivity, distance, and—at times— profound detachment. In his last book, *Day by Day*, Lowell returned once again to the lyrical and personal modes; however, despite the intimacy of subject matter, the poems continued to be marked by a kind of intellectual detachment.

Poetry

Land of Unlikeness. Cummington, Mass.: Cummington Press, 1944.   *Lord Weary's Castle*. New York: Harcourt Brace, 1946.   *The Mills of the Kavanaughs*. New York: Harcourt Brace, 1951.   *Life Studies*. New York: Farrar, Straus & Giroux, 1959.   *For the Union Dead*. New York: Farrar, Straus & Giroux, 1964.   *Near the Ocean*. New York: Farrar, Straus & Giroux, 1967.   *Notebook 1967–1968*. New York: Farrar, Straus & Giroux, 1969; augmented edition as *Notebook*, New York: Farrar, Straus & Giroux, 1970. *For Lizzie and Harriet*. New York: Farrar, Straus & Giroux, 1973.   *History*. New York: Farrar, Straus & Giroux, 1973.   *The Dolphin*. New York: Farrar, Straus & Giroux, 1973.   *Selected Poems*. New York: Farrar, Straus & Giroux, 1976.   *Day by Day*. New York: Farrar, Straus & Giroux, 1977.

Imitations, Translations, Adaptations

Imitations. New York: Farrar, Straus & Giroux, 1961.   *Phaedra* [Racine]. New York: Farrar, Straus & Giroux, 1961.   *The Old Glory*. New York: Farrar, Straus & Giroux, 1964; expanded edition, New York: Farrar, Straus & Giroux, 1968.   *The Voyage and Other Versions of Poems by Baudelaire*. New York: Farrar, Straus & Giroux, 1968.   *Prometheus Bound*. [Aeschylus]. New York: Farrar, Straus & Giroux, 1970.   *The Oresteia of Aeschylus*. New York: Farrar, Straus & Giroux, 1979.

Bibliographies

Mazzaro, Jerome. *The Achievement of Robert Lowell, 1939–1959*. Detroit: University of Detroit, 1960.   Edelstein, J. M. *Robert Lowell: A Checklist*. Detroit: Gale Research, 1973.

Critical Studies

Cooper, Philip. *The Autobiographical Myth of Robert Lowell*. Chapel Hill: University of North Carolina, 1970.   Cosgrave, Patrick. *The Public Poetry of Robert Lowell*. London: Golancz, 1970.   Crick, John. *Robert Lowell*. Barnes & Noble, 1974.   Fein, Richard J. *Robert Lowell*. New York: Twayne, 1970.   London, Michael, and Robert Boyers, eds. *Robert Lowell: A Portrait of the Artist in His Time*. New York: David Lewis, 1970.   Martin, Jay. *Robert Lowell*, Minneapolis: University of Minnesota, 1970.   Martz, William J. *The Achievement of Robert Lowell*. Glenview, Ill.: Scott, Foresman, 1966.   Mazzaro, Jerome. *The Poetic Themes of Robert Lowell*. Ann Arbor: University of Michigan, 1965.   Mazzaro, Jerome, ed. *Profile of Robert*

Lowell. Columbus, Ohio: Charles E. Merrill, 1971.   Parkinson, Thomas, ed. *Robert Lowell: A Collection of Critical Essays.* Englewood Cliffs, N.J.: Prentice-Hall, 1968.   Perloff, Marjorie. *The Poetic Art of Robert Lowell.* Ithaca, N.Y.: Cornell University Press, 1973.   Price, Jonathan, ed. *Critics on Robert Lowell.* Miami: University of Miami Press, 1974.   Simpson, Louis. *A Revolution in Taste: Studies of Dylan Thomas, Allen Ginsberg, Sylvia Plath and Robert Lowell.* New York: Morrow, 1978.   Staples, Hugh B. *Robert Lowell: The First Twenty Years.* New York: Farrar, Straus & Giroux, 1962.   Williamson, Alan. *Pity the Monsters: The Political Poetry of Robert Lowell.* New Haven: Yale University Press, 1974.   Yenser, Stephen. *Circle to Circle: The Poetry of Robert Lowell.* Berkeley: University of California Press, 1975.

JAMES MERRILL (1926)

James Merrill was born in New York City, attended Lawrenceville School, served in the U.S. Army, and graduated from Amherst College in 1947. Merrill's several awards for his poetry include the Bollingen Prize (1973), the Pulitzer Prize (1977), and the National Book Award (1967, 1979). In 1971 he was elected a member of the National Institute of Arts and Letters. Unlike most of his contemporaries, Merrill has not sought a professional teaching career; he generally divides his time between living in Greece and in Connecticut.

Most critics would agree that James Merrill's poetry has consistently reflected the influence of New Criticism and that his mentor certainly would be W. H. Auden rather than William Carlos Williams. Indeed, in Merrill's new long trilogy, Auden's spirit is Merrill's "guide." Clearly, Merrill is a masterful formalist whose manipulation of metrics and of sound—especially end rhymes—reveals the range of startling and subtle nuances in language in much the same way as Rothko unveils the nuances of color in painting. Even in what seem to be more personal poems, one is never quite sure whether the speaker is Merrill or a persona. Most of his poems are marked by a tone edged with a measure of ironic detachment that, in some literary circles—where irony is blasphemy and guts rule—might be considered indicative of high, albeit elegant, decadence.

When so many poets of this generation lead their readers into the bedlam of their tortured souls and the bedrooms of their monstrous marriages—and, indeed, into their very own and much-used beds—one emerges from the surroundings of James Merrill's poetry with the heady sense of having lingered in a rather rarified atmosphere. This is the physical, moral, and aesthetic world as perceived by Proust rather than by Baudelaire, by Henry James rather than by Walt Whitman. This is the world where, in Merrill's words, "Light into the olive entered / And was oil," an arena of human experience where it does seem that "the world beneath the world is brightening."

And yet Merrill's Weltanschauung and aesthetic seemingly always lead him—and us—to the very edge of chaos. Merrill's persona in "Laboratory Poem" knows that the heart must climb "through violence into exquisite disciplines." The handsome young man in "Charles on Fire" must view his own hand gloved in fire before the mirror reassures his beauty. And whatever entrances into immortality that art may offer, it leaves us *and* the artist with that unnerving realization that "the life it asks of us is a dog's life." Thus, if poetry, if speech "is but a mouth pressed / Lightly and humbly against the angel's hand," in a Rilkean attempt to impress the angel with the things of this world, it's distinctly possible that this very angel "does not want even these few lines written." In short, in a society where "Art, Public Spirit / Ignorance, Economics, Love of Self / Hatred of Self" are earnestly dedicated to "*sparing* us the worst" and just as earnestly *inspire* the worst, Merrill's poems stand on the edge of chaos, radiant attempts to survive its meanings—and our own.

Poetry

The Black Swan. Athens: Icaros, 1946.   *First Poems*. New York: Knopf, 1951.   *Short Stories*. Pawlet, Vt.: Banyan Press, 1954.   *The Country of a Thousand Years of Peace and Other Poems*. New York: Knopf, 1959; revised edition, New York: Atheneum, 1970.   *Water Street*. New York: Atheneum, 1962.   *Nights and Days*. New York: Atheneum, 1966.   *The Fire Screen*. New York: Atheneum, 1969.   *Braving the Elements*. New York: Atheneum, 1972.   *The Yellow Pages*. Cambridge, Mass.: Temple Bar, 1974.   *Divine Comedies*. New York: Atheneum, 1976.   *Mirabell: Books of Number*. New York: Atheneum, 1978.

Fiction

The Seraglio. New York: Knopf, 1957.   *The (Diblos) Notebook*. New York: Atheneum, 1965.

W. S. MERWIN (1927)

W. S. Merwin was born in New York City and educated at Princeton. He was tutor to Robert Graves's son for a year, but—unlike most of his contemporaries—he has not had a teaching career. Since 1951 he has devoted most of his time to writing and poetry readings and to translating from French, Spanish, Latin, Portuguese, Greek, Chinese, and Japanese originals. He has lived in the United States, England, Mexico, southern France, and currently resides in Hawaii. In addition to the

Pulitzer Prize in 1971 and the Shelley Memorial Award in 1974, he has received grants from the National Endowment for the Arts, the Rockefeller Foundation, the Academy of American Poets, the National Institute of Arts and Letters, and the Arts Council of Great Britain.

W. S. Merwin is one of the most prolific poets and poet-translators of his generation; he is among those contemporary poets whose talents were originally shaped by New Criticism and whose style has undergone a radical change in the course of his career. His early poems were elegant, controlled, symmetrical, and often concerned with myth and archetype— as the recent republication of his early work, *The First Four Books of Poems*, makes eminently clear. However, the appearance of *The Drunk in the Furnace* (1960) suggested a dissatisfaction with old techniques: his forms were looser; his language appeared less contrived and closer to the spoken word. Like other poets of the period, he too turned to family history and individual human suffering in search of larger, more immediate patterns of human experience.

However, Merwin's most radical departure—and most exciting style— appeared later only in *The Moving Target* (1963). Open and terse, these surrealistic poems—and most of the poems that Merwin has published since—are controlled not as much by a craftsman's delicate hand as by a powerful imagination. And they rise out of the depths of a more personal, sometimes enigmatic necessity. Merwin's aesthetics are clear in the statement that he wrote for *Naked Poetry* (edited by Stephen Berg and Robert Mezey): "In an age when time and technique encroach hourly, or appear to, on the source itself of poetry, it seems as though what is needed for any particular nebulous hope that may become a poem is not a manipulable, more or less predictably recurring pattern, but an unduplicatable resonance, something that would be like an echo except that it is repeating no sound. Something that always belonged to it: its sense and its conformation before it entered words."

Throughout his career, one of Merwin's dominant concerns has been death—or perhaps more specifically, extinction. The journey motif that critics have recognized in Merwin's poetry is emblematic of all life's motion toward death. However, in later poems, this concern doesn't necessarily focus on any sudden or cataclysmic end of life. Rather, it is more manifest in powerful and menacing shadows surrounding frail light, in sound struggling against the tyranny of silence, in the slow but seemingly inevitable transformation of all organic life into inert matter. And if Merwin agrees with Berryman that the individual has undertaken the biggest job of all—*son fin*—Merwin has also erected a powerful emblem of his vision in his poetic prose piece, "Tergvinder's Stone." In the presence of a mysterious, almost mystical stone in the middle of his living room and his life, Merwin's central character kneels in the darkness of the stone, converses with the stone, and even in the silence of the stone "knows that it is peace."

Poetry

A *Mask for Janus*. New Haven: Yale University, 1952.   *The Dancing Bears*. New Haven: Yale University, 1954.   *Green with Beasts*. New York: Knopf, 1956.   *The Drunk in the Furnace*. New York: Macmillan, 1960.   *The Moving Target*. New York: Atheneum, 1963.   *The Lice*. New York: Atheneum, 1967.   *Animae: Poems*. San Francisco: Kayak, 1969.   *The Carrier of Ladders*. New York: Atheneum, 1970.   *Chinese Figures: Second Series*. Mt. Horeb, Wis.: Perishable Press, 1971.   *Japanese Figures*. Santa Barbara: Unicorn, 1971.   *Asian Figures*. New York: Atheneum, 1972. *Writings to an Unfinished Accompaniment*. New York: Atheneum, 1974.   *The First Four Books of Poems* (*A Mask for Janus, The Dancing Bears, Green with Beasts, The Drunk in the Furnace*). New York: Atheneum, 1975.   *The Compass Flower*. New York: Atheneum, 1977.

Translations: Poetry and Prose

The Poem of the Cid. New York: New American Library, 1959.   *The Satires of Perseus*. Bloomington: Indiana University, 1961.   *Spanish Ballads*. New York: Doubleday, 1961.   *The Life of Lazarillo de Tormes: His Fortunes and Adversities*. New York: Doubleday, 1962.   *The Song of Roland*. New York: Modern Library, 1963.   *Selected Translations 1948–1968*. New York: Atheneum, 1968.   *Transparence of the World: Poems of Jean Follain*. New York: Atheneum, 1969.   *Products of the Perfected Civilization: Selected Writings* [Sebastian Chamfort]. New York: Macmillan, 1969.   *Voices: Selected Writings of Antonio Porchia*. Chicago: Follett, 1969.   *Twenty Love Poems and A Song of Despair* [Pablo Neruda]. London: Cape, 1969.   *Selected Poems of Osip Mandestam* (with Clarence Brown). New York: Atheneum, 1974.   *Iphigenia at Aulis* [Euripedes] (with George E. Dimmock, Jr.). New York: Oxford University, 1977.   *Selected Translations 1968–1978*. New York: Atheneum, 1979.

Prose: Fiction

The Miner's Pale Children. New York: Atheneum, 1970.   *Houses and Travellers*. New York: Atheneum, 1977.

FRANK O'HARA (1926–1966)

Before his untimely, accidental death on Fire Island, Frank O'Hara was associate curator and then curator of the international program at the Museum of Modern Art in New York and an editorial associate for *Art News*. Born in Baltimore, O'Hara was educated at the New England Conservatory of Music, Harvard, and the University of Michigan. He collaborated in various projects involving poetry and the visual arts, and in 1956 was awarded a Ford Fellowship for drama.

Before the publication of his *Collected Poems* (and the companion volume, *Poems Retrieved*), Frank O'Hara was almost a closet-poet, the product and hero of a pop-camp imagination whose seeming antipoems were light and chatty, marked by a spontaneity, exuberance, and wit that were characteristic of his contemporaries in the visual arts. His most memorable poems, like the paintings of Oldenburg and Warhol, focused on the all-too-obvious things of our urban and suburban world: hamburgers, malts, cigarettes, instant coffee. Looming above that world were its own godly artifacts: Lichtenstein's suprahuman heroes of the comic strips and Warhol's movie stars. Their mythic proportions were— and continue to be—the dimensions of contemporary human fantasies and dreams of redemption. Moreover, in O'Hara's poems there is the stinging, if somewhat hysterical, crackle of a melancholy comment on the absurdity of such hollow rites.

While it may still be too early to assess the full range of O'Hara's total opus, it's eminently clear that his scope and power as a poet extend far beyond the circumscribed world of a merely campy and gay subculture. One leaves the body of O'Hara's poetry—and his sense of what constitutes the identifiable substance and quality of our communal experience—with a verbal-emotional equivalent of Kandinsky's acute perception of "the particular spiritual perfume of the triangle." One also leaves the existential world of O'Hara's poems with a fuller understanding of the truth of Cocteau's rejection of history: "J'ais une très mauvaise mémoire de l'avenir."

Poetry

A City Winter and Other Poems. New York: Tibor de Nagy Gallery, 1952. *Meditations in an Emergency*. New York: Grove, 1957.   *Hartigan and Rivers with O'Hara: An Exhibition of Pictures, with Poems*. New York: Tibor de Nagy Gallery, 1959.   *Second Avenue*. New York: Totem Press-Corinth, 1960.   *Odes*. New York: Tiber Press, 1960.   *Lunch Poems*. San Francisco: City Lights, 1964.   *Love Poems: Tentative Title*. New York: Tibor de Nagy Gallery, 1965.   *In Memory of My Feelings: A Selection of Poems*. Edited by Bill Berkson. New York: Museum of Modern Art, 1967.   *Odes*. New York: Poets Press, 1969.   *The Collected Poems of Frank O'Hara*. Edited by Donald Allen. New York: Knopf, 1971.   *The Selected Poems of Frank O'Hara*. Edited by Donald Allen. New York: Knopf, 1974.   *Hymns of St. Bridget* (with Bill Berkson). New York: Boke Press, 1974.   *Poems Retrieved*. Edited by Donald Allen. Bolinas, Calif.: Grey Fox, 1977.

Prose

Jackson Pollack. New York: George Braziller, 1959.   *A Frank O'Hara Miscellany*. Bolinas, Calif.: Grey Fox, 1974.   *Art Chronicles 1954–1966*. New York: George Braziller, 1974.

Critical Study

Perloff, Marjorie. *Frank O'Hara: Poet Among Painters*. Austin: University of Texas, 1968.

CHARLES OLSON (1910–1970)

Charles Olson was born in Worcester, Massachusetts, educated at Wesleyan and Yale universities, and received his doctorate from Harvard. From 1951 to 1956, he was an instructor and rector at Black Mountain College in North Carolina where he worked with other artists and writers like Robert Creeley and Merce Cunningham. For varying periods of time, he also taught at Harvard, the State University of New York at Buffalo, and other universities. The recipient of two Guggenhiem Fellowships, he also received a grant from the Gren Foundation to study Mayan hieroglyphics. During much of his life, he resided in Gloucester, Massachusetts, the setting for many of his "Maximus Poems."

Clearly the most substantial theoretician and one of the most influential of the postmodernist poets, Charles Olson's criticism and speculations concerning the nature and structure of verse have become the basis for what is generally known as the *Projectivist School* in contemporary poetry. Olson's celebrated essay, "Projective Verse," originally published in 1950, articulates some of his basic attitudes toward poetry and remains one of the central documents of the "revolution" that took place in American poetry after 1945.

Complex and often refusing to yield specific meaning, "Projective Verse" is no easy essay to summarize; but some of its central ideas are worth noting. Olson's premise is that if poetry "is to be of *essential* use," it must "catch up and put into itself certain laws and possibilities of the breath, of the breathing of the man who writes, as well as of his listenings." And he posits "open" or "field composition" as an alternative to non-Projective verse with its inherited line, its stanzas, and its overall traditional form. According to Olson, field or open composition includes (1) *kinetics*: "A poem is energy transferred from where the poet got it . . . by way of the poem itself to . . . the reader"; (2) *principle*: "Form is never more than an extension of content" (as rephrased by Robert Creeley); and (3) *process*: "One perception must immediately and directly lead to a further perception." Although various poets have cited Olson as their mentor, it may well be that he is the only genuine practitioner of his own theories.

Charles Olson's major work, no doubt, is his long series of "Maximus Poems," the first ten of which were originally published in 1953. As various critics have noted, one of the characteristics of this series is Olson's delicate and all-encompassing sense of place—the vibrant details of an ever-changing landscape. But equally present are Olson's sweeping sense of history and his vast range of knowledge, which have caused some critics to compare the Maximus Poems to Pound's Cantos. From an entirely different point of view, Olson's central character in the Maximus Poems also might be compared with Henry Pussycat in John Berryman's Dream Songs.

Poetry

Corrado Cagli March 31 Through April 19 1947. New York: Knoedler, 1947. *Y & X.* Washington, D.C.: Black Sun, 1948.   *In Cold Hell, in Thicket.* Palma, Mallorca: Divers, 1953; reprint, San Francisco: Four Seasons, 1967. *The Maximus Poems 1–10.* Stuttgart, Germany: Jonathan Williams, 1953. *Anecdotes of the Late War.* Highlands, N.C.: Jargon, 1955.   *The Maximus Poems 11–22.* Stuttgart, Germany: Jonathan Williams, 1956.   *O'Ryan 2 4 6 8 10.* San Francisco: White Rabbit, 1958; expanded edition as *O'Ryan 12345678910,* 1965.   *The Maximus Poems.* New York: Jargon-Corinth, 1960.   *The Distances: Poems.* New York: Grove, 1960.   *West.* London: Cape Goliard, 1966.   *The Maximus Poems IV, V, VI.* New York: Grossman, 1968.   *Archaeologist of Morning: The Collected Poems Outside the Maximus Series.* New York: Grossman, 1970.   *The Maximus Poems, Volume Three.* Edited by Charles Boer and George F. Butterick. New York: Grossman, 1975.   *Spearmint and Rosemary.* Berkeley: Turtle Island, 1975.   *Muthologos, Vol. 1.* Bolinas, Calif.: Four Seasons, 1978.

Poetry and Prose

Charles Olson Reading at Berkeley. Transcribed by Zoe Brown. San Francisco: Coyote, 1966.   *Selected Writings of Charles Olson.* Edited by Robert Creeley. New York: New Directions, 1967.   *Causal Mythology.* San Francisco: Four Seasons, 1969.   *Poetry & Truth: The Beloit Lectures and Poems.* Transcribed and edited by George F. Butterick. San Francisco: Four Seasons, 1971.

Criticism and Other Prose

Call Me Ishmael: A Study of Melville. New York: Reynal and Hitchcock, 1947; reprint, San Francisco: City Lights, 1967.   *Projective Verse.* New York: Totem, 1959.   *Proprioception.* San Francisco: Four Seasons, 1965.   *The Human Universe and Other Essays.* Edited by Donald Allen. New York: Grove, 1967.   *The Special View of History.* Edited by Ann Charters. Berkeley: Oyez, 1970.   *Additional Prose: A Bibliography on America, Proprioception, and Other Notes and Essays.* Edited by George F. Butterick. Bolinas, Calif.: Four Seasons, 1974.   *The Post Office: A Memoir to His Father.* Bolinas, Calif.: Grey Fox, 1974.   *Charles Olson & Ezra Pound: An Encounter at St. Elizabeth's.* Edited by Catherine Seelye. New York: Grossman, 1975.

Correspondence

The Mayan Letters. Edited by Robert Creeley. Palma, Mallorca: Divers Press, 1953; reprint, New York: Grossman, 1968.   *Letters for Origin 1950–1955.* Edited by Albert Glover. New York: Grossman, 1970.

Bibliography

Butterick, George F., and Albert Glover. *A Bibliography of Works by Charles Olson*. New York: Phoenix Book Shop, 1967.

Critical Studies

Boer, Charles. *Charles Olson in Connecticut*. Chicago: Swallow, 1975.　　Butterick, George F. *Guide to The Maximus Poems of Charles Olson*. Berkeley: University of California, 1978.　　Charters, Ann. *Olson/Melville: A Study in Affinity*. Berkeley: Oyez, 1968.　　Christensen, Paul. *Charles Olson: Call Him Ishmael*. Austin: University of Texas, 1978.　　Paul, Sherman. *Olson's Push: Origin, Black Mountain and Recent American Poetry*. Baton Rouge: Louisiana State University, 1978.

SYLVIA PLATH (1932–1963)

A native of Boston and a graduate of Smith College, in 1955 Sylvia Plath won a Fulbright Scholarship to Newnham College, Cambridge. While in England, she met and married the British poet, Ted Hughes. After she taught for a year at Smith (1957–58), the couple returned to England where in 1960 she published her first book of poems and subsequently completed her novel, *The Bell Jar*. On February 11, 1963, Sylvia Plath committed suicide.

A friend of Anne Sexton and one of Robert Lowell's students, Sylvia Plath wrote poems that were intended to sound and to feel brutally personal, almost unbearably painful. Her poems are not merely *about* acute mental and emotional suffering; their very structure—the controlled flow of images, the insistent appositives—draws the reader fully into that suffering. Indeed, her later poems are so well crafted that some critics have argued, wrong-headedly, that she seemed engaged in "a murderous art"—that after writing such frighteningly honest and painfully personal poems, her suicide was virtually inevitable. As a *critical premise*, such an argument is utter nonsense, its absurdity manifestly clear when it is transferred to another artist and his or her work. If Sylvia Plath virtually had no choice but to commit suicide after writing the poems in *Ariel*, then what inevitable choice did someone like Melville have after writing *Moby Dick*?

What makes Sylvia Plath interesting as a poet is not primarily her ostensible subject matter and tone; rather, the success of the poems depends largely on her precision of observation, imagination, and language —as well as on the mastery of her craftsmanship. For example, the onion simile in "Cut" not only accurately describes the swirls of a thumb print but also serves as the entire poem's controlling metaphor. Moreover, in poems like "Cut" and "Lady Lazarus," or even in a celebrated poem like "Daddy," there is also a strong measure of wit and humor—albeit black—often conveyed through resuscitated clichés that manage to rescue the poems from pathos.

On more than one occasion, Sylvia Plath insisted that even the most personal poetry cannot be merely a *cri de coeur*; it has to be informed by and to participate in a greater historical drama. Her own poems participate fully in the vibrant Puritan tradition, not only through her preoccupation with evil (which is utterly distinct from personal suffering) but also through her metaphysical and emblematic technique. They also occur against a constant historical drama, especially the contemporary phenomenon of Nazi Germany out of which she fabricates a modern myth. In short, the pain, the suffering, the fine edge of madness—all are ultimately crafted and controlled by the poet's reasoned and careful hand flashing a measure of genius.

Poetry

The Colossus. New York: Knopf, 1962.　　　*Ariel.* New York: Harper & Row, 1966.　　　*Uncollected Poems.* London: Turret, 1965.　　　*Crossing the Water: Transitional Poems.* New York: Harper & Row, 1971.　　　*Crystal Gazer and Other Poems.* London: Rainbow, 1971.　　　*Lyonesse: Poems.* London: Rainbow, 1971.　　　*Winter Trees.* New York: Harper & Row, 1972.

Fiction and Other Prose

The Bell Jar (novel written under pseudonym of Victoria Lucas). London: Heinneman, 1963; as Sylvia Plath, New York: Harper & Row, 1971.　　　*Letters Home.* Edited by Aurelia S. Plath. New York: Harper & Row, 1975. *Johnny Panic and The Bible of Dreams: Short Stories, Prose, and Diary Excerpts.* Edited by Ted Hughes. New York: Harper & Row, 1979.

Bibliography

Land, Gary, and Stevens, Maria. *Sylvia Plath.* Metuchen, N.J.: Scarecrow Press, 1978.

Critical and Biographical Studies

Aird, Eileen. *Sylvia Plath: Her Life and Work.* New York: Harper & Row, 1973. Butscher, Edward. *Sylvia Plath: Method and Madness.* New York: The Seabury, 1976.　　　Holbrook, David. *Sylvia Plath: Poetry and Existence.* New York: Humanities Press, 1976.　　　Kroll, Judith. *Chapters in a Mythology: The Poetry of Sylvia Plath.* New York: Harper & Row, 1976.　　　Lane, Gary, ed. *Sylvia Plath: New Views on the Poetry.* Baltimore: Johns Hopkins University, 1979.　　　Newman, Charles, ed. *The Art of Sylvia Plath.* Bloomington: Indiana University, 1971.　　　Rosenblatt, Jon. *Sylvia Plath: The Poetry of Initiation.* Durham: North Carolina University, 1979.　　　Simpson, Louis. *A Revolution in Taste: Studies of Dylan Thomas, Allen Ginsberg, Robert Lowell and Sylvia Plath.* New York: Morrow, 1978.　　　Steiner, Nancy Hunter. *A Closer Look at Ariel: A Memory of Sylvia Plath.* New York: Harper's, 1973.

NOTES ON THE POETS

ADRIENNE RICH (1929)

Adrienne Rich's first book of poems won the Yale Younger Poets competition while she was completing her undergraduate studies at Radcliffe. She has taught at Brandeis, Swarthmore, Columbia, Harvard, Rutgers, and City College of New York. Rich's many honors include awards from the American Institute of Arts and Letters, the Guggenheim and Ingram Merrill Foundations, and a commission from the Bollingen Foundation for the translation of Dutch poetry. In 1974 Adrienne Rich and Allen Ginsberg were cowinners of the National Book Award for Poetry. Rich rejected her share as a personal award, but in a statement written by herself and the two other women nominated that year, she accepted the award in the name of all women.

Adrienne Rich has described her more recent poems as "a coming-home to the darkest and richest source of my poetry: sex, sexuality, sexual wounds, sexual identity, sexual politics: many names for pieces of one whole. I feel [this poetry] continues the work I've been trying to do—breaking down the artificial barriers between private and public, between Vietnam and the lovers' bed, between the deepest images we carry out of our dreams and the most daylight events 'out in the world.' This is the intention and longing behind everything I write."

Sexual identity and its profound political implications are indeed among the substantial sources of Adrienne Rich's more recent work, especially in her courageous and beautiful sequence of love poems addressed to another woman—a theme that reappears in *The Dream of a Common Language*. Moreover, even as she speaks about and for women, her poetry is informed by a vigorous intelligence that transcends any unilateral sense of sexuality and politics. At its best, Rich's poetry reaches beyond the limited periphery of any "movement" to become at once a profoundly personal statement forged into a powerful description of our common condition.

If some of Adrienne Rich's poems can be read as a "diving into the wreck," it is crucial to realize that her purpose is not only "to see the damage that was done" but also to catch a glimpse of "the treasures that prevail." Like the astronomer in "Planetarium," she is "a woman trying to translate pulsations / into images," not only for their own sake, not only for her own sake, but "for the relief of the body / and the reconstruction of the mind." Meanwhile, having found the courage to utter, "I choose to love this time for once / with all my intelligence," she also can assert and demonstrate "*a whole new poetry beginning here.*"

Poetry

A *Change of World*. New Haven: Yale University, 1952.   *The Diamond Cutters*. New York: Harper & Brothers, 1955.   *Snapshots of a Daughter-*

in-Law: Poems 1954–1962. New York: Harper & Row, 1963; revised edition, New York: Norton, 1967. *Necessities of Life: Poems 1962–1965*. New York: Norton, 1966. *Leaflets: Poems 1965–1968*. New York: Norton, 1969. *The Will to Change: Poems 1968–1970*. New York: Norton, 1971. *Diving into the Wreck: Poems 1971–1972*. New York: Norton, 1973. *Poems: Selected and New, 1950–1974*. New York: Norton, 1975. *Twenty-One Love Poems*. Emeryville, Calif.: Effie's Press, 1976. *The Dream of a Common Language: Poems 1974–1977*. New York: Norton, 1978.

Prose

Of Woman Born: Motherhood as Experience and Institution. New York: Norton, 1976. *On Lies, Secrets and Silence: Selected Prose 1966–1978*. New York: Norton, 1979.

Critical Edition

Adrienne Rich's Poetry. Selected and edited by Barbara Charlesworth Gelpi and Albert Gelpi. New York: Norton, 1975.

THEODORE ROETHKE (1908–1963)

Theodore Roethke was born in Saginaw, Michigan. The son of a florist, he received a bachelor's and a master's degree from the University of Michigan. He taught at Lafayette College (where he was also tennis coach and director of public relations), Michigan State, Pennsylvania State, Bennington, and the University of Washington where, after fifteen years of teaching and having received every major literary award in this country, he was eventually appointed poet-in-residence in 1962. Roethke's awards included two Guggenheim Fellowships, the Pulitzer Prize in 1954, both the National Book Award and the Bollingen Prize in 1958, and the National Book Award again in 1965, posthumously.

In his notebooks, Roethke repeatedly insisted on—and demonstrated with incredible brilliance—the crucial need for the poet to *look*, to be a good reporter, and to record even the most minute details of the physical world. His poems reflect not only attention to but also reverence for the glory and terror of the physical world: "Hair on a narrow wrist bone." But Roethke also insisted that it is not enough just to look and report; the poet also must learn: "It's the poet's business to be more, not less, than a man."

The range of Roethke's poems amply demonstrates his own dictum. In addition to his often masterful control of form, his poems are marked by a precise observation of natural phenomena and include a gentle, lilting humor or ironic eroticism, a quiet horror in the face of an inevitable annihilation, and a contrapuntal tension between existential despair and the hope for transcendence. If throughout much of his life Roethke was a man who walked the void, his poems are finally a prayer and an affirmation that, although the "dark comes down on what we do," the human spirit finally cannot be overwhelmed by time.

Poetry

Open House. New York: Knopf, 1941.   *The Lost Son and Other Poems*. New York: Doubleday, 1948.   *Praise to the End!* New York: Doubleday, 1951.   *The Waking: Poems 1933–1953*. New York: Doubleday, 1953. *Words for the Wind: The Collected Verse of Theodore Roethke*. New York: Doubleday, 1958.   *Sequence, Sometimes Metaphysical*. Iowa City: Stonewall Press, 1963.   *The Far Field*. New York: Doubleday, 1964.   *The Collected Poems of Theodore Roethke*. New York: Doubleday, 1966.

Prose and Other Poetry

On the Poet and His Craft: Selected Prose of Theodore Roethke. Edited by Ralph J. Mills, Jr. Seattle: University of Washington, 1965.   *Selected Letters of Theodore Roethke*. Edited by Ralph J. Mills, Jr. Seattle: University of Washington, 1968.   *Straw for the Fire: From the Notebooks of Theodore Roethke*. Selected and arranged by David Wagoner. New York: Doubleday, 1972.

Bibliographies

Lane, Gary. *A Concordance to the Poems of Theodore Roethke*. Metuchen, N.J.: Scarecrow, 1972.   McLeod, James. *Roethke: A Manuscript Checklist*. Kent, Ohio: Kent State University, 1971.   McLeod, James. *Roethke: A Bibliography*. Kent, Ohio: Kent State University, 1972.

Critical and Biographical Studies

Blessing, Richard. *Roethke's Dynamism: Vision and Technique*. Seattle: University of Washington, 1974.   Heyen, William, ed. *Profile of Theodore Roethke*. Columbus, Ohio: Charles E. Merrill, 1970.   LaBelle, Jennijoy. *The Echoing World of Theodore Roethke*. Princeton: Princeton University, 1976.   Malkoff, Karl. *Theodore Roethke: An Introduction to the Poetry*. New York: Columbia University, 1966.   Martz, William J. *The Achievement of Theodore Roethke*. Glenview, Ill.: Scott, Foresman, 1966.   Mills, Ralph J., Jr. *Theodore Roethke*. Minneapolis: University of Minnesota, 1963. Scott, Nathan A. *The Wild Prayer of Longing: Poetry and the Sacred*. New Haven: Yale University, 1971.   Seager, Allan. *The Glass House: The Life of Theodore Roethke*. New York: McGraw-Hill, 1968.   Stein, Arnold, ed. *Theodore Roethke: Essays on the Poetry*. Seattle: University of Washington, 1965.   Sullivan, Rosemary. *Theodore Roethke: The Garden Master*. Seattle: University of Washington, 1974.

ANNE SEXTON (1928–1974)

Anne Sexton was born in Newton, Massachusetts. According to the short autobiographical note she wrote for *A Controversy of Poets*, Anne Sexton received "no visible education." However, with Sylvia Plath and George Starbuck, she did attend seminars by Robert Lowell at Boston University; she participated in a summer seminar taught by W. D. Snodgrass at Antioch College; and from 1961 to 1963, she was a scholar at the Radcliffe Institute. In addition to her several books of poetry, she was coauthor with Maxine Kumin of three children's books. Her many awards included fellowships from the American Academy of Arts and Letters, the Radcliffe Institute, and the Ford Foundation. In 1967 she was awarded the Pulitzer Prize; in 1968 she was elected a fellow of the Royal Society of Literature in London. On October 4, 1974, Anne Sexton committed suicide.

Possibly the most famous of the personal-confessional poets, Anne Sexton also probably confessed to more than any of her contemporaries, recreating experiences with unabashed, almost embarrassing honesty. Indeed, it is also probable that she "confessed" to a number of events that she simply invented. In "With Mercy for the Greedy" she wrote: "I was born / doing reference work in sin, and born / confessing it." Like other confessional Puritans, she did just that. But in various interviews, she also insisted that poetry is as much fabrication as it is confession—that even the most brutal truth is shaped by imagination's energy and the artisan's hand. Moreover, doing research in sin, by necessity, must involve a commensurate search for grace, for God. That combination, for Sexton, was absolute—and as risky as a poker game.

Sexton also was a precursor of the now celebrated cause of women's liberation. When it wasn't fashionable for women to write poems about being a woman, she wrote them—openly, unashamedly, and without resorting to political rhetoric. She knew all along that the victimized woman is "misunderstood" and "not a woman, quite." But, like Hester Prynne, the first liberated woman in American literature, Sexton also knew that a relationship between a man and woman could make them gods. And she knew that she could be the ultimate survivor: "A woman like that is not ashamed to die."

Like Sylvia Plath and John Berryman, Anne Sexton chose the moment of her death. But before doing so—as Maxine Kumin has reported—she found the signs of grace and hope spelled out on her typewriter keys. Sexton knew full well that, regardless of how painful it might seem, each poem is an affirmation and celebration of life—as is all poetry.

Poetry

To Bedlam and Part Way Back. Boston: Houghton Mifflin, 1960.   *All My Pretty Ones*. Boston: Houghton Mifflin, 1962.   *Live or Die*. Boston: Houghton Mifflin, 1966.   *Love Poems*. Boston: Houghton Mifflin, 1969. *Transformations*. Boston: Houghton Mifflin, 1971.   *The Book of Folly*. Boston: Houghton Mifflin, 1973.   *The Death Notebooks*. Boston: Houghton Mifflin, 1974.   *The Awful Rowing Toward God*. Boston: Houghton

Mifflin, 1975.   *45 Mercy Street.* Edited by Linda Gray Sexton. Boston: Houghton Mifflin, 1976.   *Words for Dr. Y: Uncollected Poems with Three Stories.* Edited by Linda Gray Sexton. Boston: Houghton Mifflin, 1978.

Prose

Anne Sexton: A Self-Portrait in Letters. Edited by Linda Gray Sexton and Lois Ames. Boston: Houghton Mifflin, 1977.

Critical Study

McClatchy, J. D., ed. *Anne Sexton: The Artist and Her Critics.* Bloomington: Indiana University, 1978.

LOUIS SIMPSON (1923)

Educated at Murro College (Jamaica, West Indies) and at Columbia where he received his doctorate, Louis Simpson has taught at Columbia and the University of California at Berkeley; he is currently professor of English at the State University of New York at Stony Brook. With Donald Hall and Robert Pack, he edited the celebrated anthology *New Poets of England and America* (1957) and he is the author and editor of *An Introduction to Poetry* (St. Martin's Press, 1967). He has received the Rome Fellowship of the American Academy of Arts and Letters, a *Hudson Review* Fellowship, a Guggenheim Fellowship, and the Pulitzer Prize for poetry in 1964.

Like many other poets of his generation, Simpson began his poetic career as a formalist and gradually worked toward a verse in which content primarily determines form. In the process, his own language has become increasingly natural and closer to the colloquial idiom of American speech—a language "closely related to the language in which men actually think and speak." At the same time, both his language and his view of the American experience—the root source of much of his poetry —have retained an educated and literate edge that inform his poems with a fully conscious sense of history and tradition.

Reading Louis Simpson's poetry, one might be reminded of Robert Frost's famous aphorism about his lover's quarrel with the world. No less a lover, Simpson's quarrel is more specifically with America. It is an ongoing struggle to come to grips with the pathetic or tragic failure of the American dream and myth—especially as announced by Whitman. "Where are you, Walt? / The Open Road goes to the used-car lot," he says in "Walt Whitman at Bear Mountain." The open road also leads to the suburbs where, it seems, "You were born to waste your life." Simpson's grief is further intensified by his realization that the American dream has been perverted into a weapon capable of destroying not only supposed enemies but also America itself, which has become a foreign country where people speak a language that is strange even to themselves. "And yet there is also happiness. / Happiness . . ." A discovery of a music, even if it is "made entirely of silence."

Poetry

The Arrivistes: Poems 1940–1949. New York: Fine Editions Press, 1949. *Good News of Death and Other Poems.* In *Poets of Today II.* New York: Scribner's, 1955.   *A Dream of Governors.* Middletown: Wesleyan, 1959. *At the End of the Open Road.* Middletown: Wesleyan, 1963.   *Selected Poems.* New York: Harcourt, Brace & World, 1965.   *Adventures of the Letter I.* New York: Harper & Row, 1971.   *Searching for the Ox.* New York: Morrow, 1976.   *Armidale.* Brockport, N.Y.: BOA Editions, 1980.

Criticism and Other Prose

James Hogg: A Critical Study. New York: St. Martin's, 1963.   *Riverside Drive* (novel). New York: Atheneum, 1962.   *North of Jamaica* (autobiography). New York: Harper & Row, 1972.   *Three on a Tower: The Lives and Works of Ezra Pound, T. S. Eliot and William Carlos Williams.* New York: Morrow, 1975.   *A Revolution in Taste: Studies of Dylan Thomas, Allen Ginsberg, Sylvia Plath and Robert Lowell.* New York: Morrow, 1978.

Critical Studies

Lensing, George S., and Ronald Moran. *Four Poets of the Emotive Imagination: Robert Bly, James Wright, Louis Simpson and William Stafford.* Baton Rouge: Louisiana State University, 1976.   Moran, Ronald. *Louis Simpson.* New York: Twayne, 1972.

W. D. SNODGRASS (1926)

Born in Wilkinsburg, Pennsylvania, and educated at Geneva College and at the University of Iowa, W. D. Snodgrass has taught at the University of Rochester, Wayne State, Syracuse, and Old Dominion; he is currently a visiting professor of English at the University of Delaware. He has received fellowships from the Guggenheim and Ingram Merrill Foundations, the Academy of American Poets, and the National Institute of Arts and Letters, as well as from the National Endowment for the Arts. His first book of poems won the Pulitzer Prize in 1960.

Until recently W. D. Snodgrass has been known primarily as a personal-confessional poet; indeed, it's possible that he was primarily responsible for the emergence of that mode of poetry in the late fifties and early sixties. Unlike Lowell, Plath, and Sexton, Snodgrass made poetry not out of madness and sensationally violent suffering but rather out of the daily neuroses and everyday failures of a man—a husband, father, and teacher. Snodgrass also saw such domestic suffering as occurring against a backdrop of a more universal suffering inherent in the whole of human experience. In "Heart's Needle," he stated *and* demonstrated: "We need the landscape to repeat us." Snodgrass also shared that fundamental concern of his generation announced by Albert Camus: "There is but one truly serious philosophical problem, and that is suicide." In "April Inventory," he wrote: "I have not learned how often I / Can win, can love, but choose to die."

Although noted for their candor, Snodgrass's early poems were also controlled by an unmistakable sense of irony, directed by a highly literate imagination shaped by the New Critics and organized by a consciously formal craftsmanship. Consequently, Snodgrass achieves a good measure of distance between himself as subject and himself as poem; thus the speaker of a "personal" Snodgrass poem often sounds more like a personal-confessional "persona."

In any case, little in Snodgrass's early poetry foreshadowed the appearance of *The Führer Bunker*. A cycle of dramatic monologues, these new poems are spoken by leading figures of the Nazi regime during the last days of the Third Reich—including Albert Speer, Martin Bormann, Joseph Goebbels, Magda Goebbels, Eva Braun, and Adolf Hitler. Displaying an even more powerful range of dazzling craftsmanship, Snodgrass in *The Führer Bunker*—which unfolds like a modern-day *Inferno*—zeros in on the historical and moral landscape that modern humankind seems intent or fated to repeat. The power and the horror of this cycle do not depend on what Snodgrass has to say about the historical figures and events *per se*; he knows all too well that there is little that can be said. Rather, the emotional and moral impact of this cycle—that promises to be one of the truly great achievements of post-1945 American poetry—emerges out of the fact that, like the dark and suffering creatures Dante encountered in hell, the personages in this Nazi *Götterdämmerung* are not the monsters we have met in history books. They are all too unmistakably human, all too unmistakably recognizable.

Poetry

Heart's Needle. New York: Knopf, 1959.   *After Experience*. New York: Harper & Row, 1968.   *Remains* (published under pseudonym). Mt. Horeb, Wis.: Perishable Press, 1970.   *The Führer Bunker: A Cycle of Poems in Progress*. Brockport, N.Y.: BOA Editions, 1977.   *If Birds Build with Your Hair*. New York: Nadja, 1979.

Translations: Poetry

Gallows Songs [Christian Morgenstern] (translated with Lore Segal). Ann Arbor: University of Michigan, 1967; revised edition, Brockport, N.Y.: BOA Editions, 1980.   *Six Troubadour Songs.* Providence, R.I.: Burning Deck, 1977. *Traditional Hungarian Songs.* Newark, Vt.: Janus, 1978; printed for Charles Seluzicki, Poetry Bookseller, Baltimore, Md.   *Six Minnesinger Songs.* Providence, R.I.: Burning Deck, 1980.

Criticism

In Radical Pursuit: Critical Essays and Lectures. New York: Harper & Row, 1975.

Critical Study

Gaston, Paul. W. D. *Snodgrass.* New York: Twayne, 1978.

GARY SNYDER (1930)

Born in San Francisco, Gary Snyder received a bachelor's degree in literature and anthropology from Reed College. He did further study in oriental languages at Berkeley and later studied Zen Buddhism in a monastery in Kyoto, Japan. He has worked as a seaman, logger, and forester; and he has taught at Berkeley. The recipient of a Bollingen grant for Buddhist Studies, a grant from the National Institute of Arts and Letters, and a Guggenheim Fellowship, he was awarded the Pulitzer Prize in 1975.

In *Six San Francisco Poets*, David Kherdian quotes Snyder as saying: "As much as the books I've read, the jobs I've had have been significant in shaping me. My sense of body and language and the knowledge that intelligence and insight, sensitivity, awareness, and brilliance are not limited to educated people, or anything like it." Many of Snyder's poems are direct and simple, marked by an elemental reverence for life and salvaging poetry from the most basic human experience.

The simplicity, however, is not simplistic, for it reflects the profound influence of Zen on Snyder's sensibility and thought. As Snyder has said: "A poet faces two directions: one is the world of people and language and society, and the other is the nonhuman, nonverbal world, which is nature as nature is itself; and the world of human nature—the inner world, as it is itself, before language, before custom, before culture. There's no words in that realm."

Snyder's response to both the inner and outer worlds has resulted in the quest for a primitive identification with nature and a contemporary concern for the ecological consequences of progress and civilization.

"As a poet," Snyder has said, "I hold the most archaic values on earth. They go back to the late Paleolithic: the fertility of the soil, the magic of animals, the power-vision in solitude, the terrifying initiation and rebirth, the love and ecstasy of the dance, the common work of the tribe. I try to hold history and wilderness in mind, that my poems may approach the true measure of things and stand against the unbalance and ignorance of our times."

Among the "archaic values" that Snyder has attempted to erect "against the unbalance and ignorance of our times" are a vital and sacred reintegration of human sexuality and a full celebration of the whole sexual self. Few poets of his generation have celebrated heterosexual love as vividly as Snyder has. Fewer poets have dared explore the precarious sensual and sexual dimensions of such a simple habit as eating, as Snyder has in "Song of the Taste." And Gary Snyder's "The Bath" marks the first time that any American poet perhaps since Whitman has celebrated the pleasurable glory of the male and female bodies with such unabashed and reverential joy.

Poetry

Riprap. Kyoto, Japan: Origin, 1959. *Myths and Texts*. New York: Totem, 1960; reprint, New York: New Directions, 1978. *Hop, Skip and Jump*. Berkeley: Oyez, 1964. *Nanoa Knows*. San Francisco: Four Seasons, 1964. *Riprap and Cold Mountain Poems*. San Francisco: Four Seasons, 1965. *Six Sections from Mountains and Rivers Without End*. San Francisco: Four Seasons, 1965. *Three Worlds. Three Realms. Six Roads*. Marlboro, Vt.: Griffin, 1966. *The Back Country*. New York: New Directions, 1968. *The Blue Sky*. New York: Phoenix Book Shop, 1969. *Sours of the Hills*. Brooklyn: Portents, 1969. *Regarding Wave*. New York: New Directions, 1970. *Anasazi*. Santa Barbara: Yes Press, 1971. *Manzanita*. Bolinas, Calif.: Four Seasons, 1972. *Turtle Island*. New York: New Directions, 1974.

Essays

Earth House Hold: Technical Notes and Queries to Fellow Dharma Revolutionaries. New York: New Directions, 1969. *The Old Ways*. San Francisco: City Lights, 1977.

Critical Study

Stevding, Bob. *Gary Snyder*. New York: Twayne, 1976.

WILLIAM STAFFORD (1914)

William Stafford received his B.A. and his M.A. from the University of Kansas and his Ph.D from the University of Iowa where he was also a member of the Writers' Workshop. A conscientious objector during

World War II and active in pacifist organizations, he has taught at Manchester College and San Jose State College. From 1956 to 1979, he taught at Lewis and Clark College where he is professor emeritus of English. From 1970 to 1971, he was Consultant in Poetry at the Library of Congress. In addition to a Guggenheim Fellowship, a grant from the National Endowment for the Arts, the Shelley Memorial Award, and the Melville Cane Award, he also has received the National Book Award (1963).

In a statement for William J. Martz's *The Distinctive Voice*, William Stafford wrote: "When you make a poem you merely speak or write the language of every day, capturing as many bonuses as possible and economizing on the losses; that is, you come awake to what always goes on in the language, and you use it to the limit of your ability and your power of attention at the moment." Part of what is truly distinctive about Stafford's poetry is his sustained ability to make each poem sound as though it were, in fact, the language of everyday. But it's clear that his power as a poet arises equally out of his ability to capture an extraordinary number of bonuses—the intensity of feeling that daily speech cannot maintain. By so doing, he achieves what he considers to be the meaningful opportunity in the social process of language: "to become more aware of what being alive means."

To a large extent, this awareness also may be the primary thematic focus of Stafford's work: "Your job is to find out what the world is trying to be," he writes in his poem "Vocation." Thus his poetry reflects his attempt not only to capture the possibilities of everyday language but also to maintain "the worth of local things": the plains and small towns of the midwestern and western landscape, the often overlooked experiences of everyday life, and his relationship with his family. Stafford's is also a highly personal poetry, but one which is neither self-torturing nor confessional; rather, it is calm and gentle while remaining honest and firm. Moreover, while neither ostensibly religious nor trailing remnants of the kind of Puritanism inherent in the work of many of his contemporaries, Stafford's poems—as Richard Howard notes in *Alone with America*—occur within a *paysage moralisé* and are informed by an equally powerful moral vision.

Poetry

West of Your City. Los Gatos, Calif.: Talisman, 1961.   *Traveling Through the Dark*. New York: Harper & Row, 1963.   *The Rescued Year*. New York: Harper & Row, 1966.   *Eleven Untitled Poems*. Mt. Horeb, Wis.: Perishable Press, 1968.   *Allegiances*. New York: Harper & Row, 1970.   *Temporary Facts*. Athens, Ohio: Duane Schneider, 1970.   *Someday, Maybe*. New York: Harper & Row, 1973.   *That Other Alone: Poems*. Mt. Horeb, Wis.: Perishable Press, 1973.   *Going Places*. Reno, Nev.: West Coast Poetry Review, 1974.   *Stories That Could Be True: New and Collected Poems*.

New York: Harper & Row, 1977.   *All About Light*. Athens, Ohio: Crois-
sant, 1978.   *Smoke's Way*. Port Townsend, Wash.: Graywolf, 1978.
Things That Happen Where There Aren't Any People. Brockport, N.Y.: BOA
Editions, 1980.

Criticism and Other Prose

Down in My Heart (memoir). Elgin, Ill.: Brethren Publishing, 1947; reprint,
1971.   *The Achievement of Brother Antoninus*. Glenview, Ill.: Scott, Fores-
man, 1967.   *Leftovers, A Care Package: Two Lectures*. Washington, D.C.:
Library of Congress, 1973.   *Writing the Australian Crawl: Views of the
Writer's Vocation*. Ann Arbor: University of Michigan, 1978.

Critical Studies

Holden, Jonathan. *The Mark to Turn: A Reading of William Stafford's Poetry*.
Lawrence, Kans.: University Press of Kansas, 1976.   Lensing, George S.,
and Ronald Moran. *Four Poets of the Emotive Imagination: Robert Bly, James
Wright, Louis Simpson and William Stafford*. Baton Rouge: Louisiana State
University, 1976.

RICHARD WILBUR (1921)

A graduate of Amherst and Harvard, Richard Wilbur has taught at Har-
vard, Wellesley, and Wesleyan where he was an editor of the Wesleyan
University Press poetry series; he is currently professor of English at Smith
College. His many awards include Guggenheim and Ford Foundation
fellowships, the Prix de Rome—as well as both the Pulitzer Prize and
National Book Award in 1957.

In addition to his stunning poetry and translations, Wilbur's work
includes an operetta, *Candide* (with Lillian Hellman, 1957); poetry for
children, *Loudmouse* (1963) and *Opposites* (1973); and editions of the
poems of Keats, Poe, and Shakespeare.

Among poets whose sensibilities were shaped by the New Critics,
Wilbur continues to be the consummate artist. His poetry is marked
by grace, wit, and a kind of masterful craftsmanship equaled by few of
his contemporaries. In his statement for John Ciardi's *Mid-Century
American Poets* (1950), Wilbur affirmed the poet's need for form, for
"artistry," saying that "limitation makes for power: the strength of the
genie comes of his being confined in a bottle." Elsewhere he has stated
that the poet must move "to attempt a maximum range" and to do so
"without apparent strain." At his best, Wilbur's mastery of language and
form is not merely without strain—it is dazzling and breathtaking.

The precision of sensuous detail and the verbal *entrechats* in Wilbur's
poems are formal affirmations of his profound humanism, his belief in

humankind's potential natural grace in this "world of sensible objects." In an era when many other poets have loitered around the deterioration of social, psychic, and personal fabrics and have proclaimed us and our world to be absurd, Wilbur has consistently sought for "a reconciliation between joy and pleasure, between acceptance and transcendence"—often against strenuous odds. And he has succeeded. By so doing, his poems have found and continue to offer the possibility of human beauty and grace.

Poetry

The Beautiful Changes and Other Poems. New York: Reynal & Hitchcock, 1947. *Ceremony and Other Poems.* New York: Harcourt, Brace, 1950.   *Things of This World: Poems.* New York: Harcourt, Brace, 1956.   *Advice to a Prophet and Other Poems.* New York: Harcourt, Brace & World, 1961.   *The Poems of Richard Wilbur.* New York: Harcourt, Brace & World, 1963.   *Walking to Sleep: New Poems and Translations.* New York: Harcourt Brace Jovanovich, 1969.   *The Mind-Reader: New Poems.* New York: Harcourt Brace Jovanovich, 1976.

Translations: Poetry and Drama

The Misanthrope [Molière]. New York: Harcourt, Brace, 1955.   *Tartuffe* [Molière]. New York: Harcourt, Brace & World, 1963.   *The School for Wives* [Molière]. New York: Harcourt Brace Jovanovich, 1971.   *The Learned Ladies* [Molière]. New York: Harcourt Brace Jovanovich, 1978.   *The Whale: Uncollected Translations.* Brockport, N.Y.: BOA Editions, 1980.

Criticism

Responses: Prose Pieces, 1953–1976. New York: Harcourt Brace Jovanovich, 1976.

Bibliography

Field, John P. *Richard Wilbur: A Bibliographical Checklist.* Kent, Ohio: Kent State University, 1971.

Critical Studies

Cummins, Paul F. *Richard Wilbur.* Grand Rapids: Eerdmans, 1971.   Hill, Donald. *Richard Wilbur.* New York: Twayne, 1967.

JAMES WRIGHT (1927)

James Wright was born in Martin's Ferry, Ohio—and he subsequently transformed it into a literary landmark in the contemporary imagination. He received his B.A. from Kenyon College, his M.A. and Ph.D. from the University of Washington, and attended the University of Vienna as a Fulbright Scholar. The recipient of several awards—including the Pulitzer

Prize in 1972—he has taught at Macalester College and the University of Minnesota; he currently teaches at Hunter College.

Like many other poets of his generation, James Wright's style has undergone significant changes in the course of his career. With the publication of his first book, Wright stated that he "wanted to make [his] poems say something humanly important" and pointed to Robert Frost and E. A. Robinson as his models. Thus his early poems, such as "In Shame and Humiliation," are often concerned with his response to the life and suffering of others. After his second book, however, he asserted: "Whatever I write from now on will be entirely different."

According to Robert Bly, Wright's decision was largely the result of his having read—and translated—the work of the German poet, Georg Trakl, a contemporary of Rilke. "In Trakl," Bly writes, "a series of images makes a series of events. Because these events appear out of their 'natural' order, without the connection we have learned to expect from reading newspapers, doors silently open to unused parts of the brain." In Wright's poems such as "The Jewel," "Lying in a Hammock . . . ," and "A Blessing"—generally written between 1960 and 1970—the doors open to startling images, strange but emotionally precise. More personal than his earlier poems, these discover in his own subconscious and imagination the secret pools of human fear and joy. Moreover, the poems themselves seem to evolve quietly through layers of images until they surface with the quick thrust of a striking final image and epiphany.

In more recent poems (those written after the publication of his *Collected Poems* in 1971), Wright has sought a vital integration of his earlier concern with others—"those old Winnebago men"—and the image of epiphany—"the instant in the waterfall." The results enable us to join Wright in his assertion: "I know what we call it / Most of the time. / But I have my own song for it, / And sometimes, even today, / I call it beauty."

Poetry

The Green Wall. New Haven: Yale University, 1957.   *Saint Judas*. Middletown: Wesleyan, 1959.   *The Lion's Tail and Eyes: Poems Written out of Laziness and Silence* (with Robert Bly and William Duffy). Madison, Minn.: Sixties Press, 1962.   *The Branch Will Not Break*. Middletown: Wesleyan, 1968.   *Collected Poems*. Middletown: Wesleyan, 1971.   *Two Citizens*. New York: Farrar, Straus & Giroux, 1973.   *Moments of the Italian Summer*. Washington, D.C.: Dryad, 1976.   *To a Blossoming Pear Tree*. New York: Farrar Straus & Giroux, 1977.

Translations: Poetry and Fiction

Twenty Poems of Georg Trakl (with Robert Bly). Madison, Minn.: Sixties Press, 1961.   *Twenty Poems of Cesar Vallejo* (with Robert Bly). Madison, Minn.: Sixties Press, 1962.   *The Rider on the White Horse: Selected Short Fiction of Theodore Storm*. New York: New American Library, 1964.   *Pablo Neruda: Twenty Poems* (with Robert Bly). Madison, Minn.: Sixties Press, 1967.

Poems by Hermann Hesse. New York: Farrar, Straus & Giroux, 1970.   *Neruda and Vallejo: Selected Poems* (with Robert Bly and John Knoepfle). Boston: Beacon, 1971.   *Wandering: Notes and Sketches by Hermann Hesse* (with Franz Wright). New York: Farrar, Straus & Giroux, 1972.

Critical Study

Lensing, George S., and Ronald Moran. *Four Poets and the Emotive Imagination: Robert Bly, James Wright, Louis Simpson and William Stafford.* Baton Rouge: Louisiana State University, 1976.

Contemporary American Poetry: The Radical Tradition

American poetry since 1945 may be viewed as the product of the dialectics of generations. A recurrent phenomenon in literary as well as in much human history, the pattern of one generation's revolt against another is familiar—indeed, seemingly always close at hand. That rebellion, however, is usually not so much against the preceding generation's essential beliefs as against its excesses: principle atrophied into prejudice, freshness of thought and sensibility petrified into cliché, discipline forged into tyranny. Moreover, the revolution doesn't always realize a clean break with the immediate or distant past: the blood, the genes remain, camouflaged by a radical facade.

While emphasizing the freshness of contemporary poetry, some poets and critics have argued that it reflects a violent break with the first-generation modernist poetry of T. S. Eliot and Pound—if not with all of tradition. In the introduction to his own important anthology of contemporary American poetry (1962), Donald Hall announced that the orthodoxy of T. S. Eliot and the New Critics had ceased: "In modern art anarchy has proved preferable to the restrictions of a benevolent tyranny." The contemporary artist, Hall wrote, "has acted as if restlessness were a conviction and has destroyed his own past in order to create a future." In *The Poem in Its Skin* (1968), Paul Carroll argued that today's poets have attempted "to write poems either alien or hostile to the poem as defined and explored by Eliot and leading writers dominating the scene ten or fifteen years ago" (that is, around 1945). Later Carroll asserted: "This generation of American poets is on the high, happy adventure of creating and innovating a complex of new ways in which to view our common condition—an adventure which in its abundance, freshness, and originality is . . . as interesting as any since the Olympians of 1917."

That the adventure of today's poets has been somewhat anarchic but abundantly fresh is unquestionable. That it has produced poems entirely alien to the earlier modernist poetry is open to a good measure of debate. But the proposition that contemporary American poets have destroyed their own past as poets, for whatever reasons, is simply untenable. Admittedly, T. S. Eliot may have been aesthetically, temperamentally, and constitutionally incapable of writing such poems as Sylvia Plath's "Daddy," Maxine Kumin's "The Excrement Poem," or Frank O'Hara's campy poem to Lana Turner. And the New Critics, Allen Tate, John

577

Crowe Ransom, William Empson, who transformed the experiments of modernist poets into a legislative critical system, may not have known what to make of certain kinds of poems. When confronted by the poems in Robert Lowell's *Life Studies*, Allen Tate reportedly turned to Lowell, his former student—and known as Cal to friends—and agonizingly blurted: "But, *Cal*, it's not *poetry!*"

Although the dicta of the New Critics are no longer regarded as sacred commandments by contemporary poets, much of their valid aesthetic substance has been retained—as have some of the older and more profound literary traditions. In *The New Poets* (1967), M. L. Rosenthal convincingly traced the connections by which much of today's poetry may be considered a continuation and expansion of a strong Romantic tradition. Hyatt H. Waggoner (*American Poetry from the Puritans to the Present*, 1968) and more recently Robert Pinsky (*The Situation of Poetry*, 1976) have also explored the ways in which the contemporary American poet actively participates in various other traditions, especially the Emersonian tradition. No less important is the continuing presence of the equally profound Puritan and Whitman traditions: they are both still active and vital, influencing the formal and thematic directions of much contemporary poetry. If today's poets have achieved a unique vitality, they have done so by making full use of the past—immediate and distant, personal and communal, literary and cultural—while simultaneously contributing new and energizing elements of their own.

The characteristics of the first-generation modernist poem are obviously vital elements in the work of such poets as Richard Wilbur, Robert Lowell, John Berryman, and Stanley Kunitz, who in 1945 were the "younger" poets of the modernist generation and whose sensibilities were shaped by the New Critics. Commenting on his own work in *Poets on Poetry* (1961), Wilbur said: "Most American poets of my generation were taught to admire the English Metaphysical poets of the seventeenth century and such contemporary masters of irony as John Crowe Ransom. We were led by our teachers and by the critics whom we read to feel that the most adequate and convincing poetry is that which accommodates mixed feelings, clashing ideas, and incongruous images. Poetry could not be honest, we thought, unless it began by acknowledging the full discordancy of modern life and consciousness. I still believe that to be a true view of poetry." Written under the tutelage of John Crowe Ransom and Allen Tate, Robert Lowell's early work, in particular, was immediately hailed as a model of what the modernist poem could and should be. And John Berryman's more recent monumental series of "Dream Songs" clearly employs the essential techniques and assumptions of modernist poetry.

One of the major differences between modernist and contemporary poetry is that the latter—at least seemingly—is more intimate and personal. The elements of the modernist poem seemed consciously employed toward assuring a certain artistic distance between the poets and their subjects, the poets and their poems. From the purposeful use of persona to the conscious use of unmistakable "literary" tradition, each technique was a formal, emotional, and intellectual device for the poets' objectification of subject, emotion, and medium. The individual personality of the poets, their more intimate experiences and emotions, were not just seemingly absent: indeed, in light of Eliot's dictum that poetry was an escape from personality, what are now considered to be the "personal elements" in poetry were virtually taboo among modernist poets. And in the hands of lesser poets, such an attitude often resulted in a depersonalized and inhuman versification.

As Ralph J. Mills, Jr., has amply demonstrated in his brilliant essay "Creation's Very Self" (reprinted in *Cry of the Human*, 1974), what distinguishes the work of contemporary poets from that of their modernist predecessors is especially the presence and vitality of the "personal element." Although possibilities for objectification remain, poetry is no longer considered an escape from personality by contemporary poets but rather a fuller cultivation and use of personality. The personality of the poet is more central and more vibrant than the poetic device of the persona: "he" or "she" is now frequently replaced by "I." The speaker of the poem and the poet are often one and the same, an indivisible person; the subject of a poem is often the poet's own personal—at times intimate—experiences, which the poet does not seek to present as anything other than personal experience. Consequently, the full appreciation of some contemporary poems sometimes seems to hinge on the reader's knowledge of biographical details of the poet's personal and intimate life. For example, Robert Lowell was, in fact, jailed as a conscientious objector—as he says he was in "Memories of West Street and Lepke"; Sylvia Plath did attempt suicide—as she says she did in "Lady Lazarus." With the poet's private self as both subject and speaker of the poem, with the presence and use of the poet's own personality in the poem, the interaction between the work of art and the reader becomes proportionately more intimate: the poet seems to speak more directly to the reader, as if that reader were a confessor, psychiatrist, intimate friend, or lover.

The personalization of poetry has evolved in various ways. In the work of Robert Bly, James Wright, and W. S. Merwin, for example, a personal poetry occurs as the result of the exploration of and response to the most inner reaches of the poet's self below the rational and conscious levels. Poems grow out of images discovered in the depths of human darkness, as it were, amidst the substrata of preconscious feeling and intuition. Particularly in Galway Kinnell's later work, one senses the poet's attempt to strip away formal, linguistic, and even surface emotional constructs that might filter or impede the poet's ongoing exploration of his inmost self and experience. Through shifts of emotion, language, and tone all within the same poem, one senses in the work of John Logan the vital interaction among the various facets of an individual personality: the harmonious counterpoint between intellectual irony and corny self-deprecating humor, between religious feeling and vulgarity, between commonplace banality and high lyrical excitement—in short, an integration of the individual parts of a multidimensional personality.

Although they contain moments of private joy and grief, the poems of Allen Ginsberg and Frank O'Hara take another direction: they depend primarily on the self's discovery of the outer world and response to it. In these poems one often senses the poet's self, his personality, being shaped by the "surround" in which he finds himself. The reader hears with O'Hara's ears or touches with Ginsberg's hands. In the poetry of Louis Simpson and Richard Hugo, the personal element seems to evolve primarily out of the relationship between the poet's private self and the social as well as geographical landscape he inhabits and with which he interacts: the sophisticated suburban landscape of Simpson's poems; the bleak and desolate western landscape of Hugo's poems.

The personalization of American poetry since 1945 is probably most obvious in the work of those poets who have chosen to incorporate in their poems elements of their personal histories—and events in their individual lives usually considered intimate, private, or confidential. The sexual preferences of some of this century's great poets were among the best kept secrets in literary history—in large part because they were rightfully considered irrelevant to the poetry. Allen Ginsberg's and Robert Duncan's poems about aspects of their homosexuality, as well as Adrienne Rich's open and moving explorations of her own sexual preference in some of her more recent poems, may be somewhat startling to some readers. Indeed, most Americans still feel somewhat threatened by such sexual honesty. Private revelations of personal illness, madness, failure, and self-destruction—these are some of the recurring subjects in the work of such personal-confessional poets as Lowell, Plath, Sexton, and Snodgrass.

Today's poets, then, have succeeded in making poetry that often resonates as being radically personal; however, under closer scrutiny, other factors come into focus to temper the reader's immediate response. Subject and voice paradoxically work toward making even the most intimate poetry less personal than it first seems and result in erecting another kind of persona—the part of the private self that the poet wishes to make public. Because they have been primarily concerned with physical and psychic limitations, the personal-confessional poets have written a poetry which, to a large extent, reveals *only* the deteriorating self speaking in a chosen voice, ranging from the modulated whine of W. D. Snodgrass to the near hysteria of Sylvia Plath. Moreover, in the work of some poets, the requirements of technique and craftsmanship raise further questions about just how personal and immediate a poem can be: by drawing attention to itself, even the poem ostensibly about the most intimate subject reminds the reader that the poem, any poem, is a fabrication and takes time and calculation to complete. Like any other art, personal poetry is a selective, calculated, and public gesture, a formal utterance for which the poet *selects* a language and voice, even if they are as approximate to his or her own as the poet can manage.

In his lecture entitled "The Inward Muse," Donald Hall may have been speaking for a number of his contemporaries when he said that while working on his early poems he "could sometimes hear the voice of Mr. Ransom" reminding him of irony and that "it took ten years to get rid of that voice." Nevertheless, irony and paradox continue to be vitally present in the work of today's poets. Confronted by the quality of our common condition, the sensitive and mature human being may not survive without a strong ironic sense: although irony may thwart much genuine emotion, its absence also makes genuine emotion virtually impossible. The uses of irony in contemporary poetry can be seen in the work of two rather different poets, Sylvia Plath and Frank O'Hara. In Sylvia Plath's poetry, the presence of irony serves to temper the intensity of suffering by undercutting the vehement, and often near-Gothic imagery and the highly charged emotion. Indeed, many of Plath's more intense poems survive as *poems* specifically because her sharp ironic sense is also at play. For example, "Lady Lazarus" is protected from bathos not only by the ironic sense of humor that views the would-be suicide as "the big strip tease" in a three-ring circus of Nazi-artistic-Christian horrors but also through intonation and line-break that begin the poem by suggesting that it could be spoken by some rich Jewish lady coming out of a beauty spa like Maine Chance.

The irony in Frank O'Hara's poems may be more implicit—a pervasive impetus behind the total poem; nevertheless, it is present and crucial. In the poem to Lana Turner, for example, as well as in much of "To the Film Industry in Crisis," an ironic sensibility functions in a manner directly opposite to Plath's: it undercuts the humor by suggesting the emptiness—if not the decadence—of the emotion. In other words, in O'Hara's poems one recognizes the peculiar contemporary phenomenon of camp irony.

Because so much contemporary poetry seems so intensely personal, it also generally seems very direct and transparent; but the essential complexity of emotion, the richness of language and the potential of form—not the least of which is the organic form of free verse—make ambiguity inescapable. On a rather basic level, for example, today's reader cannot avoid the rather obvious *double-entendre* in the opening lines of John

Logan's "Love Poem": "Last night you would not come, / and you have been gone so long." John Ashbery's use of wide-open form and broken syntax in a poem like "Leaving the Atocha Station" often commands that the reader invent interpretation. The Proustian quality of James Merrill's later poems offers readers still another kind of complexity of language and texture. Robert Creeley's poems depend largely on structural ambiguity—the emotional and thematic tension between the linear unit and the syntactical unit—for their introverted effect. By eliminating punctuation in many of his poems since *The Moving Target*, W. S. Merwin succeeds in creating additional levels of ambiguity; and John Berryman achieves still another kind of ambiguity through a manipulation of pronouns referring to his schizoid persona.

One characteristic of the modernist poem that seems less prevalent in contemporary poetry is wit, especially as the word is used to refer to a kind of cerebral-aesthetic humor. A measure of this intellectual wit still can be found, most obviously, in a poem like Richard Wilbur's "Praise in Summer" in which the genuine and vibrant wit controlling the thrust of the last line paradoxically negates *and* affirms the entire poem's thematic concern. However, much of today's poetry is generally marked by a much broader brand of humor, often a buffoonish or slapstick comedy. In his "Dream Songs," Berryman consciously uses minstrel comedy, situation comedy, and burlesque techniques, including a kind of verbal double take. Kenneth Koch is the academic and symbolist Red Skelton of his generation, the innocent clown bumbling through an absurd, though sophisticated, universe where he, as poet and person, is constantly risking absurdity. As Paul Carroll has observed, Lawrence Ferlinghetti—especially when he reads his poems—sounds like a hip Will Rogers. Moreover, in contemporary poetry, comedy often belies the poet's intent: humor verges on hysteria, laughter camouflages horror: Pagliacci facing a firing squad.

The reader of modernist poetry has come to expect allusion as part and parcel of a poem: T. S. Eliot's "The Waste Land" is the archetype of the poem as footnote. However, contemporary poets have consciously avoided the excesses of literary allusion that resulted in a "poetry about poetry." Although most post–World War II poets are university graduates and professional academicians, their poems do not obviously wear their erudition on their sleeves. The reasons are varied and complex. The scarcity of allusion, in part, is the result of the democratization of poetry under the strong influence of Walt Whitman and of William Carlos Williams, both of whom advocated the use of an American language and rhythm. Moreover, because much contemporary poetry is often intensely personal, the poet responds to experience in a visceral rather than in an intellectual fashion. Response is not filtered or controlled by knowledge or formal education, nor is it shaped by a conscious sense of the formal tradition. That this is an age when the individual, the self, is threatened by the dehumanization of a technocratic society and by the overwhelming sense of imminent atomic or ecological annihilation has long been a journalistic cliché—albeit one that has recently been infused with unequaled urgency. The energy we depend on for survival, just as surely as the foetus depends on the mother's blood for survival, *is* running out. Events at the nuclear power plant on Three Mile Island reminded us too acutely that our technology is as flawed and dangerous as the human intelligence that produced it. Despite the cliché of annihilation, the phenomenon is all too real and has resulted in the poet's vehement affirmation of the individual self and in an equally intense effort to respond fully to experience as a person and as an artist. This kind of Emersonian self-reliance—with absolute stakes—is an implicit repudiation of Eliot's theory of tradition and the individual talent, perhaps in large part because of the contemporary poet's profound fear of that history, culture, and tradition, which are ultimately responsible for the deterioration of the modern self.

Compared to Eliot and his followers, today's poet is noticeably less concerned with the use of allusion. However, as Susan Sontag has written: "Language is the most impure, the most contaminated, the most exhausted of all materials out of which art is made. . . . It's scarcely possible for the artist to write a word (or render an image or make a gesture) that doesn't remind him of something already achieved." Consequently, because language is contaminated, because history shackles, and because post–World War II poets simply cannot escape their own (and our) ruthless memory, allusion—conscious or not—persists and is found in both expected and unexpected places.

The more obvious examples of allusion can be found in the early work of Lowell—such as in "Mr. Edwards and the Spider"; it can be found in such poems as Snodgrass's "April Inventory," which can be read as a retelling of an academic Prufrock's story, with intermittent references to Shakespeare's seventy-third sonnet, Hopkins's "God's Grandeur," Edward Taylor's "Meditation Six, First Series"—and with echoes of Thoreau and Camus. Ferlinghetti's "I Am Waiting," in spite of his renunciation of "poetry about poetry," relies heavily on obvious and well-known literary phrases. In Ashbery's "Leaving the Atocha Station," Paul Carroll has ferreted out mangled echoes of Pound, Eliot, Hopkins, and others. Certain critics have noted that James Dickey's famous "The Heaven of Animals" is derivative and perhaps consciously fashioned after Edwin Muir's "The Animals." A number of Louis Simpson's poems rely on the reader's being fully conversant with the work of Walt Whitman.

The burden of language and the grasp of memory result in the contemporary poet's using other kinds of allusion. For example, the presence of Rilke is clearly felt in the concluding line of James Wright's "Lying in a Hammock . . ." The position, tone, and emotional impact of Wright's line, "I have wasted my life," echoes the concluding line of Rilke's "Torso of an Archaic Apollo," which is generally translated as "You must change your life." Rilke's ninth "Duino Elegy" is present in the very title of Maxine Kumin's book, *House, Bridge, Fountain, Gate*— just as it is present in the concluding lines of Richard Hugo's poem "Montgomery Hollow." Moreover, in much of John Ashbery's more recent poetry, there is an even more all-pervasive *frisson* of Rilke's own elusive exploration of states of feeling; a specific poem like "Street Musicians" recalls the kind of vision and perspective found in Rilke's *Das Buch der Bilder* and *Neue Gedichte*. The imagery, tone, and effect of several of Robert Bly's poems reflect the more intense presence and influence of the Spanish surrealists Neruda and Vallejo.

Rather than relying on sometimes obscure literary allusions of the past, today's poet prefers to introduce more personal allusions to specific people, places, and experiences in the poet's personal life: Wichita, Missoula, Pine Island, William Duffy. The contemporary arts, especially the popular arts and popular performers, also become points of reference: movies, folk-rock, Lana Turner, Joan Baez, Bob Dylan. Contemporary poetry, then, is very much the poetry of today, requiring from the reader as much full consciousness of the present as of the past, of the banal as of the sublime.

Just as the contemporary poet is more drawn toward existential experience, he or she is also less inclined to use what Eliot understood to be "the mythical method" to organize and present experience. Indeed, except as a subconscious, elemental, and perhaps inevitable ritualistic pattern of human response, myth is virtually absent from the work of most post-1945 poets. However, if the traditional mythic method at this moment in history is not viable, the mythical vision and the need for it remain an active force in contemporary poetry. During the past quarter of a century, American poets seem to have felt an increasing need to be not simply myth users, but myth makers. Both as persons and as poets, they reflect "the instinct that their work-a-day world is interpenetrated with a super-rational or extrarational activity in which they can and do share." If the pattern of such more-than-human activity is not immediately accessible as part of a formalized tradition, then poets must dig it out of the accumulation of their experience and create myths closer to the contemporary experience than those inherited from myth makers of the past. By so doing, contemporary poets are also returning poetry to one of its primal and sacred functions.

In the poetry of W. D. Snodgrass, a rather clear pattern of extra-rational activity emerges, against which the action of the poem takes place and in which the speaker senses inevitable participation. As Snod-

grass says in "Heart's Needle": "We need the landscape to repeat us."
This pattern is quite simply Darwin's theory of evolution subsequently
transformed into the law of the survival of the fittest. Snodgrass may not
be pleased to find himself participating in this brutal dialectic, but he
recognizes its energy as one of the major determinants of human activity:
in "After Experience," he juxtaposes the rules of survival spoken softly
by the gentle philosopher Spinoza with those shouted by a military in-
structor. The same concern for survival is also the energy generating
"April Inventory," in which those who seem most fit to survive are the
"solid scholars" who get "the degrees, the jobs, the dollars." The extent
to which Darwin's law of evolution—as popularly understood—is the
extrarational pattern interpenetrating the poet's diurnal world is un-
mistakably clear in "Heart's Needle," especially in Part 9 when the
speaker of the poem walks through the local museum of natural history
and recognizes that his experience with his estranged wife is an echo
of the gesture of the primitive conflict in which the animals on display
are engaged. Rather than turn to a myth fabricated in a prescientific
age, Snodgrass has recognized and used a scientific law as a more cogent
myth for this age of science.

   In his more recent cycle of poems, *The Führer Bunker*, Snodgrass
has coupled the myth of the survival of the fittest with the drama of
Nazi Germany, and he has sought to reconstruct this contemporary
myth without subjective or moral comment. Other poets also have
discovered myth in this and other contemporary dramas and figures.
For an age of violence, Sylvia Plath has turned away from the ancient
mythology found in her earlier poetry, such as the Colossus of Rhodes,
and toward more recent history—Hiroshima, Hitler's concentration camps
—for the mythic background against which her personal suffering occurs.
For an age of media, Frank O'Hara has recognized the mythic dimen-
sions of those "stars" whose personal and public lives determine the
rhythm and quality of this civilization just as surely as the fabricated
gods of other mythologies. In the character of Henry Pussycat, Berryman
has erected a myth out of, and for, the suffering, middle-aged, white "hu-
man American man." But throughout contemporary poetry, one also senses
that the isolated self—the multifaceted and complex "I"—rises above
communal, historical, and extrarational events and assumes mythic pro-
portions of its own. Contemporary poets seem determined to accept
Wallace Stevens's words at face value and "to make of their fate an
instance of all fate." The collective impact of today's poetry, then, seems
to say: I am my own myth.

   The blood and genes inherited by contemporary poetry, however, are
not merely the formal demands of New Criticism but the full tradition
of American and British poetry. Muted, modified, transformed—none-
theless, the spirit and energy of this tradition continue as vital forces

in today's poetry. And it is not simply an aesthetic heritage, but a complex of formal and thematic stances that constitute the polarities not only of our art but also probably of our psychic and mythic life.

The polarized stances—toward humankind, its history, the substance and quality of its individual and communal life, its art, and its destiny—constituting the mainstream of American poetry are the Puritan tradition and the Whitman tradition. Of course, other less powerful currents also have contributed to the evolution of American poetry. But the life and energy of American poetry, especially in the twentieth century, spring primarily from the tension, balance, and occasional reconciliation between the microcosmic and macrocosmic vision of the Puritan and Whitman traditions. What is vitally important about these two major traditions is specifically that each is a comprehensive vision of and response to the total human and cosmic experience. The significance of such a vision cannot be stressed enough, for it strongly influences (perhaps determines) what a poet sees and how a poet responds—influencing the subjects and the themes of poems—as well as the poet's mode of expression or style—shaping the language, rhythm, structure, and form of poems.

Whether written by Edward Taylor or Robert Lowell, Puritan poetry arises out of the fundamental view of humans as the heirs of the specific history of the fallen Adam. It views humans as essentially corrupt, as seeking the contours of their lives in an equally corrupt universe, and as incapable of personal salvation. Characteristically intellectual and highly personal, seeking the speaker's place in history, this poetry focuses primarily on the individual's spiritual and physical limitations and deterioration. Its structure is usually complex, emblematic, and metaphysical; the texture of its language is intricate. Because contemporary Puritan poets have rejected the possibility of the traditional concept of salvation—the one thread of light that sustained the original Puritan—in large part because the death of God is accepted as a premise of contemporary existence, sin is therefore symbolically replaced by mental and emotional imbalance. Lacking the hope of salvation while still believing in profound personal evil, the more recent Puritan poet is threatened by madness and is tempted to self-destruction, even though the very act of writing poetry is an affirmative one, a saying *no* to any force that would destroy the human spirit. The poetry of Robert Lowell, Sylvia Plath, and Anne Sexton probably best exemplifies the aesthetic and moral dimensions of the Puritan tradition in contemporary American poetry.

The Whitman tradition in contemporary poetry stands in stark contrast to the earlier Puritan tradition. Refusing to submit humans to the bonds of history, sacred or secular, this tradition asserts the holiness of the Adamic self, inside and out, and celebrates the grace of purely human and physical activity in a holy universe. Impatient with and often scornful of intellectualization, it focuses on the unique and separate self and points to the self's limitless potential for transcendence. Open, loose, often the product of emotion rather than of intellect or conspicuous craftsmanship, its language also tends to be more recognizably "American" and earthy. However, if poets in the contemporary Puritan tradition accept the death of God as a premise of existence, so too do poets in the contemporary Whitman tradition accept the rather tragic futility of the original Whitman vision. Thus Whitman's vision and his poems often serve as the basis for lament, and the contemporary poet decries the betrayal of history since Whitman's prophetic songs. Such a sense of betrayal is at the root of Allen Ginsberg's "Howl" and serves as the aesthetic and moral background against which so much of Louis Simpson's and David Ignatow's poetry evolves.

As critics have noted, American poetry also has continued to experience a large measure of internationalization and reflects the presence of other traditions. The influence of the French symbolists persists. Rilke's presence seems to loom larger and larger. Pound's "discovery" of the East can be traced to the next generation: one can observe the influence of Japanese poetry on the work of poets like Gary Snyder and W. S. Merwin; the influence of Chinese poetry on the work of James Wright is also unmistakable. And the work of Spanish surrealists has had a profound effect on the work of poets like Philip Levine and Robert Bly. That so many of today's American poets are also active and distinguished translators—as their bibliographies in this book make obvious—has also contributed to the internationalization of contemporary poetry in America.

Clearly, then, the vitality of contemporary American poetry depends in large part on its full participation in and transformation of a rich tradition of poetry. And yet, after having posited this participation, one must also recognize the contemporary poets' real measure of dissatisfaction and restlessness not only with that tradition but also with their specific art and medium—that also accounts for the vitality and diversity of today's poetry.

The poets' restlessness with their medium is largely evident in the number of those who, for various reasons, have changed their styles radically in the course of their careers. These stylistic transformations, in turn, reflect equally radical shifts in their basic assumptions about the nature and function of their art. After having mastered the lyric rooted in the tenets of New Criticism, Robert Lowell discarded the lyric form in favor of a semi-sonnet form, which he subsequently discarded to return once again to the lyric in his last poems. From compact and trippingly anapestic poems dealing with somewhat private experience, James Dickey's poems have grown more expansive, looser, and more public—often charged by a kind of revivalist energy. On the other hand, W. S. Merwin's poems have moved from technical and structural complexity toward an imaginative and emotional density that is almost hermetic. At times savagely personal, Merwin's poems seem to refuse all further human contact. Donald Hall's poems have evolved from a relatively strict formalism to a more expansive, Whitmanesque, and commensurately more human organic form. Amiri Baraka's style and attitude have also undergone a radical shift, moving from a Projectivist, literary poetics, informed by a sense of the Black heritage and an awareness of the political situation, toward a more emphatic and political poetics of activism.

Other poets have shown a restlessness with their chosen medium by attempting the techniques of other media. Experiments with the prose poem by such writers as Robert Bly, David Ignatow, and James Wright are self-evident manifestations of discontent with the limits of more traditional poetic forms. In most of *The Anonymous Lover*, John Logan sought a closer, more obvious relationship between poetic and musical language. Some of John Ashbery's poems clearly reflect the influence of action painting; Lawrence Ferlinghetti's often explore the possibilities of poetry as a kind of verbal jazz. Underlying these stylistic transformations and experiments is not merely an obsession with originality but also a profound need to shape the structures and rhythms—as well as to explore the timbre—of the voice of the individual poet and of the times.

Each age discovers or fabricates one or two all-encompassing metaphors for the quality of human experience that it confronts or seeks. It was T. S. Eliot, of course, who fabricated the first encompassing metaphor for the twentieth century: the waste land was the image of human spiritual and cultural sterility—an image that, after Hiroshima and Nagasaki, proved to be frighteningly precise in its prophetic implications. To date, no single poet seems to have fabricated *the* central metaphor for the quality of our experience since World War II. Rather, this is what seems to have happened: although "The Waste Land" was a powerful *mise en scène* of the modern situation, to a large extent its characters were composite ghosts, unreal men and women in an unreal city. Eliot was describing the human condition, not the individual condition. In other words, Eliot set the scene, but contemporary poets have peopled that waste land, mostly with their individual selves. They have described the deterioration and sterility of the individual self, thereby fabricating a cumulative metaphor for our own age.

The language of this metaphor is as stark, brutal, and familiar as the experience. More often than not, it is the language of experience and emotion—and not recollected in tranquillity. The brutalized self responds neither in pentameters nor in euphemisms—nor, at times, even in metaphor. In the midst of unbearable suffering, Sylvia Plath, as do most of us, utters the most commonplace of clichés. In "Three Moves," at the peak of emotion and frustration, John Logan utters what in polite society would be considered vulgarities—but here transformed into lyrical epiphanies by their contextual power. And the language in Amiri Baraka's later poems not only reflects the poet's fierce emotion but indeed brutalizes the reader. In differing ways, today's poets have followed the advice and example of Walt Whitman and of William Carlos Williams who both sought to democratize the language of poetry; and they agree with George Starbuck's remark: "We've got language we haven't yet used." Above all, it is the language of today's poetry that immediately strikes us as vital, contemporary, and fresh. By making poetry out of the full range of everyday speech—including obscenity, vulgarity, and slang—contemporary poets have returned to poetry a richness of expression and experience that had been absent probably since the Renaissance.

Contemporary poets have managed to reinstate in poetry a directness and honesty toward the human tribe's sexual identity and experience, with all its ramifications. The range is virtually all-encompassing: menstruation, masturbation, love making, adultery, homosexuality, lesbianism, sodomy, abortion. Whether the cause for celebration or lamentation or both, sexuality in today's poetry is neither a programmatic metaphor, a consciously Freudian exploration, nor a pseudomystical Lawrencian Victorianism. Although clearly an essential element of the poet's theme, first and foremost it is an existential human experience, capable of being simultaneously ugly and the source of grace and, as John Berryman suggests, simultaneously lyrical and vulgar: "like the memory of a lovely fuck."

An imagination of commitment that responds directly, honestly, and morally to a broad spectrum of everyday political realities is also one of the distinguishing elements of today's poetry. The political climate has become a crucial arena within which contemporary poets have exercised their talents. This interest in politics reflects the contemporary poets' belief in a poetry engagé and thereby returns poetry to one of its long and vital traditions. The political tradition was all but ignored during the first half of the century, especially when the notion of art for art's sake virtually prohibited poetry from being anything but hermetic and when political concern had to be masked with myth, clothed with wit, and moved by indirection. Some reactionary critics still haven't forgiven Archibald MacLeish for his political involvements and concerns. But the contemporary poet agrees with Sartre and Camus that art must be committed if it is to survive. As Ferlinghetti said: "Only the dead are disengaged."

Commitment, however, does not necessitate blatant "headline" poetry. In a statement for The London Magazine (1962), Sylvia Plath suggested what an imagination of commitment really implies: "the issues of our time which preoccupy me at the moment are the incalculable genetic effects of fallout and . . . the terrifying, mad, omnipotent marriage of big business and the military in America.... [But] my poems do not turn out to be about Hiroshima, but about a child forming itself finger by finger in the dark. They are not about the terrors of mass extinction, but about the bleakness of the moon over a yew tree in a neighborhood graveyard."

The imagination of commitment is reflected in at least three obvious, though by no means exclusive, ways in today's poetry. The first includes poems informed by a general and sometimes indirect sociopolitical consciousness. Plath's preoccupation with the "incalculable genetic effects of fallout" is reflected in "Nick and the Candlestick"; addressing her young —perhaps unborn—child, she suggests the end of the world and of the universe in two stanzas that also reflect the scientific quality of her imagination:

> Let the stars
> Plummet to their dark address.
>
> Let the mercuric
> Atoms that cripple drip
> Into the terrible well. . . .

The possible destruction of the world through a nuclear holocaust is also the immediate occasion for Wilbur's "Advice to a Prophet." In "After Experience Taught Me . . ." Snodgrass suggests not only the inherent horror in any system of ideas or values carried to its logical conclusion but also that terrifying brotherhood of men—the seeming inevitability of the military-industrial-university complex. The extent to which most Americans live their conscious or subconscious lives in the constant threat of nuclear annihilation is eminently clear in Kinnell's "Vapor Trail Reflected in the Frog Pond," in Snyder's "Vapor Trails," and in Stafford's "At the Bomb Testing Site." Clearly it is an active sociopolitical consciousness that informs Gwendolyn Brooks's "The Lovers of the Poor," Robert Hayden's "El-Hajj Malik El-Shabazz," as well as so many of Louis Simpson's and David Ignatow's poems. Moreover, a poem like Ginsberg's "Howl" is a full-scale indictment of the quality of American life and the recent history that has contributed to such an experience.

In the second group, specific historical events inform the poets' imaginations. The poems from W. D. Snodgrass's The Führer Bunker are obvious examples, since Snodgrass uses specific historical personages and events to reconstruct that Nazi Götterdämmerung. Meanwhile, other poets are responding to other historical events: Wright's "Eisenhower's Visit to Franco," Hayden's poem about Frederick Douglass and his "Night, Death, Mississippi." These are only a few of the poems that suggest the imagination of commitment in contemporary poetry has not been challenged exclusively by the war in Vietnam.

However, Vietnam probably did occasion the largest number of overtly political poems, perhaps more than any other single event since World War I. Of course, World War II had generated poetry about war: Wilbur's "On the Eyes of an SS Officer," Jarrell's "The Death of a Ball Turret Gunner" and Louis Simpson's "The Heroes" are only a few examples. Despite the fact that many of today's poets were active participants in World War II—or perhaps because they were—that experience did not seem to grip their imaginations as much as the conflict in Vietnam did. The poets' opposition to the war and to the political figures responsible for it was eminently clear—in their poetry as well as in their active political lives. Poems like Bly's "Counting Small-Boned Bodies," Levertov's "The Altars in the Street," and Merwin's "The Asians Dying" reflect a profound moral outrage against this nation's participation in and support of the war in Vietnam, as well as the depth of frustration that the continued involvement in this war generated. At the root of much antiwar poetry, however, was not only moral outrage at the atrocities but also a kind of implicit belief that the war might be stopped with the language of poetry. Thus implicit in many of the antiwar poems was a silent echo of Ginsberg's courageous but disillusioning prophecy in "Wichita Vortex Sutra":

> I lift my voice aloud
>> make Mantra of American language now,
>> pronounce the words beginning my own Millennium—
>> I here declare the end of the war!

Political or moral questions aside, contemporary antiwar poetry does raise important questions—the most obvious of which is where does poetry leave off and propaganda begin? And this question raises the equally important question: can propagandistic poetry be good? (Dryden's "Mac Flecknoe" probably sets a precedent.) Moreover, contemporary antiwar poetry is the result of a peculiar set of circumstances, for, unlike the poetry that emerged out of World War I and II, the poetry generated by the war in Vietnam was written by individuals who were noncombatants, most of whom had never been in the embattled country. (One is reminded of the shocking contrast between Wilfred Owen's poems written in the trenches and Rupert Brooke's chauvinistic sonnets written in the comfort of his precious university circle.) Thus the antiwar poetry of the sixties and seventies was based not on the reality of direct experience but on the removed reality of the media: the atrocities were not *witnessed*, they were "viewed." Often this was a poetry not about the victims of war but about the perpetrators of war; not about the blood of war but about the language of war; not about the pity of war but about the policy of war. Nevertheless, if it was imperfect as poetry, as it sometimes was—an increasing number of those poems now strain our willing suspension of aesthetic disbelief—it did testify to the contemporary poets' full and human commitment to the quality of their fellow creatures' lives.

Moreover, if the political climate has become a crucial arena within which today's poets have exercised their talents, so too their work has generated an aesthetic and critical climate in which the imagination of commitment is more fully understood as a vital element in contemporary poetry. It is difficult to read much of the poetry of David Ignatow or of Philip Levine without being aware of the strong sociopolitical consciousness the work reflects. The poetry of Denise Levertov continues to reflect a refined revolutionary commitment that was so much part of the poetry she wrote during the late sixties and early seventies. In many of her recent poems, Adrienne Rich has brought her enviable powers as a poet to bear on the question of sexual identity and sexual politics. In his poetry and prose, Robert Bly has repeatedly sought to come to grips with a fuller reintegration of the feminine and masculine principles, as have Gary Snyder and John Logan. Of course, at the heart of much of Snyder's poetry is also a profound concern for this planet's ecological balance. In short, the imagination of commitment is not only a vital element in much of today's poetry but also seems to have become an essential attitude of the reader as well as of the poet.

The poets' moral stance toward sociopolitical events is only part of their more inclusive aesthetic, ethical, and spiritual concerns. It is important to note that many poets have been just as much concerned in their poems with the nature of poetry itself as with political phenomena. Indeed, the radical tradition in contemporary poetry and the poetics governing American poetry since 1945 might well be approached simply by a reading of poems that are either explicitly or implicitly about the art of poetry. Ashbery's "Leaving the Atocha Station" may well be as much an articulation of the need for a revolutionary poetic technique and a new poetic sensibility as Koch's direct statement in "Fresh Air." Many of Ammons's poems are as much about the nature of poetry as they are ostensibly about natural phenomena. Snyder's "Riprap," Ferlinghetti's "Constantly risking absurdity," Creeley's "The Language," Kunitz' "Single Vision," and many of Duncan's and Olson's poems— these are all statements of contemporary poetics, reflecting the contemporary poets' acute and ongoing concern about the nature of their art. In a less explicit manner, it is conceivable that James Dickey's "The Heaven of Animals," Donald Hall's "The Ox Cart Man," and Robert Hayden's "The Night-Blooming Cereus" are as much explorations of the poetic process as they are about animals, flowers, and a shrewd old man. If the past few decades have been called an "age of poetry" rather than an "age of criticism"—because poets have only infrequently en-

gaged in the writing of poetic theory in critical essays—they nevertheless
have wrestled with the elusive nature of their art in the poems them-
selves, which in the last analysis may offer a more essential understanding
of today's poetics than any analytical essay.

When confronting contemporary American poetry, it is also essential
to realize that what may seem to be political issues, what may seem to
be linguistic devices, and what may seem to be shockingly intimate expe-
riences of the bedroom are, in fact, profoundly moral and spiritual
explorations. Moreover, the issues of the day ought not be imposed on
poems in order to reduce them to the equivalent of buzz words or
slogans. It is clear, for example, that a poem like Gary Snyder's "Long
Hair" is not merely a statement of ecological concern any more than
Elizabeth Bishop's "The Fish," Maxine Kumin's "The Grace of Geldings
in Ripe Pastures," or Randall Jarrell's "The Black Swan" are merely poems
about the animals mentioned in the titles. The preponderance of poems
about animals in contemporary poetry suggests far more than a mere
fascination with fauna, far more than a concern for ecological balance;
rather, it suggests a moral and spiritual vision of the animal kingdom as
an emblematic, if not always totemic, kingdom. In an age noticeably
lacking in angels, saints, and heroes, certain poets seem to be returning
to more primal symbols of hierarchy in the natural world.

Meanwhile, the concern of contemporary poets for various aspects of
human sexuality is far more important than a seemingly adolescent
fascination with bedroom antics or sex and its range of dirty words;
indeed, it's more important than simply sexual politics. In a technocratic
age that would obliterate all identity, one's sexuality is at the physical
and psychic root of individual identity. The celebration of the male
torso in Robert Duncan's poem by that name is as essential to the poet's
homosexual identity as Anne Sexton's celebration of her uterus is essential
to her female identity. Moreover, a poem like Gary Snyder's "The Bath"
not only celebrates the glory of the sexual human body but also attempts
to redeem that physical glory from this society's more prevalent attitude,
described in James Wright's "Autumn Begins in Martins Ferry, Ohio,"
where "the sons grow suicidally beautiful" and therefore "gallop terribly
against each other's bodies." The sexual concerns of today's poets thus
constitute an attempt to redeem the sexual self in a society that has
traditionally suppressed it and indeed transformed it into a weapon.

These same sexual concerns extend far beyond social mores, practices,
and weaponry. Since an explicit or implicit belief in the death of God
necessarily posits the end of belief in a supernatural life or life force, it
simultaneously necessitates a greater understanding of what is ostensibly
the most powerful manifestation of the human life force, sexuality. In
the past, the spiritual and cultural heritage of the West has been such
that the traditional affirmation of the supernatural life force has been

at the expense of the natural life force. Indeed, we have no comfortable language for our sexuality except for precise scientific terms or the more graphic language of the street. And so in a language that may sometimes be awkward or fumbling, the contemporary poets' celebration of sexuality may well be equivalent to a celebration of the god within as well as an implicit affirmation of the sexual nature of poetry itself—thereby suggesting a double measure of the sacred. Clearly, the sexual concerns in a poem like James Dickey's "The Sheep Child" extend far beyond the level of the dirty joke, far beyond the matter of sexual politics; they reach into the very heart of the god and of the creator within.

Although none of these poets has publicly proclaimed allegiance to any formal ethical or religious system to date, and although some have been members of the Catholic church, for example, and later quietly left it, one can point to a diversity of profound religious experiences in the work of most contemporary poets. In some of Richard Wilbur's poems—"A Dubious Night," for example—the existence of God is at best irrelevant, at worst a handicap to the discovery of that more profound salvation discovered in purely human activity. The ending of Lawrence Ferlinghetti's "Sometime during eternity" affirms—but implicitly laments—the contemporary theological stance that God is dead; his "I Am Waiting" humorously reveals the poet's quest for and anticipation of salvation. A profound mystical sense is clearly at the heart of Allen Ginsberg's "Wales Visitation," just as it is at the heart of much of Roethke's poetry. In "Mary's Song" Sylvia Plath sees the cycle of Christian salvation reflected in contemporary history's need for sacrificial victims. Moreover, in much of her poetry one senses the ancient mysticism that affirms salvation through suffering: "The fire makes it precious." Whereas the existence of God seems either irrelevant or impossible in much of Merwin's poetry, "Lemuel's Blessing" is nevertheless one of the powerful prayer poems of the generation.

To a large extent, most contemporary poets—like many of their modernist predecessors—view traditional, formal, and established religious belief as impossible. Rather, they affirm a personal and vital religious or mystical, spiritual sense. John Berryman is one of the few who uses the traditional Judaic-Christian mythology—complete with God, Saint Peter, and Satan—as a potentially legitimate framework for religious experience. However, the work of John Logan, perhaps one of the most truly religious poets of the generation, is a clearer example of the contemporary poet's evolution from a formal and established religious belief to a more personal one. Logan's early work relied primarily on what James Dickey called an "orthodox symbology" and a religious sense. His later work, having shed the formal accouterments of religion, also has gained in intensity—tempered by a greater human complexity. The mystery of salvation is seen in its human incarnation. Grace is discovered and given and received specifically through human and incarnate acts. Thus "White Pass Ski Patrol" is a secular and sporty account of the ascension. The member of the ski patrol continually rises and then caroms down—speeding, dancing, balancing, taking all human risks, and ministering to others, even in danger. And he rises again; he "vanishes in air!" But only after he has come down, after he has learned what the body can do, what grace the body can realize on its own. And finally, like Teilhard de Chardin's fully evolved human, the central figure in Logan's poem moves through the final process into pure light.

Politics, sex, and religion in all their complex ramifications—the outdated taboos of so-called civilized society and polite conversation—are only a few of the primary concerns to which today's poets have addressed themselves. They are also only a few of the themes that contribute to the freshness and especially to the relevance of contemporary poetry. Alive with the blood and genes of the immediate and distant tradition of poetry, rebelling against all that is petrified and dead in that heritage, and asserting their fierce personal response to all that is demanded of a human being at this moment in history, contemporary American poets repeatedly affirm, with Louis Simpson, that American poetry:

> Whatever it is . . . must have
> A stomach that can digest
> Rubber, coal, uranium, moons, poems. . . .
>
> It must swim for miles through the desert
> Uttering cries that are almost human.

Criticism: A Selected Bibliography

Most of the following books and pamphlets contain substantial discussions of the work of individual American poets, especially those represented in this book; some also include critical essays or statements of poetics by these poets. A few books in this bibliography, however, are primarily concerned with American poetry before 1945; still others focus on various aspects of the art of American poetry in the twentieth century. Book-length critical studies written by individual poets generally appear both in this bibliography and in the "Notes on the Poets"; book-length critical studies devoted *to* individual poets appear only in the "Notes."

With the exception of Norman Friedman's unique study of the "Wesleyan Poets," individual essays aren't included here, for most bibliographies of critical essays quickly become outdated and incomplete. I trust that serious readers of poetry will turn to book-length bibliographies devoted to individual poets and to such standard bibliographical sources as: *Contemporary Poets* (St. Martin's Press); *Contemporary Authors* (Gale Research Co.); the annual bibliographies published in *PMLA*, *American Literature*, and *Journal of Modern Literature*; the regular bibliographies in *Twentieth Century Literature*; and *Contemporary Literary Criticism* (Gale Research Co.), an annual volume of critical excerpts. Of course, many of the books listed below also include their own individual bibliographies of varying lengths.

Lastly, readers should be aware that even some of the seminal books of criticism devoted to post-1945 American poetry listed below are presently out of print and therefore available only in some of the larger libraries.

Allen, Donald M., and Warren Tallman, eds. *The Poetics of the New American Poetry*. New York: Grove, 1973.

Bloom, Harold. *The Anxiety of Influence: A Theory of Poetry*. New York: Oxford University, 1973.

Bloom, Harold. *A Map of Misreading*. New York: Oxford University, 1975.

Boyers, Robert, ed. *Contemporary Poetry in America: Essays and Interviews*. New York: Shocken, 1974.

Boyers, Robert. *Excursions: Selected Literary Essays*. Port Washington, N.Y.: Kennikat, 1977.

Cambon, Glauco. *Recent American Poetry*. Minneapolis: University of Minnesota, 1962.

Carroll, Paul. *The Poem in Its Skin*. Chicago: Follett, 1968.

Charters, Samuel. *Some Poems/Poets: Studies in American Underground Poetry Since 1945*. Berkeley: Oyez, 1971.

Dickey, James. *Babel to Byzantium: Poets and Poetry Now*. New York: Farrar, Straus & Giroux, 1968.

Faas, Ekbert, ed. *Towards a New American Poetics: Essays and Interviews*. Santa Barbara: Black Sparrow, 1978.

Friedman, Norman. "The Wesleyan Poets I–IV," *Chicago Review*, vol. 18, nos. 3–4; vol. 19, nos. 1, 2, 3, 1966–1967.

Heyen, William, ed. *American Poets in 1976*. Indianapolis: Bobbs-Merrill, 1975.

Hungerford, Edward B., ed. *Poets in Progress: Critical Prefaces to Thirteen Modern American Poets*. Evanston: Northwestern University, 1967.

Howard, Richard. *Alone with America: Studies in the Art of Poetry in the United States Since World War II*. New York: Atheneum, 1969.

Jarrell, Randall. *Poetry and the Age*. New York: Knopf, 1965.

Kherdian, David. *Six San Francisco Poets*. Fresno: Giligia, 1969.

Lensing, George S., and Ronald Moran. *Four Poets and the Emotive Imagination: Robert Bly, James Wright, Louis Simpson and William Stafford*. Baton Rouge: Louisiana State University, 1976.

Lieberman, Laurence. *Unassigned Frequencies: American Poetry in Review 1964–77*. Urbana: University of Illinois, 1977.

Malkoff, Karl. *Crowell's Handbook of Contemporary American Poetry: A Critical Handbook of American Poetry Since 1940*. New York: Crowell, 1973.

Mazzaro, Jerome, ed. *Modern American Poetry: Essays in Criticism*. New York: David McKay, 1970.

Meltzer, David, ed. *The San Francisco Poets*. New York: Ballantine, 1971.

Mersmann, James F. *Out of the Vietnam Vortex: A Study of Poets and Poetry Against the War*. Lawrence: University Press of Kansas, 1974.

Mills, Ralph J. Jr. *Contemporary American Poetry*. New York: Random House, 1965.

Mills, Ralph J. Jr. *Creation's Very Self: On the Personal Element in Recent American Poetry*. Fort Worth: Texas Christian University, 1969.

Mills, Ralph J. Jr. *Cry of the Human: Essays on Contemporary American Poetry*. Urbana: University of Illinois, 1974.

Nemerov, Howard, ed. *Poets on Poetry*. New York: Basic Books, 1961.

Nemerov, Howard. *Reflexions on Poetry and Poetics*. New Brunswick: Rutgers University, 1972.

Ossman, David. *The Sullen Art: Interviews by David Ossman with Modern American Poets*. New York: Corinth, 1963.

Ostroff, Anthony, ed. *The Contemporary Poet as Artist and Critic*. Boston: Little, Brown, 1964.

Packard, William, ed. *The Craft of Poetry: Interviews from The New York Quarterly*. New York: Doubleday, 1974.

Parkinson, Thomas, ed. *A Casebook on the Beat*. New York: Crowell, 1961.

Pierce, Roy Harvey. *The Continuity of American Poetry*. Princeton: Princeton University, 1961.

Phillips, Robert. *The Confessional Poets*. Carbondale: Southern Illinois University, 1973.

Pinsky, Robert. *The Situation of Poetry: Contemporary Poetry and Its Traditions*. Princeton: Princeton University, 1977.

Rexroth, Kenneth. *American Poetry in the Twentieth Century*. New York: Seabury, 1973.

Rosenthal, M. L. *The Modern Poets: A Critical Introduction*. New York: Oxford University, 1962.

Rosenthal, M. L. *The New Poets: American and British Poetry Since World War II*. New York: Oxford University, 1967.

Shaw, Robert B., ed. *American Poetry Since 1960: Some Critical Perspectives*. Chester Springs, Pa.: Dufour, 1974.

Simpson, Louis. *A Revolution in Taste: Studies of Dylan Thomas, Allen Ginsberg, Sylvia Plath and Robert Lowell*. New York: Macmillan, 1978.

Stepanchev, Stephen. *American Poetry Since 1945: A Critical Survey*. New York: Harper & Row, 1965.

Waggoner, Hyatt H. *American Poetry from the Puritans to the Present*. Boston: Houghton Mifflin, 1968; paperback edition, New York: Dell, 1970.

Writers at Work: The Paris Review Interviews. Second Series. New York: Viking, 1965. Third Series, 1967. Fourth Series, 1974.

A Note on the Editor

A. Poulin, Jr. was born in Lisbon, Maine, and received a B.A. from St. Francis College, an M.A. from Loyola University, and an M.F.A. from the University of Iowa; he did additional postgraduate work at the State University of New York at Buffalo. He has taught for the European Division of the University of Maryland, at the University of New Hampshire, and at St. Francis College where he was chairman of the Division of Humanities and assistant to the president for Curriculum Planning and Development. He is currently a professor of English at the State University College at Brockport and faculty exchange scholar of the State University of New York. He has also served as director of the Writer's Forum at Brockport and has recorded videotape interviews with more than twenty contemporary poets, including John Ashbery, Robert Bly, Robert Creeley, Lawrence Ferlinghetti, Allen Ginsberg, Robert Hayden, David Ignatow, Galway Kinnell, Stanley Kunitz, John Logan, Adrienne Rich, Anne Sexton, Louis Simpson, Gary Snyder, and William Stafford—some of the poets represented in this edition of *Contemporary American Poetry*.

A poet, translator, and editor, Poulin has received a Creative Writing Fellowship from the National Endowment for the Arts, a translation award from Columbia University's Translation Center, and fellowships from the Research Foundation of the State University of New York for writing and translating poetry. He also has received program grants from the National Endowment for the Arts, the New York State Council on the Arts, and the Ford Foundation.

During the past few years, Poulin has served as a member of the State University of New York's University-Wide Committee on the Arts and as a member of the Literature Panel of the New York State Council on the Arts. In addition, Poulin is the founder and acting executive director of the New York State Literary Center in Rochester, New York, as well as founder, editor, and publisher of BOA Editions, an alternative publishing house devoted to poetry and poetry in translation.

Poulin's own books of poetry include: *In Advent* (1972); *Catawba: Omens, Prayers & Songs* (1977); *The Widow's Taboo: Poems After the Catawba* (1977); and *The Nameless Garden* (1978). His books of translations include: *Duino Elegies and The Sonnets to Orpheus* by Rainer Maria Rilke (1977); two collections of Rilke's French poems, *Saltimbanques* and *The Roses and The Windows* (1979); and *Eve: Poems* by Anne Hébert (1980).

599

Credits

601

with the permission of Farrar, Straus & Giroux, Inc., "North Haven" appeared originally in *The New Yorker*. "One Art" reprinted with the permission of Farrar, Straus & Giroux, Inc. from *Geography III* by Elizabeth Bishop. Copyright © 1976 by Elizabeth Bishop. "One Art" appeared originally in *The New Yorker*.
◻ **Robert Bly:** "Surprised by Evening," "Waking from Sleep," "Poem in Three Parts," "Snowfall in the Afternoon," "In a Train," "Driving to Town Late to Mail a Letter," and "Watering the Horse" reprinted from *Silence in the Snowy Fields* by Robert Bly (as published by Wesleyan University Press) by permission of Robert Bly. Copyright © 1962 by Robert Bly. "After Long Busyness" reprinted from *Jumping Out of Bed* by Robert Bly (as published by Barre Publishers) by permission of Robert Bly. Copyright © 1973 by Robert Bly. From *The Light Around the Body* by Robert Bly: "The Busy Man Speaks" (p. 60) copyright © 1962 by Robert Bly; "War and Silence" (p. 61) copyright © 1966 by Robert Bly; "Counting Small-Boned Bodies" (p. 61) copyright © 1967 by Robert Bly; "Looking Into a Face" (p. 62) copyright © 1965 by Robert Bly; "The Hermit" (p. 62) copyright © 1967 by Robert Bly; "Come with Me" (p. 62) copyright © 1964 by Robert Bly, reprinted by permission of Harper & Row, Publishers, Inc. "Looking into a Tide Pool" reprinted from *The Morning Glory* by Robert Bly (as published by Kayak Books) by permission of Robert Bly. Copyright © 1970 by Robert Bly. "Shack Poem" (p. 63) from *Sleepers Joining Hands* by Robert Bly. Copyright © 1971 by Robert Bly. Reprinted by permission of Harper & Row, Publishers, Inc. From *This Body is Made of Camphor and Gopherwood* by Robert Bly: "When the Wheel Does Not Move" (p. 64) copyright © 1977 by Robert Bly. Reprinted by permission of Harper & Row, Publishers, Inc.
◻ **Gwendolyn Brooks:** From *The World of Gwendolyn Brooks by* Gwendolyn Brooks: "kitchenette building" (p. 67), "a song in the front yard" (p. 68), "the ballad of chocolate Mabbie" (p. 69), "the independent man" (p. 70), "of DeWitt Williams on his way to Lincoln Cemetery" (p. 70), "Negro Hero" (p. 71), copyright 1945 by Gwendolyn Brooks Blakely. "We Real Cool" (p. 72), copyright © by Gwendolyn Brooks; "The Lovers of the Poor" (p. 73), copyright © 1960 by Gwendolyn Brooks. By permission of Harper & Row, Publishers, Inc. "Riot" and "An Aspect of Love, Alive in the Ice and Fire" from *Riot* © 1970 by Gwendolyn Brooks Blakely. Reprinted by permission of Broadside/Crummel Press. "To Don at Salaam" from *Family Pictures* © 1970 by Gwendolyn Brooks Blakely. Reprinted by permission of Broadside/Crummel Press.
◻ **Robert Creeley:** Reprinted by permission of Charles Scribner's Sons: "The Business" and "I Know a Man" from *For Love* by Robert Creeley, copyright © 1962 by Robert Creeley. First published in *The Whip* (Migrant Books, 1957) by Robert Creeley. "A Form of Women," "A Wicker Basket," and "The Flower" from *For Love* by Robert Creeley, copyright © 1962 by Robert Creeley. First published in *A Form of Women* by Robert Creeley (Jargon Books in association with Corinth Books, copyright 1959 Robert Creeley). "The Rain," "The Memory," and "The Rescue" from *For Love*, copyright © 1962 Robert Creeley. "The Language" and "The Window" from *Words* by Robert Creeley, copyright © 1962 Robert Creeley. First published in *Poetry* (copyright © 1962, 1964, 1965, 1966, 1967 Robert Creeley). "The Act of Love," "On Vacation," and "Moment" from *A Day Book* by Robert Creeley, copyright © 1972 by Robert Creeley, reprinted by permission of Charles Scribner's Sons and Robert Creeley.
◻ **James Dickey:** "The Heaven of Animals," "In the Lupanar at Pompeii," "A Screened Porch in the Country," "The Hospital Window," "In the Mountain Tent," "The Firebombing," "Sled Burial, Dream Ceremony," "The Sheep Child," "Adultery," and "Deer Among Cattle" copyright © 1961, 1962, 1964,

1965, 1966 by James Dickey. Reprinted from *Poems 1957–1967* by permission of Wesleyan University Press. "The Heaven of Animals" and "In the Mountain Tent" originally appeared in *The New Yorker*. "The Hospital Window" and "The Firebombing" originally appeared in *Poetry*.

□   **Alan Dugan:** "Love Song: I and Thou," "Tribute to Kafka for Someone Taken," "Elegy," "To a Red Headed Do-Good Waitress," "For Masturbation," "Fabrication of Ancestors," "American Against Solitude," "Poem," and "Elegy for a Puritan Conscience" from *Collected Poems* (Yale University Press). Copyright © 1969 by Alan Dugan. Reprinted with the permission of Alan Dugan. "Prayer," "On Leaving Town," and "Moral Dream" from *Poems 4* by Alan Dugan, by permission of Little, Brown and Co. in association with the Atlantic Monthly Press. Copyright © 1962, 1968, 1972, 1973, 1974 by Alan Dugan.

□   **Robert Duncan:** "Often I Am Permitted to Return to a Meadow," "The Structure of Rime II," "Poetry, A Natural Thing," and "Ingmar Bergman's *Seventh Seal*"; Robert Duncan, *The Opening of the Field*. Copyright © 1960 by Robert Duncan. Reprinted by permission of New Directions Publishing Corporation. "Such Is the Sickness of Many a Good Thing," "Bending the Bow," "Tribal Memories, Passages 1," "The Structure of Rime XXIII," "My Mother Would Be a Falconress," and "The Torso, Passages 18," Robert Duncan, *Bending the Bow*. Copyright © 1963, 1966, 1968 by Robert Duncan. Reprinted by permission of New Directions Publishing Corporation.

□   **Lawrence Ferlinghetti:** "Constantly risking absurdity," "Sometime during eternity," "The pennycandystore behind the El," and "I Am Waiting," Lawrence Ferlinghetti, *A Coney Island of the Mind*. Copyright 1955, © 1957 by Lawrence Ferlinghetti. Reprinted by permission of New Directions Publishing Corporation. "A Phoenix at Fifty," and "Pound at Spoleto"; Lawrence Ferlinghetti, *Open Eye, Open Heart*. Copyright © 1973 by Lawrence Ferlinghetti. Reprinted by permission of New Directions Publishing Corporation. "Monet's Lilies Shuddering," Lawrence Ferlinghetti, *Who Are We Now?* Copyright © 1976 by Lawrence Ferlinghetti. Reprinted by permission of New Directions Publishing Corporation.

□   **Allen Ginsberg:** "Howl" and "America," copyright © 1956, 1959 by Allen Ginsberg. Reprinted from *Howl and Other Poems* by permission of City Lights Books. "Love Poem on Theme by Whitman" and "Psalm III"; copyright © 1963 by Allen Ginsberg. Reprinted from *Reality Sandwiches* by permission of City Lights Books. "Wales Visitation," copyright © 1968 by Allen Ginsberg. Reprinted from *Planet News* by permission of City Lights Books. "On Neal's Ashes" and "Flashback," copyright © 1972 by Allen Ginsberg. Reprinted from *The Fall of America* by permission of City Lights Books. "Ego Confession" and "The Rune" from "Contest of the Bards," copyright © 1977 by Allen Ginsberg. Reprinted from *Mind Breaths* by permission of City Lights Books.

□   **Donald Hall:** "My Son, My Executioner," "Digging," and "The Man in the Dead Machine" from *The Alligator Bride: Poems New and Selected*. Copyright © 1969 by Donald Hall. Reprinted with the permission of Donald Hall. From *The Yellow Room* by Donald Hall: "Gold" (p. 165) copyright © 1969 by Donald Hall. By permission of Harper & Row, Publishers, Inc. "Stories" and "The Town of Hill" are from *The Town of Hill* by Donald Hall. Copyright © 1971, 1972, 1973, 1974, 1975 by Donald Hall. Reprinted by permission of David R. Godine, Publisher. "Maple Syrup" copyright © 1978 by Donald Hall. This version of "Maple Syrup" reprinted with the permission of Donald Hall. "Kicking the Leaves" (p. 169) from *Kicking the Leaves* by Donald Hall. Copyright © 1975 by Donald Hall. By permission of Harper & Row, Publishers, Inc. "The Toy Bone" from *The Toy Bone* (BOA Editions) copyright © 1979 by Donald Hall. Reprinted with the permission of BOA Editions and Donald Hall.

in the Ruins," "Vapor Trail Reflected in the Frog Pond," "The Bear," and "Last Songs." From *The Book of Nightmares*, copyright © 1971 by Galway Kinnell, "Under the Maud Moon" and "The Hen Flower." All above poems reprinted by permission of Houghton Mifflin Company. "The Still Time," from *Three Poems* (Phoenix Book Shop), copyright © 1976 by Galway Kinnell. Reprinted by permission of Galway Kinnell.

◻   **Kenneth Koch:** "Fresh Air," "Variations on a Theme by William Carlos Williams," "Permanently," and "To You" from *Thank You and Other Poems* by Kenneth Koch. Reprinted by permission of Grove Press, Inc. Copyright © 1962 by Kenneth Koch. "Poem" from *The Pleasures of Peace* by Kenneth Koch. Reprinted by permission of Grove Press, Inc. Copyright © 1969 by Kenneth Koch. "Alive for an Instant" from *The Art of Love*, by Kenneth Koch. Copyright © 1972, 1974, 1975 by Kenneth Koch. Reprinted by permission of Random House, Inc.

◻   **Stanley Kunitz:** "Single Vision," "Father and Son," "End of Summer," "The War Against the Trees," and "Reflection by a Mailbox" from *Selected Poems 1928–1958* by Stanley Kunitz, by permission of Little, Brown and Co. in association with The Atlantic Monthly Press. Copyright 1929, 1930, 1944, 1951, 1953, 1954, © 1956, 1957, 1958 by Stanley Kunitz. "Indian Summer at Land's End," "The Artist," and "The Portrait" from *The Testing-Tree* by Stanley Kunitz, by permission of Little, Brown and Co. in association with The Atlantic Monthly Press. Copyright © 1962, 1963, 1965, 1966, 1967, 1968, 1969, 1970, 1971 by Stanley Kunitz. "The Unquiet Ones" and "The Quarrel" copyright © 1978, by The Atlantic Monthly Company, Boston, Mass. Reprinted with permission. "The Knot" copyright © 1973 by Stanley Kunitz. Reprinted by permission of Stanley Kunitz.

◻   **Maxine Kumin:** From *Up Country* by Maxine Kumin: "Morning Swim" (p. 249) copyright © 1962 by Maxine Kumin; "Stones" (p. 250) copyright © 1972 by Maxine Kumin; "Woodchucks" (p. 250) copyright © 1971 by Maxine Kumin. "Thinking of Death and Dogfood" and "The Absent Ones" from *House, Bridge, Gate* by Maxine Kumin. Copyright © 1975 by Maxine Kumin. Reprinted by permission of Viking Penguin Inc. "Seeing the Bones," "How It Is," "The Longing To Be Saved," "The Excrement Poem," and "The Grace of Geldings in Ripe Pastures" from *The Retrieval System* by Maxine Kumin. Copyright © 1978 by Maxine Kumin. Reprinted by permission of Viking Penguin Inc.

◻   **Denise Levertov:** "The Jacob's Ladder," from Denise Levertov, *The Jacob's Ladder*, copyright © 1961 by Denise Levertov Goodman. "Hypocrite Women" and "A Psalm Praising the Hair of Man's Body" from Denise Levertov, *O Taste and See*, copyright © 1964 by Denise Levertov Goodman. "The Wings," "Stepping Westward," and "The Altars in the Street" from Denise Levertov, *The Sorrow Dance*, copyright © 1966 by Denise Levertov Goodman. "Revolutionary" and "Entr'acte, 'Let us Sing Unto the Lord a New Song' " from Denise Levertov, *To Stay Alive*, copyright © 1971 by Denise Levertov Goodman. "Intrusion," "The Poem Unwritten," and "Man Alone" from Denise Levertov, *Footprints*, copyright © 1970, 1972 by Denise Levertov. "Ways of Conquest" from Denise Levertov, *The Freeing of the Dust*, copyright © 1975 by Denise Levertov. "Wedding Ring" from Denise Levertov, *Life in the Forest*, copyright © 1975 by Denise Levertov. All poems reprinted by permission of New Directions Publishing Corporation.

◻   **Philip Levine:** "Animals Are Passing from Our Lives" and "To a Child Trapped in a Barber Shop" copyright © 1966, 1968 by Philip Levine. Reprinted from *Not This Pig* by Philip Levine, by permission of Wesleyan University Press. "Coming Home," "Angel Butcher," and "They Feed They Lion" from

They Feed They Lion, copyright © 1972 by Philip Levine. "Coming Home" appeared originally in the *Hudson Review*; "They Feed They Lion" in *Kayak*. Reprinted by permission of Atheneum Publishers. All rights reserved. "Zaydee" from *1933*, copyright © 1974 by Philip Levine, appeared originally in the *Iowa Review*. Reprinted by permission of Atheneum Publishers. All rights reserved. "Starlight" and "Ashes" from *Ashes*, copyright © 1971, 1979 by Philip Levine. "Ashes" appeared originally in the *Iowa Review*. Reprinted by permission of Atheneum Publishers. All rights reserved. "Let Me Begin Again" and "You Can Have It" from *7 Years from Somewhere*, copyright © 1979 by Philip Levine. "Let Me Begin Again" appeared originally in *The New Yorker*, and "You Can Have It" in *Antaeus*. Reprinted by permission of Atheneum Publishers. All rights reserved.

□   **John Logan:** "Three Moves," "White Pass Ski Patrol," "Suzanne," and "Love Poem" from *The Zigzag Walk: Poems: 1963–1968* by John Logan. Copyright © 1963, 1964, 1965, 1966, 1967, 1968, 1969 by John Logan. Reprinted by permission of the publisher, E. P. Dutton. "To a Young Poet Who Fled" and "Spring of the Thief" from *Spring of the Thief*, Alfred A. Knopf. Copyright © 1963 by John Logan. Reprinted with the permission of John Logan. "Poem for My Brother" reprinted by permission of John Logan. Copyright © 1978 by John Logan. "The Bridge of Change" reprinted from *The Bridge of Change* by John Logan, by permission of John Logan and BOA Editions, A. Poulin, Jr. Publisher. Copyright © 1979 by John Logan. "First Reunion in New Orleans: The Father as King of Revels" reprinted from *Poem in Progress* by John Logan, by permission of Dryad Press and John Logan. Copyright © 1975 by John Logan. "Dawn and a Woman" is reprinted from *The Anonymous Lover, New Poems by John Logan*, with the permission of Liveright Publishing Corporation. Copyright © 1969, 1970, 1971, 1972, 1973 by John Logan.

□   **Robert Lowell:** "Colloquy in Black Rock," "Christmas Eve under Hooker's Statue," and "Mr. Edwards and the Spider" from *Lord Weary's Castle*, copyright 1946, 1974 by Robert Lowell. Reprinted by permission of Harcourt Brace Jovanovich, Inc. "Memories of West Street and Lepke," "Man and Wife," "To Speak of Woe That Is in Marriage," and "Skunk Hour" reprinted with the permission of Farrar, Straus & Giroux, Inc. From *Life Studies* by Robert Lowell. Copyright © 1956, 1959 by Robert Lowell. "Eye and Tooth" reprinted with the permission of Farrar, Straus & Giroux, Inc. From *For the Union Dead* by Robert Lowell. Copyright © 1962, 1964 by Robert Lowell. "Long Summer" and "Reading Myself" reprinted with the permission of Farrar, Straus & Giroux, Inc. From *Notebook* by Robert Lowell. Copyright © 1967, 1968, 1969, 1970 by Robert Lowell. "History" reprinted with the permission of Farrar, Straus & Giroux, Inc. from *History* by Robert Lowell, copyright © 1967, 1968, 1969, 1970, 1973 by Robert Lowell. "Homecoming," and "Epilogue" reprinted with the permission of Farrar, Straus & Giroux, Inc. From *Day by Day* by Robert Lowell. Copyright © 1975, 1976, 1977 by Robert Lowell.

□   **James Merrill:** "After Greece" and "Angel" from *Water Street*, copyright © 1960, 1962 by James Merrill. "After Greece" appeared originally in *The New Yorker*, and "Angel" in *Poetry*. "The Octopus," "Laboratory Poem," and "A Dedication" from *The Country of a Thousand Years of Peace*, copyright 1951, © 1958, 1970 by James Merrill. "The Octopus" and "Laboratory Poem" appeared originally in *Poetry*. "Charles on Fire" from *Nights and Days*, copyright © 1965, 1966 by James Merrill. "Nike" from *The Fire Screen*, copyright © 1968, 1969 by James Merrill. "The Emerald" from the poem "Up and Down" and "The Victor Dog" are from *Braving the Elements*, copyright © 1972 by

James Merrill. "Up and Down" appeared originally in *The New Yorker*. All reprinted by permission of Atheneum Publishers. All rights reserved.

□   **W. S. Merwin:** "The Drunk in the Furnace" from *The First Four Books of Poems* by W. S. Merwin, copyright © 1956, 1957, 1958, 1959, 1960, 1975 by W. S. Merwin. "Lemuel's Blessing," "Dead Hand," "Air," and "We Continue from *The Moving Target*, copyright © 1962, 1963 by W. S. Merwin. "Lemuel's Blessing" appeared originally in *The New Yorker;* "Air" in *Poetry;* and "We Continue" in the *Evergreen Review.* "Some Last Questions," "December Night," and "For the Anniversary of My Death" from *The Lice,* copyright © 1963, 1964, 1965, 1966, 1967 by W. S. Merwin. "Some Last Questions" appeared originally in *Poetry;* "December Night" in the *Atlantic Monthly;* and "For the Anniversary of My Death" in the *Southern Review.* "Tergvinder's Stone" from *The Miner's Pale Children* by W. S. Merwin, copyright © 1969, 1970 by W. S. Merwin, appeared originally in the *Quarterly Review of Literature.* "The Hands," "Do Not Die" and "Animula" from *The Carrier of Ladders,* copyright © 1967, 1968, 1970 by W. S. Merwin. "The Hands" appeared originally in *The New Yorker;* "Do Not Die" in *Poetry;* and "Animula" in *The Nation.* "Eyes of Summer," "Habits," and "A Door" from *Writings to an Unfinished Accompaniment,* copyright © 1971, 1972, 1973 by W. S. Merwin. "Eyes of Summer" appeared originally in the *Quarterly Review of Literature;* "Habits" in *Field,* and "A Door" in the *Atlantic Monthly.* "The Falcons" from *The Compass Flower,* copyright © 1977 by W. S. Merwin. All reprinted by permission of Atheneum Publishers. All rights reserved.

□   **Frank O'Hara:** "Autobiographia Literaria" copyright © 1967 by Maureen Granville-Smith, Administratrix of the Estate of Frank O'Hara. Reprinted from *The Collected Poems of Frank O'Hara,"* edited by Donald Allen, by permission of Alfred A. Knopf, Inc. "Poem," "To My Dead Father," and "To John Ashbery" from *The Collected Poems of Frank O'Hara,* edited by Donald Allen. Copyright © 1967 by Maureen Granville-Smith, Administratrix of the Estate of Frank O'Hara. Reprinted by permission of Alfred A. Knopf, Inc. "Why I Am Not a Painter" copyright 1951 by Maureen Granville-Smith, Administratrix of the Estate of Frank O'Hara. Reprinted from *The Collected Poems of Frank O'Hara,* edited by Donald Allen, by permission of Alfred A. Knopf, Inc. "Poem" and "Meditations in an Emergency" reprinted by permission of Grove Press, Inc., from *Meditations in an Emergency* by Frank O'Hara. Copyright © 1957 by Frank O'Hara. "The Day Lady Died," "Steps," "Yesterday Down at the Canal," and "Poem" copyright © 1964 by Frank O'Hara. Reprinted by permission of City Lights Books from *Lunch Poems* by Frank O'Hara.

□   **Charles Olson:** "Maximus, to Himself," "I, Maximus of Gloucester, to You," "Maximus, to Gloucester, Letter 19 (A Pastoral Letter" copyright © 1960 by Charles Olson. Reprinted by permission of Corinth Books, Inc., from *The Maximus Poems* by Charles Olson. "Maximus to Gloucester, Letter 27 (Withheld)" and "A Later Note on Letter #15" from *Maximus Poems IV, V, VI* by Charles Olson. Copyright © 1968 by Charles Olson. Reprinted by permission of the Estate of Charles Olson, George F. Butterick, Literary Executor. "The Librarian" and "Moonset, Gloucester, December 1, 1957, 1:58 am," copyright © 1960 by Charles Olson. Reprinted from *The Distances* by Charles Olson (as published by Grove Press) by permission of the Estate of Charles Olson, George F. Butterick, Literary Executor.

□   **Sylvia Plath:** "The Colossus" (p. 375) copyright © 1961 by Sylvia Plath. Reprinted from *The Colossus* by Sylvia Plath, by permission of Alfred A. Knopf, Inc. From *Ariel* by Sylvia Plath: "Lady Lazarus" (p. 381), "Cut" (p. 379),

Simpson. By permission of Harper & Row, Publishers, Inc. "The Mannequins," and "The Street" from *Searching for the Ox* by Louis Simpson. Copyright © 1976 by Louis Simpson. By permission of William Morrow & Company.

◻   **W. D. Snodgrass:** "April Inventory" copyright © 1957 by W. D. Snodgrass. Reprinted from *Heart's Needle*, by W. D. Snodgrass, by permission of Alfred A. Knopf, Inc. "Heart's Needle" copyright © 1959 by W. D. Snodgrass. Reprinted from *Heart's Needle*, by W. D. Snodgrass, by permission of Alfred A. Knopf, Inc. From *After Experience* by W. D. Snodgrass: "After Experience Taught Me . . ." (p. 460) copyright © 1964 by W. D. Snodgrass; "A Flat One" (p. 457) copyright © 1960 by W. D. Snodgrass. By permission of Harper & Row, Publishers, Inc. "Eva Braun (22 April, 1945)" and "Dr. Joseph Goebbels (1 May, 1945; 2800 hours)" from *The Führer Bunker: A Cycle of Poems in Progress* (BOA Editions), copyright © 1977 by W. D. Snodgrass. Reprinted by permission of BOA Editions and W. D. Snodgrass. "Magda Goebbels (30 April, 1945)" copyright © 1979 by W. D. Snodgrass. Reprinted by permission of W. D. Snodgrass.

◻   **Gary Snyder:** "Riprap" and "Milton by Firelight" from *Riprap & Cold Mountain Poems* (Four Seasons Foundation), copyright © 1965 by Gary Snyder. Reprinted with the permission of Gary Snyder. "Hunting #16" from Gary Snyder, *Myths and Texts*. Copyright © 1960, 1978 by Gary Snyder. Reprinted by permission of New Directions Publishing Corporation. "Vapor Trails" from Gary Snyder, *The Back Country*. Copyright © 1968 by Gary Snyder. Reprinted by permission of New Directions Publishing Corporation. "Song of the Taste" and "Long Hair" from Gary Snyder, *Regarding Wave*. "Song of the Taste" was first published in *Poetry*. Copyright © 1968, 1970 by Gary Snyder. Reprinted by permission of New Directions Publishing Corporation. "I Went Into the Maverick Bar," "The Bath," "Bedrock," and "As for Poets" from Gary Snyder, *Turtle Island*. Copyright © 1972, 1974 by Gary Snyder. Reprinted by permission of New Directions Publishing Corporation.

◻   **William Stafford:** From *Stories That Could Be True: New and Collected Poems* by William Stafford: "At the Bomb Testing Site" (p. 483) copyright © 1960 by William E. Stafford; "Traveling Through the Dark" (p. 483) copyright © 1960 by William E. Stafford; "Vocation" (p. 484) copyright © 1962 by William E. Stafford; "My Father: October 1942" (p. 484) copyright © 1963 by William E. Stafford; "Across Kansas" (p. 485) copyright © 1963 by William E. Stafford; "A Family Turn" (p. 485) copyright © 1966 by William E. Stafford; "An Introduction to Some Poems" (p. 486) copyright © 1968 by William E. Stafford; "For a Child Gone to Live in a Commune" (p. 487) copyright © 1972 by William E. Stafford; "Touches" (p. 487) copyright © 1970 by William E. Stafford; "Report from a Far Place" (p. 488) copyright © 1970 by William E. Stafford; "The Stick in the Forest" (p. 488) copyright © 1969 by William E. Stafford. By permission of Harper & Row, Publishers, Inc. "Finding Out" and "Assurance" from *Smoke's Way* (Graywolf Press, 1978), copyright © 1978 by William Stafford. Reprinted with the permission of the Graywolf Press. "A Certain Bend," "Answerers," and "Things That Happen Where There Aren't Any People" from *Things That Happen Where There Aren't Any People*, BOA Editions, copyright © 1979 by William Stafford. Reprinted with the permission of BOA Editions and William Stafford.

◻   **Richard Wilbur:** "Advice to a Prophet" © 1959 by Richard Wilbur. Reprinted from his volume *Advice to a Prophet and Other Poems* by permission of Harcourt Brace Jovanovich, Inc. First published in *The New Yorker* magazine. "Love Calls Us to the Things of This World" and "A Baroque Wall-Fountain in the Villa Sciarra" from *Things of This World*, © 1956 by Richard Wilbur.

ited by permission of Harcourt Brace Jovanovich, Inc. "Year's End" copy-
1949, 1977 by Richard Wilbur. Reprinted from his volume *Ceremony and
er Poems* by permission of Harcourt Brace Jovanovich, Inc. "Potato," "On
e Eyes of an SS Officer," "A Dubious Night," and "Praise in Summer" from
he Beautiful Changes and Other Poems, copyright 1947, 1975 by Richard Wil-
bur. Reprinted by permission of Harcourt Brace Jovanovich, Inc. "On the Mar-
ginal Way" copyright © 1965 by Richard Wilbur. Reprinted from his volume
Walking to Sleep by permission of Harcourt Brace Jovanovich, Inc. Originally
published in *The New Yorker* magazine. "Cottage Street, 1953" copyright © 1972
by Richard Wilbur. Reprinted from his volume *The Mind-Reader* by permission
of Harcourt Brace Jovanovich, Inc. "The Writer" copyright © 1971 by Richard
Wilbur. Reprinted from his volume *The Mind-Reader* by permission of Harcourt
Brace Jovanovich, Inc.

❑ **James Wright:** "As I Step Over a Puddle at the End of Winter, I Think
of an Ancient Chinese Governor," "Goodbye to the Poetry of Calcium," "Au-
tumn Begins in Martins Ferry, Ohio," "Lying in a Hammock at William Duffy's
Farm in Pine Island, Minnesota," "The Jewel," "Fear Is What Quickens Me,"
"Eisenhower's Visit to Franco, 1959," "A Blessing," "Late November in a Field,"
"The Lights in the Hallway," "In Response to a Rumor that the Oldest Whore-
house in Wheeling, West Virginia, Has Been Condemned," and "A Moral Poem
Freely Accepted from Sappho" copyright © 1950, 1961, 1962, 1966, 1968, 1969,
1971 by James Wright. Reprinted from *Collected Poems* by James Wright by
permission of Wesleyan University Press. "A Blessing" and "The Lights in the
Hallway" first appeared in *Poetry.* "A Poem of Towers" reprinted with the per-
mission of Farrar, Straus & Giroux, Inc., from *Two Citizens* by James Wright.
Copyright © 1970, 1971, 1972, 1973 by James Wright. "To a Blossoming Pear
Tree" and "Beautiful Ohio" reprinted with the permission of Farrar, Straus &
Giroux, Inc., from *To a Blossoming Pear Tree* by James Wright. Copyright ©
1973, 1974, 1975, 1976, 1977 by James Wright.

ABCDEFGHIJ-BP-8210/80